KU-644-577

Reading Myth

Classical Mythology and Its Interpretations in Medieval French Literature

Figurae

ADVISORY BOARD

Teodolinda Barolini, Margaret Bent, R. Howard Bloch,

Kevin Brownlee, Marina Scordilis Brownlee,

Brigitte Cazelles, Jacqueline Cerquiglini-Toulet, Georges Didi-Huberman,

Hans Ulrich Gumbrecht, Rachel Jacoff, Sarah Kay, V. A. Kolve,

Seth Lerer, Charles Méla, Jan-Dirk Müller,

Stephen G. Nichols, Lee Patterson, Jeffrey Schnapp, Linda Seidel,

Gabrielle Spiegel, Brian Stock,

Karla Taylor, David Wallace, Rainer Warning, Michel Zink

Reading Myth

Classical Mythology and Its Interpretations in Medieval French Literature

Renate Blumenfeld-Kosinski

Stanford University Press, Stanford, California, 1997

Stanford University Press
Stanford, California
© 1997 by the Board of Trustees of
the Leland Stanford Junior University
Printed in the United States of America

Library of Congress Cataloging-in-Publication Data
Blumenfeld-Kosinski, Renate
Reading myth : classical mythology and its interpretations in medieval French literature / Renate Blumenfeld-Kosinski.
p. cm. — (Figurae)
Includes bibliographical references and index.
ISBN 0-8047-2810-0 (cloth : alk. paper)
1. French literature—to 1500—History and criticism.
2. Mythology in literature. I. Title. II. Series: Figurae (Stanford, Calif.)
PQ155.M94B58 1997
840.9′15—dc21 97-718
CIP

∞ This book is printed on acid-free, recycled paper.

Original printing 1997
Last figure below indicates year of this printing:
06 05 04 03 02 01 00 99 98 97

For Antoni

Acknowledgments

This book has taken shape over many years. Questions on the nature and function of classical myth in medieval culture first began to intrigue me during my graduate school years. In my dissertation, completed in 1980, I addressed some of the issues surrounding myth in relation to the twelfth-century romances of antiquity, and I remain grateful to Karl D. Uitti of Princeton University for making me think along different lines. Many other projects occupied me between my dissertation and the current book, however—some of them spawned in rather unexpected ways by my interest in the afterlife of antiquity. My book *Not of Woman Born* (Cornell University Press, 1990), for example, did not originally grow out of an interest in medieval medicine but rather centered around the figure of Julius Caesar as one of the prime "survivors" of antiquity. Several graduate courses I taught at Columbia University helped broaden and define the topic of the afterlife of classical myth. My students there were an inspiration and wrote many stimulating papers that I profited from. The audiences of the public lectures I gave at the University of Minnesota, New York University, and my present home, the University of Pittsburgh, further enriched my thinking.

Several colleagues have read parts or all of the present manuscript (some of them several times), and I would like to thank Kevin Brownlee, David Damrosch, Sylvia Huot, and Nancy Freeman Regalado for their generous input. Parts of Chapters 1 and 5 appeared in somewhat different form as, respectively, "The Gods as Metaphor in the *Roman de Thèbes*," *Modern Philology* 83 (1985): 1–11 (© 1985 by The University of Chicago), and "Christine de Pizan and Classical Mythology: Some Examples from the *Mutacion de Fortune*," in Margarete Zimmermann and Dina De Rentiis, eds., *The City of Scholars: New Approaches to Christine de Pizan* (Berlin and New York: Walter de Gruyter, 1994), pp. 3–14.

A research grant from the National Endowment for the Humanities supported a year's work on the project in 1991–92, just when I needed such support most. That I am still in the profession of thinking about medieval things—despite the events of that year—is due to the support of many friends and colleagues and, most of all, that of my husband, Antoni, whose love has sustained me for the last 24 years. To him I dedicate this book.

Contents

Reading Myth

Classical Mythology and Its Interpretations in Medieval French Literature

Introduction

When medieval poets and clerks encountered mythological narratives by such classical authors as Virgil, Ovid, or Statius, they not only read the narratives themselves but layer upon layer of commentary and interpretation. Woven into the very fabric of the text, filling every available square inch of the margin, or appended to the text itself, the interpretive tradition constantly insinuated itself into the act of reading. There were many ways to interpret myths: the historical, which claimed that the ancient gods and goddesses had been kings and queens in remote times; the physical, which saw in the gods the forces of nature, such as the sun, heat, or cold; the astrological, which linked the gods to the constellations; and the moral, which considered the actions in mythological narratives expressions of good and evil.[1] But, like any others, medieval readers could pick and choose between these different possibilities. In fact, they could even choose to read literally, although this road was fraught with dangers, as the early Homeric commentators had already realized.

One of the aims of the early commentators was to cleanse mythology of supposed indecencies, while later Christian commentators saw it as their task to justify their use of such pagan material in a Christian culture. They did so by using three dramatic images. Saint Jerome borrowed from Origen the idea that pagan mythology could be likened to a "beautiful gentile captive," who, with a few cosmetic adjustments, could become an Israelite. Jerome's contemporary, the Greek Basilius, highlighted the educational value of pagan literature by comparing the process of exploiting it to the activity of bees, who choose only those flowers and parts of plants that will bring them profit. Finally, one of the most enduring images—that of the "gold of the Egyptians"—was Augustine's preferred comparison: just as the Hebrew people transformed the gold vessels they had taken with them on the flight from Egypt for use in their religious ceremonies, so the Christian writer is authorized to draw on pagan material if he employs it in the service of the true Gospel.[2] These images provided a powerful authorization for the integration of at least parts of pagan culture. And yet all the authors who dealt with pagan subject matter had to be aware of the potential riskiness of their endeavor, namely, to graft something essentially alien (that is, not Christian)—something that embodied "dread of idolatry, danger to morals, and the fear of attraction to wordly values"—onto the shoots of their Christian imagination.[3]

This is not to say that every medieval writer christianized ancient mythology—far from it. It simply means that the consciousness of having to make a choice was there. In the ninth century Rabanus Maurus expressed this consciousness perfectly when, after making a reference to the "beautiful captive," he wrote: "In the same way, if, when we read the pagan poets, [or] when books of secular wisdom come into our hands, we discover in them something that is useful, we have to turn it into our dogma; if there is something superfluous about idols, love or the cares for this world, we have to erase it."[4] It was not only philosophers and theologians who dealt with pagan myth, of course. Since the teaching of Latin rhetoric and grammar in the schools relied heavily on the pagan classics, every educated clerk routinely encountered authors like Horace, Cicero, Virgil, Ovid, and Statius.[5] If one looks at the production of manuscripts of these authors' works, one can discern distinct patterns. Virgil's *Aeneid*, *Georgics*, and *Eclogues*, for example, experienced two waves of popularity, the first in the Carolingian era and the second in the twelfth century, whereas Ovid's *Metamorphoses* and Statius's *Thebaid* did not come into their own until the twelfth century.[6] In France and the Anglo-Norman territories, this period saw not only a renewed interest in the Latin classics but also, for the first time, the vernacularization of texts such as the *Aeneid* and the *Thebaid*. This decisive entry of classical subject matter into French literature provides the starting point of the present study.

Conditioned by their education in the classics, vernacular poets started, in the twelfth century, to become interested in adapting the ancient epics and with them the mythological material they contained. Some of them translated whole works; others chose to integrate certain parts of such works, often mythological stories, into their own texts. In each case, their reception and representation of ancient mythology reflects a manner of reading; that is, the new texts reflect the specific choices the poets-clerks had made while reading myths in their source texts.

A hermeneutic act is thus bound up with the creative act.[7] Unlike the epic, which had no textual interpretive tradition, the retelling of ancient myths could thus lead to a hermeneutic awareness, hitherto unknown in vernacular literature. But although authors like Rabanus Maurus had emphasized the need to erase everything that did not pertain to Christian dogma, the twelfth-century poets highlighted exactly the "love" and "cares for this world" that ancient myth could convey. In this way, vernacular poets could recuperate some of the undercurrents of threat and anxiety present in so many myths but often dissipated in a Christianized moral framework.

At the same time, vernacular poets could profit from the preceding Latin interpretive traditions without necessarily referring to them explicitly. For example, when Chrétien de Troyes depicts the story of Dido and Aeneas on Enide's saddle in *Erec et Enide*, he evokes the destructive potential of passionate love, which could constitute a threat to the courtly order. The story is given prominence through the ekphrasis, a poetic representation of a work of art, that calls for interpretation, and it gains complexity through the echoes of the moral philosophy and psychology of Bernardus Silvestris (the presumed author of a commentary on the *Aeneid*).[8]

Chrétien used ekphrasis as the means to weave a myth into his text, but mythological narratives could be integrated into vernacular texts in many other ways. From brief allusions to full-fledged translations or adaptations, anything was possible. However, after the first generation of poets, the authors of the romances of antiquity, who were the first to turn the texts of Virgil, Statius, or Ovid into thoroughly medievalized versions of their former selves, the use of myth is largely fragmentary. Not until the *Ovide moralisé*, in the fourteenth century, do we find another attempt to translate or adapt an entire Latin poem.

The texts discussed in this book illustrate the wide variety of approaches to the interpretation of classical myths and their integration into medieval French narrative.[9] We begin in the twelfth century with the *romans antiques*, which prefer historical interpretations to the various allegorical interpretations available in the mythographic tradition, and at the same time offer mythological stories as interpretive aids or even programs for reading the entire romance. Our next stop will be the *Roman de la Rose*, where myth is linked to language and sexuality, and new and old ways of interpreting myth are combined and problematized. The center of the book will be occupied by the early-fourteenth-century *Ovide moralisé*, a most unusual and extremely long text. Consisting of a rather creative translation of the *Metamorphoses*, along with thousands of lines of interpretation, it is a perfect example of medieval allegoresis in action and provides by its very excesses a test case for techniques of interpretation. Indeed, the *Ovide moralisé* became the major source for Ovidian fables among subsequent writers. We then turn to a more allusive use of myth in the narrative works of Machaut and Froissart, where, in a very subtle form, myth is linked to love experiences and creative activity in a kind of literary bricolage. Finally, the works of Christine de Pizan will illustrate the tension a late medieval writer experienced in the treatment of classical myth: was she a mythographer or a mythmaker?

The texts chosen do not, of course, constitute an exhaustive list. Anybody who has done a thematic study of a given myth can come up with dozens of texts in which the myth appears. But completeness is not my aim here. Rather, I have chosen those texts that mark turning points in the treatment of ancient myth and that best exemplify certain prevalent methods—for both the interpretation and the integration of myths—in use over several centuries. Thus, each text represents its period in a certain way. The approach of the *romans antiques* is at once historical-political and sophisticated from a literary perspective. The *Roman de la Rose* gives us a programmatic use of myths linked to issues of poetic creativity and sexuality, while the *Ovide moralisé* constitutes a summa of interpretations that made available the whole range of received interpretations, together with a large number of new ones. A moral and consciously artistic orientation toward myth dominates in Machaut, Froissart, and some of Christine de Pizan's works, although Christine will be the one, finally, to draw freely on all possible approaches and, like Froissart, she will come up with some new myths of her own.

The presence of classical mythology in medieval literary production raises a number of interesting historical and theoretical issues. But while the historical problems of the transmission of myths have been treated at length in a number of first-rate studies,[10] many of the theoretical questions have not been very clearly defined. This may be because the dominant approach to myth criticism has been that of *Stoffgeschichte*, or the tracing of a given myth. Most practitioners of this approach choose the same texts for their surveys and on the whole consider only textual fragments, that is, the portion of the text that features their chosen myth.[11] Another problem with some of these studies is that authors do not always distinguish sufficiently between the mythographic Latin and the vernacular traditions. Not every mythographic interpretation can be successfully transferred to, say, a vernacular romance text.

Yet there are a number of theoretical issues that can be illuminated through a study of mythological narratives. In the present context, the most pertinent ones are the theory—or aesthetics—of reception; intertextuality; the function of "indexes" of interpretation; and the allegory versus allegoresis debate.[12] From a formal perspective, the most important techniques are ekphrasis and *mise en abyme*.[13] Here, these issues will not be treated separately but will appear in the context of "reading." That is, we will ask: How did the way medieval clerks read ancient myth condition the ways they rewrote these myths and made them meaningful, not only for the subject matter at hand but also for a definition of the medieval writing process? Let us therefore take a brief look at how medieval clerks became familiar with classical authors and what they were taught to do with them.

John of Salisbury's *Metalogicon* gives us some important information on how medieval clerks used the classics in education. Here, as Michelle Freeman pointed out some years ago, the concept of *translatio* occupies a central place. *Translatio* is seen as a creative reading that could lead to a "renewal of a text or body of texts."[14] This renewal could, of course, also involve actual translation, as is the case for the twelfth-century *romans antiques*, the first texts to offer vernacular translations and adaptations of the classics. Through the example of the *romans antiques*, vernacular literature received a powerful impetus: pagan mythology suddenly became part of the Old French repertory. When Jean Bodel classified the three subject matters of French literature, around 1200, he drew a clear distinction between the epic (the matter of France) which is "true," Arthurian literature (the matter of Bretagne) which is "vain and pleasant," and the "matter of Rome," represented by the *romans antiques*. The latter was "de sens aprendrant" (teaching wisdom).[15] What Bodel did not reflect on is what makes the "matter of Rome" dramatically different from the other two: the long interpretive tradition that had attached itself to the ancient epics and that each author had to come to terms with.

The texts a twelfth-century clerk would have encountered were not in their "pure" state but were already encrusted with many layers of commentary and glosses. The most important of these layers were the *accessus ad auctores*, prologues which, in the twelfth century, featured a paradigm consisting of *titulus* (title), *nomen auctoris* (name of the author), *intentio auctoris* (author's intention), *materia libri* (subject matter of the book), *modus agendi* or *tractandi* (way of proceeding), *utilitas* (usefulness), and *cui parti philosophiae supponitur* (part of philosophy to which it belongs).[16]

This list is of extreme importance because it circumscribes what could be called the literary theory of interest to medieval clerks.[17] The *titulus* gave the title of the work, frequently with what Minnis calls "specious etymologies," a specialty of the medieval period.[18] The second category gave the name of the author, sometimes a brief biography, and a discussion of the authenticity of the work. The *intentio* was defined as the moral or didactic purpose. It is here that we often find allegorical interpretations of the work in question that direct the reader's attention away from the literal level. The subject matter is then described, as well as the method and organization of the work. In the *utilitas* section one could find justifications as to why this work was part of a Christian curriculum, and the last part defined which "aspect of philosophy the work pertained to."[19]

The thirteenth century saw a new type of prologue, "which was based on the Aristotelian concept of the four causes," and which—under different headings—dealt with issues very similar to those of the twelfth-century prologues, thus keeping the focus on the purpose and usefulness of the text.[20]

Thus, before medieval clerks read the text of a given author their minds were already conditioned. They moved in an interpretive mode, and, most important, that mode had moved away from the literal level and toward the moral one.[21] The poetic merit of a text played little part in the assessment of its value; rather, the work was judged by its usefulness.

Turning now to the medieval commentaries we see that they frequently adopted the method of multiple interpretation evident in such late antique authors as Servius (late fourth century), Fulgentius (d. ca. 533) and Isidore of Seville (d. 636). All of these interpreters of the classics were extremely influential in the middle ages. The third of the important Vatican mythographers, for example, relied heavily on Fulgentius.[22]

The commentaries of Fulgentius on Virgil and Ovid have the most bearing on our interests here. In these works he presented his search for hidden meanings in the ancient texts—he found many.[23] In his treatment of the pagan fables he followed Macrobius, who in his famous *Commentary on the Dream of Scipio* (ca. 400) had expounded the idea that some fables could have philosophical usefulness. Such fables Macrobius called *narratio fabulosa*.[24] He thus justified the use of fiction in philosophical and moral teaching. At the beginning of Fulgentius's *Vergiliana continentia* (Content of Virgil), it is Virgil himself who appears to the mythographer and explains the true meaning of the *Aeneid* and the method to get at this meaning: to expound the epic allegorically, that is, to go beyond fiction into the realm of moral philosophy.

In the prologue to his *Mythologies* Fulgentius tells us that "once the fictional invention of lying Greeks has been disposed of, I may infer what allegorical significance we should understand in such matters."[25] Fulgentius adumbrates here the crucial terms used for the interpretation of myths in the twelfth century, *integument* (or sometimes *involucrum*), the veil or covering of philosophical, and even Christian, truths by means of fabulous narrative. Through the notion of integument modes of interpreting fictional texts and sacred scripture could coalesce. As Brian Stock observes, "Scholars commenting on classical texts during the intellectual revival of the twelfth century introduced their theories of the hidden meanings of myth from a framework for exegesis most highly refined by theologians. The methods being developed for the sacred texts became, with slight modifications, those employed for secular texts."[26] The "fictional invention" one can dispose of, then, is the veil or covering, as Bernardus Silvestris proclaims.[27] Together with William of Conches, Bernardus makes a forceful case for the importance of the notion of integument.[28] Once the interpreter has stripped it away, what remains is the true meaning of the text. The consequences of this method for the interpretation of myth are extremely important, for, in theory, it opens up any and every text to a Christian interpretation or allegoresis, an "imposed allegory" in Rosemond Tuve's term.[29] Second, this mode of interpretation requires no direct interpretive index (an explicit invitation to interpretation within the text) in the Todorovian sense: the pagan author was considered to have been unaware of the hidden meaning of his text.[30] It was up to the interpreter to decide whether and what to interpret. Third, the veil could not be lifted from everything, so selective interpretation became necessary.

Thus, most texts were divided into segments seen as suitable for interpretation, or as Ralph Hexter puts it, "segmentation is a precondition for interpretation."[31] Segmentation destroyed the poetic coherence—in fact, the very artistry—of the classical texts and reduced them to mere instruments for the exercise of the interpreter's ingenuity. It also reinforced the kind of "catalog" thinking so influential in the use of mythological figures as exempla.[32] Once separated from their narrative context, gods and goddesses, heroes and heroines, were often read in a one-dimensional moral way.

John of Garland, in his thirteenth-century *Integumenta Ovidii*, provides some telling examples of this method. Hercules is the virtue of an active life; Midas stands for avarice.[33] Arnulf of Orléans, his predecessor, had given somewhat more importance to the literal level in his allegories on the *Metamorphoses* (ca. 1175) but had offered equally reductive, if much more ample readings of the myths.[34] Both commentaries were often appended to manuscripts of the *Metamorphoses*. Interestingly, the two, the first in verse, the second in prose, were segmented just as much as Ovid's text itself.[35] A section of each of the two commentaries followed each metamorphosis, so that a triple-layered text was the result. Another form of gloss, generally called "Lactantian," also often encumbered the text.[36] It is in this complex form, then, that a medieval clerk might read the *Metamorphoses*.

Laden with such commentaries as with so many chains, the pagan myths, which for centuries had led "an existence in the shadow of allegorical ornamentation," made their way to and through the middle ages.[37] Paradoxically, it was this very captivity in the chains of allegory that liberated myth. As Reinhart Herzog points out, the very devaluation of myth, its reduction to "mere metaphor," led to an unprecedented freedom of interpretation, opening these works up to *Remythisierung* (remythisization) and bricolage.[38] The term *remythisization* brings us to some of the theoretical issues surrounding the reception of myth.

The desacralization of myth—necessitated by its introduction into a Christian culture—entailed its *Literarisierung*, its transformation into literature.[39] This transformation is the crucial fact of its reception history. Received as texts, not as religion, the ancient myths provoked not worship but commentary. The myths, then, had become texts, mythological narratives that existed in a large number of versions, none of which was particularly privileged. Hans Blumenberg defines myths as "stories that are distinguished by a high degree of constancy in their narrative core and by an equally pronounced capacity for marginal variation."[40] In this study the term *myth* will be used interchangeably with the terms *fable* (especially Ovidian) and *story* but will refer to a story that always carries within it the signifying potential of its mythic roots.

Mythological narratives in their variability and flexibility can be said to occupy the place of *parole* in a Saussurian *langue-parole* schema transposed to mythology.[41] Where the storehouse of myths resembles the system of *langue*, any given manifestation, such as the story of Pygmalion in the *Roman de la Rose*, is a *parole* and as such is both indebted to and independent from the system that produced it. In a give-and-take process, a kind of dialogue central to the notion of the aesthetics of reception, each use and reuse of myth slightly modifies the system and pushes its frontiers farther.[42]

Equally important is the distinction between diachronic and synchronic analyses of myths. The diachronic perspective will be helpful in defining both the myth's relation to tradition and the dialogue the text engages in with preceding texts, indispensable for a definition of the otherness of vernacular myths. The synchronic approach surfaces in a syntagmatic analysis of myths, highlighted by Weinrich.[43] This approach will allow us to see myths as systems in medieval narratives. In a system like the one in the *Roman de la Rose* or the one in Machaut's *Voir-Dit* the myths comment on each other and cohere in programmatic ways.

Myths are multifaceted, and so is their interpretation. There is no overriding interpretive system—such as the moral or Christianizing—that applies equally to all mythological texts. To reduce each myth's significance to an illustration of Christian dogma would be to completely misunderstand the function of myth in vernacular narrative. The multiple interpretation of myth, practiced by the early commentators, did not suddenly vanish in vernacular literature to be replaced by a one-dimensional moral or Christian interpretation, centering on, say, the notion of Christian charity.

Myths were received by Latin medieval authors as texts and subjected to the treatment that classical texts received. Our brief consideration of the commentary tradition confirms this point. But how did myths appear in narratives that had nothing to do with commentaries and glosses? How did they function intertextually? It is in this context that the formal and interpretive aspects of mythological texts interact in the most interesting way. For myth is almost always a "work of art" set off from the narrative line. Rather than being folded directly into the story, myths tend to be integrated into the new texts in self-consciously "artistic" ways. As parts of exemplary stories, dreams, inscriptions, works of art (ekphrasis of objects such as plaques, shields, saddles, or cups), or invocations, they resolutely assert their function as intertext; they resist a complete fusion with the text that receives them. The mythological text is thus set off from the narrative diegesis or story line and provokes, in the medieval as well as in the modern reader, a desire to interpret.[44] But the definition I give here of an intertext differs from the standard one of the "absent" or "unknown" intertext that hovers in the back of the reader's mind and surfaces through a textual trigger. Rather, the intertext is present through an often fragmented inserted text that is grafted onto the diegesis and evokes the complete text from which it has been severed.

The narratives I discuss in this book were written between 1150 and 1430. During these centuries mythology as used in vernacular literature moves along a kind of curve that sometimes approaches the mythographic tradition and sometimes moves away from it. How medieval poets used this tradition will become a touchstone for an analysis of their interpretive methods and attitudes.

A preliminary consideration of the curve's shape shows that in the twelfth century the *romans antiques* poets, the focus of Chapter 1, set themselves off from mythographic traditions by rehistoricizing the classical epics of Thebes, Rome, and Troy. But while they generally refused to integrate the available interpretive, that is, mostly allegorical, models,[45] they do participate—at least to a certain extent—in the process of remythisization described by Jauss. Poirion sees in the *Roman d'Enéas* a redistribution of the functions of the different deities, a new type of moral related to a founding myth, which could have had a significance for twelfth-century Anglo-Norman England.[46]

The *romans antiques* also provide paradigms or models both for the interpretation of classical mythology and its integration into the vernacular. Thus, on the one hand, the *romans antiques* mark a step on the long path of demythisization,[47] in the sense that they contribute to making classical epic a part of history, sometimes even of medieval national history;[48] on the other, they remythisize by showing new ways of using myths in the composition and interpretation of vernacular literature. In this period, then, an important transformation in the reception of classical myth takes place: a refusal of allegorization goes hand in hand with a new historicization and literarization of myth.

There is a crucial difference between the new type of historicization and the other, traditional, way of historicizing myth: euhemerism.[49] Euhemerism explained away the divinity of the pagan gods, as it were; they were "really" rulers of ancient times who were deified for their perceived merits. The *romans antiques*, on the other hand, offer quite a different view of the gods and pagan religion: pagan religion is medievalized. It begins to resemble Christian rites, while the gods become actors in a historical drama. They are neither deified humans nor expressions of moral forces; rather, they intervene in history.

When the *romans antiques* were reworked in prose in the early-thirteenth-century *Histoire ancienne jusqu'à César*, a peculiar thing happened. As they became even more "historical," a function of the use of prose, they also reacquired moralizations that came straight from the mythographic tradition.[50] The *Histoire ancienne* was very popular; it often appeared in manuscripts with the *Faits des Romains*, an equally popular text that is essentially a life of Julius Caesar. The *Histoire ancienne* was used as a source throughout the middle ages, as, for example, Christine de Pizan's *Mutacion de fortune* demonstrates.

The interest of the *romans antiques* to *Histoire ancienne* sequence lies in its influence, which illustrates the dialectical nature of reception and production. Because the *romans antiques* were received largely as "history" they reappeared in the *Histoire ancienne*. The author of the *Histoire ancienne* had quite a different mind-set than the authors of the *romans antiques*, however. To demonstrate the usefulness of "history" and to cleanse, once again, pagan narrative from inconsistencies and indecencies,[51] the author had recourse to the mythographic tradition and thus reintroduced the very elements the twelfth-century poets had so studiously avoided.

It was not only the *romans antiques* that avoided allegorical interpretation of classical myth. Other full-scale mythological narratives of the same period like the *Narcisus* or *Pyramus and Thisbe* also show no traces of the allegorical interpretations evident in so many commentaries. And while Ovidian myths surface in Marie de France's *Lais*, no overt moral or Christian allegories appear. In light of the learnedness of her Prologue, which seems to present scholarly methods of interpretation, one can think of Marie de France, and of the authors of other vernacular texts, as consciously refusing to allegorize.

In the *Roman de la Rose*, a text replete with classical myth, no overt allegorization of myth is discernible either, as we will see in Chapter 2. Nevertheless, many critics would like to read mythographic moralizations into the *Rose*.[52] In the *Rose*, myths are arranged in artful patterns.[53] Each speaker, and occasionally even the narrator,[54] uses mythological exempla or allusions, demarcated as intertexts. Here, the absence of known mythological stories on the diegetic level suggests that the *Rose* offers us a paradigm for the use of myth in medieval culture. That is, the different functions each speaker assigns to his or her myths cover the spectrum of myth's exemplary usefulness. Unlike, say, the twelfth-century *Narcisus*, which transposes the Narcissus myth into a courtly milieu and plays out a drama of unrequited love, the Narcissus myth in the first part of the *Rose* appears in an immobilized form: it is an inscription, a text.[55] This fact points to the necessity of *reading* myth, as seeing it as an interpretable object. That the moral of the Narcissus story runs counter to that found in the mythographic tradition underlines the originality of the *Rose*. That is, although the *Rose* is written with a clear awareness of the mythographic tradition, it also contains a refusal—though a different sort of refusal than that in the *romans antiques*—to use mythography in traditional ways.

Of course, we have to make a distinction between "traditional mythological stories" and the whole framework of classical myth supplied by figures like Venus and Cupid and "newer" figures like Genius and Nature. As Jauss shows very clearly, these figures participate in the important process of remythisization, that is, they acquire a new density and complexity that shapes them for centuries to come. Thus, for example, the apple-cheeked Cupid familiar from classical literature is replaced in the *Rose* by a suave adult: a capable strategist and an avid reader of love poetry. In the second part of the *Rose*, he is as aware of Ovid, Catullus, and Tibullus as he is of Guillaume de Lorris. The *Rose* represents a dramatic revitalization of mythology, which, as Jauss argues, had come to an almost complete standstill and had begun to atrophy in its "Babylonian captivity" of allegorization. But this particular kind of revitalization extends only to certain mythological figures, for in general the myths appear *as* stories, told by individual characters as by so many prophets, and each speaker conditions the myth he or she tells. The form in which the myths appear further conditions their meaning: interruptions, truncations, and connections between myths all contribute to their signification. Together the myths in the *Rose* provide an illustration of the possibilities of mythological narrative in the thirteenth century.

If we return to our image of the curve approaching and distancing itself from the mythographic commentary tradition, we see, in Chapter 3, the curves approach dramatically with the *Ovide moralisé*. Not only is its author aware of the mythographic tradition and more than willing to accept it and incorporate it into his vast oeuvre, he also expands the entire notion of commentary to hitherto unknown dimensions. His interpretive techniques, vocabulary, and convictions will be at the center of Chapter 3. Growing out of the fourteenth-century fascination with the classics,[56] the

Ovide moralisé represents a massive infusion of mythographic material and Christian allegorizations into vernacular literature. It is also a touchstone of medieval interpretive theory and practice. It illuminates like no other text the difference between allegory and allegoresis, and establishes allegoresis as a thoroughly medieval genre.

Polysemous and often contradictory interpretations are the rule in the *Ovide moralisé*. While many of these interpretations draw on the allegorical tradition as well as on what Herzog calls an *Einheitsmythologie*, a uniting of biblical and mythological figures (a practice that dates back as far as the second century before Christ, when Eupolemos equated the giants with the builders of the tower of Babel, and certainly as far as the *Ecloga Theoduli* [ca. 786],[57] the *Ovide moralisé* also contains many inventive and new associations of myth and interpretation. Although Old Testament figures had been paired with mythological ones, by the authors I just mentioned and others, such as Dante, the multiple pronouncedly Christian correspondences, which could turn almost every figure into Christ, were certainly new.

In Chapter 4 we see whether the impact of the *Ovide moralisé* was as dramatic on fourteenth-century literature as it has been on criticism of fourteenth-century literature. Critics love to read the texts by Machaut and Froissart, for example, through the moral grid of the *Ovide moralisé*.[58] But the *Ovide moralisé*'s interpretations are not exclusively moral: they also exhibit an interest in the poetic aspects of the myths. Such concerns also surface in Machaut's and Froissart's work.

The *Ovide moralisé* must be read in all its complexity and multiple resonances, and, when used in intertextual criticism, its multilayered interpretations should not be reduced to a one-dimensional moral. Altogether, it seems to me that the influence of the *Ovide moralisé* may be found in the interpretive just as much as in the strictly moral realm. That is, the very polysemousness, the almost unbelievable excess of interpretation practiced by the *Ovide* poet liberated myth, opened it up to totally new and apparently limitless interpretive possibilities.

The *Ovide moralisé* thus smoothed the way for the kind of literary bricolage we find in such texts as Machaut's *Fontaine amoureuse* (in which Narcissus's fountain is claimed to have been constructed by Pygmalion) and Froissart's *Prison amoureuse* (which offers counterfeit Ovidian myths invented by the author, yet attributed to Ovid). As in the *Rose*, the myths in Machaut and Froissart treated in Chapter 4 do not generally appear on the diegetic level but rather in ekphrastic constructions, dreams, or exemplary discourses, that is, as inserted texts. This appropriation of myth—its use as a structural device or key to a programmatic reading of the text—is a hallmark of fourteenth-century literature.

These processes also highlight the differences between mythography and this type of use of myth. In mythography myths are interpreted (based on segments drawn from the classical texts), but in the *dits* of Machaut and Froissart, for example, myth is an aid to the interpretation of the new text. Thus the hermeneutic act is doubled: in order to understand the text, the reader first has to understand the myth and recognize the kind of system the myths form in a given text. Fiction is different from mythography—that may very well be the lesson learned in the fourteenth century by poets like Machaut and Froissart and that we can learn from them.

All the more interesting, therefore, is Christine de Pizan's use of myth, the focus of Chapter 5. Her many works present the whole spectrum of late-medieval attitudes toward classical myth. Each text we will consider constitutes a different meditation on the function and value of classical mythology not only for Christine's life and works but for medieval culture as a whole. Autobiographical, moral, hermeneutic, and political issues are figured in the ancient myths Christine uses so profusely. Appropriately, Christine's work ends with the creation of a powerful myth in her *Ditié de Jehanne d'Arc*, written in 1429 at the height of Joan of Arc's glory. Christine did not live to see Joan's end and the end of her myth of national unity and salvation. But Joan of Arc leads us into the realm of new myths, indebted to yet somewhat remote from the classical mythology that this study centers on.

Christine marks the end of our trajectory from the twelfth to the fifteenth century. On the threshold of the Renaissance this book will come to an end. There is no doubt that such a study could go on, and there is no doubt that the stops along the way could have been chosen differently. But like selective medieval pilgrims we will only stop at those points designated—in an imaginary medieval *Guide Michelin*—as worth the trip.

Chapter I

Reading Classical Mythology in the Romances of Antiquity

The history of classical mythology in French literature begins with the romances of antiquity in the third quarter of the twelfth century. Daniel Poirion singles out this moment of cultural transference as "the proud image of a culture's genealogy."[1] The *Roman de Thèbes*, the *Roman d'Enéas*, and the *Roman de Troie* provide their culture's prehistory, centering on the destruction and founding of empires, and they do so not only in genealogical terms (Aeneas's descendant Brutus, for example, was believed to have settled Britain) but also in terms of a literary heritage.[2] Texts that had long circulated in a learned Latin environment now made their way into the vernacular and began to reach courtly and aristocratic audiences.[3] Indeed, the three romances are situated at a most interesting nexus of history, politics, and new intellectual and literary currents. Literature's political potential comes to the fore at the same time as the conscious decision to renew and transform materials of the Latin tradition.

In the areas of politics and literary history the romances of antiquity offer something dramatically new: a shift of the political import of literary texts from the French to the Anglo-Norman domain;[4] and, vis-à-vis the Latin mythographic and commentary traditions that had preserved the very texts the new vernacular poets chose for their ventures, a rejection of overt allegorization and the segmentation of texts that such allegorization usually entailed.[5] Rather, the *romans antiques* poets chose to tell coherent narratives, interrupted occasionally by digressions or ekphrastic pauses. These privileged moments were often used for the display of the poets' mythological knowledge. Thus, while much of the action concerning the pagan gods was eliminated,[6] they appeared in constructions that highlighted their "artificial" nature; they could become literary devices, used to organize and reorient the narrative. Thus the *romans antiques* not only made mythological material available to a French vernacular audience, they also offered innovative literary techniques for making the most of the pagan subject matter in new contexts. They established paradigms for the integration and interpretation of ancient myth that remained influential throughout the middle ages. In this chapter I will consider some of the theoretical and thematic directions the romances of antiquity provided for future generations of vernacular poets, including guidelines that pertain to poetic voice, narrative form, and treatment of sexual threat and transgression.

Classical mythology offered a basis for the establishment of an authoritative voice in the vernacular, but it also had a more far-reaching function. By virtue of its being "a tool for the analysis and explanation of the real through the imaginary" it could also provide ways of speaking about forbidden, transgressive, and dangerous topics. The privileged locus for such topics was Ovid's *Metamorphoses,* where "self-love, homosexuality, and incest account for much of the depiction of human love."[7] Thus the introduction of Ovidian elements into the epics of Statius, Virgil, and Dares and Dictys decisively colored a French-speaking audience's view of pagan antiquity. The epics were anchored in history, but they also offered vistas into forbidden territories, most often in the form of Ovidian myths of problematic passion. As Leonard Barkan observes: "Myths of magical change . . . will be stories celebrating the unfamiliar forms of the sexual impulse, with all their terror and allure."[8] Thus both the affinity of myth and love (a theme that later became quite pronounced in the *Roman de la Rose* and in Machaut and Froissart) and the use of myth as historical legitimation had their origin in the romances of antiquity.

By the time the authors of the romances of antiquity decided to translate and adapt the Latin epics, paganism no longer existed as an actual threat to Christianity. (Although traces of some cults, such as that of Diana, persisted here and there.) Rather, the subject matter of the classical epics was perceived as a part of history and of school learning. In the historical tradition, the idea that the French were the descendants of Francio, a survivor of the Trojan War, dates back to the seventh and eighth centuries.[9] Aeneas, in turn, was believed to have been the founding father of the Britons through his great-grandson Brutus, who had settled in Britain, as Geoffrey of Monmouth told in his *Historia regum Britanniae* (ca. 1139) and Wace in his *Roman de Brut,* based on Geoffrey (ca. 1155).[10] The history of Thebes had not been popular before the *RTh,* yet it was known that Diomedes, one of the Greek adversaries of the Trojans, was the son of Thideus, one of the Seven against Thebes. Thus the link between Thebes and Troy was evident and encouraged people to think in terms of an ancient trilogy: Thebes, Troy, Rome (Aeneas).

The romances of antiquity were created in an Anglo-Norman milieu, possibly for the court of Henry II Plantagenet.[11] Bernard Guenée has shown that Plantagenet historiography fits into a pattern of the emergence of national history in the twelfth century and is particularly tendentious. It also presents events and human behavior of ancient history as repeatable and falling into certain models, such as "feuds between brothers, . . . the illicit loves of kings etc.—which have far-reaching national consequences."[12]

The *RE* and the *RTr* fit rather well into a legitimizing scheme for the new Angevin dynasty: one celebrates a founding myth and an advantageous marriage (in 1152 Henry married Eleanor of Aquitaine with her vast territories); the other functions as a kind of prelude to the *Roman de Brut* (and thus "British" history) by providing a detailed account of the Trojan War and its aftermath. By contrast, the *RTh* with its bleak view of parricide and fratricidal war is not really a tribute to the skills of the new ruler of England. Rather, it should be read as an exhortation against civil war addressed to the royal family of Henry II, designated so aptly by the chronicler Richard of Devizes as "the troubled house of Oedipus."[13]

For the *RTh* and the *RE* in particular, an analysis of the suppression, addition, and reorientation of mythological material can help us to characterize the political mission of these texts. Intertwined with any political purposes the romances of antiquity may have had are the literary innovations they proposed. For future generations of poets it was primarily the literary treatment of mythology found in these romances that provided models to imitate and react against. It is this lineage of classical mythology that is the primary focus of our study.

It is hard to overestimate the effect the vernacularization of classical subject matter must have had. Poets like Chrétien de Troyes and Marie de France quickly became aware of the *romans antiques*. Audiences who may have known the *Chanson de Roland* and some saints' lives were suddenly confronted with a wealth of figures, events, and new literary techniques that must have astonished and delighted them. The pagans, with whom such audiences had most often associated the saracens of the epic (that is, the enemy) and Apollo, who was conflated with the "angel of the bottomless pit" Apollyon of Revelation 9.11 and was reduced to an idol invoked to aid Charlemagne's enemies, for example, were now invested with new identities and new functions. The pagans were real people, loving, suffering, and dying. They were not Christians, it is true, but was the pagan Dido in the *RE* not the most unfortunate and the best of women anyway?[14] The word *pagan*, used frequently in the romances of antiquity, sets the characters of ancient times off from their medieval admirers, yet their humanity is never denied.

It was a different story with the gods. A medieval audience may have heard the name of Apollo/Apollyon in the *Chanson de Roland* and have seen him as an incarnation of pagan evil and idol worship, but of course this figure did not resemble in the least the powerful sun god with oracular powers presented in the earliest romances. Early on in vernacular literature a distinction was made between mythological characters like Medea, Oedipus, or even Circe, who act on the diegetic level like any other person, and the Olympian gods, who do not. The gods of the *romans antiques* are in many ways quite unlike their counterparts in the Latin texts of Virgil and Statius, where they appear as flesh and blood and intervene in the action at every possible moment. Yet, this partial removal of the gods and goddesses from the diegesis did not result in allegorization, nor were the *romans antiques* poets attracted by one of the other possibilities available for the treatment of ancient myth at the time: the cosmological allegories of the poets associated with the School of Chartres.[15]

Certainly, the activities of the Neoplatonic Chartrian poets had helped to prepare the ground for new ventures involving classical myth. There was, after all, something that could be called the "renaissance of the twelfth century," a revalorization of and a new interest in classical texts. But while the *romans antiques* poets undoubtedly benefited from these currents, they did not subscribe to the same tenets. They were much more firmly grounded in history, and they were not interested in the same type of remythisization, which involved the creation of new figures, like Genius and Nature, and which became so influential later on.[16] The *romans antiques* poet did engage in some remythisization, however; that is, the gods are no longer the personifications they had become in the mythographic and particularly the epithalamic traditions[17] but rather agents that serve new purposes designed by the medieval poets. Thus, for example, in the *RE*, as Daniel Poirion has shown, the gods become partial to Enéas as the representative of a new founding myth; in the *RTh* Jupiter becomes a mouthpiece for the poet's antiwar message.[18] In short, the *romans antiques* poets undoubtedly felt that they were part of a tradition that gave classical mythology a new dignity in this period, but they also consciously separated themselves from this tradition; they were innovators, the founding fathers of a new genre: romance.

The *Roman de Thèbes*

Even if Sigmund Freud had not given the Oedipus myth a new lease on life,[19] the Theban story of parricide and fratricide with its powerful—and eternal—implications for human history would probably have survived till our present era. It has as much meaning in modern as in medieval times, though this meaning may have changed. While for us moderns the threats of incest and parricide are most often internalized parts of our troubled psyches, for a medieval audience these threats could have had a more immediate political impact. Daniel Poirion has shown how the mysterious story of Oedipus, involving as it does not only parricide but also attempted infanticide, incest, and the inability to establish a viable lineage, could represent a mise-en-scène of the myriad threats to the feudal order.[20]

In the middle ages the Oedipus myth was reworked a number of times,[21] but the first version that a French-speaking audience became acquainted with was the "pre-text" of the *RTh*.[22] Statius in the *Thebaid* had clearly assumed his audience's familiarity with the story and could therefore content himself with a few references to what had "already" happened.[23] The only lengthy development involving Oedipus is the curse against his sons, which contains a number of details that make the prehistory intelligible to Statius's audience. They learn, for example, that Oedipus was brought up by Polybius, who turned out not to be his father; that he consulted the oracle at Delphi in order to find his real father; that he solved the riddle of the Sphinx; that he "cleft the visage of the trembling dotard" (his father, Laius); that he joined himself to his mother in an incestuous union and had sons with her; that he blinded himself when he found out what he had done; and that his sons mocked his blindness. This last outrage provoked the curse in which Oedipus calls on the gods to avenge him through the destruction of his sons.[24] The *RTh* poet found some other details regarding the exposing of Oedipus in a forest and his early life in the *Second Vatican Mythographer*, as L. G. Donovan has shown.[25]

Why did the medieval poet expand the information found in the *The-*

baid? Jean-Charles Huchet suggests that the poet wanted to provide a "narrative matrix," accentuating the killing of multiple father figures and their substitutes: "the final destruction of Thebes is already present in the oracle of Apollo." The Oedipus story, according to Huchet, participates in a kind of archeological project the *RTh* proposes: the search for the originating fault or sin.[26] Further, the story highlights the concept of the sin "against nature," the incest that brings about the final destruction of the Theban realm. The Oedipus myth is a locus for forbidden destructive forces; prefacing the *RTh* with the explicit narration of this myth thus orients the audience's reception of the entire romance, which ends precisely with an exhortation against sins "against nature" (ll. 10,555–62).[27]

But could the rather radical rewriting of the *Thebaid* also be related to the poet's attitude vis-à-vis Statius: a parricide of the *auctor* so to speak? The surprising way of citing Statius for precisely those moments in the narrative that are either not in the *Thebaid* or substantially modified could suggest this. Indeed, the medieval poet's voice usurps that of Statius just as he usurps that of a variety of mythical figures throughout the text.[28] One such figure is Apollo, whose oracle, prophesying parricide, plays a central role in the *RTh*'s pre-text. It is here that the poet first gains authority through an inscription of his own voice into a divine mythical one.

One of the most dramatic changes with regard to the *Thebaid* is the transposition of Oedipus's curse, in which he recounts his own sinful life (ll. 56–87) from his prayer and invocation of the gods to the diegetic level. The story of Oedipus is thus removed from its overtly polemical purpose and becomes functional on a narrative level. From a formal perspective, the story of Oedipus is a digression because it interrupts the résumé of the plot, which the poet begins with "des deus freres parleré" (I will speak of the two brothers; l. 19), but soon interrupts:

Des deus freres ore em present
ne parleré plus longuement,
car ma reson veul conmencier
a leur ayol dont voil treitier. (ll. 33–36)

Of the two brothers I will at this moment speak no longer, for I want to begin my story by treating of their ancestor.

As in the *RE*, where, as we will see, the poet has to take a step backward in order to proceed, in the *RTh* the poet undoes the very sequence of events he has just proposed in order to give us some important background.

This digressive technique, often justified by a "reason" that has to be given for some of the plot's elements, will become typical as a method for the integration of mythological subject matter in romance narrative texts. It allows for the establishment of more explicit thematic links between different temporal dimensions of a text: the reference to the "ayol" (ancestor) of line 36, for example, highlights the genealogical aspects of a doomed race much more than Oedipus's direct speech in the *Thebaid* could have done.

Thus the medieval poet steps back two generations, for the first event recounted in the pre-text-digression is Laius's visit to Apollo to inquire about the gods' purpose for him. Apollo's prophecy follows, vouched for by the narrator: everything happened just as Apollo had predicted, he states (ll. 45–48). The narrator uses Apollo's divine voice for laying out the plot to come, an astute proleptic device. The narrator also offers his own prophecies and represents the plot to come as a contest between Laius's and Apollo's willpower.[29] Since the shaping of the plot depends on no one but the narrator, and since Apollo's prediction comes true, the poet's voice is clearly equal to that of the divine oracle; he is in control of the narrative, while a mere mortal such as Laius vainly tries to avoid the inevitable. The narrator also assumes the role of the interpreter of the oracle when he says (this time for Oedipus): "Mes du respons n'entendi mot, / car dit li a par couverture / tel respons de quoi cil n'ot cure" (But he did not understand one word of the answer, for he [Apollo] gave him such an answer in a covered way that he did not care for it; ll. 208–10). The term "par couverture" suggests, of course, the twelfth-century notion of the integument, a fiction or fable covering a deeper moral meaning. The poet signals Laius's incomprehension of this device, while he, the poet, presumably knows how to interpret the oracle. Interestingly, though, the *RTh* remains grounded in history and narrative: what lies beneath the poet's "couverture" is the plot, not allegorical significance.[30]

The medieval poet continues to play games of interpretation when he reinforces the emphasis on decoding oracles with the repeated appearance of riddles. He insists much more strongly than Statius on the multiple riddles only briefly evoked in the *Thebaid*.[31] Indeed, the riddle of the "beast" that walks first on four legs, then on two, and finally on three occurs twice in the *RTh*. Initially Oedipus solves it and thus saves Thebes from the monstrous sphinx (ll. 269–364); later on Thideus has to solve the same riddle, this time posed by a devil named Astarot (ll. 2889–938). Thideus first wants to disqualify himself: he is a chevalier and knows more about carrying arms than solving riddles. But eventually he solves it without difficulty and the old she-devil collapses and dies.

Since this episode is absent from the *Thebaid*, its presence here underscores the poet's predilection for having his characters take on tricky problems of interpretation. Thideus's initial insistence that a chevalier cannot be expected to solve riddles seems to suggest that riddles belong to the interpretive domain of *clergie*, the kind of book learning inaccessible to a mere knight. His successful solution to the riddle, then, aligns *clergie* with *chevalerie*, a solidarity suggested in the Prologue (ll. 13–16), where the poet excludes all those who are neither clerks nor knights from his potential audience, a situation that of course reflects the conditions of production and reception of the *romans antiques*.

From the obscure prophecy of Apollo to the sphinx's riddle to the riddle of Astarot, the characters must use their powers of interpretation, and in most cases, lives depend on the correctness of their interpretive efforts. This dramatization of interpretation has repercussions for the treatment of myth in the *RTh*, particularly in light of the implicit refusal on the part of the poet to espouse preceding allegorical modes of interpretation. Myths must be interpreted: this had always been a precondition for their survival in a Christian culture. But in the *RTh* their interpretation remains on the narrative level. Answers to riddles shape the plot and not what is hidden under any "couverture" (l. 209) or "responsse obcure" (l. 192). This does not mean, of course, that myth is merely part of the romance narrative. It rather means that from the beginning, the poet appropriates the myths of Thebes by proposing correct (Apollo's) and incorrect (Laius's) interpretations of them, pitting (as he will do for the Arachne story) divine power and cleverness against human efforts. Since he is aligning himself with Apollo, he is invested with a quasi-divine authority to deal with myth as he sees fit. And indeed, the other principal episodes we will consider here will demonstrate the poet's independence not only from Statius but from any other tradition that had turned the Theban heroes into schematic, one-dimensional allegorizations.[32] Rather, the gods will play a part in a drama, reoriented with regard to the *Thebaid* and devised by the medieval poet.

It has often been remarked that in comparison to their treatment in the *Thebaid* the role the gods play in the *RTh* is minimal.[33] While they are still responsible for prophecies and dreams (as in the case of Adrastus's dream announcing the coming of his future sons-in-law), they no longer swoop down from the heavens in order to intervene directly in the business of warfare. This fundamental change with regard to Statius sets the tone for many future treatments of mythology in medieval texts.

The *RTh* poet turned to other figures, drawn from Ovidian myth and the historical tradition, in order to articulate some essential ideas as well as conflicts and dangers that had not been present in the ancient texts. In the *RTh* two female figures who do not appear in the *Thebaid* give a new richness to Statius's text: Arachne and Semiramis. Both are skilled and powerful women who are finally undone by their presumption. Here they are conjoined as the producer and the giver of some marvelous curtains in the palace of Adrastus, king of the Argives and the future enemy of the Thebans (ll. 913–18). Arachne, a well-known Ovidian figure, is not actually named but identified by her contest with Minerva and her fate: suicide by hanging.[34] Semiramis built the city of Babylon, assumed the role of male warrior in her kingdom, had an incestuous relationship with her son, and was said to have been killed by him.[35] The stories of these two women offer a number of thematic correspondences to the *RTh*; some of these are explicit, others are evoked intertextually. Both women exemplify transgressive behavior, linked to sexuality and human ambition, that threatens the established order.

Arachne represents a human whose ambition brings about divine punishment. Arachne's crime was her "ignorance of the limits of humanity,"[36] as well as her exposing of the sexual activities of the gods. For while Pallas's tapestry emphasized the power and authority of the gods, Arachne's concentrated on the victims of divine seduction. The presence of the curtains thus signals the dangers of human presumption, and it does so early on in the romance before this very theme takes center stage in the episode of Capaneus, defier of the gods. But the allusion to Arachne also anticipates the engulfment of Amphiares's marvelous chariot, a superior work of art, emblematic of human striving for civilization. As we will see below, the chariot can be equated with human learning and skill. Similarly, there is a connection between weaving and poetry; the texture of the fabric is analogous to the poetic text.[37] Arachne's cruel fate, brought about by her hubris and disregard for divine will, thus announces the disappearance of human art and accomplishments: the impending doom of Thebes as well as that of its adversaries.

Semiramis and her son, for their part, embody the sins of Oedipus in a kind of mirror image: incest between mother (founder of a city) and son, with the difference that this crime was committed knowingly at the mother's instigation; and matricide, an act of vengeance on the son's part. By evoking the Semiramis legend the medieval poet replays the events of the pre-text, contrasting implicitly sins committed consciously with those committed unknowingly. Moreover, a story of incest now also hovers in the background of Adrastus's court, pointing perhaps to unarticulated conflicts on the Argive side. Since the *RTh* poet tries to assign the guilt for the fratricidal war more evenly than did Statius,[38] the allusions to Arachne and Semiramis clarify that blasphemy and incest are not the exclusive sins of the Thebans.

Arachne's tapestry, the doomed achievement of human industry and skill, finds an equivalent in Amphiares's chariot. Amphiares, designated as an archbishop knowledgeable in the Seven Liberal Arts in the *RTh*,[39] fought against the Thebans as an ally of Adrastus. Though he knew from an oracle that he would die during the first battle (ll. 5053–56), he is an exemplar of heroism. This dual nature of learned clerk and chivalric hero makes him emblematic of the "clerc" and "chevalier" of the Prologue, defining the *RTh*'s cultural environment.

The centerpiece of the Amphiares episode is the description of his chariot.[40] It was made by Vulcan, the divine master craftsman:

Vulcans le fist par grant porpens
et a lui faire mist lonc tens.
Par estuide et par grant conseil
i mist la lune et le soleill
et tresgita le firmament
par art et par enchantement. (ll. 4953–58)

. . .

Qui des set arz set rien entendre,
iluec em puet assez aprendre.
Li jaiant sunt en l'autre pan. (ll. 4967–69)

. . .

Jupiter est de l'autre part,
unne foudre tient et un dart.
Mars et Pallas sont en aprés, (ll. 4979–81)

. . .

Tuit se combatent par le trone, (l. 4986)

. . .

paintes i furent les set Arz (l. 4989)

. . .

L'euvre du curre et la matire
vaut bien Thebes a tot l'empire. (ll. 5007–8)

Vulcan made it [the chariot] very thoughtfully and spent a long time making it. After much study and reflection he put the sun and the moon there and forged the firmament, through his art and magic. Whoever wants to know something about the Seven Arts can learn quite a lot here. The giants are on the other side. Jupiter is on another side, he holds a lightning bolt and a spear. Mars and Pallas are [painted] after him. They [the gods] all fight for the throne. The workmanship and the material of the chariot are well worth as much as the entire empire of Thebes.

This description of the chariot, absent from the *Thebaid*, can be read as an ekphrastic transposition of the essential elements that make up the *RTh*: the focus on artistry, on encyclopedic knowledge,[41] and on the Seven Arts; as well as the mythological pantheon, represented by the giants and the gods. The only action highlighted is that of fighting for the throne, which, of course, the characters in the *RTh* do. I suggested earlier that while in the romances of antiquity the gods still appear, they are frequently removed from the diegetic level. The chariot confirms this: "all" (tuit; ll. 4983 and 4986) the gods appear on the chariot, with Jupiter, Mars, and Pallas singled out; that is, the highest god, and the gods of warfare and chivalry in particular define the chariot. Up to this point these gods have only appeared in invocations (another paradigm for the transposition of the gods from the plot level); now they appear in images. In a proleptic move on the poet's part, Jupiter appears with the very weapons he will use later to destroy Capaneus.

What the poet is doing here is transposing the direct intervention of the gods found in Statius onto a work of art whose author is—via Vulcan—the poet. The vocabulary of this passage establishes an analogy between the creation of the chariot and writing poetry. "Porpens," "estuide," "conseil," "art," "enchantement" (reflection, study, deliberation, artistic skill, incantation)—all these terms could be read as referring to the technical terms of poetic creation. The first two could correspond to *inventio*, with its emphasis on deliberation and study, which lead to finding a suitable subject matter; "conseil" could designate *dispositio*, the ordering of textual elements. The last two terms evoke *elocutio*, the enunciation of the text, while "matire" of line 5007 suggests a parallel with poetic subject matter. The text has a didactic function, as the poet indicates by using the word "aprendre" (to learn) in conjunction with the Seven Arts. In contrast, we are not explicitly exhorted to learn anything from the gods' conduct depicted here. On the different sides of the chariot, the poet thus pits the behavior of the gods against the education that makes knowledge of them possible. The "old" gods, exhibiting the behavior that already made the Homeric commentators call for some nonliteral, more acceptable meaning, need to be integrated into new frameworks, a new epistemology, based on the type of education proposed by our medieval poet. Only the "new" gods, those re-created by our poet, can play a meaningful role for the medieval audience.

Like Achilles's shield in the *Iliad* (bk. 18), or Aeneas's in the *Aeneid* (bk. 8), the chariot presents a crystallization of a society's values, glory, and dangers as depicted by master artists. And just as Vulcan fashioned the chariot, which displays not only the very type of education the medieval poet had received but also an internecine war, the poet made the romance, drawing on his traditional clerical education and offering the dramatic story of a fratricidal war. The positive (learning) and the negative (warfare) are neatly balanced on the different sides of the chariot. The chariot provides a forceful commentary on the contest between the power of culture and civilization and that of the desire for mutual destruction. Eventually, though, Amphiares's engulfment together with his chariot does not signal a complete destruction of the civilization emblematized by the images on it. Vulcan's masterpiece perishes, but, and this is important, the romance endures.

While Amphiares is a wise and learned figure who accepts his death and the engulfment of his chariot, Capaneus, another ally of Adrastus fighting on the Argive side, is a blasphemer who in his determination to win the battle against the Thebans challenges the gods. In another important addition to Statius's *Thebaid*, the medieval poet introduces another set piece, the Theban temple, which Capaneus seeks to destroy. This image transports us deep into the mythology of Thebes itself. The ekphrasis of the temple offers another moment of crystallization: the links to Thebes's problematic past highlight its present dangers. This could be read as a *mise en abyme* of *RTh*'s global function, for in depicting eternal repeatable patterns of human behavior and pointing to their potential consequences, the romance—like the temple—makes history and its lessons visible.

The poet makes the description part of his remarks on a feast celebrated within the Theban walls in honor of Cadmus, Thebes's founding father. Again, artistic and poetic accomplishments occupy center stage. In fact, the temple has many features that evoke a medieval manuscript. The paintings on it present *estoires* executed in gold and silver (ll. 9182–83), recalling illuminations and historiated initials. The decorations of enamel and precious stones and the ebony panel resemble the wooden cases in which medieval books were kept. Mars and Venus, ekphrastic images of a well-known mythological story, are depicted on this panel. Just as well known is the story of Cadmus, the brother of Europa, a woman abducted and raped by Jupiter. Cadmus's exploits of slaying the serpent; of sowing its teeth, which brought forth warriors who promptly killed each other; of founding Thebes; and of marrying Mars's daughter Hermione are the subject matter of the paintings on the temple. The Theban myths link transgression (the adultery of Mars and Venus, the rape of Europa) to the founding of the city and thus undercut the celebratory atmosphere of the Theban feast day.

Through his ekphrastic technique the poet emphasizes the notion of memory: this entire story, the founding history of Thebes, is "digne de memoire" (worthy of being remembered; l. 9226).[42] This commemoration was also the function of texts: to be read in a celebratory or ceremonial context. As Wace puts it in the *Roman de Rou*:

> Pur remembrer des ancessurs
> Les faiz e les diz e les murs
> Deit l'um les liures et les gestes
> E les estoires lire as festes.[43]

In order to remember the deeds, the sayings, and the customs of the ancestors one should read the books and epics and stories on feast days.

This sort of reading and celebrating is exactly what is happening at this point in the *RTh*: the story of Cadmus and Amphion is being read and celebrated by the Theban population. Both of these founding fathers were also ancestors of anyone engaged in writing: Cadmus was the inventor of the alphabet; Amphion used "gramaire" (l. 9323) to construct the city of Thebes.

The temple is thus a mythological artifact, an emblem recalling the past of Thebes couched in an elaborate artistic vocabulary. It embodies not so much Theban history as *writing* about Theban history. Once again the transposition of mythological material from the diegetic to an "artistic" level is functional: the diegetic function assigned to mythological characters in the *Thebaid* is replaced by a memorial and emblematic function.

Invocation is a further nondiegetic representation of the gods that becomes functional in the general design of *RTh*. Capaneus's blasphemous speech, challenging the gods, skillfully transposes elements from the *Thebaid* in order to rewrite the myth of Thebes and to articulate the threat against Theban culture.[44]

The defiant speech of Capaneus follows the description of the temple and makes mention of some of the same characters and events, notably Mars and Venus, and Hermione (l. 9334). Most of the many Theban figures, almost all of them victims of the gods' vengeance, evoked by Capaneus come from the speech of Aletes in the *Thebaid* 3.179–213. In an interesting move, the medieval poet has transposed this speech by a Theban elder to the enemy of Thebes, Capaneus.[45] In the *Thebaid* the speech, evoking the past misfortunes of Thebes, is addressed to the mourners of the 50 knights who have been killed in the treacherous ambush of Thideus after his diplomatic mission in Thebes. Aletes has contrasted the guilt of some of the early "mythological" Thebans with the innocence of Etheocles's men killed in the ambush. But whatever its function, Aletes's speech clearly articulates that the doom of Thebes reaches back deep into a mythological past.

Capaneus's tirade is extremely complex:

N'i vaudra rien deu ne deesse,
lire sautier ne chanter messe;
n'i vaudra rien veu ne promesse
que clers en face ne clergesse.
Ou sont ore tuit vostre dé,
Mars, Venus et Hermÿoné,
Juno et Leüthocoé,
et Palamon et Agavé
qui pour le despit de lor dé
furent puis mort et forsené? (ll. 9329–38)

Neither god nor goddess will do you any good now, nor will the reading of the psalter or saying mass; nor will any vow or promise that a clerk or a female clerk may make. Where are now all your gods? Mars, Venus, and Hermione, Juno and Leucothea, and Palamon and Agave, who for their defiance of the gods were killed and driven mad?[46]

Capaneus freely mixes pagan and Christian religion, exhibiting the syncretism so characteristic of the *RTh*. He then goes on to list the unfortunate forebears of the current inhabitants of Thebes, some of whom were —as Arachne was and Capaneus will be—punished for their presumption and defiance of the gods. In addition to the ones just cited, Capaneus enumerates Bacchus, Semele, Amphion, Niobe, Echion (Cadmus's friend), Calchas, Juno, Pallas, Manto, Tiresias, Pentheus, Athamas, and finally "all the gods" of this town. This list is meant to illustrate that Thebes has "tante paine . . . enduree" (has suffered such pain; l. 9318).

Why did the medieval poet move this speech from Aletes's to Capaneus's mouth? Capaneus represents the current doom of Thebes. Although he himself will not live to see the death of the two royal brothers Etheocles and Polynices, their fate is sealed. Like the description of the temple, the speech is a vehicle for conveying the mythological history of Thebes, and here, unlike in the *Thebaid*, it is articulated by their enemy. Rather than a consolation, as in the *Thebaid*, the history here is more a threat. As in the Amphiares episode, the focus of this story is the dire consequences of warfare. In that warning Capaneus's speech mirrors the function of the *RTh* as a whole. Nothing less than the continuity of (Theban) history is at stake here. The connection to the medieval audience is established through the syncretism in the representation of religion. Capaneus defies gods and goddesses in the same breath as clerks and the psalter. According to him all of them are equally useless in averting Thebes's doom.

Yet Capaneus does not have the last word. Right after his blasphemous speech (in which he ultimately sets his own prowess and strength over the power of the gods) the gods convene a council, which results in Capaneus's violent death (ll. 9377–9630). This dramatic scene is amplified with regard to the *Thebaid*: it draws not only on 10.883–920 but also on other council scenes from Books 1 and 7. Much of the material is original to the medieval text. Most important, it is the first and only scene in which the gods—both those supporting the Greeks and those in favor of Thebes (ll. 9377–78)—appear on the diegetic level. Their function here is that of seekers of peace, clearly stated in line 9383: "[pour] . . . savoir se pes en porroit estre" (to know whether peace could be brought about). Jupiter, designated by the medieval terms "danz" and "mestre" (sir, master; l. 9380), first identifies himself by his achievements: he devised languages and kingdoms; he conferred divinity on the gods; and he controls animals and humans (ll. 9407–14). He decrees that there must be battle and proceeds to listen to the arguments of the supporters of the different sides. Juno appeals in the Greeks' favor (and threatens to withhold her sexual favors from Jupiter); Bacchus and Hercules plead for Thebes by evoking their mothers. Jupiter finally decides that Capaneus's blasphemy was worse than that of the giants (who also appear on Amphiares's chariot) and that Capaneus deserves to die (ll. 9589–600). He wants to send a signal ("enseignes"; l. 9597) to humans that such outrage will not be suffered by the gods, and he does so in the form of a thunderbolt that kills Capaneus. Thus Jupiter's warnings against the serious consequences of war, and in particular civil war, which run through the entire council scene, are realized in a most dramatic manner.

Since, as I argued earlier, the central message of the *RTh* is that war must be avoided, the poet again aligns himself with a god. In the opening scene he usurps the oracular voice of Apollo; here, he makes the highest god (*the* authority figure for the characters in the romance) the mouthpiece for the message of his entire text. Jupiter and the *RTh* dramatically decry the folly of fratricidal war.

By adding the prehistory of the Theban war and the descriptions of Amphiares's chariot and of the temple, by putting the speech dwelling on the mythological history of Thebes into Capaneus's mouth, and finally by moving the gods onto the diegetic level only in the vastly expanded council scene, the medieval poet reorients, in fact reinvents, the mythological basis of the *Thebaid.* The mythological past of Thebes is integrated into digression, ekphrasis, and invocation, thus providing a model for future romances for how to include mythological material. The only appearance of the gods on the diegetic level shows that the pagan divine voices within the text can in fact be put to the same service as the romance as a whole: to warn against civil war. As for the poet himself, he constructs his authority through his reliance on a Latin authority as well as through the inscription of his own voice into that of the supreme god, Jupiter. The earliest romance text thus demonstrates the usefulness of classical mythology as historical exemplar and as literary model, a means for the creation of a new vernacular authority.

Both formally and functionally, then, the *RTh* proposes new models for the use of the mythological elements present in the classical texts the romances of antiquity adapted. This lesson was well learned by the *RE* poet, who used some of the same methods as the *RTh* poet but added new and different ones in his reorientation of the *Aeneid*'s mythology.[47]

The *Roman d'Enéas*

The *Roman d'Enéas* reorchestrates Virgil's relationship between love and power through a transformation and reorientation of some of the *Aeneid*'s mythological material, notably through the introduction of Ovidian myths. Thus the medieval poet opens the text to new themes and concerns that not only proved influential for the development of vernacular romance but also offered formal and functional models for the use of mythological elements.

Like the poet of the *RTh*, the *Enéas* poet rejects overt allegorization, and that despite the fact that the *Aeneid*, much more than the *Thebaid*, had been the subject of commentaries and allegorizations. In late antiquity Servius had written his detailed commentary on the *Aeneid*, and Fulgentius had the *Aeneid* explained to him by an authoritative Virgil figure in his *Exposition of the Content of Virgil*.[48] In the twelfth century the commentary attributed to Bernardus Silvestris, equating the first six Virgilian books with the six ages of man, was the most influential.[49] No direct echo of this tradition can be found in the *RE*. While the marginalia and glosses of *Aeneid* manuscripts left some traces and while the commentary tradition undoubtedly hovered in the back of the medieval poet's mind, the *RE* features no explicit allegorization.[50] The poet clearly felt no need to allegorize the pagan gods, but he did feel compelled to rewrite and to reorient Virgilian mythology. In the process the *RE* poet picked up some of the methods for the integration of myth proposed by the *RTh* but also added new ones, particularly in the realm of amorous myth. His linking of Virgilian and Ovidian mythology was the most influential and far-reaching innovation in vernacular literature.[51] But the medieval poet's use of Ovid goes beyond the introduction of amorous vocabulary and psychology. Ovid's opening "towards the feminine" allows the medieval poet to approach a different problematic: he transforms the roles of Venus and Lavinia. In line with Ovid's view of Lavinia in *Amores* 2.12 as "setting the war afoot," her role is enhanced by comparison with her role in the *Aeneid*. Moreover, Ovidian intertexts allow the surfacing of feminine threats to the established order.[52]

Unlike in the *RTh*, where the gods appear on the diegetic level only in the Council scene, in the *RE* some of the gods intervene on the plot level, although less frequently than in the *Aeneid*.[53] Echoing the *RTh*, the *RE* also uses digression and ekphrasis as means of conveying mythological material; in some instances intertextual allusions allow the threatening aspects of myth to surface. We will focus on only a few episodes that illustrate the effectiveness of the manipulation of myth for a reorientation or enrichment of some of Virgil's major themes.

The *Roman d'Enéas* opens with a brief summary of the Trojan war and then turns to a lengthy elaboration of the Judgment of Paris (ll. 99–182). Virgil mentioned the Judgment of Paris only briefly in *Aeneid* 1.27 in order to explain Juno's wrath against the Trojans. Not even the detail that Paris had preferred Venus, or rather her bribe, Helen, to Juno and had awarded her the coveted golden apple appears in the *Aeneid*.

Nevertheless, a more detailed version of the Judgment had attached itself rather early on to the *Aeneid* in the form of marginal glosses that offered the interpretive possibility of the choice between the three goddesses as a choice between three lives: the active (Juno), the contemplative (Pallas), and the voluptuous (Venus).[54] However, since the *RE* essentially rejected the allegorizing tradition, the question remains why the *RE* poet, who otherwise follows Virgil rather faithfully, chose to devote so much space to the Judgment.

We saw that in the *RTh* the pre-text of Oedipus also takes the form of a digression. The function of this type of digression can be both backward and forward looking. That is, it provides explanatory background material and at the same time may offer a structuring or a proleptic device for the text to come.[55] Both of these functions are evident in the Judgment of Paris episode.

The opening sequence of the *RE* has often been contrasted with Virgil's beginning his epic in medias res with Aeneas's shipwreck after his escape from Troy.[56] The *RE* begins with these lines:

> Quant Menelaus ot Troie asise,
> onc n'en torna tresqu'il l'ot prise,
> gasta la terre et tot lo regne
> por la vanjance de sa fenne. (ll. 1–4)

When Menelaus had besieged Troy he did not depart from it until he had conquered it; he laid waste the land and the whole kingdom as a revenge for his wife.

Then the poet tells of the sack of Troy and Enéas's escape. When he and his men are at sea, Juno's wrath descends on them. It is here that the Judgment of Paris appears as a digression: because of Paris Juno hated all Trojans. The reason ("l'acheison"; l. 99) for this hatred lies in the Judgment, and it will be explained now. The poet does not mention the wedding of Peleus and Thetis, which often forms the background for Discord's throwing of the golden apple. Rather, Juno, Pallas, and Venus are in "un parlemant" (a conversation; l. 103), when Discord appears with the apple. The apple has an inscription "an grezois" (in Greek; l. 107) that it should be given to the most beautiful. Since each one desires the apple, they finally agree to ask Paris "qui molt savoit des lois" (who was very knowledgeable in the laws; l. 120) to choose between them. Paris "par grant engin" (with great cunning; l. 131) decides to wait and see what each goddess might offer him as a bribe.[57] Juno offers him riches, Pallas "pris de chevalerie" (the highest prowess), and Venus the most beautiful woman in the world. Paris covets all three things offered to him but finally prefers the woman offered by Venus. This woman turns out to be Helen for "plus bele fame ne trova" (she [Venus] found no more beautiful woman; l. 178). The episode closes with a repetition of the word "acheison" (reason; l. 181), and thus we learn that it was because of Paris that Pallas and Juno hated Troy.

There can be no doubt that Paris's choice offers us a program for reading the romance.[58] Michel Rousse has associated the three goddesses and their bribes with the three important women of the *RE*: Dido is linked to Juno and riches; Camille belongs to the realm of Pallas and knightly prowess; and Lavine is associated with Venus and love. Thus, Rousse argues, because the romance can be divided into three parts, each part has a patron goddess.[59] This scheme is tempting, if perhaps too clear-cut. To associate Dido only with Juno because of her riches and not with Venus or, conversely, to link Lavine with Venus but not with Juno (when Lavine brings plenty of riches to Enéas) is too reductive. I agree with Rousse that the goddesses and their promised gifts provide a structural device, but I would see the fulfillment of the announced structure as less schematic: the goddesses announce the major themes of the romance—riches, chivalry, and conquests and love—and a variety of characters and situations can be attached to each of these themes.[60]

What the Judgment suggests is that Enéas should be read as reenacting and most likely correcting Paris's choice. Virgil hints at the link between Paris and Aeneas in the most disparaging terms: King Iarbas, one of Dido's rejected suitors, hears of Aeneas's arrival in Carthage and comments: "And now that Paris with his eunuch train . . . grasps the spoil" (4.215–17). In this equation of Paris and Aeneas the latter is clearly associated with lechery and homosexuality, a theme that also surfaces in the *RE*.[61] The extended treatment of the Judgment invites readers to reconsider the link between Paris and Enéas, especially in light of the romance's ending, at which time the poet closes the circle and again evokes Paris. In an ironic move, he compares Enéas's happiness to that of Paris:

> Unques Paris n'ot graignor joie,
> quant Eloine tint dedanz Troie,
> qu'Eneas ot, quant tint s'amie
> en Laurente (ll. 10,109–12)

Never did Paris have greater joy when he held Helen in Troy than had Enéas when he held his beloved in Laurente.

At the end of the trajectory from Troy to Rome Enéas thus not only outdoes Paris, he *un*does him: the threat of homosexuality has vanished in a legitimate marriage; the joy of Rome must clearly be contrasted with the disaster of Troy.[62]

Enéas's progress can be read against the Judgment of Paris in a variety of ways. In terms of the choice of Venus we have to ask What is the Judgment of Paris after all, if not the choice of Venus? But is Paris's Venus the same as Enéas's? Enéas, of course, is Venus's son; the love goddess thus plays a central role in Enéas's career. Daniel Poirion has pointed out that most of the Virgilian pantheon is missing in the *RE*; by contrast the role of Venus is more complex.[63] Her functions are multiple and often motivated by maternal concerns; furthermore, as in Ovid's *Fasti*, Venus can be "the builder of the *civitas*, not its disrupter."[64] As we will see, she uses her powers over love mostly in order to protect her son so that he can bring *civitas* to the region dominated by the savage Turnus.

This maternal-protective thematic dramatically contrasts with Paris's choice of Venus and its consequences, and this contrast seems to be one of the fundamental reasons for the inclusion of the Judgment episode. The poet essentially offers a rehabilitation and a rewriting of Venus. This does not mean that the libidinous Venus of the Judgment becomes chaste.[65] It is not so much a question of two Venuses as that of an added complexity to Venus and her son Cupid. As one of the few divine figures left in this medieval mythological pantheon her function is primarily to see to it that Enéas survives and gets what he is destined to receive: the kingdom *and* the woman (Lavine). The founding myth will be supplemented by that of a legitimate marriage based on passion. The insistence on marriage and especially married love is more clearly articulated in the *RE* than in the *Aeneid*, making the *RE* particularly relevant to the married couple of rulers, Henry II and Eleanor of Aquitaine. Love has moved from the realm of destruction (Troy and Carthage) to that of construction (Rome).

In the Dido episode Venus intends love to be essentially a protective device for her son:

> La mere Eneas sot et vit
> que ses fiz estoit an Cartage;
> molt redotoit an son corage
> qu'il nel menassent malement:
> molt ert antre salvage gent.
> Ele ot d'amor la poësté. (ll. 764–69)

Enéas's mother knew and saw that her son was in Carthage. She feared greatly in her heart that they might treat him badly, for he was among a savage people. She held the power of love.

Venus then goes on to give Ascanius the power to incite love in whoever kisses him and instructs those who take care of him that only the queen (Dido) and Enéas should be allowed to kiss him. This action represents a curious overlapping of the human and divine realms. Rather than sending Cupid in the shape of Ascanius, Venus embraces and empowers Ascanius himself.[66] Venus herself is shown in a much more favorable light here than in the *Aeneid*, where Virgil describes her motivations as follows: "But the Cytherean revolves in her breast new wiles, new schemes; how Cupid, changed in face and form, may come in the stead of sweet Ascanius, and by his gifts kindle the queen to madness. . . . In truth, she fears the uncertain house and double-tongued Tyrians; Juno's hate chafes her" (1.656–62). Venus's desire to protect Aeneas is also evident in this passage, but the French text insists much more on her maternal role by identifying her as "la mere Eneas" instead of "the Cytherean." The love she inspires via Ascanius is just as raging and destructive to Dido, yet Venus's motives seem more honorable.

That Venus was the guiding light of his mission had also been recognized by Enéas himself who, echoing *Aeneid* 2.588–620, explains to Dido:

> Venus ma mere me vint dire,
> de par les deus, que m'en tornasse,
> et an la terre m'en alasse
> dont Dardanus vint nostre ancestre. (ll. 1186–89)

Venus, my mother, came to tell me on behalf of the gods that I should go away from there [Troy] and set out for the land from which Dardanus, our ancestor, came.

Unlike in the *Aeneid*, however, in the *RE* it is immediately after this passage that Dido feels the pangs of love. Thus the connection between Venus's protectiveness of Enéas (by having Dido fall in love with him) and her articulation of Enéas's mission is much clearer here: the shaping of the *RE*'s action is more obviously a result of Venus's design and intervention.

Venus is a full-fledged mythological figure. In contrast, "les deus" (the gods) who appear frequently are much shadowier. Dirk Blask has shown in his careful study of the notion of destiny in the *RE* that Fortune and the gods coexist, but that the gods seem to be a subcategory of destiny, in charge primarily of the Trojans' well-being.[67] It is therefore the gods collectively—and not Jupiter via Mercury as in the *Aeneid*—who urge Enéas's departure from Carthage. But rather than departing in a clandestine fashion, as does Virgil's hero, the medieval Enéas engages in a discussion on the gods' commands with Dido.[68] In a touching exchange Dido asks:

> Destruis ge Troie? — Nenil, Greus.
> Fu ce par moi? — Mes par les deus.
> . . .
> Sire, por coi me fuiez donc?
> Ce n'est par moi. — Et par cui donc?
> C'est par les deus. (ll. 1753–54, 1757–59)

Did I destroy Troy? No, the Greeks did. Because of me? No, because of the gods. Sire, why do you flee me, then? Not because I want to. Why then? Because of the gods.

Enéas is more concerned about Dido; he values her love more highly than the Virgilian Aeneas. Nevertheless, Dido doubts the gods' command when she says "Mais par ma foi ne lor an chalt / se il remaint ou s'il s'en alt" (But by my faith, they don't care whether he stays or leaves; ll. 1841–42). Clearly, Dido is not privy—or does not want to be—to the grand scheme governing Enéas's destiny. When Enéas finally leaves, Dido commits suicide as in the *Aeneid*, but unlike in that text, in the *RE* she forgives Enéas before she dies (l. 2064).

The Dido episode shows to what extent the *RE* poet retained the notion of divine intervention from the *Aeneid* but also how far he went in modifying it. Enéas's Venus is maternal and protective; she is in charge of his destiny. The other gods remain unspecified forces whose intentions accord with those of Venus. Venus thus has come to dominate not only the sphere of love but also that of the founding myth. At the end of the Dido episode we can see already that Paris's choice has been turned upside down: from the destruction of a realm Venus unerringly moves her son to the founding of a new one.

This determination on Venus's part is highlighted again in one of the other significant mythological *micro-récits*, the production of Enéas's arms.[69] The motivation for Venus's intervention recalls that of the Dido episode: Enéas is being besieged in Montalban, and Venus is afraid for her son's safety (ll. 4299–301). She approaches her husband, Vulcan, and asks him what he intends to do about her son's predicament. Before he can answer, Venus determines that her son needs the kind of arms only her husband can fashion. In return she offers him a night of love, something, the narrator tells us, Vulcan has not enjoyed in seven years. The poet immediately explains the reason ("l'acheison"; l. 4353) for this forced abstinence: Venus had been in bed with Mars when Vulcan caught the two in a fine net and exposed them to the denizens of Mount Olympus, who were not too pleased at the sight. The gods were jealous because many of them wanted to be equally intimate with Venus. Since that day Venus has been angry with her husband and has refused him her love (ll. 4355–78).[70]

Formally, the story of Mars and Venus, based on several Ovidian texts, is a digression;[71] the word "acheison" links it to the Judgment of Paris digression. Both instances are returns to the characters' mythological past; both function as a program for the reading of the text; both present a kind of antitype for what is happening in the *RE*.[72]

If we read the *RE* in part as a rehabilitation and a transformation of Venus we can see that the present episode confirms some of the changes we have already observed. Venus reaffirms her strong maternal role and now adds the role as the rehabilitated wife, if only for reasons of expediency.

Significantly, the *RE* poet omits a striking detail from the *Metamorphoses* version of the Mars and Venus story: the gods laughed.[73] Instead, the *RE* focuses on the jealousy felt by the other gods. Jealousy implies discord, while laughter is a communal experience. As Discord threw the apple to the three goddesses and caused not only discord between the three but a destructive war, discord reigned among the gods because of Venus. The scene of the reconciliation between Vulcan and Venus must be set against the scene of divine discord in order to acquire its full meaning: the union of married love contrasts with the disunion caused by lascivious love.[74]

Thus the Mars and Venus digression encourages us to read the *RE* as a progression toward married love, a theme that is certainly not as important in the *Aeneid*. Where Rome looms on the horizon of the *Aeneid*—and Lavine is little more than a pawn to this end—Rome *and* Lavine are the desired endpoints of Enéas's wanderings in the *RE*. This may be the reason that there is no depiction of Roman history on Enéas's armor as there is in the *Aeneid*. The focus thus remains on the armor as the product of a couple: Vulcan makes it and signs it in gold[75] and Venus adds the pennon, which by its being attached to her husband's work of art loses the subversive elements of its origin (not only had it been a gift of Mars, her lover, it had also been fashioned by Arachne, challenger of the goddess Pallas, who had revealed the predatory sexual practices of the gods).[76] The pennon reminds us of Venus's past transgressions as well as Arachne's lesson that humans do not do well to challenge the gods' power. Like Capaneus in the *RTh*, Turnus, the enemy who will be the victim of the power of these arms, would have done well to learn that lesson. Although he is aware that the gods are on Enéas's side, Turnus persists in fighting him, and, not unlike Arachne, he is punished for his shortsightedness.[77]

The episode of the fabrication of the arms with its two mythological *micro-récits* thus lies at the core of the romance's themes and highlights the thematic shifts with regard to the *Aeneid*. Through the evocation of the Mars and Venus story this section dramatizes Venus's rehabilitation, her refound marital love in the service of her son; the Arachne myth underlines the futility of even the most talented human competing with the gods; and, more globally, viewing the arms as the product of a renewed union (as opposed to discord), marriage, makes us anticipate marriage as a major constructive theme in the *RE*. The episode thus functions both analeptically (as a contrast to Paris's illicit love) and proleptically (anticipating the appearance of Lavine). But it also introduces the use of Ovidian intertexts as an allusive articulation of threats of subversion: Venus's infidelity and Arachne's pride.

This use of the intertext becomes especially significant in the development of Lavine's love for Enéas (ll. 7857–9274). Lavine's long dialogue with her mother and her monologue, so suffused with Ovidian diction and themes that it would be impossible to list all of them here,[78] marked medieval romance for generations to come. Here, the *RE* establishes the connection between love and valor, indeed, establishes love as a worthy goal for the heroic founding father of Rome. But the love between Lavine and Enéas is problematic in a number of ways: he is the enemy, she is ignorant of love, and Enéas is suspected by her mother to be a homosexual, to name only a few potential problems. Significantly, it is in the Ovidian intertexts that surface in the Lavine episode that the *RE* poet evokes, confronts, and resolves some of these problems.

The *RE* skillfully evokes the three stories of Myrrha, Byblis, and Scylla by using the Ovidian techniques that characterized the declaration and evolution of love in them: fragmented revelations of the beloved's name; gazing from towers; and tortured redactions of letters. All of the stories deal with incestuous love or love leading to a father's destruction. As Joan Cadden observes for Alan of Lille's telling of some of these Ovidian tales, "women's disobedience of Nature's laws comes primarily in forms that attack the integrity of the family."[79] Lavine is thus placed at the center of a whole web of Ovidian tales that articulate threats to the very order she is supposed to represent: married love, family, and legitimate rule. But significantly Lavine does not reenact these stories. Rather, as Enéas does for Paris, she offers a correction: while her emotions echo those of the three unfortunate women from the *Metamorphoses*, the chosen object of her love is neither her brother (as for Byblis) nor her father (as for Myrrha); nor will her love require her to destroy her father (as did Scylla).

The opening of Book 8 of the *Metamorphoses* shows Scylla, the daughter of the Megarian King Nisus, on top of a tower watching the battle between her father's troops and those of King Minos of Crete. The sight of that handsome king kindles Scylla's passion, and she is determined to gain his love. She believes that by cutting off her father's miraculous lock of hair and offering it to Minos she will reach this goal. This "horrid crime, [this] unnatural act" (*Met* 8.85, 96), however, has the opposite effect. Minos recoils from Scylla in horror and curses her. Now banished from her homeland, her only recourse is to accompany Minos to Crete, something he absolutely refuses. In despair she swims after the Cretan ship, reaches it, but has to let go of it when attacked by her father, now in the shape of an osprey. At that moment she herself is changed into a bird.

The appearance of Lavine on the tower recalls very closely the scene of Scylla watching Minos. As she gazed upon the man who, according to her mother, should be her enemy "Amors l'a de son dart ferue" (Love struck her with his arrow; l. 8057). From that moment on she can think of nothing else. Although she does not realize yet that her symptoms are those of love, she begins to have an inkling of what is wrong with her by naming that which she supposedly does not know: "ne sai Amors ou com a nom" (I do not know Love or whatever his name is; l. 8095). After a lengthy meditation on love she returns to the window to take another look at her beloved. The next order of business is to conceal her love from her mother, who urges her to love Turnus (ll. 8479–82). It is here that the intertextual scene shifts from the story of Scylla to that of Myrrha.

Myrrha reveals her guilty passion for her father to her nurse, but only after many promptings. The "confused sound" (*Met* 10.382) of Myrrha's voice the nurse hears before Myrrha's attempted suicide, the slow hesitant way in which she reveals the name of the object of her love—all this reappears in the scene in which Lavine's mother seeks to uncover her daughter's secret. Syllable by syllable the name "Enéas" emerges from the trembling girl (ll. 8553–60). Her mother reacts violently and accuses Enéas of being a homosexual (sodomite; l. 8583), thus repeating King Iarbas's accusation in the *Aeneid*. Lavine picks up this idea later when she, wrongly it turns out, believes herself spurned by Enéas: "Son Ganymede a avec soi" (he has his Ganymede with him; l. 9135).[80] But at this moment, Lavine refuses to listen to her mother and determines that she must write a letter to Enéas to reveal her love to him and thus slips into the role of Byblis.

In Ovid, Byblis, in love with her brother Caunus, decides to tell him of her love: "a private letter shall confess my secret love" (*Met* 9.516). She puts great care into the writing of this letter: "She begins, then hesitates and stops; writes on and hates what she has written; writes and erases; changes, condemns, approves" (9.523–24). She manages to finish the letter, sends it through a messenger to her brother (despite a fateful omen—she drops the letter—warning her not to do so), and then learns of her brother's response of horror and outrage. In despair, she roams the countryside in a kind of Dionysian madness and is finally transformed into a fountain.

The three Ovidian stories offer many parallels with the Lavine episode. But for each case, Lavine manages to "correct" the Ovidian model, to avert the cruel fate awaiting Scylla, Myrrha, and Byblis. Although in a similar position as Scylla and falling in love in exactly the same way, Lavine is not tempted to undo her father in order to gain her love (though she does oppose her mother's choice of Turnus). Scylla had hoped that her offer of love would bring an end to the war between Nisus and Minos but was sadly mistaken. Lavine knows that her love will be sanctioned and bring peace; consequently Scylla's fateful mistake of judgment is not repeated because Lavine's father Latinus is aware of Enéas's divinely ordained right to his daughter. The story significantly diverges from the Ovidian intertext: it evokes the threat of impious behavior yet averts it. Lavine's affinity to Myrrha emerges in the revelation scene with Lavine's mother. Lavine, however, is afraid to divulge her beloved's name not because he is her father but because he is not the man her mother has chosen for her. Incest and familial disaster lurk in the Ovidian intertext but are not allowed to surface because Lavine plans for a legitimate marriage, not an incestuous one.[81] Finally, Lavine reenacts the scene of Byblis's writing her letter to Caunus—with the big difference that this letter does not express an incestuous passion but a heterosexual love that will be reciprocated. For all the Ovidian dilemmas, then, legitimate love and marriage provide the answers. All along the audience is encouraged to look for exactly these values. Now these values are reinforced by their juxtaposition to possible threats emerging from the Ovidian intertexts.

The recognition of these intertexts and the subversive significance they bring with them is of course dependent on acts of interpretation. Interestingly, the text itself offers a model for the interpretation of a mythological figure, specifically, Amors or Cupid, so central to the developments in the Lavine and Enéas episode. As Daniel Poirion has shown, in the last part of the romance Enéas's love life is governed more by Cupid than by Venus.[82] But the *RE* does not see Cupid so much as replacing Venus than as part of the family coming to the aid of Enéas by kindling Lavine's love. This point is confirmed by Lavine's knowledge that Cupid is indeed Enéas's brother: "N'est Cupido frere Eneas, / li deus d'amor qui m'a conquise?" (Is not Cupid, the god of love who has conquered me, the brother of Enéas? ll. 8630–31). Love and conquest are clearly a family affair for Venus and her two sons. Even though Cupid seems to take over in the Lavine and Enéas story, Venus remains the most complex mythological figure in the *RE*. She has a past history:[83] the digressions on the Judgment of Paris and the Mars and Venus story saw to that. She interacts with other characters in the romance, both human (Ascanius, for example) and divine. She is the mastermind behind Enéas's success. Cupid, by contrast, has disappeared from the Dido episode, where, in the *Aeneid*, he plays an important role. In the *RE*, then, he is not a full-fledged mythological figure but is still more than a mere personification of love because as Venus's son and Enéas's brother he is part of the family.

In addition to being a sometime actor on the stage of the *RE*, Cupid is part of a shared mythological knowledge that can be interpreted, as becomes clear in his appearance in an ekphrasis. For when Lavine's mother first wants to teach her about love she does not evoke love as an abstract force but rather as an image, more specifically an image painted on a temple (ll. 7975–86). We saw in the *RTh* how important such images and their interpretation can be. Indeed, they function as interpretive indexes. In the image, Amors holds two arrows in his right hand and a box with a healing ointment in his left. One arrow is made of gold and makes people fall in love; the other is made of lead and makes love change. These attributes, Lavine's mother instructs her, show "par figure" (figuratively; l. 7983) that Amors is capable of wounding people; the box, on the other hand, signifies that he can also heal.[84]

As in the *RTh* a god is thus transposed into an ekphrastic representation, a representation that needs to be interpreted. Lavine's mother proves to be a most capable interpreter. Although mistaken as to the identity of the beloved her daughter will choose, she masters the mythographic tradition regarding the significance of each attribute. She thus establishes for her daughter the connection between the confused sentiments Lavine will experience later on and a tradition that has invented a pictorial expression for the explanation of exactly those feelings. What Lavine experiences in her love for Enéas serves to confirm her mother's interpretation of the temple image, while at the same time it subverts her mother's plans. In any case, her feelings are not spontaneous but rather well-orchestrated responses to a tradition represented by Cupid's image. Passion is contained by order and learning.

Thus the whole Ovidian vocabulary, which would lead us to expect an Ovidian type of love, that is, a finally unstable love relationship, is put to the service of creating a stable marriage. For Enéas responds to Lavine's overtures as Cupid's brother would: he reciprocates the love offered him by Lavine, which is, as he knows well, in his best interest. Not even his lovesickness can blind us to the utterly utilitarian motives in this love. Enéas meditates on the love he had for Dido and how different his current love is: if he had had that same kind of love for Dido he would have never left her (ll. 9038–46). Yet, as Christiane Marchello-Nizia makes clear, it was not so much that he did not have the right kind of love for Dido but that she held a realm and power that he would perhaps have been allowed to share but never to possess completely.[85] Lavine's father, on the other hand, is only too ready to hand over his power to Enéas.

This view of the Lavine and Enéas story is perhaps not especially romantic since it emphasizes expediency over spontaneous emotions. In this respect, it echoes the reconciliation of Venus and Vulcan, which was also more expedient than deeply emotional. Nevertheless, as we have seen, throughout the *RE* and, in particular, the mythological *micro-récits* the poet creates an expectation in the audience that marriage will be a key component in Enéas's quest for Rome and contrasts legitimate love with illegitimate love in its various guises. This contrast, inherent in the Dido/Lavine opposition, is dramatized and highlighted toward the end of the romance by the three Ovidian intertexts evoking Scylla, Myrrha, and Byblis as Lavine's antitypes.

In this context the final irony of the comparison between Enéas and Lavine and Paris and Helen becomes only too evident.[86] Certainly, Paris was happy, but look what it got him, the poet seems to be saying. Enéas, on the other hand, will be the founding father of an important lineage, as he learns through the prophecies of his father in the underworld. Thus, as in the Judgment of Paris, Venus has won, but here it is not only Venus who has won but her sons. In an effective familial cooperation, Enéas's father predicts the lineage to come and Enéas in the here and now can rely on his already existing lineage: his mother and his brother. This family alliance achieves a victory that turns out to be considerably more permanent than Venus's winning of the apple.

Thus, like the characters from mythology in the *RTh*, the mythological figures of the *RE* serve the romance's central themes. In the *RTh*, myth emphasizes the seriousness of the threat war poses to a civilized human existence; in the *RE* the founding myth and the myth of love merge. The figure of Venus orchestrates this merger, and other mythological figures, such as Paris, Arachne, Myrrha, Scylla, and Byblis, represent the threats to the new order that are one by one undone by Venus and her family. While the *RTh* is a "family romance" in the most disturbing sense, the *RE* is a "family romance" in the best sense of the term. The two romances thus stage the move from Theban gloom to Roman glory just as the Angevin dynasty at different periods staged both the "confused house of Oedipus" and "greater joy" of Enéas and Lavine.

The *Roman de Troie*

In the prologue to his *RTr* Benoît de Sainte-Maure confronts one of the problems classical mythology presented for a Christian audience: Homer made the gods act on the narrative level and thus gave them a status that is no longer acceptable in a nonpagan environment. Indeed, Benoît argues, already the wise Athenians condemned Homer for this transgression, but they were finally won over by Homer's authority and accepted his text nonetheless:

> Dampner le voustrent par reison,
> Por ço qu'ot fait les damedeus
> Combatre o les homes charneus.
> Tenu li fu a desverie
> E a merveillose folie
> Que les deus come homes humains
> Faiseit combatre as Troïains,
> Et les deuesses ensement
> Faiseit combatre avuec la gent;

E quant son livre reciterent,
Plusor por ço le refuserent.
Mais tant fu Omers de grant pris
E tant fist puis, si com jo truis,
Que ses livres fu receüz
E en autorité tenuz. (ll. 60–74)

They wanted to condemn it [his book] for the reason that he had made the gods do battle with human beings. It was considered craziness and unbelievable folly that he had the gods like human men do battle with the Trojans and also made the goddesses fight with people. And when his book was read aloud, many rejected it for that reason. But Homer had so much merit and did so many things later, as I found out, that his book was accepted and considered an authority.

Benoît himself, however, feels compelled to reject Homer because the latter was not an eyewitness to the events (l. 56), in spite of his being a "clers merveillos / e sages e esciëntios" (a marvelous scholar, learned and knowledgeable; ll. 45–46). In the fourteenth century the *Ovide moralisé* poet faults Benoît for this attitude. Benoît, he claims, did not recognize that Homer "parla par metafore."[87] Yet, Benoît's rejection of Homeric forms and functions of mythology was appropriate for the spirit of his period. The "metafore" adduced by the *Ovide moralisé* poet would not work in Benoît's program for reading the ancient myths, which includes the rejection of allegorization. Rather, Benoît reveals a sensibility for the reading of myth in ways that both echo the intertextual use of Ovidian myths in the *RE* and adumbrate the psychological, internalized dimension of myths that marked medieval literature for centuries to come.

The *RTr* has been the stepchild of criticism on twelfth-century romance. This may be because with 30,316 verses it is three times as long as the other romances of antiquity. Another reason for its relative neglect may be the mediocre quality of the texts it is based on. There is simply no comparison between the epics by Virgil and Statius and the colorless accounts of the Trojan War by Dares and Dictys. Nevertheless, Benoît de Sainte-Maure turns these flat texts into a full-bodied and exciting romance.[88] It is true, vast stretches of the text are occupied by somewhat repetitive battle scenes. But there is much to admire in this text. The Prologue, for example, details not only the reasons for rejecting Homer we just discussed, but it is also a most interesting dramatization of the *translatio studii* topos, describing the linguistic and geographic peregrinations of the text, now in the hands of Benoît.[89]

Benoît's argument against Homer supports the movement of the gods away from the diegetic level that we have already observed in the *RTh* and the *RE*, and which is even more evident here. What is significant for the Prologue of the *RTr* is that what was implicit in the two earlier romances becomes explicit here. Just as the story of the transmission of the text is told explicitly, Homer's treatment of the gods is the subject of explicit reflection. Benoît follows Dares and Dictys rather faithfully when it comes to pagan mythology, and, as in their texts, the gods and goddesses appear almost exclusively in invocations, prayers, and images.[90] In a few instances Benoît introduces additional mythological elements or motivations. Jason, for example takes an oath to the gods more elaborately than in Dares's text; Achilles's religious duties are fleshed out in great detail;[91] and Andromache's warning dream is, as it is not in Dares, sent by the gods (ll. 15,284–86).

But it is the amorous realm that shows the most evidence of divine presence, if mostly in the form of the personification of love, Amors.[92] Benoît thus also helps to forge the link between myth and love that came to dominate the use of mythology in medieval texts.

Amors first appears as Medea is attracted to Jason: "Esprise l'a forment Amors" (Love has forcefully taken command of her; l. 1465). Amors is also responsible for the love between Paris and Helen: "Navra Amors e lui e li" (Love wounded both him and her; l. 4357). Diomedes, as well, falls into Amors's snares when he sees Briseide, newly separated from Troilus: "Quant Amors vueut qu'a vos m'otrei, / Nel contredi ne nel denei" (When Love wants me to give myself to you, I will not contradict him or refuse him; ll. 13,691–92). The love story between Diomedes and Briseide is one of the most important innovations of the *RTr*. It allows Benoît to comment on the nature of women (they are fickle, don't trust them; ll. 13,441–56).[93] It also allows him to display once more his knowledge of Ovidian love casuistry. Finally, the new story raises the thorny question of loyalty and love during war.

But while powerful, Amors is not really a mythological figure in these stories. He is neither associated with Venus nor is he called Enéas's brother, as he is in the *RE*.[94] Further, he has not yet acquired the personality he will be given in the *Roman de la Rose*. In the *RTr* he remains at all times in the realm of personification, thus confirming Benoît's rejection of having gods intervene directly in human affairs.

Benoît certainly sees the gods as the objects of his characters' religious devotion, but when he turns to Ovidian myth his approach is psychologizing. Ovidian intertexts with their rich resonances serve to illuminate the characters' anxieties and amorous emotions. Achilles's psychological portrait, nonexistent in Benoît's model texts, gains particular complexity through the intertexts of Narcissus and Hero and Leander.[95] But the intertexts also bring something to the reader: myth's power to evoke the forbidden and transgressive aspects of human existence creates a textual undercurrent that the characters remain unaware of.

When Achilles says "Narcisus sui" (I am Narcissus; l. 17,691) he thinks of the shadow that Narcissus was in love with and the death that ensued. But anyone who knows Ovid would also see the ambiguous sexuality of Narcissus, pursued by both "many youths and many maidens" (*Met* 3. 354). Readers of the *RTr* had already heard Hector's accusation of Achilles as having had a homosexual relationship with Patroclus:

> Que tantes feiz avez sentu
> Entre voz braz tot nu a nu,
> Et autres gieus vis e hontos. (ll. 13,183–85)

Whom you have felt so many times naked in your arms, and [with whom you have played] other vile and shameful games.

Although Achilles gives a different focus to his reading of the story, Narcissus nonetheless evokes the accusation of Achilles's homosexuality. Thus his love for Polyxene must be read under the sign of the struggle for heterosexual love in the *RTr.* On the surface his love for Polyxene fits into a purely heterosexual model: Benoît amplifies Dares's terse narrative to thousands of lines.[96] Unlike Dares, Benoît immediately alerts his audience to the unhappy end this love will have:

> Veüe i a Polixenain
> Apertement en mi la chiere:
> C'est l'acheison e la maniere
> Par qu'il sera getez de vie
> E l'ame de son cors partie. (ll. 17,540–44)
> . . .
> Il fu destreiz por fine amor
> Mar vi onc ajorner le jor.
> Mout est fort chose d'Aventure
> Mout est as plusors aspre et dure. (ll. 17,547–50)

There he looked at Polyxene, directly into her face. This is the reason and the manner by which he will lose his life; his soul will depart from his body. He was being pressed by "fine amor"; it was too bad that he had to see the dawn of that day [that he saw Polyxene]. Chance is something very powerful; to many people it is bitter and hard.

In the next few hundred lines the term "Amors" appears many times, used both by the narrator and by Achilles. Amors "bites" him, "burdens" him, "snares" him. Achilles finally realizes "Bien sai de veir que jo sui mort" (I truly know that I am dying; l. 17,689). This thought culminates in the realization, "Narcisus sui."

Achilles's version of Narcissus's sad story is brief: he loved his "ombre" (shadow or reflection) so much that he died of this love by the fountain. In the same way, Achilles says, he loves "his shadow, his death, and his burden," for he too cannot kiss and embrace that which he loves. Thus he must do the same thing that Narcissus did: cry, scream for mercy, and finally die. Narcissus died for love, and so will he. Narcissus was deceived by his appearance, and he, Achilles, can expect nothing better. No more help will come to him, Achilles, than came to Narcissus (ll. 17,692–717). But, and this is the crucial turning point, Achilles reflects that there may be something that "a pro me tornast" (could change things for the better; l. 17,717). He argues that a person who feels a sickness coming on should do everything to avert it. In a possible allusion to the Tiresias of Ovid's Narcissus story, Achilles states that he would like to be a prophet and know how it will all turn out. Finally, he resolves to pray to God to give him some advice on how to win Polyxene. He promptly finds a messenger to send to Hecuba, Polyxene's mother, to ask for her daughter's hand in marriage. In return, Achilles promises to withdraw from the war (ll. 17,720–72).

Achilles shows an intimate familiarity with the story of Narcissus, yet he leaves out Echo and thus the element of heterosexual love. Nevertheless Achilles seems to read the Narcissus story in a manner similar to that of courtly poets, that is, the unattainable reflection is not a reflection of himself but of his lady:

> Ne plus que il la pot baillier
> Ne acoler ne embracier
> . . .
> Plus ne puis jo aveir leisor
> De li aveir ne de s'amor.

Just as he [Narcissus] cannot attain it, or kiss or embrace it [his shadow], I may not have her or her love. (ll. 17,697–98; 17,701–2)

But the identity of Achilles's beloved remains ambiguous. The threats of self-love and of homosexuality do not disappear completely in this particular reading of the Narcissus myth, though Achilles attempts to interpret the myth not as a reference to self-love but to reciprocal love—not yet reciprocated, however. Achilles's reading spurs him to action, which for the moment at least saves him from Narcissus's fate, and the accusation of homosexuality, so clearly articulated by Hector earlier in the romance, is not allowed to resurface.

Achilles is only temporarily saved, however, by his interpretation of the Narcissus myth. Many thousands of lines later (after having gone through all the stages of love for Polyxene) he will be treacherously killed by Paris in Apollo's temple, where he goes for what he believes is a rendezvous with Polyxene, but is actually a trap set by Paris. Again an Ovidian intertext and an allusion to homosexuality converge (Achilles is accompanied by a young beloved knight).

At this point, the narrator evokes the story of Hero and Leander, based on Ovid's *Heroides* 18 and 19, to bring home his point. Barbara Nolan argues that "no letter in the *Heroides* initiates a love that is legitimate" and shows that medieval commentaries on the *Heroides* "explored the political *problem* of sexual love in their texts."[97] Thus the evocation of Hero and Leander's passionate but doomed love puts the love of Achilles and Polyxene into a context that, like the love of Enéas, Dido, and Lavine, would have some relevance for a twelfth-century audience interested in the links between power, illegitimate passion, and legitimate marriage.

The episode of Achilles's death begins with a trap laid for him at the request of Hecuba, who cannot forgive Achilles for reentering the war. (Of course, earlier he had also killed her son Hector.) But even earlier, at the very beginning of the Achilles and Polyxene story, the narrator prophesies Achilles's violent end, thus linking passion (the foolish, unreasonable emotion targeted by the moralizing commentaries on the *Heroides*) and death. As Achilles prepares for his meeting with Polyxene, Amors makes him lose all reason. The narrator comments:

> Tot autresi com Leandès,
> Cil qui neia en mer Ellès,
> Qui tant ama Ero s'amie
> Que senz batel e senz navie,
> Se mist en mer par nuit oscure,
> Ne redota mesaventure:
> Tot autresi Achillès fait. (ll. 22,121–27)

Just like Leander, who drowned in the Hellespont, who loved his beloved Hero so much that without boat or ship he plunged into the sea in the dark night and did not fear misfortune, Achilles does exactly the same thing.

This passage makes the reader despair for Achilles. Death is as certain for him as it was for Leander; what the Hellespont was for Leander, the enemy camp is for Achilles.

Interestingly, it is not Achilles who tells or interprets the story here but the narrator. Although Achilles had managed earlier on to avert Narcissus's fate for himself through a reading of the Narcissus story, here he is helpless: he does not *know* that he is a second Leander, only the narrator—and consequently the audience—does. Moreover, medieval Ovidian commentaries had established that Leander's love is "stultus" (foolish), and thus the audience may take a view of Achilles's love that is quite different from his own perception. The foolishness and danger of loving the enemy's daughter quite elude him.[98]

But again an apparently perfect heterosexual passion is juxtaposed to an undercurrent of homosexuality. For immediately after the evocation of Hero and Leander Achilles enters the temple with "uns chevaliers [qui] esteit sis druz" (a knight who was his beloved; l. 22,144): Antilocus, young and smooth-faced.[99] Thus, just like Narcissus, Achilles remains a sexually ambiguous figure who dies through foolish passion.

There is no doubt that the text gains depth through the use of the Ovidian figures: narrative possibilities are opened up before the audience, and stories are read and interpreted for them. Fates can be averted through the knowledge of the appropriate exemplary stories;[100] but fate may have to be reenacted, a point the narrator can make implicitly by evoking a myth that parallels the characters' own stories.

Formally, the two Ovidian intertexts are exempla, not part of the diegesis. This formal possibility will be one of the most frequently used in medieval literature. Like the *RTh* and the *RE*, then, the *RTr* helps establish important paradigms for the integration and the interpretation of mythological stories. In addition, Benoît shows us the difference between modes of interpretation: Achilles's interpretation of the Narcissus story leads to only a provisional averting of Narcissus's fate; the narrator's more authoritative interpretation of the Hero and Leander story spells Achilles's perdition. And both stories add a moral dimension: self-love, sexual ambiguity, and boundless but unreasonable passion are the models of behavior presented and criticized through the Ovidian intertexts.

The achievement of the *RTr*, then, is not only the introduction of the Trojan subject matter into the mainstream of medieval literature. Benoît was the only author within the cycle of the romances of antiquity to reflect explicitly on the use of the gods by a pagan author, Homer. Thus what had been accepted, if in a modified form, by the other romancers, but especially by the *RE* poet, could no longer remain unquestioned for Benoît. Benoît does not show us gods intervening as if they were humans. The gods are clearly present as part of the characters' world, in which they have a valid function: they occupy temples, they are represented in images, people pray to them, and some of them, such as Apollo, offer prophecies.[101] Benoît supplements the mythology appearing in his sources. He insists more than Dares and Dictys on the ritual required to win the gods' favor. And, most important, he introduces and exploits Ovidian mythology in the form of exemplary stories. Here, once again, Benoît is more explicit than his predecessors in that he has one of his principal characters, Achilles, recite, reflect on, and interpret one of Ovid's most intriguing tales, that of Narcissus. From both a formal and an interpretive perspective, Benoît is indebted to the other two romances of antiquity, yet he also points in new directions.

Clergie, *chevalerie*, and love—these three elements define the earliest romances and became the paradigm for future generations of romancers. The first element is concentrated in the figure of the poet, whose self-representation includes all the qualities of a learned clerk: the establishment of authority by citing ancient *auctores*; the anchoring of their texts in tradition by referring to sources and models; and the display of encyclopedic learning and stylistic virtuosity. The second element is represented by the characters who demonstrate that, like *clergie*, *chevalerie* had its origin in antiquity: for every Homer there is a Hector. No one would know about Hector without Homer, and Homer would have nothing to write about without Hector. Yet the relationship between clerk and knight is only seemingly symbiotic, for it is finally the poet who incarnates memory, without which our world would be a desert. Love, the third element of romance, grows in importance as time progresses. It becomes more complex, more introspective than in the Latin model texts. As we saw, the great innovation of the romances of antiquity was the fusion of Ovidian mythology with the epic subject matter of the model texts.

Each element we have been discussing is bound up with mythology. The clerk's knowledge of the pagan texts allows him to transmit them to a new audience: he becomes the purveyor of mythological knowledge, which up to that time had been the sole property of the learned class. The gods and the meanings attached to them now enter vernacular literature.

Liberated from centuries of moralizing allegorizations, the gods and goddesses become part of romances and lyric poems; there is a new openness and availability to the mythological subject matter. New techniques are developed, such as digressions functioning as programs for reading the text, or mythological exempla used intertextually to give the romance new dimensions. The focus on mythological artist figures allowed poets to inscribe themselves into the text in a new way: epic narrators had been passionate witnesses to a communal experience; the new romance narrator is a proud and skilled poetic craftsman, grounded in the authority of antiquity.[102]

The *chevaliers* could recognize themselves in the heroes of antiquity. The myths of Troy and Rome are suddenly transferred to their own time and place—and to their own language—the twelfth-century knights *are* the descendants of Aeneas and Brutus. By historicizing the mythological universes of the ancients, the romancers of antiquity showed their audiences new horizons. The myth of Trojan origins began to inform almost every European culture. That myths could be appropriated for contemporary purposes became an idea no longer limited to the most rarefied learned circles.

As for love, the introduction of an Ovidian vocabulary, of the figure of Amors, and of a number of Ovidian exemplary stories of great psychological complexity, was probably the most revolutionary step for future generations of poets. To make woman's love a goal to strive for, to link *chevalerie* and love, to contrast the love of Dido with that of Lavinia—these became the classical themes of romance. They turned the love depicted in the ancient texts into a new myth of love. The literary revolution in the realm of love, initiated by the romances of antiquity, had an effect that reached far beyond the middle ages, for it is still part of Western culture.

In the twelfth century, then, the pagan gods and goddesses were changed: they were neither what they had been for the ancient authors nor what they had been for the later commentators and glossators. The romances of antiquity "remythisized" them into new poetic figures that felt thoroughly at home in the medieval world.

Chapter 2

The Myths of the *Roman de la Rose*

Classical mythology plays a crucial role in the interpretation of the *Roman de la Rose* (= *Rose*),[1] particularly in the second part by Jean de Meun. Building on some of the mythological foundations of *Rose I*, Jean creates intricate networks that bring together Ovidian myths, mythographic traditions, and new myths of his own making in original and newly meaningful combinations. More than Guillaume de Lorris, who chose one myth, that of Narcissus, as the centerpiece of his garden, Jean displays an immense learnedness and playfulness in his exploitation of the storehouse of ancient mythology for his own ends.

Myth's centrality—and at the same time its playfulness—is perhaps nowhere better expressed than in the famous passage, located at the midpoint of the conjoined *Rose* texts, where the God of Love, or Amors, addresses his assembled troops and announces to them the future birth of Jean de Meun. In order to prevent any mishaps in this poet's appearance, Amors pronounces a prayer:

> Pri je Lucina, la deesse
> d'enfantement, qu'el doint qu'il nesse
> sanz mal et sanz enconbrement (ll. 10,593–95)

I pray to Lucina, the goddess of childbirth, that he may be born without any mishaps or obstacles.

Amors then goes on to invoke Jupiter, who, with his two barrels of good and evil, shall "abevrer" (drench) Jean immediately after his birth.[2] After that Amors will take over and so indoctrinate him with his "science" that Jean will then "fleuter" (flute) around roads and schools and will do so in French (as Amors specifies: "selonc le langage de France"; l. 10,613).

Thus Jean de Meun will be born, "baptized" (for surely the drenching is a parody of baptism), and instructed under the sign of classical mythology. What he has learned he will convey in French. This passage is a most effective *mise en abyme* of the ways mythology can become part of a vernacular text like the *Rose*. First, Amors/Love is seen as the inspiration of the poet's use of classical mythology, reenacting the affinity of love and myth that had already become apparent in the *romans antiques* and subsequently in lyric poetry.[3] Second, within the fictional framework of the romance, Jean, and by extension his poem, is a protégé of the pagan gods,[4] reflecting the extraordinary mythological richness of the text. And finally, Amors's selection of the French language points to the ongoing process of the vernacularization of myth.

More often than not in the *Rose*, familiar myths are presented in unexpected circumstances. Their lessons surprise us by their subversion of traditional readings of fables such as those about Saturn, Mars and Venus, Hercules, and Adonis. Overtly Christian interpretations of classical myths are notably absent from the *Rose*, as are indeed almost all traditional interpretations attached to mythological stories over the centuries. When an explicit moralization of a story appears it is often unexpected or even inappropriate (at least at first sight) and thus questions the very processes by which myth had been perpetuated in Christian culture.[5]

The *Rose* provides a model for the primarily nonallegorical use of myth in a new allegorical framework: that of the dream vision of love. Myths here are not in need of interpretation in the traditional sense. On the contrary, they themselves are aids to the interpretation of the romance as a whole. As Armand Strubel observes, rather than being glossed, they gloss the romance.[6] Mythological stories and allusions form part of a vast system of references that illuminate the central themes of the *Rose*: love, sexuality, language, art, and nature.

Within the new myth of the courtly universe in *Rose I* one "old" myth, that of Narcissus, occupies the ideological center.[7] In contrast, a multiplicity of myths are woven into the encyclopedic display of learning by the speakers of *Rose II*, signaling the expansion of the closed courtly world of *Rose I* not only in geographical and temporal but also in hermeneutic terms. Some of these myths tend to form systems or programs, like that of eroticism and petrification crystallized around the figure of Medusa in a later interpolation, analyzed brilliantly by Sylvia Huot.[8] Others appear several times with changing meanings, as do the myth of the Golden

Age and the story of Mars and Venus. Yet others play off each other or provide commentaries on each other, as do Pygmalion's evocation of the Narcissus myth and Genius's criticism of that same story.

I will consider the myths and their interpretive functions under three major headings: myths as stories produced by the author figures, readings of myths by other characters, and finally the creation of new myths in *Rose II.*

Most mythological characters appear in intercalated tales and are thus one step removed from the diegesis, but some also appear in the story proper. Amors and Venus are after all the masterminds behind the quest for, or the assault on, the Rose, which constitutes the plot. Armand Strubel offers the useful model of an "*axe de montage*," an axis, onto which a variety of figures, events, and places—many of them only tangentially related to the quest proper—are grafted.[9]

Thus, those mythological figures that act on the *axe* proper emerge as complex fictional characters, leaving behind the chains of allegorization that over the past centuries had reduced them to mere personifications.[10] This process of remythisization had begun in the *Roman d'Enéas*; one of the important achievements of that text had been to give new life to these figures, to transport them from the realm of personification to that of romance, to have them act in the plot of a vernacular text.[11] As a mere personification Venus would be opposed to chastity, and this opposition would exhaust her meaning. But in the *Rose*, Venus and her son—all grown up now—have a past and an agenda; they have become actors on the diegetic level, and we may well ask whether the *RE* hovers somewhere in the background here.

The *Rose* as an allegory can accommodate a large variety of figures on the diegetic level: one-dimensional personifications, such as Poor (Fear) or Faim (Hunger); allegorical figures, ranging from La Vieille and Ami to such slippery characters as Faux Semblant and the apparently reasonable Raison; and complex mythological figures. Other characters are not part of the diegesis and cannot easily be classified, such as the Jaloux as a kind of emanation of Ami or Pygmalion as an exemplum slipped into the text as part of a negative comparison.

As varied as the natures of the *Rose*'s characters are the forms that mythological stories take in that text. How do myths formally and temporally relate to the plot? How are their formal characteristics indicative of the *Rose*'s methods of integrating and interpreting myths?

Form, Temporality, and Interpretation

The *Rose*'s narrative structure is governed by Amant's quest for the Rose, which provides the unity of the two *Rose* texts. Among the figures that are most closely linked to the experiences of Amant's quest are those that represent lyric constructs, such as Douz Regart or Esperance. There are also more complex figures, such as Deduit and Oiseuse (respectively, ruler and guardian of Guillaume de Lorris's garden), whose functions go beyond the purely psychological. Some figures seem at first to be mere personifications but then take on their own life, like La Vieille. And finally there are a very large number of mythological figures that emerge in stories (mostly exempla) told by the many narrators—including *the* narrator—of the *Rose*.

The events that overflow from the diegesis as defined above take up thousands of lines, particularly in *Rose II*. Nature's confession to Genius and Venus's tryst with Adonis are good examples. Their relation to the Rose quest is not obvious at first sight; nor is it clear how the narrator could be a witness to these scenes. Many of the events that appear at first sight to be extraneous to the quest proper will take us into the realm of classical mythology. Thus, the geography of the *Rose* expands vastly from *Rose I* to *Rose II*. While the garden of Deduit provides the parameters of Amant's universe in *Rose I*, *Rose II* expands his universe to include the palace of Fortune, Nature's forge, Venus's habitat, and even the spheres of the cosmos.[12]

For each of the categories just listed it seems that the mythological elements, except for Amors and Venus, who act on the diegetic level, are the ones at the furthest remove from the *axe de montage*. They add an immense richness to the initial quest-conquest motif and constitute a large part of the huge *amplificatio* visible in *Rose II*. But it is not only by means of the ancient myths as intercalated stories that Jean de Meun can build his amplified text; the interpretations of the myths also constitute important building blocks in Jean's universe.[13]

The opening up of the *Rose*—in the realms of textual construction and interpretation—is accomplished to a large extent through the use of classical mythology, which contributes amplifying figures and events as well as geographical locations and temporal depth. The artful integration of myths also offers a more general model for the absorption of diverse, largely poeticized "pagan" materials into a new work of art. In the *Rose* the threat of the spiritual, temporal, and geographical dislocation once represented by ancient myth is no longer visible. For Jean ancient myth is part of a prestigious cultural heritage, and he can thus complete the process of the vernacularization and literarization of myth begun in the *romans antiques*. In many ways, then, the *Rose* is emblematic of the processes and methods by which Christian culture absorbed pagan subject matter.[14]

Narcissus

At first sight there is nothing strange about Guillaume de Lorris's inclusion of the Narcissus story in his account of Amant's quest.[15] Basing their work on Ovid's *Metamorphoses* 3.339–510, courtly lyric poets had proposed a reading of the myth in which Narcissus's reflection came to stand as an image of the inaccessible lady rather than as the "shadow" (umbra) of Narcissus himself.[16] If we read *Rose I* as a lyric poem transposed into a narrative context,[17] the presence of Narcissus signals a decisive moment of revelation and *inamoramento*, a passionate falling in love. This is indeed what happens in the *Rose*'s Narcissus episode, yet there are a number of strange twists to the story, highlighting the problematic nature of the temporality and geography of classical myth. Let us follow the steps by which the fountain appears in and becomes part of *Rose I*.

Amant arrives in a beautiful place and perceives a fountain under a pine tree.[18] Nature has arranged this fountain within a marble enclosure. Before we learn any details about Narcissus, the narrator tells us that the following is written in small letters on the fountain: "ilec desus / estoit morz li biau Narcisus" (here the beautiful Narcissus died; ll. 1435–36). This inscription signals more than the identification of the fountain in the garden with that of Narcissus: it tells us in effect that Amant has been introduced into the realm of classical mythology, and he learns this by way of reading a text, all that is left of Narcissus.[19] The garden that seemed to be located not far from his own home is in fact part of a mythical universe with a mythological past that is still present and that Amant had not at first perceived.[20] The narrator insists on the geographical coincidence: the fountain in Deduit's garden is the *same* fountain as the one that was Narcissus's undoing and that subsequently became his memorial. That is, the garden is the potential locus for a reenactment of the myth; it still contains its past in a written record.

It is only after these facts are established that the narrator tells us Narcissus's and Echo's stories in a digression that recalls the digressions in the *romans antiques*; there, digressions often served to explain the reason ("l'acheison"), located in the past, for events located in the present. This is also the function of the story here: the story will explain how Narcissus died and how he came to be commemorated by the inscription on the fountain. For the present, and thus for Amant, the story serves as a cautionary tale, explaining the dangers of the fountain. Whether Amant, guided by the rather surprising explicit moral drawn from the story,[21] learns a useful lesson here remains to be seen. For the moment we will concentrate on the formal and temporal characteristics of the episode that constitute a paradigm for the use of myth in the *Rose* and by extension in thirteenth-century French culture.

The order of the elements is as follows: a brief inscription identifying the mythological character and story; an extended narrative ending with Narcissus's death;[22] and then an explicit timeless moral appended to the story and addressed to the audience of "dames" (l. 1505). This sequence recalls texts like Arnulf of Orléans's allegories of the *Metamorphoses*, which first briefly announces the text to come and then tells the story and draws out the allegory.[23] Formally the Narcissus episode suggests a traditional allegorizing handbook in miniature; yet we are not allowed to allegorize for long, for the initial impression is quickly undercut by the moral, which in fact subverts the overt lesson of Narcissus's story. The narrator steps out of the poetic framework of the garden, adopts a didactic voice, and addresses himself to his audience. However, instead of the expected lesson for the gentlemen—that self-love and pride lead to destruction—the ladies are supposed to learn to be merciful toward their lovers if they want to avoid divine punishment. A self-consciously courtly didacticism, centering on the disdainful courtly lady and the pining male lover, thus undoes the traditional allegorization. The surprise of the moral makes the reader realize that the structure of text and gloss can produce any number of meanings.

Furthermore, in contradistinction to the traditional timeless and generalizing allegorization of myth, the inscription on the fountain highlights the geographical congruence between the mythological locus and that of present specific events, thereby opening up the garden to a vast mythological past that, unlike its counterpart in mythography or allegorization, could physically resurface and confront Amant at any moment. This making present of myth distinguishes the poetic from the purely didactic with its universal application. That is, Amant, as an individual in a particular situation, must read and interpret not only the mythological narrative but also the moral, which presents him with a surprising gender reversal: the ladies now occupy the structural place of Narcissus, and Amant must now strive for ways to make the myth meaningful for his own experience. By going beyond one-dimensional moralization, the poet creates a thematic density in this passage that sets in motion new readings of the familiar myth.

As for the prophetic dimension, represented in Ovid by Tiresias's foretelling of Narcissus's death, it here applies to Amant: he sees his future—the rosebud—reflected in the fountain's crystals and, in the voice of the narrator, who has a more mature perspective, speaks of his own future that was then still to come:

> Cil miroërs m'a deceü:
> se j'eüsse avant coneü
> quex ert sa force et sa vertuz,
> ne m'i fusse ja enbatuz,
> que maintenant ou laz cheï
> qui maint home a pris et traï. (ll. 1607–12)

This mirror deceived me: if I had known beforehand what its power and force were, I would never have gotten into this, for now I have fallen into the nets that trapped many a man and betrayed him.

This passage highlights the futility of the supposed lesson—indeed, it dramatizes the uselessness of the moralization of myth—by pitting didacticism against future experience analyzed in retrospect. Thus an extremely complex temporality results from the interplay of myth, moralization, and experience: past, present, and future are fused in the myth of Narcissus.

We have seen that from a formal perspective the Narcissus myth is neatly framed by two markers: a written inscription that gives us the gist of the story and a lesson—both static expressions of myth. The center by contrast is taken up by a fast-moving narrative. This interplay between stasis and motion reproduces to a certain extent the genres of lyric and narrative that make up the *Rose*: where the lyric turns in on itself, the narrative must progress.[24] The voices of the *Rose*, lyric, narrative, and didactic, are already contained in the Narcissus myth, thus creating a paradigm that proved influential not only in *Rose II* but for texts well into the fourteenth century.[25]

Venus

Like Narcissus, the figure of Venus is at the center of geographical and temporal expansions and of new interpretations in the *Rose*. But unlike

Narcissus, imprisoned in the inscription on a fountain, Venus is an active, heterogeneous character and thus illustrates particularly well the variegated uses of myth in the *Rose*. Formally she participates in all the major manifestations of mythology in the *Rose*: on the diegetic level, in exempla, and in a curious episode that takes place in Cythera and has a most problematic temporal and geographical relationship to the *Rose*'s story line. Indeed, it represents a fusion of diegesis, exemplum, and moralization.

Venus first appears as the enemy of Chasteez (Chastity), her traditional role in personification allegory. Raison demands of her daughter Chasteez that she "exile" Venus (ll. 2830–38). As a personification Venus had come to stand for *luxuria*, a kind of lecherous sensuality,[26] and that is clearly the only function she has here; at this point nothing is said about her background or family relationships. She is a woman without a past. This status changes in the description Amant gives of her while yearning for the first kiss of the Rose. Significantly she is again first identified as the enemy of Chasteez, but she quickly becomes more complex. We learn that she is the mother of the God of Love, that she has a habit of helping lovers, that she holds a torch in her hand with which she has inflamed many a lady, and finally that she is so beautiful that she resembles a goddess or a fairy and is clearly not a religious (ll. 3402–14). She has now acquired a family (the God of Love) and an iconography (the torch in her right hand); as for her looks, she seems to hover between classical antiquity and the middle ages (goddess or fairy).

Thus in *Rose I* the process of the remythisization of Venus has begun, and in *Rose II* each speaker who brings up her story adds a new dimension. Of course, each mention of Venus, particularly her adulterous relationship with Mars, has a specific function in each speaker's discourse. For the moment, however, we are interested in the ways Venus exemplifies the different forms myth and mythological figures take in the *Rose*.

The first time that Venus appears in *Rose II* is in Raison's discussion of the relative value of love and justice. In order to prove that love is more valuable than justice she evokes the castration of Saturn by his son Jupiter, using in the process the word "coilles" (testicles) that so horrifies Amant that he will—much later—demand an explanation. In any case, Venus is born from Saturn's severed genitals.[27] That is all we learn at this point. The next installment of Venus's history is offered by her son, the God of Love. Here, Venus appears in all her complexity: her birth is alluded to again, albeit in a veiled manner ("Saturnus . . . l'angendra . . . mes non pas de sa feme espouse"; Saturn engendered her but not in his wife; ll. 10,798–800), and Amors speaks of his countless brothers of (at least to him) unknown fathers. But Amors also represents Venus very much as part of the allegory. She is the one who can conquer "fortresses" without him, that is, without L/love, but with money (ll. 10,735–44). Here, Venus is an allegorical representation of mercenary sexuality.

In the four evocations of Venus's affair with Mars, the goddess is not seen as participating in the diegesis but is rather part of exempla illustrating a variety of points.[28] La Vieille uses the story of the adultery of Mars and Venus and their being caught in Vulcan's fine metal net in the context of the ruses women should employ when they want to cheat on their husbands.[29] Some husbands, especially if they are as ugly as Vulcan, La Vieille concludes, can simply not be loved. A few hundred lines later, after a digression on "free love," La Vieille refers to Mars and Venus in a tirade on the uselessness of jealousy: had Vulcan kept quiet rather than exposing his wife and her lover, Venus would have cherished him more. Echoing Ovid's *Ars amatoria* 2.589–90, La Vieille claims that the only result of Vulcan's folly was that now Mars and Venus did openly what hitherto they had done in secret.[30]

The theme of open versus hidden is pursued by Nature and Genius, who speak of Mars and Venus in the context of mirrors (ll. 18,031–99). Here the two speakers offer in effect an alternate version of the myth in a lengthy conditional phrase dependent on "If Mars and Venus had had such magnifying mirrors as the ones we are speaking of, then . . ." First, Nature contends, they would have avoided detection because they would have perceived the delicate strings of Vulcan's net as if they were gigantic beams. Second, Genius adds, if they had seen the net they would have met elsewhere or at least they would have had time to cover up and invent some lies.

Thus, while La Vieille gives a thoroughly literal reading of the myth—and thus adheres to the uses of the exemplum at the simplest level—Nature and Genius in keeping with the more complex character of their discourses offer a hypothetical mythical plot that unfolds under their control: they do it with mirrors. The myth appears here in a completely new form, not as what happened but as what might have happened. Mirrors are presented as if they had the potential to change the past, even the mythological past. Thus myth is revealed as fiction, for if the mirror of Narcissus was a place of psychological revelation and of poetic fecundity, the mirrors discussed here reflect back into classical mythology and create new versions of familiar stories.

This questioning of a well-known mythological story becomes especially significant in light of the subsequent discussion of dreams and visions (ll. 18,258–484). The intense questioning of the veracity of dreams encourages us to reexamine the premise of *Rose I*, where, in the Prologue, the narrator made a strong case for the truth of dreams in general and his dream in particular. Here, Nature and Genius use exactly the kind of dream that Amant supposedly dreamed—as a kind of case history—to prove the falsehood and illusion of dreams in general (ll. 18,327–74). As Nature and Genius engage in a reevaluation of the poetic constructs of *Rose I*, they create, with their version of the story of Mars and Venus, a kind of mini-fabliau that, by going counter to the traditional version of the story, questions the traditions of myth and mythography. Implicitly the critique also extends to the Narcissus myth, the only evocation of classical mythology in *Rose I*, which will be at the center of Genius's myth criticism later on.[31] Jean de Meun as author thus uses his characters' reading and rewriting of well-known mythological stories to highlight the malleability of myth as fiction.

Let us now turn from the exempla involving Venus to a more complex formal and temporal arrangement: the interlocking of diegesis and exemplum in the passage of Venus's tryst with Adonis.

After the crucial psychomachia-like battle between personifications such as Honte and Peur with the likes of Delit, described in great and amusing detail, Jean de Meun shows us the God of Love in a crisis. Things are going badly for his army, and he needs his mother's active support. Amors decides to send messengers to his mother, Venus, who is spending some time with Adonis in Cythera. Basing his work on *Metamorphoses* 10.519–739, Jean shows us a hunting scene reminiscent of that in Guillaume's Narcissus episode (ll. 1470–72), thus linking the two moments where an awareness of imminent danger should lead to appropriate moral behavior. Tired from the hunt, Venus and Adonis rest, and it is at that moment that Venus warns her lover against hunting animals that are too wild and dangerous. (Jean omits the Atalanta story, a lengthy digression Venus uses in Ovid to make her point.) Yet her warning has no effect, for Adonis will be killed by a wild boar. The moral that is drawn from the story is addressed to "Biau seigneur" (gentle men; l. 15,721) and urges them to believe their girlfriends' warnings because they are as true as "estoire."[32]

This story explodes the temporal and geographical parameters of *Rose II*. Initially, the story is part of the diegesis, since Amors dispatches his messengers at a precise moment in the battle, yet quite unexpectedly it turns into a timeless exemplum with an attached moral at the end. Moreover, it is almost impossible to pinpoint the story in time: it clearly begins before Adonis's death, and it ends with the narrator telling us—in the past tense—that Adonis did not heed her warnings: "Ne la crut pas, puis an mourut" (he did not believe her and then died because of it; l. 15,709). Thus, the narrator points to an extratextual future whose exact temporality remains unclear.[33] But, and this is the important point, even the future beyond the borders of the text lies in the realm of classical mythology. The story thus reorients the entire narrative of the *Rose*. We are shown that it takes place in a mythological past and that this past is represented by the dream vision. Through the psychomachia that preceded the story of Venus and Adonis, the vision thus has taken on a new complexity: the forces of Amant and the Lady's psyche battle it out on the diegetic level. The mythological figures of Amors and Venus, clearly parts of the diegesis, are supplemented here with the figure of Adonis, who becomes part of both the *Rose*'s diegesis and of its network of mythological exempla. As with Narcissus, the coincidence between Amant's experience and the realm of mythology is dramatized.

Furthermore, the Adonis story stages the transformation of a mythological story into an exemplum by problematizing the relationship between the telling of a story and the drawing out of a moral. But the markers that usually identify an exemplum, such as the inscription on Narcissus's fountain or a term of comparison (for example, just as . . . so . . .), are missing here. We are led in a seamless move from the diegesis to the moral, from a precise moment in time to the timelessness of moralization, from narration to commentary. The direct address of the audience, of course, recalls the moral drawn from the Narcissus story—explicitly addressed to women—and thus links these two crucial moments. Both open up the text to a mythological past, link Amant's experience with that past, and, at the same time, open up the text to the audience, which, although fictional or inscribed, must nevertheless be considered contemporaneous with the "real" audience.

Pygmalion

Like Venus, Pygmalion appears in a wide variety of contexts and functions in *Rose II* and thus illustrates the interplay between Ovidian myth and the *Rose*'s diegesis, but unlike Venus, Pygmalion never acts on the diegetic level. The various appearances of Pygmalion's story help construct clusters of ideas on art, love, and sexuality.[34] His story also furnishes extremely interesting examples of the many shapes Ovidian myth takes in the *Rose*. Its formal characteristics are unusual: his story is at first fragmented and used only allusively, but toward the end of the romance it is told directly by the narrator and at such length that the audience sees it inevitably as one of the major informing episodes of the entire text.

The very first mention of Pygmalion by La Vieille, however, is somewhat mysterious. She refers to a "chançon" of Pygmalion's "ymage" or statue that her interlocutor Bel Acueil supposedly knows well.[35] This song, La Vieille claims, gives plenty of advice on how to ornament oneself in order to attract lovers. Like some of the explicit morals drawn from mythological exempla in the *Rose*, this advice has a certain surprise effect: neither Pygmalion's artistic skill, nor his misogyny (so important in Ovid), nor the danger of idolatry, the mythographic commonplace, surface here. La Vieille refocuses the story on the statue as if it had decorated itself and gives it a didactic value that has nothing in common with traditional lessons.[36]

Significantly we find several intricate gender changes that recall the unexpected moral drawn from the fable of Narcissus. While in the preceding interpretive tradition Pygmalion had been at the center, here it is his statue, a "woman." And though the exemplar, the female statue who will eventually become the live Galatea, is a "woman," La Vieille's advice on beautification is addressed to Bel Acueil, a male figure, but one who in turn stands for the "Fair Welcome" of the Rose, representing certain aspects of a woman. As we will see shortly, La Vieille is a tendentious reader of myth who reinterprets traditional fables in light of her own agenda. The unexpected lesson drawn from the story of Pygmalion thus shows us that through La Vieille, Jean de Meun can play with the meaning of the Pygmalion myth and, by extension, with the interpretation of myth in more general terms.

A further very important consequence of the reference to the "Song of Pygmalion" is again an expansion of the allegory. In *Rose I* La Vieille is primarily a personification of old age that appears on the garden wall as one of the qualities that is excluded from the *locus amoenus*, the enchanted space of the garden. (Although she can be glimpsed as Bel Acueil's guardian toward the end of *Rose I* [ll. 3902–8].) But in *Rose II* La Vieille becomes a full-blown character, presumably within the world of the garden, who interacts with Bel Acueil by drawing extensively on Ovid's *Ars amatoria* and on her own experience: she is a person with a past and is well read to boot. Her evocation of the "Song of Pygmalion" as a known text first of all underlines the appearance of myth *as* text in the *Rose*, a text produced and interpreted by a character important within the *Rose*'s diegesis. The recital of the "Song of Pygmalion" also creates a complicity between La Vieille and Bel Acueil that excludes the audience. The audience must wait until the end of the romance to hear Pygmalion's story. The reference thus functions proleptically within *Rose II*: what La Vieille and Bel Acueil already know the narrator will deliver later to his expectant audience. Jean again plays with the temporality of the text and ties his thematic knots well in advance.

Pygmalion, the master artist, marginalized in La Vieille's version of the story at the expense of his statue, does not fare much better in the next evocation of the myth: the narrator claims that not even an artist like Pygmalion would be capable of making a life-like statue of Nature (ll. 16,147–48). This passage forms part of the extensive discussion on art versus nature in the *Rose*.[37] Here, the narrator uses a variation of the *Unsagbarkeitstopos* (the impossibility of representation topos) to underline Nature's singularity. Neither philosophers nor writers, nor sculptors, nor painters, can do justice to Nature. Yet, the choice of Pygmalion for this series of exempla finally undercuts the claims in favor of nature: for it is precisely Pygmalion who through his desire and Venus's intervention succeeds in bringing art to life.

But here the name of Pygmalion has a purely evocative function. Nothing is told of the story: the name and his activity, "entaillier" (sculpting; l. 16,147), suffice. The narrator proposes no overt moral but rather uses Pygmalion in a whole series of figures of writers and artists. This allusive use of myth is typical for medieval texts: the name of a mythological character could evoke not only his or her story but also the interpretive tradition attached to it. Thematically, the narrator refers to the insufficiency of Pygmalion and thus provides the link to the full-blown story that appears in a curious construction—as part of negative comparison.

The anomaly of the location of this elaborate version of the myth should not be overlooked. It is as if Jean created a kind of fold in the text into which he inserts the story. This fold is the result of a comparison: as Venus and her troops approach the castle, they perceive "une ymage" (l. 20,769) of a woman. This representation is so perfect that Pygmalion's statue would be like a mouse compared to a lion with respect to it (ll. 20,781–86). This negative introduction of the story recalls the narrator's remarks in his description of Nature and thus provides a thematic link. At the same time, we can read the story as the "Song of Pygmalion" mentioned by La Vieille thousands of lines before. The narrator will now fill the empty textual space that had been created by the previous fragmentary allusions, and he does so, as I suggested, by telling the well-known fable in a curious formal and temporal set-up.

As in the *Roman de Troie*, where Achilles compares himself to Narcissus,[38] a kind of doubling of classical culture is at work here. Pygmalion also compares himself to Narcissus, thus establishing a link to the central myth of *Rose I* and to a more general tradition in which the Narcissus myth was interpreted morally and psychologically. Pygmalion attempts to define his own predicament by contrasting it with that of Narcissus. He first alludes to Narcissus by saying "J'aime une ymage sourde et mue" (I love a deaf and dumb statue; l. 20,821) and then mentions him explicitly:

> Si n'ain je pas trop folement,
> car, se l'escriture ne ment,
> maint ont plus folement amé.
> N'ama jadis ou bois ramé,
> a la fonteine clere et pure,
> Narcisus sa propre figure,
> quant cuida sa saif estanchier? (ll. 20,843–49)

Thus I do not love in too mad a fashion. For, unless the text lies, there were quite a few people who loved even more madly. Did not Narcissus long ago love his own appearance in the woods when he meant to alleviate his thirst in the clear and pure fountain?

The crucial reference here is to "escriture": the Narcissus myth is presented as a text that Pygmalion knows and from which he can learn. While his love may be just as crazy and idolatrous as that of Narcissus,[39] it nevertheless bears fruit. His creation is animated through Venus's intervention, and Pygmalion is spared Narcissus's fate. In *Rose I* the Narcissus story receives a definite closure as narration (Narcissus the character dies) but continues to live as commentary, as moralization. As we saw, his story appears in *Rose I* as an engraved text from which the narrator draws an explicit moral.

This balance between narration and overt commentary is absent from the Pygmalion story. Here the commentary remains implicit in the coda to the story proper. Galatea's offspring Paphos brings forth Cinyras, the father of Myrrha. Myrrha in turn gives birth to Adonis, engendered in an incestuous relationship with her father. The narrator refuses to tell

Adonis's story because this would take him too far from his "matire" (l. 21,181) and instead returns to the comparison that opened the story: Pygmalion's statue is like a mouse to the lion of the tower image (ll. 21,188–98).

This tying up of the story is extremely complex. First of all, the return to the negative comparison closes the "fold" that had been opened at the beginning of the Pygmalion story. That is, the most elaborate myth told in *Rose II* exists only in a kind of ellipsis with respect to the diegesis. Yet, in an important move, the narrator ties the myth back into the diegesis by means of the mythic genealogy that resulted from Pygmalion's procreative efforts. Thus the text doubles back on itself: the strange temporal space of the Adonis story can now be located more precisely as that of four generations past Pygmalion.

Pygmalion is thus the ancestor of a character at the margins of the diegesis, a double of the protagonist (as artist-lover), part of a series of exempla involving artist figures, and the subject of a "Song" with which La Vieille and Bel Acueil are familiar as well as of the most extended mythological story told by the narrator. Pygmalion can be seen as emblematic of the vast expansion of the allegory—in large part through the use of myth—visible in *Rose II*.

Thus the mythological stories of Narcissus, Venus and Adonis, and Pygmalion function in very complex ways. The first two open up the dream allegory to the realm of classical mythology by positing an identity or congruence between the textual space of the *Rose* and that of myth. Their links to the diegesis are both spatial and temporal. In *Rose I* Oiseuse's garden *is* the locus of Narcissus's death, and in *Rose II* Venus and Adonis can be reached by messengers from the castle where Bel Acueil is imprisoned. From a temporal perspective, Narcissus was physically present in the garden and is still there, in that his story is commemorated on a marble plaque. Venus and Adonis exist in a time preceding Adonis's death. The narrator, however, can refer to his death and draw out its lesson. Thus, narration and commentary coexist in this story, as they do in most mythographic texts.

I suggested that the Narcissus story represents—formally—a mythographic text in miniature and that the episode of Venus and Adonis dramatizes the interplay between mythological exemplum and moralization, revealing a very skilfull *mise en abyme*. The "essential property [of this technique] is that it brings out the meaning and the form of the work."[40] Each story does exactly that. The Narcissus myth, as many critics have shown, is central to the idea of the courtly lyric, ultimately sterile and turned in on itself. Yet critics have not concentrated on the form and temporality of the story, which, in a more general way, provide a *mise en abyme* of the *Rose*'s integration of mythology. The unexpected moral drawn from Narcissus's tale, in turn, exemplifies the subversion of a traditional mythographic interpretation under the influence of the vernacular courtly lyric. *Rose I* thus already authorizes the unexpected interpretations given to myths that Jean de Meun capitalizes on in *Rose II*.

It is in this interpretive domain that we can see the link between the stories of Narcissus and that of Venus and Adonis. Here as well, the lesson is somewhat surprising because of what precedes it: the evocation of the girlfriends' "gospel truth" that every lover should believe (ll. 15,721–28) appears after the long discourse of La Vieille, who counsels nothing but lies and deceit in love. Thus we can read the moralization in light of exactly that discourse. The myth's lesson moves away from the mythographic tradition by means of an interior conditioning by the discourse that precedes it in *Rose II*. That is, although lovers must know by now that their girlfriends lie, they should believe them nonetheless in order to demonstrate their love.

Finally, it has become a critical commonplace that the Pygmalion story is a *mise en abyme* of the creative process, the animation of the loved object through art. And if we look at the formal aspects of the story as part of a series leading from "song" to exemplum to full-blown story, we can see that it also represents the whole range of the forms myth can take in the *Rose*.

Characters in the *Rose* as Interpreters of Myth

For the Narcissus story the narrator himself drew out the surprising moral, but the myths of *Rose II* are interpreted by a wide range of characters, indeed there is hardly a speaker who does not mention a mythological story at one point or another.[41] The choice of stories and their interpretations is conditioned by the agenda of each speaker: they highlight certain features and suppress others. Raison, Ami, and La Vieille, our focal points here, exemplify the flexibility in the interpretation of myth in the *Rose*.

Raison

Raison's structural significance for Jean de Meun derives from her role as the speaker of the first long discourse in *Rose II*. Of all the speakers Raison reflects most explicitly on problems of interpretation. What kinds of interpretive models does she propose and to what extent do her theoretical reflections govern the actual use and interpretation of myths in her own discourse and those of other speakers?

The crucial passage for an understanding of Raison's methods of interpretation is the end of her discourse.[42] The point of departure for the long discussion of language, sexuality, and euphemism is Raison's telling of the myth of the castration of Saturn, which leads to Amant's reproach that Raison, a courtly lady in his estimation, has used an indecent expression when she referred to Saturn's "coilles" (testicles) in her account. Amant insists that she should have used some "cortaise parole" (courtly expression; l. 6905) to gloss the word. Raison counters Amant's attack by arguing that since God made the things in question, one is perfectly justified in using the proper names for them. No gloss is necessary to speak of natural things. Amant replies that while God made the things, He did not make the names, and therefore human beings presumably have a choice between decent and indecent words.

For Raison there is no linguistic concept of indecency; the only thing that should not be pronounced is something superfluous. She considers it "dyablie" (work of the devil; l. 7006) to say things that should be kept silent (presumably garrulousness is bad) and adds "langue doit estre refrenee" (speech should be curbed; l. 7007), that is, Amant should stop interrupting her. Moreover, she states, if a word like "coilles" were to be glossed, another, superfluous, textual level would appear, since Saturn's castration is already a figure for the severing of a primal (including linguistic) harmony. Raison thus is not an advocate of unrestrained expression nor of impoliteness but of a reasonable use of language.

As for God not making the names, she adds, did He not charge Raison with naming things? And did not Plato teach that these names were made to facilitate communication?[43] Consequently, the right word should be used to designate things. Raison then lists some of the metaphoric expressions women use to designate men's sexual organs.

This list of metaphors leads Raison to questions of interpretation. Essentially, Raison proposes a way of reading or interpreting texts that combines free expression with deeper meanings. In the schools, she states, some speak in "paraboles" (parables; l. 7124), and therefore one should not take things literally. Similarly, she states that "En ma parole autre sen ot, / au mains quant des coillons parloie" (there is another sense in what I said, at least when I spoke of testicles; ll. 7128–29). Thus in her own words, at least as far as her use of the term "coilles" is concerned, there is another sense: the literal sense of sexuality is integrated into the deeper sense of the fable. The "fable occure" (obscure fable; l. 7134) will eventually take on a clear meaning.

Here Raison uses the crucial term "integumanz" (l. 7138). We saw in the Introduction that integument became in the twelfth century the most important term in the interpretation of fables: the removal of the covering or veil would expose the fable's true and profound meaning. Raison aligns herself with this method of interpretation, while at the same time insisting on her literal use of individual words:

> Mes puis t'ai tex .II. moz renduz,
> et tu les as bien entenduz,
> qui pris doivent estre a la letre,
> tout proprement, sanz glose metre. (ll. 7151–54)

But I gave you these two words and you heard them well; these must be taken literally, in their proper sense, without a gloss.

Raison offers a model of interpretation of mythological fables in which the literal level is noneuphemistic.[44] Thus she proposes a reading in which the parable derives its sense from open or literal representation on the textual level of integument. Amant, however, is singularly uninterested in these intricate interpretive processes: he is not in a mood for fables, metaphors, or glosses, he states. Perhaps once he has been successful in his quest he will feel like glossing something, but not now (ll. 7160–68).[45] Clearly, the kind of open expression of sexuality Raison advocates has not gained Amant's favor; he is still advocating the courtly euphemism of *Rose I*.

As Nancy F. Regalado has shown, the mythological exempla provide an especially privileged locus for the expression of sexuality that was banned from the courtly allegorical level.[46] The debate between Raison and Amant thus spells out the profound transformation and expansion in *Rose II*. The courtly diction of *Rose I* is shown as insufficient, as removed from linguistic truth; it is too concerned with words. Raison offers a wide range of interpretive techniques and acknowledges the usefulness of parables and integuments for the conveying of philosophical truths.

The fable in which Raison uses noneuphemistic language is that of

Saturn's castration by Jupiter, in which she not only names Saturn's testicles but also compares them to sausages (l. 5508). But what is most remarkable here is that Raison offers a new combination and conceptualization of the Fulgentian version of the ancient fable in which Uranus is castrated by Chronos. In Fulgentius, it is Saturn who is castrated and not Uranus (though he does not name Jupiter as the castrator). Following this version, Raison combines this myth with that of the end of the Golden Age and the reigns of love and justice.

For Raison, the meaning of the fable of Saturn is an explanation of the necessity of love on earth, for without love justice is worth nothing (ll. 5510–20). As Jean-Marie Fritz has shown, the originality of Jean de Meun lies in his reorientation of the myth away from the physical, historical, and moral mythographic interpretations toward the position that morals, politics, and history all appear in opposition to the goodness of the natural state.[47]

From this complex reinterpretation of the myth of Saturn's castration, Raison extracts a clear message for Amant with which she wants to dissuade him from his foolish love for the Rose: "Mes l'amor qui te tient ou laz / charnex deliz te represente" (but the love that holds you captive in its nets represents carnal delights for you; ll. 4570–71). Instead, Raison proposes the good kinds of love: friendship and charity. Yet, when it comes to explaining the importance of love, her recourse to the fables of Saturn and of the birth of Venus seems to undercut the very message she hopes to convey. For the connection between the birth of Venus and the appearance of love on earth remains ambiguous. Though Raison overtly rejects Venus's type of love, the sequence of events as presented by her seems to imply that Venus's birth was somehow linked to the emergence of the good love that is more important than justice.[48]

Thus Raison is both a subtle and biased reader of myth. To recapitulate her interpretive method: she uses a fable within which she employs "plain speech" as a form of expression. The fable may mean "something else," that is, the end of the Golden Age and the necessity for love, but the word, as an isolated element, is plain and literal. Noneuphemistic language appears on the level of what is generally considered the integument, that is, the level of fable, and the fable itself reveals a deeper truth, though that truth may not be exactly what Raison had in mind. In any case, Raison practices the interpretive methods she identifies at the end of her discourse. The important point is, as David Hult emphasizes, that the fable precedes, in fact provokes, the discussion on language.[49] Of course, the fable plays a role in Raison's argumentation and is related to the diegesis because it is addressed to Amant. But with its innovative interpretations, its focus on language, and its place in the creation of new mythological clusters it also serves to highlight the fundamental questions concerning the reading of myth in the thirteenth century.

But Raison does more than just tell myths; she also inscribes herself into a mythological fable, that of Echo. As the allegorical figure of reason, Raison offers Amant a different type of love from that of the Rose: she wants to become Amant's "amie" and offers herself to him as a beautiful and desirable woman (ll. 5765–71). In her wooing of Amant she appeals to the myth of Echo, evoking the plight of rejected women (ll. 5803–8). In this instance, Raison follows the interpretive model she later discusses with Amant: she uses a fable to convey her views and ideas. Yet she does not overtly follow the mythographic tradition that saw in Echo "good reputation" (though Amant's reputation would be enhanced in the type of love she offers him) but presents Echo simply as a spurned and unhappy young woman. Raison's identification with Echo may be motivated by a web of allusions: in French, both the Ovidian "resonabilis Echo" (resounding Echo; *Met* 3.358) and the "priere resnable" uttered by Echo in *Rose I* (reasonable prayer; l. 1465) evoke Raison's name.

The mere mention of Echo of course brings with it the myth of Narcissus. "Don't make me a second Echo," Raison seems to caution, "or you may very well find yourself to be a second Narcissus." Raison thus ties her own use of myth to the central myth of *Rose I*, and like the courtly moral attached to that fable the myth is seen from the woman's perspective. This brief evocation of Echo thus emphasizes the importance of the context for the interpretation of myth. In the Narcissus myth the courtly woman who resists her lover's advances is cast in the role of Narcissus. Raison interprets the same myth as that of a man spurning the good love of a woman (which corresponds to Amant's rejection of Raison's good love).

Interestingly Raison is also evoked at the very moment another lesson is drawn from a myth (the story of Adonis) that seems rather surprising to us—the overt moralization of the episode (believe your girlfriends like the gospel; ll. 15,723–28) is not quite congruent with the gravity of Adonis's fate of violent death. Here the audience is warned against Raison: "Se Reson vient, point n'an creez" (if Reason appears, don't believe her; ll. 15,730). Because Raison is the only character to reflect explicitly on the interpretation of myths, the fact that she is mentioned at this very moment of playful and surprising interpretation is surely significant. As in the case of her ambiguous message derived from the fable of Saturn, her position on the philosophical use of fables is called into question here—as is her fundamental message, which does not fit in at all with love's illusions!

Ami

Tendentious and contextual interpretation of myth is also a hallmark of Ami's discourse. He and, as we will see, La Vieille are particularly prolific users of myths. Their interpretive techniques are especially interesting and complex: both of them use the device of dividing a myth and using it as a framing device for a digression, thus conditioning the interpretation of the myth by a different type of discourse. This tripartite structure helps to produce a meaning that is more complex than that of the mythological story alone. Thus Ami inserts the Jaloux's speech between the two halves of his evocation of the Golden Age,[50] and La Vieille digresses on free love in the middle of the Mars and Venus story.

Ami as a descendant of Ovid's "praeceptor amoris" is the supreme adviser in the field of amorous hypocrisy, though he himself has ended up without either love or money.[51] He evokes the myth of the Golden Age in a nostalgic mode: there was a time before money and deceit ruled the world.[52] People foraged for food, they slept on moss, they enjoyed bird song and flowers, they wore beautiful garlands made from flowers (ll. 8325–424). Indeed, it seems that what Ami describes here is the first impression Amant had when entering the garden, when he believed he was in an earthly paradise (l. 634). Ami ends the first part of his description by insisting that at that time there was no mastery in love, rather equality and harmony. "Seigneurie" (mastery; l. 8421) separates lovers, and it is here that the Jaloux's intercalated discourse is introduced.

As mastery severs lovers, so the Jaloux with his diatribe on women cuts into two parts the evocation of the Golden Age. He is the physical embodiment of those human characteristics that brought about the end of that age: small-mindedness, suspiciousness, total incomprehension of the true nature of love. He is also a thoroughly nonmythological character. His roots are in the lyric, where he is a type, and in the fabliau. Indeed, he identifies himself as a traveling merchant (ll. 8445–46) and thus as the kind of husband whose absence fosters his wife's adulterous ambitions. He wants to be his wife's master, and his tirade draws on the proverbial misogynist sources, such as Juvenal, Theophrastus, and even Heloise's arguments against marriage (ll. 8437–9390).[53]

The Jaloux represents the extreme counterpoint to the Golden Age, an experience different from that of this ideal mythic past and that would fit better into what could be called the Age of Suspicion. Interestingly, the Jaloux himself implicitly evokes the loss of the Golden Age by a reference that recalls Ovid's Age of Iron. When he speaks of Juvenal's negative depiction of female nature he specifies: "Ne voit l'en comment les marrastres / cuisent venins a leur fillastres?" (Does one not see how stepmothers cook up poisons for their stepdaughters? ll. 9119–20). In Ovid's Age of Iron "stepmothers brewed deadly poisons" (*Met* 1.147). Although this idea may have become a commonplace at that time,[54] the Jaloux's discourse nonetheless illustrates the transference of ideas and motifs initially associated with mythology into a new, vernacular context.

As I suggested earlier, the Jaloux also represents a type—as his very name indicates—from the vernacular genres of the fabliau and lyric. The intercalation of his discourse into the myth of the Golden Age thus signals the interaction between the realms of mythology and vernacular literature that pervades the entire *Rose*.[55]

When Ami reappears as narrator he draws the moral from the Jaloux's examples: "Amor ne peut durer ne vivre, / s'el n'est en queur franc et delivre" (Love can not last and survive unless it exists in a free and frank heart; ll. 9411–12). To illustrate this point, Ami describes how in marriage the man who used to be his mistress's servant now becomes her master (ll. 9413–62). These arguments allow him to return to the Golden Age, where no servitude spoiled love. There was no travel and no wealth and were no wars caused by greed (ll. 9463–9634). Money, of course, is one of the principal means to gain love nowadays, as Ami explains to Amant in his advice on bribery. Thus, for Ami the myth of the Golden Age is the counterpoint to the world we live in today, a world that makes counselors like Ami necessary. He tells in detail how the current world, that in which his methods work, came about. The Jaloux serves as the catalyst in that he interrupts Ami's nostalgic evocation of the Golden Age and reorients the discourse: the Golden Age is revealed as nothing but a myth, which he exposes in order to destroy Amant's illusions. (Amant, however, seems to remain as unchanged as he did after Raison's discourse.) As a result of the Jaloux's intervention, dramatizing the loss of the Golden Age in misogynistic terms, the world of the garden as depicted in *Rose I*, which so closely resembles Ami's description of the Golden Age, is also revealed as a myth. As Genius will do after him, Ami attempts to destroy Amant's naive belief in a courtly myth leading to perfect love.

La Vieille

La Vieille's discourse and her interpretation of myth are also colored by her particular purpose, that is, teaching women how to deceive. Confirming all the misogynist commonplaces regarding women's deceitfulness, her speech supposedly has a warning function. Addressed as it is to Bel Acueil, it tries to exhort young women to seize the day and take advantage of their beauty as long as it lasts. A number of mythological fables support her lessons of deception and her demonstration of why women have to look out for themselves. For example, she offers the traditional catalog of false lovers, including Aeneas, Demophon, Paris (with regard to Oenone), and Jason (ll. 13,143–234). At times, she invents a new moral for a known story, such as the one of Argus and Io, in which the moral—women must "guard" themselves; even Argus cannot do it for them (ll. 14,351–64)—precedes the fable.[56] Two other stories illustrate La Vieille's approach to myth: that of Mars and Venus (told in two parts) and that of Palinurus.

For the Mars and Venus story La Vieille uses the framing technique or ring structure we just observed in Ami's discourse. The story is cut in two, with a digression on free love in the middle. Where Ami advocates free love in the frame story of the Golden Age, La Vieille extolls free love in the middle of a frame story about jealousy and its consequences.[57] La Vieille introduces the story with a gender reversal reminiscent of the reversal we saw in the overt moralization of the Narcissus myth: women should pretend to be as jealous as Vulcan was of his wife, Venus (ll. 13,805–12). Thus the mythological story appears in the context of jealousy, feigned in La Vieille's advice, real for Vulcan.

The traditional mythographic interpretation of the myth was based on Fulgentius and saw in Venus's love affair with Mars "valor corrupted by lust," stating that Vulcan's chains represented the fetters of habit.[58] It is precisely with Vulcan's chains that the first segment of the story ends. The two lovers are caught and exposed to the gods. Venus, whose beauty is admired by all, feels shame and anger (ll. 13,810–31). The commentary of La Vieille follows. No wonder Venus preferred Mars, she says, since Vulcan was so ugly. However, even if he had been as beautiful as Absalom or Paris, she would not have loved him (presumably because he was her husband), for "el savoit bien, la debonere, / que toutes fames sevent fere" (she, the sweet one, knew well what all women know how to do; ll. 13,843–44). This leads to La Vieille's excursus on the free nature of love. Led by instinct, women know that they are made for more than one man. She adduces many examples from the animal world to illustrate the force of instinct.[59] Of course, free love can also lead to trouble, such as the Trojan War (ll. 13,893–910), but basically nature governs us and will win—she draws our hearts to unfettered delights (ll. 14,127–28).

After this excursus La Vieille returns to the Mars and Venus story at exactly the point where she had left off. But now the lovers' shame vanishes: henceforth they do openly what they had done in secret before.[60] Vulcan's act of jealousy thus has backfired. As we saw earlier, La Vieille uses the story as an exemplum. Now we see how the bipartition of the tale conditions its interpretation. The first part, ending with Mars and Venus in chains, suggests the traditional moralizing interpretation of humankind in the bonds of corruption. The digression rejects this interpretation and advocates a free (albeit morally doubtful) love. It thus sets the stage for the second segment of the story—Venus's liberation—and the moral drawn from it: displays of jealousy have no effect on women who are determined to pursue free love. La Vieille interprets the story literally here, since Venus, Vulcan, and Mars represent a love triangle well known from the Ovidian as well as from the fabliau traditions.

The structure of the Mars and Venus story thus first suggests a provisional interpretation of the story, derived from the moralizing interpretive tradition, and then, through the digression, offers the definitive literal interpretation of a wife liberated from her husband's chains. Again, the mythological story is interrupted by a different type of discourse, which serves as an aid to a literal reinterpretation. La Vieille's perspective colors the interpretation of the myth. Women are deceivers, men are cuckolds, and both play tricks on each other. The myth has neither a cosmological nor a deeply moral meaning but resembles a fabliau whose moral has no deeper meaning than that of strategy in the battle of the sexes.

Another reinterpretation of a mythological fable, indicating a more playful use of myth and validating the literal level, is visible in the story of Palinurus, Aeneas's helmsman swept overboard to drown and finally encountered by Aeneas during his descent to the underworld in Book 6 of the *Aeneid.* Here again, La Vieille's didactic purpose governs the interpretation.

Palinurus's story was not a mythographic staple like the story of Mars and Venus. It was Bernardus Silvestris in the twelfth century who had attached the most profound allegorical meaning to the character: Palinurus is the "wandering vision" that the rational spirit must abandon in order to rule desire with reason.[61] La Vieille transposes his story into the context of advice on table manners addressed to women: women should not fall asleep at the table for all sorts of accidents and ill fortune could befall them if they do. They should remember Palinurus, who steered well when awake but drowned when he fell asleep (ll. 13,438–44). La Vieille thus plays not only with the figure of Palinurus but also with the traditional negative moral implications of sleep. Here, sleep is seen simply as a danger for a woman at the dinner table, which La Vieille's advice can prevent.

La Vieille's playing with known myths and their interpretations for her own purposes illustrates the flexibility of mythology in the *Rose*. The redirection of the moral and philosophical implications of myth visible in La Vieille's interpretive activity and, in Katherine Heinrich's words, the "perverse mythographic exegesis" inserted into La Vieille's misogynistic lessons,[62] dramatize to what extent Jean de Meun removed his text's overt meaning from preceding mythographic and interpretive traditions. By using a sophisticated triptych structure in their discourses, Jean's sly counselors illuminate mythological fables from all possible angles and dramatize the flexibility of myth through the contextual interpretations they provide.

Interpretations of Hercules

La Vieille repositions the story of Palinurus by removing it from a philosophically moralizing context and using it for her own purposes of teaching etiquette. One further example will buttress the points I have made for La Vieille's speech: the story of Hercules, which in *Rose II* is pried loose from the mythographic allegorizing tradition.

In the middle ages the figure of Hercules appeared in two major contexts: he was one of a series of lovers destroyed by women; and because his labors had earned him deification he was seen as a figure for Christ. Hercules makes three appearances in *Rose II*.[63] The Jaloux evokes Hercules—seven feet tall, according to Solinus (ll. 9157–58)—as a comparison for the young men who pursue women such as his wife. They believe themselves to be like Hercules or Samson. Then the Jaloux points out that Hercules, just like Samson, was brought down by a woman. He thus includes even the young men that threaten him in the generalization that all men will sooner or later be victimized by women. Against women's wiles men have to stick together, states the quintessential misogynist. Hercules's exemplary role is thus determined solely by the Jaloux's hatred and fear of women.

Hercules makes a second appearance when Seurte (Security) wants to revile Poor (Fear). She also has recourse to the example of the hero. Poor, Seurte claims, is as fearful as Cacus when he fled from Hercules (ll. 15,543–58).[64] The playfulness of this passage becomes apparent when we consider its construction: an allegorical figure reprimands another allegorical figure for embodying exactly the quality she is meant to represent, for Fear is indeed fearful. To buttress her argument, Seurte disparagingly compares her allegorical adversary to Cacus, a figure from classical mythology. Jean stands the interplay between myth and allegory on its head here: instead of using mythological figures as allegories of moral virtues or vices, he has one allegorical character compare another to a mythological figure. Cacus does not stand for fear, rather Fear resembles Cacus. In this brief episode, then, the traditional relationship between myth and allegory as it had been established in mythography is reversed.

Finally, Hercules and Cacus reappear at the very end of the romance, at the taking of the Rose. The fence representing the lady's hymen is the last obstacle Amant must overcome to attain his desires. Three times he throws himself against it, and three times he has to sit down to catch his breath. Similarly, Hercules banged three times on the doors of Cacus's cave (ll. 21,589–602). But the comparison of Amant's final "success" to one of Hercules's labors makes the reader think of Hercules's violent death at the hands of a woman as described many thousands of lines earlier by the Jaloux. Through its multiple treatments in various contexts, the myth now brings interpretive baggage with it. Thus, while watching Amant reach his goal, readers may well wonder whether he, like Hercules, will not in the end be brought down by a woman.[65]

The final assault on the Rose brings together a number of themes and techniques used throughout *Rose II* and gives them a final twist. First of all, the pilgrim's garb Amant dons for the assault reminds us of the "relics" Raison mentioned in her discussion on language. If I had called "couilles" relics and vice versa, she asked Amant at that point, would you have taken offense (ll. 7079–85)? The example used by Raison to illustrate the arbitrariness of language comes to life here, as it were. Only now it is the female genitals that play the role of relics that the pilgrim aspires to and not the male genitals as in Raison's example. Amant, who had refused to gloss anything at the end of Raison's discourse, now becomes an actor on the textual level, which equates amorous pursuits and pilgrimages. Second, when Nature had spoken of dreams she mentioned that some people dream that they set out on journeys equipped with pilgrims' staffs, undoubtedly a phallic image here, and knapsacks (ll. 18,274–96). Amant now realizes this dream on the diegetic level. Thus Raison's metaphors and Nature's images coalesce in this final scene.

The appearance of Hercules and Cacus adds a further element to this convergence of the central images of the quest of love as pilgrimage and the adored woman as relic. The use of myth in an erotic context and its literal reading by Amant lead to the subversion of a potential Christ figure, which is not out of place in this mock-Christian pilgrimage. Again, the traditional moral and philosophical implications of the story, transmitted by such writers as Boethius and his commentator William of Conches,[66] have vanished in the creative and subversive use of myth typical of *Rose II*.

Myth Criticism and Some New Myths

As we just saw, the large number of traditional myths woven into *Rose II* receive the most varied and often innovative interpretations. But there are also episodes that could be construed as "new myths," defined by Hans-Robert Jauss as a story that encompasses the entire world, that symbolizes man's relationship with superior forces and that answers a fundamental question; the *récit* can give the answer figuratively by introducing a new god in place of an old one (in Jean, Nature and Genius replace Guillaume's God of Love); or, in a polemical manner, it can give a new answer to an old question differently posed.[67]

The most important new myth introduced in the period preceding the *Rose* was that of the courtly universe peopled with allegorical personifications, a kind of earthly paradise of love.[68] It drew its elements from the biblical myth of the Garden of Eden and the ancient myth of the Golden Age.[69] Guillaume de Lorris had adopted this construct and further expanded it, as we saw, through his use of the fountain of Narcissus. Jean de Meun in his vast expansion of *Rose I* retained Guillaume's initial construct of the garden of Deduit as a mythic framework, but he also introduced a large number of additional classical mythological stories. In many cases he makes his audience question the traditional interpretations and functions of these myths. Throughout *Rose II* Jean plays with some of the basic assumptions of the courtly universe, criticizes and reinterprets them, and in the process creates new mythic constructs.

Jean uses two mythic characters, Amors and Genius, to question, comment on, and re-create some of the underpinnings of courtly poetics. Amors questions the idea, fundamental to the courtly lyric, that the experience of love gives birth to poetry by substituting a bookish creation myth for the love experience. Genius redefines the relationship between love, sex, and religion, evident in the courtly universe in the expression of desire and at the same time adoration for the loved object. His overt criticism of Guillaume's garden brings forth, by opposition, a new myth, that of the "parc du champ joli." The two crucial passages where a reinterpretation of *Rose I* brings forth new mythic constructs are the midpoint of the conjoined *Rose* texts (ll. 10,465–648) and the sermon of Genius (ll. 19,475–20,637).

The two passages just mentioned fulfill the requirements of Jauss's definition of new myths in more ways than one. The new myths are enunciated by mythical figures: the first by the God of Love, ostensibly an "old god," the second by Genius, a "new god" who had gained prominence in Alan of Lille's twelfth-century *De planctu Naturae*. These figures show how superior forces shape human actions, and they give new answers to such old questions as what is the origin of love and what is the purpose of human existence. In each case the new myths of *Rose II* introduce a twist with respect to the tradition represented in *Rose I*: love is revealed to be really love poetry, that is, we find a questioning of the claim to the experiential basis of love and a dramatization of the transformation of love into poetry. Genius intertwines sex and elements from Christian religion and unveils the carnal reality underlying courtly euphemism.[70] Thus while Jean uses the "old myths" like that of Saturn or Pygmalion to articulate, and in some cases redefine, fundamental ideas on language, sexuality, and art, he also creates new myths that will reorient the very bases of Guillaume's text.

The Creation Myth of the Book: The Midpoint

In order to defeat Jalousie, the God of Love rallies his troops and delivers a speech, which, as we saw at the opening of this chapter, includes a detailed *récit* of the creation of the *Rose* as text.[71] The function of this passage corresponds to the second mythical function outlined by Jauss: it responds to the old question Where did we (or, in this case, the text) come from? in a new way by bringing to life the central courtly construct of love inspiring and thus creating poetry. What we have here is a creation myth that explains the genealogy of the book in terms of a genealogy of poets.

Amors's military enterprise of storming the castle in which Bel Acueil is imprisoned seems to be faltering because the support of the love poets of old is lacking: Tibullus, Gallus, Catullus, and Ovid are all dead and "porriz" (rotten; l. 10,495). The rhyme pair "porriz/Lorriz" is significant here.[72] Since Guillaume is still on the scene at this point, the rhyme has both an analeptic and a proleptic function. Amors's "Vez ci Guillaume de Lorriz" (here is Guillaume de Lorris; l. 10,496) indicates his presence at the moment of the address to the troops, but at that moment Guillaume is Amant and not the writer of the romance, who still lies in the future: "Doit il conmancier le romant / ou seront mis tuit mi conmant" (He shall begin the romance where all my commandments shall be put; ll. 10,519–20). The word "porriz" thus points backward to the dead Roman poets whose successor is Guillaume; but it also points forward to the moment of Guillaume's death (l. 10,531), which will, however, be preceded by his composition of the romance. Guillaume's disappearance will then make the appearance of Jean de Meun necessary. The temporal complexity and expansion that Jean had achieved in other instances through his use of mythological fables now develops on the diegetic level through Amors's placement of Guillaume into a poetic genealogy.

Genealogy is one of the fundamental structures of myth, and we can see here how Jean carefully develops the line of descent that will finally lead to him as the last in the tradition of the Roman love poets. These men were both lovers and love poets—as was Guillaume, whose identity as Amant Amors establishes in this passage.[73] But Jean will exclusively be a poet who will write about Guillaume's love; he will not experience it. This separation underlines the bookish character of *Rose II*. For Jean, the experience of reading replaces the experience of love; in fact, his experience *is* his vast book learning.[74]

In addition, we witness the profound transformation of the "old" God of Love. For when Love says "Puis vendra Johans Chopinel . . . / qui . . . / me servira toute sa vie" (then Jean Chopinel will come who will serve me all his life; ll. 10,535–39), the service he refers to is not loving but writing poetry. The creation myth of the *Rose* dramatizes the crucial realization that the clerk has come to replace the lover.[75]

Jauss's idea of remythisization can be taken one step further here. For Jauss, Amors was remythisized in the *Rose* as a more complex mythical figure after a long stasis in allegorization. A truly mythical figure, he argued, always leaves a surplus of meaning after the allegorical equation has been completed. Thus, although Amors loses in *Rose II* the supreme hierarchical position he had occupied in *Rose I*—for now Venus gains the ascendancy—he acquires a new literary function by becoming a mythmaker and creator in the realm of bookishness.

Amors's renaming the *Romanz de la Rose* (l. 37) the *Miroër aus Amoreus* (Mirror for Lovers; l. 10,621) confirms his role of being instrumental in the creation of the book. Where in *Rose I* the mirror appears as the object associated with Narcissus's death, here the term *mirror* has a didactic meaning evoking the summa-like character of *Rose II*, which, with its multiplicity of voices, refuses to espouse any one point of view.[76] The title *Miroër* most likely also plays with the negative connotations of the mirror in *Rose I*. Readers will wonder whether this *Miroër* will be more useful than the mirror of Narcissus; the fountain and its lesson did not deter Amant from embarking on the path of love, but at least it prevented self-love in favor of love of the Rose. The *Miroër* teaches so many contradictory lessons that Amant cannot follow them all, yet he preserves a singleness of purpose that leads him to the successful final assault. Thus, by renaming the text Amors engages in a polemic with *Rose I*. The emphasis shifts from the Rose to the mirror; it shifts from love to learning and *ingenium*, the skillful pursuit of a goal. Thus, just as love as an experience gives way to love as writing,[77] the lover's objective seems to be as much the text, the *Miroër*, as the Rose.

Genius's *Parc du Champ Joli*

Jean continues the process of the revision and replacement of values central to *Rose I* in the sermon Genius delivers to Amors's barons. Genius systematically replaces one mythic universe with another; he undoes Guillaume's garden step by step by creating the vision of an enchanted park that will in all respects be the contrary of Deduit's garden of delight.[78] And he does this in a context of writing and reading.

First, at the end of Nature's complaint she insists that her wishes regarding humans' loyal behavior, that is, to multiply their lineage, should be written "an mon livre" (in my book; l. 19,354). Her pardon and sentence, she adds, should also be written there (ll. 19,374–75). Genius then writes everything down, seals it, hands it to Nature, absolves her, and dispatches her back to her forge. Genius proceeds to address Amors's troops by stepping onto a kind of pulpit and unfolding his charter (ll. 19,376–474). Genius is thus a reader, but he is also a writer. One should not forget that the "parc" that forms the centerpiece of his speech seems to be a purely verbal construct; for when Genius likens the relationship between Deduit's garden and his "parc" to the relationship between fable/falsehood and truth, he says: "ce biau parc que je devise" (the beautiful park that I am describing [or narrating]; l. 20,253), indicating that he is the author or creator of the park.

In its most general outline, Genius's sermon represents a subversion both of Alan of Lille's allegorical world—which had given a quasi-sacramental function to procreation—and of the courtly, still sublimated, world of *Rose I*.[79] The first instance of subversion works through the adoption and subsequent exaggeration of a number of themes (in particular, the equation of writing and sexual activity) from Alan's *De planctu Naturae*.[80] The second instance works, as Kevin Brownlee has shown, through a threefold rhetorical strategy of rewriting, denigration, and correction.[81] It is in this second area that we find "internal myth criticism," since one of the major objects of Genius's scorn is the fountain of Narcissus, and it is this myth criticism that generates the new myth of the park.

In the opening section of his sermon Genius emphasizes the dangers of sterile sex in a whole series of images relating sexual activity to writing and agriculture. Nature gave men styluses to use on (presumably female) writing tablets, hammers to use on anvils, as well as well-sharpened plowshares to till the soil, so why do men not use them and procreate? (ll. 19,513–30). As in the *De planctu Naturae*, homosexual love is condemned and homosexuals themselves (represented by Orpheus) threatened with emasculation. The story of Cadmus becomes the key myth here. He is the exemplar of the man who did the right thing: he knew how to "arer" (plow) (ll. 19,706–22). Cadmus thus becomes a pivotal figure, for his approved activity of "arer" comprises three important meanings: he literally plowed (in the legend he sowed dragon teeth that then became warriors); he procreated (plowing is thus a metaphor); and he wrote (he is credited with the invention of the alphabet). Thus plowing becomes a double metaphor here, denoting actual writing and sexual activity. The example of Cadmus thus highlights one of the problems inherent in the entire metaphorical discourse of figurative and literal language that equates writing and sexuality: the connection between words, acts, and objects.

The relationship between deeds and words is a recurrent theme in the *Rose*. Earlier in the text, in his so-called "excusacion," his apology to his readers, Jean's narrator insists that no one should be offended by his language because he, the narrator, must choose his words in accordance with his subject matter.[82] In support of this view, he quotes Sallust, who underlines the desirable concordance between words and deeds:

> li diz doit le fet resambler;
> car les voiz aus choses voisines
> doivent estre a leur fez cousines. (ll. 15,160–62)

The word must resemble the deed, for the words that are neighbors to things, must be cousins to their deeds.

Interestingly, it is precisely this concordance that will allow people to enter Genius's park:

> Et se vos ainsinc preeschiez,
> ja ne seroiz anpeeschiez,
> selonc mon dit et mon acort,
> mes que li fez au dit s'acort,
> d'antrer ou parc du champ joli. (ll. 19,901–5)

And if you preach like this you will never be prevented, according to my word and promise—and as long as deeds agree with words—from entering the park of the beautiful field.

Thus Genius translates Sallust's desirable congruence of words and deeds into a command for active procreation: only those who preach procreation and practice it, those who can deduce correct behavior from a string of metaphors, will be permitted into this new paradise. Of course, the concordance of words and deeds is problematized in allegory as a construct in which words "mean something else."[83] Genius himself highlights this problem when he calls Guillaume's garden a "fable" and his own park "voir" (true). Thus, underlying the comparison between the garden and the park is the opposition between the figurative and the literal, the false and the true, euphemistic and direct language.

Genius's deconstruction of the garden of Deduit focuses on its shape, its outside decoration, and in particular on the fountain—its surrounding landscape, its waters, its crystals, and its qualities. The focus on Narcissus's fountain reveals that Genius, as a reader of *Rose I*, sees this embodiment of myth as the central feature of the garden and the courtly ideology it stands for. In accordance with the terminology used for literal truth as opposed to figurative language, which can hide falsehoods, the term "apertement" appears at several crucial junctures.[84]

First, Genius compares the outsides of garden and park. On the garden wall there are ten ugly images of the vices excluded from it; but outside the park, as is fitting for "paradise," there is the entire universe, including the stars and hell. Genius ends his enumeration of the things found outside the park by saying:

> Qui la seroit, toutes ces choses
> verroit de ce biau parc forcloses
> ausint apertemant portretes
> con propremant aperent fetes. (ll. 20,301–4)

Whoever would be there would see all these things outside the beautiful park so openly portrayed that they appeared to actually be there.

Thus the flat wall paintings of the garden wall contrast with the lifelike depiction of the universe. "Apertement" denotes that Genius's universe is what it is: not painted allegorical figures—twice removed from their true meaning—but the true and literal.

As the true and false are opposed, so are the light and dark. Here again Genius's use of "apertement," this time in the context of the fountain and its crystals, is illuminating.[85] After describing Guillaume's garden as "corrumpable" (corruptible) and stressing that nothing "estable" (stable) exists in it (ll. 20,323–24), Genius turns to the good things to be found in his park. Its prize feature is the fountain, which is quite different from the "perilleus miraill" (perilous mirror; l. 20,386) of *Rose I* that made healthy people ill. Amant, Genius says, insisted repeatedly that the fountain is clearer than pure silver (ll. 20,401–2), but in reality it is dark and cloudy, and no one sees anything when he looks into it.

The reader may ask: So how could Narcissus see himself? How could the lover make out the rosebush? Genius does not answer these questions but instead introduces an allusion to Tiresias's warning concerning Narcissus's death in Ovid's *Metamorphoses*, "si se non noverit" (if he never knows himself; 3.348), which had not been part of the Narcissus story proper in *Rose I*: "Tuit s'i forsanent et s'angoissent / por ce que point ne s'i connoissent" (they all go crazy and experience anguish there because they don't manage to know themselves; ll. 20,407–8).[86] That is, try as they might, they cannot know or see themselves because the fountain does not reflect anything. As for the crystals, they afford some kind of vision, but only a partial one, precisely "la moitié des choses" (half of everything; l. 20,413). Perfect vision is precluded "par l'occurté qui les obnuble" (by the darkness that clouds them [the crystals]; l. 20,423). This charge becomes especially damning when we look at how glowingly the narrator of *Rose I* describes the fountain and the crystals. In order for us to understand how the crystals work, he offers us "un essample" (an example; l. 1552):

> ausi con li mireors montre
> les choses qui sont a l'encontre
> et i voit l'en sanz coverture
> et lor color et lor figure,
> tot autresi vos di por voir
> que li cristaus sanz decevoir
> tot l'estre dou vergier encuse
> a celui qui en l'eve muse;
> car torjors, quel que part qu'il soit,
> l'une moitié dou vergier voit;
> et c'il se torne, maintenant
> porra veoir le remenant. (ll. 1553–64)

just as the mirror shows the things that are in front of it, and one sees without a covering both their color and their shape, in the same way, I tell you truly, the crystal shows, without deception, the whole being of the garden to whoever gazes into the water; for always, no matter where he stands, he sees one half of the garden; and if he turns, then he will be able to see the rest.

Thus Genius negates the claims of a clear vision put forward by *Rose I* by insisting on the fact that only half of the garden is visible at any one time. At the same time, Genius shows that Amant as narrator of *Rose I* tried to trick his audience when he used the terms "voir" (true) and "sanz coverture."

A further important point is that, unlike the garden fountain, the park fountain has its origin in itself: it has three ducts that seem to be one, with no external source. This trinitarian imagery leads to the identification of the fountain (by a convenient label attached to it) as the "fonteine de vie" (fountain of life; l. 20,491). The olive tree replaces the pine tree of *Rose I*.[87] Most important is the carbuncle at the bottom of the fountain, round with three facets (some people might think this description is a fable, Genius adds [ll. 20,496–97]) of which each one is worth the other two; indeed, one cannot separate them. This carbuncle "siet an mi si hautement / que l'an le voit apertement / par tout le parc reflamboier" (sits in the middle so high that one sees it clearly glow throughout the park; ll. 20,501–3). Through the carbuncle, which is its own source of light, night is banished (and thus dreams?), and everything in the park can be seen by everyone wherever he may be. The people who can profit from the carbuncle will not only know all the things in the park but also themselves (ll. 20,539–44)—and they will be saved by this knowledge, thus reversing once and for all Tiresias's dire prediction that self-knowledge will lead to death. Finally, Genius closes his praise of the park by comparing it to the Garden of Eden: "onques en si biau paradis / ne fu fourmez Adan jadis" (Adam, in the olden days, was not formed in such a beautiful paradise; ll. 20,565–66). Thus, where Amant believes he is in an earthly paradise when he enters the garden, Genius promises those who follow Nature's commands a place that surpasses even Adam's paradise and thus God's perfect creation.

Is Genius a "lewd humorist" here; is "his blending of Golden Age and Elysium with the Christian paradise" merely "a medieval commonplace"; does he "play innocently into the bawdy hands of Venus and Amors"?[88] He certainly is something of a humorist and not altogether innocent, for when he throws the candle that "makes all women burn" right after his discourse Genius surely knows its effects (ll. 20,640–48). As for his lewdness, after the initial tour de force of metaphors pointing to sexuality, it recedes as his sermon progresses. The humor persists, however; for his paradise, with all its christological imagery of the Trinity, the good shepherd, and the countless sheep, remains a curious mixture of funny and serious ideas. But more than anything, he seems to be interested in demolishing the courtly myth underlying *Rose I* by replacing it with his own myth of the park, where language and light are *apert* (open), where sexuality is a means of salvation.

Can Genius, as a new mythmaker, do without classical myth? Is the language of the integument and of fable no longer valid or necessary? Despite his overt rejection of those whose words and deeds do not correspond to each other (ll. 19,901–5), Genius uses fables himself, notably that of the castration of Saturn, a veritable guiding thread in *Rose II.* When stressing that in his park eternal day reigns, he has recourse to that fable to explain the beginning of time. Before Saturn's castration there was no time. A digression on castration seems to represent a challenge to Amant's earlier misgivings about the use of the word "coillons" (l. 20,006).[89] But more important, in this digression Genius insists on the literal meaning of the myth. That is, before interpreting the myth in the traditional sense as the end of the Golden Age, Genius spends about 40 lines enumerating the horrible consequences of castration, which set the myth into a literal, historical framework.[90] Thus the literal precedes the figurative, and the insistence on the term "coilles" ties this passage to the long discussion on the relationship between words and things that Raison and Amant had involving exactly that term.

The one myth told and interpreted explicitly in Genius's sermon, that of Saturn and Jupiter, thus explores the crucial questions on language, sexuality, and interpretation that appear again and again throughout *Rose II.* Despite his insistence on the value of the nonfigurative—the "apert"—Genius relies on an integument in the shape of a myth from classical antiquity to illustrate his theses on the timelessness of his park. In one sense one can consider this the culmination of the temporal expansions effected by ancient myth in both parts of the *Rose.* In Genius's speech, as we saw, the old myths and their often critical interpretations generate the new myth of the park.

In his telling of the fable of Saturn and Jupiter Genius strives to highlight the literal, castration, but he ends up by expounding at length on the Golden Age, the truth hidden by the integument of the fable. Genius insists that the interpretation of the integument should be translated to the level of action in people's lives. That is, the right understanding of figurative language leads to real and true deeds. Genius offers a mythical discourse that initially pretends to be able to dispense with the covert language of fable, that valorizes "le voir" (the true) over the "fable" of *Rose I* (l. 20,258). Yet Genius demonstrates that a discourse entirely without integument is an impossibility.

The final episode of the *Rose* illustrates the intricacy of Genius's advice concerning literal meanings and real deeds. He highlights the necessity of correct interpretation before any metaphorical lessons can be translated into action. The excessive accumulation of metaphors in the final assault on the Rose illustrates the richness of figurative language and dramatizes the move from metaphor to action. Thus, Amant finally follows Nature's commands—for he does seem to procreate in the end—and he does so in a way that would, by Genius's own command on words and deeds, make him a model citizen of the paradoxical "parc du champ joli": he has sex *both* figuratively and literally.

In the end, the garden of Deduit in *Rose I* has been unveiled as the garden of death. Time, night, and dreams have been banned from the *parc*; thus Amant, as the hero of his own dream, can find no place there. He must stop dreaming and enter the world of experience. Genius condemns the type of figurative language that sustained the courtly discourse of *Rose I* as false and instead introduces another kind of metaphorics, derived from the *De planctu Naturae*, which equates the activities of sex and writing. In this context, Genius as a writer figure replaces the fruitless pining of the courtly Amant with pointed advice on the desirability of sex. This sexuality is couched in a language filled with Christian imagery; it is a construct that attempts to reconcile what, in medieval culture, is only reconcilable in marriage: religion and sexuality (as long as its goal is procreation). But Amant never overtly contemplates marriage. The final assault on the Rose, when Amant appears to be a pilgrim entering a shrine, makes us rethink Genius's utopian fantasy. The violence, callousness, and obscenity of this last passage seem to bear no resemblance to Genius's vision of a sexuality rewarded by a sojourn in a garden with gentle lambs. The taking of the Rose finally unveils all figurative language as hiding the same thing: sex.[91] Genius's recapitulation of existing myths as part of his new myth is thus a means to express the sexuality that appeared in such a sublimated form in *Rose I*.

Jean de Meun was an innovator who built on and transformed what Guillaume de Lorris had offered him in *Rose I*. *Rose II* became a summa, embracing many different types of discourse and many of the philosophical currents of Jean's time. He experimented with new forms and introduced new complexities of temporality, which largely resulted from his flexible use of ancient myths. Mythological figures now appeared on all the levels of the text: they acted on the diegetic level; they appeared in exempla; and their stories, like those of Adonis and Pygmalion, could appear in textual spaces that had a problematic relation to the rest of the text. Moreover, Jean had a variety of characters narrate myths and interpret them in surprising ways. One can speculate whether Guillaume's unexpected moral drawn from the Narcissus myth—which redirected the myth's meaning from a purely moral to a courtly milieu—did not authorize Jean's new approaches to a number of traditional myths; for the recontextualization of known mythological stories is one of the hallmarks of *Rose II*.

Jean exploited the polyphony of his own text for an exposition of how one type of discourse can condition another. This is particularly clear in the interpretations of mythological fables. Thus the triptych structure in Ami and La Vieille's speeches shows how the meaning of the myth of the Golden Age or the fable of Mars and Venus can be reoriented by other types of discourse, derived in part from vernacular literature. Through the allegorical characters turned interpreters and glossators of myths, the interpretation of myth is thematized and invites us to pose questions on interpretive traditions and their validity. In the end, Jean managed to recast the myths' meanings and substitute his own glosses, which emerge from both narrative and his characters' overt interpretations, for those dictated by tradition. In this manner he led the way to the *Ovide moralisé*, where interpretation and the interpreter in the shape of the medieval poet finally displace the ancient text.

Chapter 3

The Hermeneutics of the *Ovide moralisé*

Of all the medieval texts dealing with pagan mythology in general and with Ovid in particular the *Ovide moralisé* (= *OM*) is by far the most excessive. It is excessive in its length (close to 72,000 lines) and in its "interpretive delirium,"[1] vastly surpassing any previous attempts at allegorizing, moralizing, or christianizing Ovid's *Metamorphoses*. Written probably between 1316 and 1328 by a Franciscan friar,[2] this work has attracted critical attention most often not for itself but rather as an example of the continued influence of the mythographic tradition and, because it was the first complete French translation of the *Metamorphoses*, as an important source for subsequent texts, both poetic and nonpoetic.[3]

Neither of these two critical directions will preoccupy us in the present chapter (although a brief survey of the *OM*'s antecedents will follow). Rather, I will consider the text of the *OM* as a hermeneutic system. How does it work? This apparently simple question has received a partial answer in Paule Demats's *Fabula*, but no one has studied the text as a whole: its interpretive vocabulary, its structure, its interpretive choices and mechanisms.[4] In fact, the segmentation the text has undergone in critical discourse resembles nothing more than the segmentation Ovid's *Metamorphoses* itself was subjected to by the mythographers over centuries.[5] This chapter will attempt to bring a comprehensive view to the *OM* and show that the driving principle behind the text is "allegoresis in action,"[6] that a mode of reading in fact became a mode of composition.[7] Moreover, we will discover that issues of sexuality and transgression are often bound up with issues of interpretation in the text. Reflections on the problematic and sometimes bizarre nature of much of the *Metamorphoses*'s sexuality frequently leads the poet to what one could call a hermeneutic *prise de conscience*, a moment of reflection and self-awareness.

While Ovid's texts had been given Christian interpretations before, this was never done in such a systematic and consistent fashion as in the *OM*. Furthermore, because Ovid's *Metamorphoses* had been transmitted in manuscripts full of glosses, *accessus*, and other notations and explanations, we do not find in the *OM* simply a translation of the *Metamorphoses* with appended interpretations. The commentary tradition frequently insinuates itself into the base text, a phenomenon studied by Paule Demats. This base text—and this is quite stunning—is treated like the Scriptures as far as the exegetical methods are concerned. The "abyss" that Henri de Lubac sees between scriptural and profane allegory is bridged by the *OM*; through euhemerism the poet establishes a "true" basis for his allegorizations and, as we will see, treats Ovid's text like an Old Testament to which he adds "his" New Testament: the *OM*.[8] Concomitantly, we can observe a growing respect for Ovid's text. As the *OM* progresses, the patterns of the alternation between base text and interpretation change, and the poet exhibits a new concern with preserving the integrity of Ovidian speakers such as Orpheus or Pythagoras.

The allegoresis of the *OM* is thus constructive in different ways: it adds a vast system of Christian interpretations to Ovid, a sure means to preserve the text for many different purposes (such as preaching, a particularly Franciscan concern); it highlights the importance of the base text by a growing refusal to segment it further and further; and it accords a new dignity to the Ovidian text by treating it essentially like the Scriptures.

From Ovid to the *Ovide moralisé*

In the Introduction I traced some of the ways by which classical learning was transmitted to the middle ages. Ovid was, by the twelfth century, the most popular *auctor*. His tales found their way into many romances and lyric poems. But before the *OM* vernacular texts shunned the interpretive baggage that had accumulated around Ovid's works. The antecedents of the *OM* can thus be found not in the vernacular tradition but in such Latin works as Fulgentius's *Mythologies* (sixth century) and the compilations of the three Vatican Mythographers (seventh or eighth century to twelfth century). Of particular importance are Arnulf of Orléans, who wrote his allegory of the *Metamorphoses* in the second half of the twelfth century and was the first to attach a specifically Christian, rather than merely moral, meaning to the fables of the *Metamorphoses*, and John of Garland, author of the *Integumenta Ovidii* (ca. 1234).

In order to appreciate the innovative nature of the *OM* we will briefly look at one of Ovid's fables, the story of Myrrha, and see how it was treated by various authors.

In *Metamorphoses* 10 Orpheus sings of Pygmalion and his descendants, among them Cinyras, Pygmalion's grandson and the father of Myrrha. The tale is called "horrible" (10.301), for it deals with Myrrha's unquenchable incestuous desire for her own father. Ovid uses a powerful image to describe Myrrha's mad desire, which is as yet incapable of action:

> just as a great tree, smitten by the axe, when all but the last blow has been struck, wavers which way to fall and threatens every side, so her mind, weakened by many blows leans unsteadily now this way and now that, and falteringly turns in both directions; and no end nor rest for her passion can she find save death. (10.372–78)

Of course, death is deferred, for the nurse finds a way to smuggle Myrrha into her father's bed, where she promptly conceives a child. After many amorous meetings the father discovers the truth (he finally brings a light into the bedroom [10.473]), falls into a rage, draws his sword, and chases his daughter into the night. She escapes but in the despair of her advanced pregnancy prays to the gods to "change me and refuse me both life and death" (10.487). A beautiful description of her transformation into the myrrh tree follows (with an aside that the tree bears its name from her), which culminates in the dramatic sequence of her giving birth to Adonis when already half changed into a tree: "The tree cracked open, the bark was rent asunder, and it gave forth its burden, a wailing baby-boy" (10.512–13).

Ovid's beautifully wrought tale appears in a much abbreviated version in Hyginus's *Fabulae* (first or second century A.D.). In six lines (fable 164, 21–26) the author summarizes Myrrha's tragic story. He adds one interesting detail, which will reappear in later versions, although not in the *OM*: the father strikes the myrrh tree with his sword and Adonis is born. A naturalistic detail appears in the context of fable 58, another version of the story: myrrh flows from this tree.[9] Would it be giving too much credit to Hyginus to suggest that the detail of the father's cutting open the tree may have been suggested by the extended tree simile used by

Ovid to dramatize Myrrha's love pangs? Of course, Ovid's simile skillfully announced Myrrha's future transformation into a tree. But to have the father violently deliver his own incestuous offspring heightens the drama and gives some life to the otherwise colorless fable in Hyginus.

Fulgentius devotes three sentences to the story, picking up on Hyginus's detail concerning the father's sword, and then goes on to explain what it all means.[10] He first juxtaposes a naturalistic observation ("the myrrh is a kind of tree from which the sap oozes out") and an encapsulated version of the story ("she is said to have fallen in love with her father").[11] The father, in this context, is the sun who is loved by the tree. The sweet sap oozing out is "Adonis" because the Greek word for a "sweet savor" is *adon*. Venus's falling in love with him can be explained by the fiery nature of myrrh. Fulgentius then quotes various texts, including Petronius's *Satyricon*, in which myrrh is associated with sexual desire.[12]

Thus, in this particular instance, there is no trace of a moralizing or allegorizing interpretation. The interpretation is etymological (whence the name "myrrh") and physical. In the *Vatican Mythographers I and II* we find basically the same version as in Fulgentius, minus the citations.[13] *Mythographer III* reintroduces the reference to Petronius; otherwise the story remains the same.[14]

In Alan of Lille's *De planctu Naturae*, to cite just one example outside the strictly mythographic tradition, Myrrha forms part of a catalog of unworthy women blessed with beauty.[15] Nature regrets her decision to give beauty to Myrrha, who "goaded by the sting of the myrrh-scented Cyprian, in her love for her father corrupted a daughter's affection and played a mother's role with her father."[16] Here, no attempt at interpretation is made, although the connection between myrrh and Myrrha is present.

Arnulf of Orléans, unlike the authors cited so far, reflects extensively on Ovid's possible intentions in the *Metamorphoses*. Did the fables illustrate and analyze people's emotional life? Or guide us to divine truth? Or simply justify Caesar's apotheosis? Or did Ovid merely want to compile fables dispersed in other works?[17] Arnulf's conclusion contains a crucial innovation for the interpretation of Ovid. He states: "the study of the *Metamorphoses* has a two-fold usefulness, bringing us the knowledge of the ancient fables and that of divine things."[18] But while the story of Orpheus receives a Christian interpretation, that of Myrrha is based directly on Fulgentius and offers no Christian meanings.[19] In fact, the subheading *allegoria* is missing in the Myrrha story.

It was the allegorical interpretation that represented Arnulf's most important contribution to interpretive techniques used on the *Metamorphoses*.[20] Arnulf announces his three interpretive strategies at the beginning of his *Allegoriae*: "We will interpret in an allegorical, a moral and a historical manner."[21] He then lists the different "mutations" of each book, gives a brief summary, and appends his interpretations. (But not every fable receives all three types of interpretation, as we saw for the story of Myrrha.) The result is a text of 28 pages in Ghisalberti's quarto-sized edition.

The thirteenth century offers us one more interpretation of the *Metamorphoses* in John of Garland's *Integumenta Ovidii*. He promises his readers that "Ovid's *Metamorphoses* will be opened up with John's little key . . . , the secret knots will be undone, he will reveal what is hidden, clear up the fog: he will sing the 'integumenta.'"[22] His version of the Myrrha story is essentially a *jeu de mots* playing on the sweetness of the myrrh and the bitterness of love.[23] Other stories are interpreted much more dryly, as are the fables of Midas or Atalanta, for example. John simply tells us "the gold of Midas signifies avarice" or "the lion (in the Atalanta story) stands for luxuriousness."[24] These brief equations, encompassing all fifteen books of the *Metamorphoses*, add up to a total of 520 lines.

The biggest difference between the *OM* and its predecessors is the fact that the *OM* poet tells Ovid's fables at length. As I indicated earlier, he provides the first French translation of the entire *Metamorphoses*.[25] Thus, in the *OM*, Myrrha's story itself takes up almost 900 lines and its interpretations another 300. Let us first look at the structure of Book 10 to understand the interaction between the fable and its interpretations.[26]

Book 10 of the *OM* has 4141 lines (of which 1000 are devoted to the allegorization of Orpheus's "harp"), while Ovid's has 739. The poet begins by recalling that he just told the fable of Iphis.[27] He then tells of Eurydice's death (including the mourning of other inmates of the underworld). Orpheus then loses Eurydice through his own fault, and the story progresses to the point where Orpheus prefers young men to women. Here the first break occurs: the poet will now interpret the story in the "historial sens" (10.196). Eurydice was bitten by a snake during her wedding to Orpheus; he despaired and became a homosexual. Thus the "historical sense" represents a literal reading and not a euhemeristic one, as one might expect. The next interpretation is a mixture of moral and spiritual exposition. Orpheus is correct understanding; Eurydice represents the soul's sensuality; and the serpent stands for sin (10.220–46) and later for the devil (10.469). Citing Macrobius, the poet now offers a moral-spiritual interpretation of each of the five rivers in the underworld as well as of the underworld as a whole (a moral morass), from which Orpheus wanted to liberate the sinful soul, figured by Eurydice. One of the poet's more remarkable interpretations is that of Orpheus's homosexuality: it signifies that Orpheus, as "correct understanding," shuns female corrupted nature and turns toward the pure and virtuous masculine one (10.558–77).[28]

Now the poet returns to the story line (he reminds us that "above we heard the story of the one who dies from a snake bite" [10.578–79]), and we learn about Attis metamorphosed into a pine tree and Cyparissus into a cypress. Orpheus's song begins at line 724. Here the *OM* more or less follows Ovid until he gets to the story of Myrrha. Interestingly the child of Pygmalion and of his "statue" is a son here, although the name Paphos is retained (10.1076). Did the firstborn have to be a boy in the middle ages or was it just that the name Paphos sounded like a boy's name to the poet?

In the context of the Myrrha story we find one of the rare direct addresses to a female audience, rather faithfully translating Ovid, except that Ovid also addresses fathers:

> Ce samble cruel chose à dire
> Mes puis qu'il chiet en ma matire
> Dire en vueil. Ensus vous traiez,
> Filletes, que vous ne l'oiez,
> Mes s'il vous delite à savoir,
> ne crees pas cest conte à voir.
> Se le crees, si soies certes
> Qu'ele en reçut crueulz desertes. (10.1096–1103)

This seems a horrible thing to tell. But because it belongs to my subject matter, I will tell of it. Go away, young girls, that you do not hear it, but if it is your pleasure to hear it, don't think that this tale is true. If you believe it, you can be certain that she received a cruel reward for all this.

The one telling addition to Ovid is the reference to the "matire," which requires the poet to tell the story. Along with the word "fabula," "matire" frequently denotes Ovid's text.[29] The poet feels compelled by his source to tell of something that is morally repugnant to him. In Ovid, Orpheus makes no such excuses.

The story then progresses through Adonis's birth and Venus's falling in love with him to his death and metamorphosis into a flower. At line 2494 the poet breaks in by saying:

> Ces fables ordeneement
> Veuil espondre et premierement
> Dou poete, dou harpeour
> Orpheüs, le bon chanteour (10.2494–97)

I wish to interpret these fables in order, beginning with the poet, the harp player Orpheus, the good singer.

He then gives a brief résumé of the story.

The first interpretation is literal (Orpheus became a homosexual out of grief). The next is allegorical and requires "autre sentence" (another interpretation): Orpheus is Christ (10.2540–60). Approximately a thousand lines are devoted to the allegorization of the harp. The highlight of this passage is the identification of the "new song" sung by Orpheus with the New Testament. In Ovid, Orpheus proclaims: "But now I need the gentler touch, for I would sing of boys beloved by gods, and maidens inflamed by unnatural love and paying the penalty of their lust" (10.152–54). In a move that is typical for the medieval poet's approach to the many striking examples of "unnatural love" in the *Metamorphoses*, the *OM* only insists on the love that will fill the new song as opposed to the warfare of the old, which is, of course, the Old Testament. In this radical allegorization of Ovid—worthy of Saint Augustine—the *OM* poet defuses threatening sexuality or "cupidity" by subsuming it into Christian charity.

I will skip the interpretations of the Ganymede, Pygmalion, and other stories to return to the Myrrha story. The poet states: "Or vueil plus especialment / De la mirre espondre autrement" (now I want to interpret myrrh differently; 10.3678–79), although he had not interpreted Myrrha in any way at this point. Presumably, the poet follows here his own rhetoric of interpretation established for other stories without realizing that for Myrrha he now offers only the first interpretation. The series of interpretations that follows will allow us a first look at the poet's method and the justification of this method.

The series begins with the natural interpretation, which we already know from Fulgentius and others. The next one is moral: Adonis is Myrrha's son; he stands for sweetness and sexual appetite. Venus is luxuriousness enamored of the delights represented by Adonis (10.3712).

But there is also an "autre sentence . . . / Mieudre et plus digne de savoir" (another interpretation, better and more worthy of being known; 10.3748–49). Myrrha is the Virgin Mary, and Adonis is Christ. Note that here the poet establishes a definite hierarchy of interpretations: this one is *better* and *more* worthy. But that is not all: "Autre sentence i puet avoir, / Qui assez est semblable à voir" (there is another interpretation that has the appearance of truth; 10.3810–11). In this case, Myrrha stands for the sinful soul of any Christian, layman, or clerk (10.3812–14) who receives God wrongly. Such a Christian needs the savory fruit of repentance (Adonis), which will redeem the sinner's soul.

The last interpretation is introduced as follows:

De ceste fable or l'exposons
En autre sentence, et posons,
Ausi com li autours parole,
Que feme eüst esté si fole,
Plaine de tel forsenerie
Qu'el onc amast par puterie
Son pere et o lui se jeüst
Et de son pere conceüst,
Si com dist de Mirre la fable. (10.3878–86)

Of this fable we now offer another interpretation, and we propose, just as the author tells it, that a woman was so crazy, full of such madness, that she loved her father in a whorish way and lay with him and conceived from him, just as the fable tells of Myrrha.

The poet adds, however, that true confession and repentance can save even such a sinner and that good works (Adonis) will be born of her. This is a literal yet generalizing interpretation. It deals with real incest, certainly not an unknown phenomenon in the middle ages. The story thus has an exemplary and consoling function for women, a function that runs counter to the direct address to young girls adapted from Ovid. This last instance, then, is an example of the poet's inventiveness coupled with thoughtfulness. The positive view of Myrrha's giving birth as bringing forth good works is quite original. This juxtaposition of extremes, an incestuous woman and the Virgin Mary, also defuses the transgressive nature of Myrrha's sexual life. As for the case of Orpheus's new song, the poet seems to apply an Augustinian scheme of interpretation here. Augustine, of course, did not speak of Ovid but of the Scriptures when he said, "Those things which seem almost shameful to the inexperienced . . . are all figurative, and their secrets are to be removed as kernels from the husk as nourishment for charity."[30] The exhortation to read "shameful" things figuratively clearly inspired the *OM* poet. But, as we have just seen, he also preserves the literal level of shameful acts, such as incest, when he insists on the importance of repentance.

The poet goes on to offer multiple interpretations for the rest of the stories of Book 10. The structure of this book thus leaves most of the song of Orpheus uninterrupted and appends the interpretations in a series. In other books, as we will see, the poet shifts constantly back and forth between story line and interpretation.

Book 10 and in particular the Myrrha story serve as an example of the poet's methodology and preoccupations. The segmentation of the mythological story and the multiple interpretations rejoin the mythographic tradition, although they are more ample than previous attempts at interpretation and introduce new meanings. What is also new is the indication that the interpretations are ordered hierarchically. For example, the equation of Myrrha and the Virgin Mary, with the Virgin occupying the highest spiritual level, is accorded pride of place. Let us now see how the *OM* poet himself defines his project, both in the Prologue and in various direct interventions in the narrative.

The Prologue

The very first line of the Prologue evokes the Bible ("escripture"), which states that everything that is written in books is for our instruction (Rom. 15.4). It does not matter whether these books contain good or bad things, for the bad ones are there so that we can guard against them, and the good ones so that we can imitate them.[31] The next theme is that "he who has knowledge should not hide it away but rather share it so that it can fructify" (1.8–14). This was a rhetorical commonplace of Latin texts and even of vernacular texts as early as the *Roman de Thèbes* (ca. 1150).[32] The poet goes on to describe his project: "Pour ce me plaist que je commans / Traire de latin en romans / Les fables de l'ancien temps" (For this reason it pleases me to translate from Latin into French the fables from old times; 1.15–17).[33] He stresses that he will tell his readers how *he* understands the fables that Ovid offers him (1.18–19). What the *OM* poet's predecessors had done to a much smaller extent he will now do at great length—and better. Some have tried to explain Ovid's fables before him, but in vain; and although he might not have more sense than they, the poet trusts God in this matter, because while He may not reveal His secrets to the wise, He often reveals them to the "apprentis," as long as he eagerly searches for the hidden sense (1.20–30).[34]

Thus the *OM* poet hopes to compose a text ("un ditié"; 1.31) that can serve as a moral exemplar. His subject matter extends from the creation of the world to the coming of Christ, and, although these fables seem to be lies, they contain nothing but the truth: "La veritez seroit aperte / Qui souz les fables gist couverte" (the truth that lies hidden under the fables will become apparent; 1.45–46). However, the poet will not give us all possible interpretations because that would lengthen his text excessively. "Les mutacions des fables" (the transformations of the fables; 1.53) will be explained as briefly as possible.[35] Any reader should feel free to correct the poet as long as the suggestions conform to the teachings of the Church (1.47–70).

So ends the Prologue proper, although one could include the next 27 lines, which seem to target one of the poet's predecessors, Arnulf of Orléans, who said that Ovid should not have written "Mes cuers vieult dire / Les formes qui muees furent / En nouviaux cors" (My mind is bent to tell of forms changed into new bodies"; 1.72–73),[36] but rather "les cors qui en formes noveles / Furent muez" (bodies that were changed into new forms; 1.79–80).[37] The latter cannot be correct, so the *OM* poet says, because God made the bodies and hence they cannot be changed into new forms. What interests me here is not so much doctrinal questions as the fact that the very beginning of this text takes issue with one of the earlier commentators of the *Metamorphoses*. For despite the humble appearance of the Prologue (such as the poet asking his readers for criticisms), the *OM* contains an underlying polemic contrasting the *OM* poet with earlier unsuccessful attempts at interpreting Ovid.

The poet uses the traditional vocabulary of the explication of fable and allegory: what is hidden will become apparent.[38] But by tying this hermeneutic activity to biblical examples, the poet actually participates in a divine process. Just as God revealed the hidden truth of His secrets, so the poet will reveal the truth covered by the Ovidian fables. The big difference is, of course, that here the base text is the *Metamorphoses* and not the divine Word. The poet is careful to distance himself from the polytheism of the Ovidian world:

> Que que li paien creüssent
> Des dieus que pluisors en fussent,
> Nous devons croire fermement
> Qu'il n'est fors uns Dieus seulement. (1.107–10)

Although the pagans believed that there were several gods, we have to believe firmly that there is only one God.

The text is thus put immediately on a firm doctrinal footing.[39]

Another point worth noting in the Prologue is the reference to the "surplus" of interpretations in lines 47–51, a notion that we will encounter again below. Thus while the *OM* seems to offer an almost unbelievable plenitude of interpretations, it is still not complete. This admission certainly invites the enterprising reader to add yet more meanings to each fable. From a methodological perspective, these lines point to the inexhaustibility of interpretation, which in fact dramatically opens up the rigid fourfold scheme of traditional exegesis.

The last lines of the Prologue that I would like to highlight are the following:

> Si ne porroie tant escrire,
> Mes les mutacions des fables,
> Qui sont bones et profitables,
> Se Dieus le m'otroie, esclorrai. (1.52–55)

I can't really write that much, but, if God wants me to, I will explain [open up] the mutations of the fables that are good and profitable.

Thus a selection principle governs his choice of interpretations, again pointing to the possibility of any number of other interpretations that will not be included because they are not worthwhile. Nevertheless, they are "out there."

Line 53 is ambiguous: is the poet referring to the metamorphoses as they take place on the diegetic level or is he speaking of the metamorphosis of interpretation? Leonard Barkan shows that a much earlier reader of Ovid, the eighth-century bishop Theodulf of Orléans, "has adopted an Ovidian, and specifically metamorphic, scenario for the conversion of lies into truth." The metamorphosis of form thus equals the metamorphosis effected by interpretation, which turns lies into truth. What Barkan calls the "rhetorical permission given by metamorphosis" authorizes the extreme variety and multiplicity of interpretations found in the *OM*.[40] Just as the Ovidian beings are transmuted into forms and substances that have a sometimes tenuous and sometimes logical connection to their former selves, so the interpretations that follow each Ovidian fable in the *OM* are sometimes well motivated and sometimes completely disconnected from the preceding story. I believe that the ambiguity of the term "mutacion" is intended. The *OM* poet is another Ovid in that he metamorphoses meanings rather than creatures.

The Interpretive Vocabulary

In his *Mittelalterliche Hermeneutik* Hennig Brinkmann studies the principles of medieval interpretive and explanatory techniques through an analysis of the commentaries, glosses, and allegories in which medieval scholars reflect upon their hermeneutic enterprise.[41] In a similar approach this section will concentrate on words like "allegorie," "fable," "exposicion," and "estoire" in order to show how the *OM* poet defined his own interpretive task and which problems of interpretation he might have considered especially important.

The first crucial task for the *OM* poet (here in the context of the giants and their fall) is to demonstrate that the "estoire" and the fable are "acordable" (compatible; 1.1101–2); his second task is to prove that the "fable" and the "Divinité s'acordent" (the fable and the Holy Scripture are reconcilable; 1.1154–55). The poet thus posits three distinct realms—fable (poetry), "estoire" (true history), and Holy Scripture—that all have to agree with each other. The only way these disparate realms can be reconciled is through interpretation. Interpretation is a kind of bridge that ties apparently unreconcilable things together.[42]

The poet thus needs to establish equivalencies, and he does so through the use of words like "est," "veut dire," "signifie," and "note," indicating that one thing or figure stands for another. This is, of course, part of the rescue mission that the various interpretive traditions undertook for classical mythology as early as the sixth century B.C. and which Wilhelm Nestle aptly compared to the efforts of "physicians" attempting to save an ailing religion.[43] The Ovidian myths themselves had no religious connotation for the *OM* poet (as they most likely did not for Ovid), but he reintroduces religious elements in the form of Christian allegorizations, thus relinking the Ovidian fables to the origins of myth, which—though already remote even in Ovid's time—had been religious. If figures like Adonis or Orpheus can stand for Christ, there is at least an implicit acknowledgment of the religious potential (even in an orthodox sense) of these fabulous characters.

Although a number of these equivalencies had surfaced in preceding mythographic texts, the absolute insistence on the Christian connection and particularly on salvation history in the *OM* establishes extensive new parallels between the pagan and the Christian worlds and thus rebuilds the ties of myth to religion in quite a new way. For the *OM* poet the Incarnation of Christ may represent the ultimate metamorphosis. Through the vast Christian grid imposed on the *Metamorphoses* its meaning has come full circle, as it were; but while the origins were in pagan religion, the final destination of the text is Christian orthodoxy.

Despite this underlying Christian structure, the term *fable* dominates the interpretive vocabulary. The huge preponderance of its use (approximately 300 times; "exposicion" and "espondre" appear 71 times) dramatizes that the text of Ovid's *Metamorphoses* provides the base on which the interpretations are constructed. Demats has calculated that 36,092 verses (approximately half of the text) are taken up by the fables translated from Ovid, whereas about 8000 lines are additions from various glosses, signaling an invasion of the commentary tradition into the base text.[44] This leaves almost 28,000 lines of interpretations and explanations, which use the term "estoire" approximately 60 times and "allegorie" about 50 times, suggesting, at least superficially, an even distribution between historical and allegorical interpretations. Let us first look at the word "fable."

I will not rehearse here the origins and uses of the term "fable" or "fabula" prior to the *OM*,[45] but rather see in which contexts the word is used in the text. In the section on the Prologue we saw that the poet is aware of the accusations against fables, namely that they are lies (1.41) but that he himself considers some of them—or at least their "mutations"—good and profitable (1.53–54). The defense of fable runs like this:

Si com la fable nous enseigne,
Qui nous done example et enseigne
Et signe et vraie demonstrance
Dou baptesme et de la creance
Qui lors estoit à avenir. (1.2297–2301)

As the fable teaches us which gives us an example and a signpost and a sign and a true demonstration of baptism and the belief that then was still to come.

This is an extremely important passage because it accumulates terms like *sign*, *signpost*, and so forth, that designate the function of fable. It also highlights the temporal aspect: like the scriptural *figura*, in which events in the Old Testament announce events of the New, fables announce the Christian doctrine to come. In the context of late medieval allegoreses of Ovid, Friedrich Ohly rightly observes that "just like the Old Testament books, texts from antiquity—often belatedly—were sucked into the vortex of an irresistible desire to penetrate their 'surface' in order to find the meaning hidden in their depth."[46] It is the poet's task to reveal typological relationships predicated on the Old Testament–New Testament relationship in a figurative reading model based on the concept of *allegoria in verbis* (that is, an allegory of poets). The poet must ensure that the fable yields its meaning to a Christian audience.

Thus the fable of Jupiter, which is the text as Ovid wrote it, is worth little without the deeper meaning that can be supplied by the poet. The poet introduces this activity, "Or vous vueil espondre briement / De ces fables l'entendement" (now I will briefly explain to you the meaning of these fables; 1.719–20), and informs us that Jupiter is heaven and fire, he represents a planet, and Thursday ("juefdis"; 1.724) is named after him. This reading of the gods as planets is most traditional. Continuing along these lines, the poet explains why Saturn is said to have had several children and to have been mutilated:

Pour ce faint la fable, sans faille,
Que les genitaires li taille.
Il fait divers effez en terre,
Selonc ce qu'il s'appresse et serre
Des autres planetes errables:
Pour ce contreuverent les fables
Qu'à divers enfans qu'il avoit
Aprist divers ars qu'il savoit,
Si com la fable le raconte,
Et l'estoire de l'autre conte
Dont je vous ferai mencion
Emprez ceste exposicion. (1.789–800)

Undoubtedly it is for this reason that the fable pretends that his genitals were cut off. He has different effects on the earth, depending on whether he approaches and clings to other moving planets. For this reason they invented the fables that he taught the different arts he knew to the different children he had, as the fable tells it and as the story tells of the other one [Jupiter] whom I will mention after this explanation.

This passage features a variety of recurring interpretive terms: "fable," here the Ovidian *récit* of Saturn's teaching and of his emasculation; "estoire," used here not in the sense of history (in a euhemeristic interpretation) but rather in the sense of story; and finally "exposicion," denoting the poet's own contribution (which is still indebted to the mythographic tradition). In an earlier passage, however, "estoire" referred to a rationalizing explanation (Neptune was drowned by his father; 1.606–7) that explains the fable of Neptune's being the god of the sea. In 12.1205, in contrast, "estoire" refers to the base text (the story of Menelaus) and not to any of the interpretive levels. "Estoire" thus plays a somewhat ambiguous role in the interpretive vocabulary.

The terms "fable" and "exposicion" have a tendency to occur together, since "espondre la fable" (to explain or interpret the fable) is the poet's principal occupation in the *OM*. These terms are often paired with "signification" or "sentence" (interpretation). There is also an occasional blurring between fable and exposition. In Book 3, for example, we find:

> Double signification
> Puet avoir l'exposition
> de la fable c'avez oie. (3.571–73)

The explanation of this fable [of Actaeon] can have a double meaning.

Here, the poet insists on the multiple meanings not of the fable itself but of its explanation. Or, for the story of Bacchus, the line "Autre sentence i puis escrivre" (I can write here another meaning; 3.905) indicates that "sentence" is another term for exposition, one that has the added connotation of didacticism. Another typical formula is "Autre sens puet la fable avoir" (the fable can have another meaning; 4.1756).

Without listing any more of the hundreds of available examples, we can see that the fable has multiple meanings, which the poet has to uncover. He does this by *writing* interpretations of the fables his audience has *heard* (3.573). In a significant move, the poet undermines here the received status of the *Metamorphoses* as a written Latin text and assigns it to the popular realm. Another term for fable, "conte," also has oral and aural connotations: "Dessuz avez oï le conte" (above you have heard the story [of Hermaphroditus]; 4.1924). Thus the domain of fable can be seen as a popular one, that is, one accessible to an audience of listeners. The realm of interpretation, in contrast, is one of writing, of privileged learned activity reserved for the *OM* poet.

The realm of fable that the unlearned are privy to is also frequently equated with lies. We saw that the Prologue already tackled this problem in lines 41–42, where "fables" rhymes with "mencoignables" (lying). In Book 4 the word "faindre" (to pretend) characterizes the function of fable. In an allusion to several characters metamorphosed into flowers the poet says: "dont la fable / Faint qu'il fussent devenus flors" (of whom the fable pretends that they were changed into flowers; 4.1995–96). Fable can also be paired with "truffe," a colloquial Old French term for nonsense, as in Book 8:

Mes ne croit pas Pirithoüs
Que ce qu'il dist soit veritable,
Ains le tient à truffe et à fable (8.2892–94)

But Pirithous did not believe what he (the river god Achelous) said and considered it nonsense and lies.

It is interesting that this equation of lie and fable occurs in the context of Pirithous's disbelief in metamorphosis: he cannot believe that Perimele was transformed by Neptune into an island at the request of Achelous (who also tells the story). This passage is a rather faithful translation of Ovid,[47] but while Ovid uses the word "ficta" here (in the sense of fiction), the *OM* uses "fable," thus dramatizing in this scene of Pirithous's disbelief the problematic status of *Metamorphoses*/metamorphosis in the realm of Christian belief, which was first addressed in the Prologue.

Also in Book 8 we find in the allegorization of the Achelous story a lengthy reflection on truth and lies introduced by

Souvent est faulz et mecognable
Ce qui samble estre veritable,
Et tel chose i puet estre voir
Ou ne samble que fable avoir. (8.3655–58)
. . .
Ainsi li faulz pour decevoir
Se coile et tapist sous le voir
Et le voir sous le faulz se cueuvre. (8.3663–65)

Often that which seems to be true is false and lying. And such a thing can be true that seems to be nothing but fable. . . . Thus the false, in order to deceive, conceals and hides itself under the truth, and the true hides away under the false.

This passage is followed by remarks on the duties of the wise man, who should be indefatigable in looking for the truth. But the use of the word "fable" leads us as well into another—more globally interpretive—direction.[48] Clearly, these reflections on truth and fable rejoin the Prologue and other places where the poet muses on the nature of fable. What is interesting here is the image of both truth and lies as both cover and the covered, suggesting that all surface meanings are deceptive. For while the traditional notion of integument claims that the fable is the veil under which the truth is covered, here the poet states—in an innovative move—that the truth can also be the cover or veil. What does this mean for the *OM*? I suggested earlier that the *OM* poet could be seen as another Ovid, who metamorphoses meanings rather than creatures. The seemingly convoluted statement illustrates the complicated nature of the *OM* poet's interpretive techniques. As we will see, for him, not only the fables can be interpreted, but the interpretations themselves can become base texts for further interpretation or allegorization. An examination of this technique will appear in the section "The Mechanics of Interpretation." For now, I would like to pursue the analysis of the interpretive vocabulary by turning to the term *allegory*.

There is hardly a term in critical vocabulary that has caused as much confusion and debate as the term *allegory*.[49] In a sense, all interpretation is allegory, or rather allegoresis. What Harald Steinhagen says about Walter Benjamin also holds true for the *OM*: "For Benjamin all interpretation, criticism, or exegesis is allegoresis that pushes or projects its own interpretation on texts."[50] Steinhagen's term *unterschieben* (literally "to push or slip under") is eloquent here because it picks up on the cover or veil image of the notion of integument. Allegoresis, according to Benjamin, slips its own interpretation under the text. Thus the truth that is uncovered in the interpretive process is in fact the truth the interpreter slipped there in the first place. This is, of course, exactly what happens in the *OM*, for Ovid would not in his wildest dreams have imagined some of the interpretations the *OM* attributes to the *Metamorphoses*: the *Metamorphoses* was not an "intended allegory." I will discuss the mechanics of allegoresis in the next section, but first I will examine how the terms "allegorie" and "estoire" are used throughout the *OM*.

In the traditional fourfold scheme of scriptural interpretation the level of allegory is that of belief, "quid credas" (that which you should believe).[51] But is that the sense of "allegorie" in the *OM*? If we look at the 50 or so occurrences of the term it becomes apparent very quickly that allegory is something much broader here; in fact, it seems to designate all types of interpretation except the historical and the physical. The latter two have their own special terminology and are usually announced as "historial" and "phisique." In this context, the term "estoire" (or "istoire") is problematic because it sometimes stands for the historical sense (as in 1.1101, for example) and sometimes for the Ovidian story. Thus for the figures Phrixus and Helle (mentioned in *Heroides* 18 in the letter from Leander to Hero but not explicitly mentioned in the *Metamorphoses*), the poet lines up his interpretations by announcing: "Ore est drois que nous vous conton / L'istoire et puis l'allegorie / Que ceste fable signifie" (Now it is in order that we tell you the history [or story] and then the allegory that this fable signifies; 4.2929–31), which makes us expect first a historical and then an allegorical interpretation. Yet there follow a moral and a spiritual interpretation, and no historical explanation. But for the interpretations of the story of Pomona and Vertumnus in 14.5289–644 we do indeed have a sequence of a historical explanation ("historial sens"; 14.5289), then a naturalistic or physical explanation ("naturelment selonc phisique"; 14.5312–13), and finally an "allegorie" (14.5377), which is by far the longest interpretation.

For the story of Phaeton we find a further interesting use of "estoire": "Or vous espondrai par estoire / Coment la fable sera voire" (Now I will explain through history how the fable will be true; 2.631–32). Note the use of the future tense here: history will enable the fable to be understandable as true. This temporal image will be supplemented, as we will see below, by a spatial image for the allegorical interpretation. But sometimes fable and history agree, as for the story of Phrixus and Helle, where the poet states at the end, with reference to the sacrifice of the ram that had transported Phrixus to the island of Colchis: "La fu . . . / Sacrifiez, selonc l'estoire, / Et selonc la fable ensement" (There it was sacrificed, according to history and fable together; 4.2924–26). It is possible that because this story came from the *Heroides* and not from the *Metamorphoses* it was considered more "historical." Or else, the poet uses "estoire" here simply in the sense of story. A final example, from the Medusa story, underlines this ambiguity: "Or vous vueil la fable exposer / Par istoire, et le sens gloser" (Now I want to explain to you the fable through history and gloss its meaning; 4.5714–15). The one eye of the gorgons, we learn, stands for their kingdom. Fable and history are curiously intermingled in the subsequent explanations.[52]

To conclude: throughout the text "estoire" has the double meaning of story (fable) and of euhemeristic interpretations (which are also designated "historial sens"). Now let us return to "allegorie."

The most common formulas involving the term "allegorie" are of this sort: "Or espondrai l'alegorie / Que ceste fable signifie" (Now I will explain the allegory that this fable signifies; 11.2401–2) or "Tel allegorie y puis metre" (I can add here such an allegory; 1.1185).[53] The most important property of this allegory is that it is reconcilable with the truth ("acordable à voir"; 1.3905). In this particular instance this truth lies in the equivalence between Io and any virgin who stops doing good deeds. This is a moral meaning, then, with a spiritual touch, for virginity generally stands for spiritual purity. A further, predominantly moral, meaning is the one for the Judgment of Paris story, where the choice between the three goddesses has the Fulgentian sense of a choice between three types of life (11.2421–531). The poet manages, however, to infuse each of the three lives (the active, the contemplative, and the voluptuous) with an added Christian meaning. This combination of the moral and spiritual occurs in many of the allegorical interpretations.

Another formula involving the term *allegory* expresses the extremely interesting idea of interpretive movement: "Allegorie i puet avoir / Pour la fable amener à voir" (We can put an allegory here in order to move the fable toward the truth; 5.3844–45). Interpreting spiritually in this case, the poet wants to show that Ceres's grain equals Jesus's grace. The word "amener" recalls our image of the different realms of fable, belief, and so on, that are connected by the bridge of interpretation. On one side of the bridge is truth, on the other, falsehood. Interpretation allows the poet to lead ("amener") the meaning from one domain to the other.

Biblical allegory often reveals a mysterious sense, and in the *OM* allegory and "mistere" are often equivalent, as in this example from Book 14: "Or est drois que je vous espoigne / L'alegorie et le mistere / De la dame orgueilleuse et fiere" (Now it is in order that I explain to you the allegory and the mysterious sense of the proud and forbidding lady; 14.5590–92).[54] This is the last in a series of interpretations that involve both the story of Pomona and Vertumnus and the story within this story, that of Iphis and Anaxarete, told by Vertumnus (disguised as an old woman) in order to persuade Pomona not to reject his love. A historical, a naturalistic, and also an allegorical interpretation (Pomona as the "plant" of the Holy Church) have already appeared. The sense designated as "allegorie et mistere" derives from a mixture of the Pomona and Vertumnus fable and the story of Iphis and Anaxarete, which tells how Iphis hanged himself out of grief over his unrequited love and how Anaxarete was metamorphosed into marble. The elements chosen for the allegory come from both stories and lead to rather convoluted reflections on the time it took the deity to decide to become incarnated (Pomona hesitated for a long time before giving in to Vertumnus) and on the "hanging" of Jesus (prefigured, as it were, by Iphis). The conclusion states that God disdains the proud and favors those that love him dearly. Thus, the allegory clearly exposes the spiritual meaning of these stories, the "mistere."

The same holds true for the story of Iphis in Book 9, to give just one more example.[55] Here Iphis (the name is androgynous) is a girl who was disguised as a boy to escape her father's wrath at her being born female. Finally, at her mother's prayer, she is transformed into a young man just before her wedding. Here the *OM* poet offers an allegory, which is introduced as follows:

> Meillour sentence, ce m'est vis,
> Par allegorie y puis metre
> Et gloser autrement la letre,
> Si doit ceste estre miex amee (9.3158–61)

It seems to me that I can put a better meaning there by allegory and gloss the text differently; this (meaning) should be preferred.

Because the previous interpretation had claimed that Iphis was a woman who disguised herself as a man (with an "attached member") in order to seduce young girls, we can easily see that the new interpretation—in which the gender metamorphosis is equated with the Incarnation—is preferable. But this is not all; there is yet another allegory, which this time is equated with the "verité" (truth; 9.3190) of the fable. Now, Iphis's father, Ligdus, is God, her mother, Theletusa, is the Holy Church, and Iphis, the sinful soul. Out of this equation the poet spins an allegory of several hundred lines.

The term *allegory*, then, does not designate *the* spiritual meaning of a fable but one of many (mostly spiritual) meanings, which are sometimes designated as being "more worthy" than the other meanings. And even within the allegories we sometimes find a hierarchy of meanings. Neither Fulgentius, nor John of Garland, nor Arnulf of Orléans—the *OM* poet's methodological forebears—used this type of hierarchization.[56] The *OM* poet thus explodes traditional schemes of interpretation (in particular the fourfold scriptural exegesis) and introduces instead a web of overlapping and often interlocking interpretations.

The Mechanics of Interpretation

The principal topics that will occupy us in this section are the structure of the *OM* in terms of the balance between base text and interpretation in selected books; the notion of hierarchy; the complicated technique of what I call "interpretation to the second degree," in which the poet interprets not the Ovidian text itself but rather his own (or inherited) interpretations of Ovid; and finally the use of intertexts as an aid to interpretation.

Interpretive Structures

My remarks on the interpretive structure of the *OM* will concentrate on Books 3, 7, 10, and 15, which feature the principal patterns of the interplay between text and interpretation. We will observe a significant change in the rhythm between text and interpretation from the first half to the second half of the *OM* as well as a growing awareness of the poetic coherence of stories told by important Ovidian narrators.

Book 3 is Ovid's Theban book. The stories are tied together by the theme of the forbidden glance. In the *OM* it is, with 2914 lines, one of the shortest. Narration predominates, at least in terms of lines, but interpretation is nevertheless important. The basic pattern is alternation between portions of the stories proper and various interpretations. Unlike some of the other books, Book 3 does not include explicit transitions between text and interpretation. Thus the poet tells the story of Cadmus and then explains that Cadmus stands for "clergie" (learning), that his companions are those who try to tame the "serpent of philosophy," and the city of Thebes is "divine culture" (3.266).[57] Actaeon's story is directly followed by multiple interpretations: a moral against hunting and an ingenious spiritual word play on "cerf" (stag) and "serf" (servant [= Jesus]) (3.593–670). After this passage the poet reminds his audience that earlier they had heard the story of Actaeon (which he summarizes together with Cadmus's) and then goes on to tell of Semele.

The multiple interpretations of that story are followed by the fable of Tiresias, whose interpretation begins with a tirade against powerful women (3.1060–83). Here the poet seems to adopt Tiresias's function in the dispute on sex between Jupiter and Juno. For in the allegory, the *OM* poet, and not Tiresias, resolves the fight: women love God more ardently than men, he concludes (3.1274–75). This substitution of the poet for Tiresias makes sense, for at the end of Book 3 Tiresias stands for the prophets. The poet thus skillfully buttresses his own authority.

The story of Echo and Narcissus follows.[58] Echo is good reputation, we learn, and Narcissus pride (both traditional interpretations). Then come Bacchus and Pentheus, where Bacchus stands for the gluttons and Pentheus for Jesus, torn to pieces by the Jews (3.2528–649). In an interesting move, the poet also historically interprets a minor element of the story, the fate of the sailors who transported Bacchus: they were not really changed into fish but rather their carcasses were eaten by fish (3.2688–714).

Finally, at the end of Book 3 the poet wants to explain "toutes ces fables ensamble" (all these fables together; 3.2743). Tiresias stands for the prophets, and Bacchus, who earlier stood for the gluttons, now signifies Christ, while Pentheus, who earlier had been Christ, now stands for the Jews who want to kill Christ (as Bacchus stands for Christ).[59] The interpretive rhythm of this book is thus alternating, with a reprise of some of the fables at the end.

Book 7 deals mostly with the stories of the Argonauts, in particular the stories of Jason and Medea, Theseus and Pirithous, and finally Cephalus and Procris.[60] Here we have an interpretive rhythm that has even more of a staccato character than Book 3. Altogether, narration dominates. Thus, while the story of Jason runs from line 8 to line 682, the allegories occupy only 130 lines, and the equation between Theseus and Jesus occupies only 52 lines. After Jason's story the narrative elements shrink until we get to the story of Cephalus and Procris, told by the unlucky husband himself, who by mistake killed his wife with a javelin. He is allowed about 500 lines to tell his story uninterrupted (7.2782–3281). The interpretations begin only after the story's conclusion. Book 7 allows us two preliminary conclusions: that in the first half of the *OM* the poet has tended to alternate shorter portions of text and interpretation and that he seems reluctant to interrupt a story if it is told by one of the protagonists.

The interpretive rhythm changes dramatically by Book 10, where our second observation seems to be confirmed: Book 10 contains the song of Orpheus, which begins at line 724 and continues uninterrupted until line 2492. As in Ovid, Orpheus announces a "new song," which will focus on love instead of on war.[61] This subject matter will be "lighter" and "more amiable" (10.737). Orpheus then sings of Ganymede, Hyacinthus, the Cerastes, the Propoetides, Pygmalion, Myrrha (analyzed above), and Adonis; and Venus tells the story of Atalanta. All this takes us to line 2493, when the *OM* poet announces: "Ces fables ordeneement / Vueil espondre et premierement / dou poete, dou harpeour" (These fables I want to explain in order, and first of the poet, the harp player; 10.2494–95). This "explanation" then goes on until line 3361, where the poet turns his interpretive attention to Ganymede.

The interpretation of Orpheus is probably the most excessive in the entire *OM*; it not only repeats the traditional equation between Orpheus and Christ but explains Orpheus's "harp" detail by detail. Thus the different tuning pegs where the strings are attached all stand for concepts such as the Virgin Birth, marriage, baptism, and the Passion, while the strings themselves are the cardinal virtues. This detailed list suggests a model for meditation, such as Philippe de Mézières's *Livre de la vertu du sacrement de mariage*, which came later in the century, and may offer us a clue to one of the *OM*'s purposes: to serve as a storehouse for meditation that would link the world of classical learning with a Christian piety of an intellectual nature.[62]

Orpheus's "new song" turning toward "unnatural love" is, as we saw earlier, the New Testament (10.3323–29). Thus it makes sense that the *OM* poet after this tour de force on the harp goes on to Ganymede who, so goes the historical interpretation (here called the "paiene geste" [pagan tales]; 10.3369), was a homosexual who had a love relationship with a king named Jupiter. The allegory posits, by contrast, that the pair Jupiter and Ganymede represent Jesus, that is, divinity and flesh together (10.3406–42). For the *OM* both the homosexual act and the Incarnation are "contre nature" (10.3385), in a negative and in a positive sense, and this notion allows him to equate the two, a rather startling equation (given the condemnations of homosexuality in the later middle ages) and one that deepens the mystery surrounding the *OM* poet.[63] To return to the interpretive rhythm: after the interpretation of the Ganymede story follow multiple interpretations of all the other fables.

Book 10, then, has a structure completely different from that of Book 3 or 7: all the fables come first followed by all the interpretations. While this does not become a completely consistent pattern in the subsequent books, we do see a growing reluctance to interrupt stories that are seen as coherent entities and that feature strong internal narrator figures, such as the "Song of Orpheus" in Book 10 and the Judgment of Paris in Book 11. By the time we get to the huge Book 15 (7548 lines), fables (the first 2300 lines or so), interpretations (about 5000 lines), and "literary criticism" (which will occupy us later) are strictly divided.

In its outline, Book 15 follows, like most of the books of the *OM*, the *Metamorphoses*. Thus we find the story of Numa and an exposition of the Pythagorean doctrine on metempsychosis and the passing and changing of all things. This is followed by the death of Numa, his wife's transformation into a fountain, various other metamorphoses, the story of Aesculapius, and finally the apotheosis of Caesar. Thus up to line 2308, Book 15 is a straight translation of Ovid without any interruptions, except references to the *auctor*. Any real additions, such as the story of Veronica's veil, triggered by remarks in the allegorizations of Aesculapius's story, appear in the allegories.

Yet the poet continues to use the rhetorical devices he had used in the other books in order to structure his narrative. For example, the poet tells how Numa's widow, Egeria, is transformed into a fountain. Only one line later, he says: "Dessuz avez la fable oïe / Coment fu muee Egerie / En fontaine" (Above you have heard how Egeria was changed into a fountain; 15.1453–55). The poet uses this formula throughout the *OM*, but generally many allegorizations divide the end of the fable proper from this kind of reprise, which normally introduces the next portion of the narrative proper. The same holds true for the end of the story of Aesculapius, which is immediately referred to as "Dessus vous ai conté le conte / Si com li auctors le raconte / Dou dieu qui d'Epidaure vint" (Above I told you the story, just as the author tells it, of the god who came from Epidaurus; 15.1899–901). These apparently minute changes do show, though, that this last book is caught between the structural traditions the poet had established for himself in Books 1–14 and a move away from the segmentation and fragmentation that had been the hallmark of all previous commentaries on classical texts. Book 15 thus proposes a new method of reading the Ovidian text, a method that shows greater respect for the integrity of the base text.

Interpretive Logic and Principles of Selection

Some years ago Judson B. Allen raised some critical issues concerning the *Fulgentius metaforalis* of John Ridewall that are also pertinent to our text. When speaking of the signification attached to each pagan god or goddess, Allen states: "Either these meanings are entirely arbitrary, or meaning did not mean in the Middle Ages what it does now." He also detected a new kind of allegory, which has certain parallels with what we find in the *OM*, which predates Ridewall by only a few years: "It is the kind of allegory that creates structures rather than references, by which all things and systems that are true are necessarily therefore equivalent—equivalent, that is, in that they become mutually illuminating when placed in ordered parallel."[64]

If meaning in the "modern" sense may emerge through logical—or even intuitive—connections that are made between certain properties or qualities of a person, an object, or a story and a set of philosophical, psychological, or other significations, we have to ask ourselves how meanings might emerge in a text like the *OM*, which is saturated with interpretations arranged in various series, characterized by constant contradictions. If Myrrha stands for the Virgin one moment, she stands for the sinful soul or an incestuous sinner the next. What kinds of parallels, in the sense that Allen uses the term, do we find in such stories and their interpretations?

Of course, apparent contradiction in interpretation or allegoresis is not a privilege of medieval times. The lack of what we would call logic in these contradictory interpretations, can be likened to Walter Benjamin's judgment on Baudelaire in the *Passagenwerk*, a judgment that at first sight seems to apply to the entire corpus of interpretations in the *OM*: "The allegorist chooses—sometimes here, sometimes there—a piece from the disordered storehouse made available to him by his learning; he then places it next to another [piece] and tries to see if they fit together: that meaning to this image, or this image to that meaning. One can never foresee the result."[65] It seems, then, that the parallel systems juxtaposing text and allegoresis can rest on a completely arbitrary basis. Yet we have already seen that the poet frequently unites extremes: sinful figures can stand for holy ones; the concept "contre nature" can equate homosexual union with the Incarnation. To get a more detailed view we will select a few examples from the many thousands of lines of interpretation and see which elements of each myth the poet chooses to interpret and what might be the links connecting these textual elements and their interpretation.

Our first example is the story of Deucalion and Pyrrha, who, in Book 1 of the *Metamorphoses*, repopulated the earth after the great flood by following Themis's command to throw "the bones of your great mother" (which Deucalion realizes means stones) behind them.[66] The first meaning the poet extracts from this fable is rather obvious: human generation, where the stones represent the male semen received by the mother (earth). The interpretation of the stones as "gent dure et male" (hard and bad people; 1.2181) also emerges logically from Ovid's "inde genus durum sumus" (hence come[s] the hardness of our race; 1.414). But then the poet launches into a long discussion of sin and its effects in which the connection between text and interpretation centers on the semantic field "water." There is no one-to-one equivalence between elements of the story and the interpretation.

The key words of this passage are "affondrer" (to swallow up, in reference to water), "floter" (to float), "noier" (to drown), "nagier" (to swim), and "plonger" (to dive, to plunge). With these terms the poet builds a frightening vision of the power of sin, which submerges humans. Only the Ship of the Church ("la nef sainte yglise"; 1.2255) can save humans from this deluge of or submersion ("sumercion"; 1.2249) into sin. The poet makes the obvious connection between this story and the Deluge in the Old Testament, but the interpretation here is mostly semantically motivated. So is the equation between "semence" (seed; 1.2239) and holy doctrine. Since "to sow holy doctrine" is a common expression, the word "semer" naturally brings the word *doctrine* with it.

The poet then presents interpretations of the other elements in the story. The mountain on which Deucalion and Pyrrha survive the flood is "perfect charity" (1.2264) because it touches the sky (so does charity, presumably). Next, Deucalion is interpreted as "gent de droite entencion" (right-thinking people; 1.2270). The poet does not explicitly motivate this interpretation, although he could have done so, since Deucalion is the one who interprets Themis's command correctly. But the poet does not lose sight of the theme of water, for he returns to it by speaking of baptism (1.2296), this time referring to the water of Cephisus's stream, and continues with another tirade on sin, which drowns and swallows up humans.

The poet finally emerges from all this water imagery by speaking of the goddess Themis who, of course, stands for "devine parole" (the divine Word; 1.2326). After this rather logical equation we turn to the notion of "vesteüre" (clothes), which stands for our mores and virtues (1.2339). The only reference to "vesteüre" in the story proper had been line 2031, which stated that—as in Ovid—Deucalion and Pyrrha ritually sprinkled some water on their clothes. The interpretation of these clothes as the virtues that we should clothe ourselves in (the poet even speaks of the headscarf of salvation) have no particular connection to the base text.

The last element to appear in the interpretation are the stones that stand for "malices" (maliciousness; 1.2351) that we should throw far from us. The connection between stones and moral hardness is a traditional one.[67] The same stones had earlier represented human semen, a change that is an example of the poet's technique of assigning multiple meanings to one and the same story element. In an injunction that combines allusions to both the story of Lot's wife and that of Orpheus and Eurydice, the *OM* poet insists that people should not turn around so that "Les malices et les pechiez / De quoi nous sommes entechiez, / Si lessons tries nostre derriere" (we shall leave behind us all malice and sin with which we are stained; 1.2357–59), for only in this way can we become all new, clean, saintly, and acceptable to God (1.2360–64).

We can see that most of the interpretations seem not very clearly motivated. Certainly the interpretation is not a running commentary on the fable as earlier commentaries on classical texts, such as Servius's notes on the *Aeneid*, had been. Rather, the poet constructs a second text that follows its own logic. The interpretive elements are not in the same order as the narrative ones; for example, the clothes are mentioned before Themis in the fable but are interpreted after the goddess. The dominant image is that of water, and it is the semantic field of that element that connects most of the allegorizations to the fable. The other details selected for interpretation were the "sowing" of the stones, the stones themselves, Deucalion (but not Pyrrha), the stream, Themis, the clothes, and once more, the stones. The one incident that we find most interesting from a modern perspective, Pyrrha's and Deucalion's differing interpretation of the goddess's command,[68] finds no place in the poet's interpretive scheme.

The story of Pasiphae and its interpretation in Book 8 provide examples of a different interpretive approach: not only is the story vastly amplified by comparison with the few allusions in the *Metamorphoses* (while the Deucalion and Pyrrha story was faithful to Ovid's version), the interpretation has not much to do with the story.[69] The mythographic tradition offered a number of possible interpretations. Fulgentius, for example, speaks of the five daughters of the sun in *Mythologies* 2.7, where he equates Pasiphae with sight, Medea with hearing, Circe with touch, Phaedra with smell, and Dirce with taste. The second Vatican mythographer follows the ancient Greek rationalization of seeing in the Minotaur Minos's secretary, who was one of the fathers (the other one was Minos) of Pasiphae's twin children.[70] Interestingly, the *OM* poet does not use any of these interpretations but rather offers only the most general musings on the sins of the flesh. But let us first see what he does with the story.

Pasiphae's story in the *OM* is a drama of a woman's (at first) unrequited love for a bull. The way the poet describes her falling in love with the bull, her jealousy of the cows he prefers, her ingenious idea of inserting herself into a wooden heifer in order to deceive the bull into loving her—all this is told in romance style reminiscent of courtly scenes, like Lavine's falling in love with Enéas in the *Roman d'Enéas*. Were it not for the perverse participants this would be a perfect little courtly romance. Indeed, Ovid's brief remarks have been expanded to 369 lines of narrative, including love monologues and commentaries of the poet, such as "Le buef contre nature ama / Ama? Non fist! Ce ne fu mie / Amours! Quoi donc? Forsenerie" (She loved the bull against nature. Loved? No!

This was not love! What then? Madness; 8.718–20). Of course, Pasiphae finally succeeds and, as a consequence of her "madness," gives birth to the Minotaur. The poet continues the story up to the point where Minos imprisons the monster in Daedalus's maze.

We saw that for the Deucalion and Pyrrha story the poet selected various narrative elements for interpretation. The balance between story and interpretation was almost one to one (173/200 lines). Here, although the story proper is longer than many others in the *OM*, the allegory occupies only 95 lines. Furthermore, there is only one level of interpretation: the spiritual one. None of the traditional interpretations I mentioned above makes an appearance. The poet chooses no particular details of Pasiphae's story for his interpretation. He starts with the usual interpretive formula, "Or vous vueil ceste fable espondre" (Now I wish to explain this fable to you; 8.986), which leads to "A sa forme et à sa figure / Crea Diex humaine nature" (God created human nature in His form and image; 8.987–88).

The first negative note is sounded when the poet says "Mes ore est humaine nature / Si vil et si se desnature" (But now human nature is so vile and so unnatural; 8.999–1000) that it has forgotten all honor and God's love. The passage continues in this vein, speaking of Israel and Judaea, who should ask for forgiveness; of the spread of the true religion; and of the evil nature of most humans, who love nothing but their flesh. The only clear link to the story is line 1055, which states that humans submit to their fleshly desires "contre nature" (against nature), recalling line 718, where Pasiphae's behavior had been described in those terms. The poet also mentions "la beste gloute" (the gluttonous beast; 8.1079) who is the devil, without, however, making the explicit connection to that other beast, the bull.[71]

The interpretive logic thus hinges on the term "contre nature," which leads to the idea that human nature is perverted in its lack of love for God. None of the other spiritual meanings (the references to Israel, and so forth) have any basis in the fable. No person, object, or event is directly interpreted. Pasiphae's story thus shows us a completely different approach to interpretation, one that has separated itself from the base text, offers only one level of interpretation, and relies on remote verbal echo for its allegorical themes. The extreme sexual transgression represented by Pasiphae's bestiality may have determined this reluctance to establish precise links between the narrative and its allegorization.[72]

Our last example is the story of Dido, well known in the middle ages through the *Roman d'Enéas*, Ovid's *Heroides*, and other texts. In the *Metamorphoses* Dido is not named, but referred to as "the Sidonian queen" (14.79–80). The narrative part in the *OM* begins with the storm that throws Aeneas's ship off course and brings it to Carthage, where Dido reigns. The love story develops quickly, and soon Aeneas leaves Dido, who embarks on a long complaint, derived in part from *Heroides* 7 (the speech includes the detail that Dido is pregnant [*Her* 7.133]). Her sister, Anna, makes an appearance in the scene of Dido's suicide. The inhabitants of Carthage mourn their queen who died through "fole amor" (mad love; 14.525). Only then does the poet tell the story of the founding of Carthage, of Dido's brother, and of her husband.

Traditionally Dido was interpreted as a figure of passion or libido. In Fulgentius's *Content of Virgil* she stands for adultery in Book 4 (although her name is not mentioned), and in Book 6 she is a shade "now devoid of lust," a lust that is tearfully recalled by the repentant man.[73] In the commentary on the *Aeneid* attributed to Bernardus Silvestris Dido stands for a passion that will soon be burnt out or exhausted.[74]

In a very original move, the *OM* poet does not explicitly use any of these interpretive possibilities. Rather, he centers his interpretation around the image of Aeneas's ship as the Holy Church ("Saint Yglise"). This ship had escaped from two perils, Scylla and Charybdis, that is, the Jews and the pagans,[75] when a storm (heresy) brings it to a dry and sandy country, which stands for those people without the fructifying benefit of holy doctrine. Finally, "raisons" and "desputoisons" (reasoned discourse, disputations; 14.567–68), presumably standing for Mercury's intervention, bring the ship back to sea and on the right course. This saddens Dame Heresie (Dido), pregnant with foolish error, whose company God (Aeneas) flees. In despair heresy kills herself spiritually just as "bougres et herites" (Bogomils [a dualist sect of heretics originating in tenth-century Bulgaria] and heretics; 14.590) are burnt. "Sainte Yglise" sails off in the direction of "voire creance" (true faith; 14.542). There is no interpretive formula leading into the allegory.

Unlike in the Pasiphae story, in this episode the poet selects a number of narrative elements for interpretation. Again, there is essentially only one level of interpretation—the spiritual—which is, however, linked up with a vaguely historical level by the reference to the burning of heretics, particularly the Bogomils. The thread holding the interpretation together is that of the voyage, that is, a spatial scheme: a ship is thrown off course, and then its passengers are endangered and finally saved. Dido's interpretive heritage as a figure of libido might have prepared her for her fate as Dame Heresie, but essentially this interpretation is innovative. The poet also chooses to elaborate on certain words, such as Dido's reference to her pregnancy, which reappears as the heretics being "pregnant" with error.

From a structural perspective, story and interpretation follow the same order. Unlike our two previous examples, this interpretation is more of a running commentary on the narrative. But again, not all elements are interpreted. Dido's sister, Anna, for example, does not appear in the allegory, nor does Dido's founding of the city, her brother, or her husband. The poet selected only those elements that fit into the ship allegory or can be linked to heresy. We can thus discern one of the principles of the poet's methodology: frequently one dominant image or idea gives shape to an extended allegorization that is generated by semantic fields, such as that of water or navigation.

An analysis of all the stories and their interpretations in the *OM* from the points of view of interpretive logic and selection shows a large number of different patterns.[76] From running commentary to loosely connected associations anything is possible. The elements selected for interpretations range from single words to whole narrative structures. Sometimes, as we just saw, in what one could call an "aesthetics of semantics," a whole semantic field, like that of water, is explored through series of images and associations. But for many stories, the principles that govern the poet's selection of certain elements for interpretation resist easy explanation. What the poet was seeking was undoubtedly variety, and although reading some of the endless allegorizations, mostly those on sin and redemption, can plunge the reader into a kind of stupor, the large variety of interpretive methods is a testimony to the poet's inventiveness. Multiple interpretations uniting apparently contradictory elements are the norm. They work through verbal triggers, through association, through sometimes belabored parallel constructions, and finally through an overriding faith that imposes similar spiritual messages on stories that appear quite dissimilar. The unity of the Christian message imposes an implacable order on the teeming magical world of the *Metamorphoses*.

Interpretive Hierarchies

As I mentioned briefly above, the *OM* poet's idea to introduce interpretive hierarchies is an innovation in the Ovidian commentary tradition.[77] Even those commentators who had proposed Christian meanings for the Ovidian fables, such as John of Garland and Arnulf of Orléans, did not explicitly set them above any other meanings. In the *OM*, the terms used to indicate the superiority of one meaning over others are "plus noble" (nobler), "meillour" (better), "plus digne" (worthier), and even "plus saine" (healthier or more reasonable). Yet, structurally, they do not always represent a climax, because sometimes they occur in the middle of a series of interpretations and only sometimes as a kind of culmination. I will analyze those examples that best illustrate the poet's approach to hierarchization, which, like other hermeneutic problems in the *OM*, is frequently bound up with issues of sexuality.

A long interpretive tradition existed for the fable of Actaeon, who was transformed into a stag for having seen Diana nude in her bath and was finally torn to pieces by his own hounds. In the fourth century B.C. the Greek commentator Palaiphatos interpreted the story as a warning for men against ruining themselves with their love for hunting and raising dogs.[78] The *OM* attributes a double meaning ("double signification"; 3.571) to the fable. For the first, the poet picks up on tradition by stating that Actaeon's story cautions us against an excessive love of hunting and against being idle (hunting is seen here as a pastime, not a necessity; 3.593–603). But there is an "autre sens" (other meaning; 3.604), and this meaning is "plus noble et de meillor sentence" (nobler and a better teaching; 3.605). Here, both Diana and Actaeon stand for Christ. The equation for Diana is made through the adjective *nude* ("nue . . . filz Dieu, sans couverture" [nude . . . the Son of God, uncovered; 3.633, 638–39]) and the one for Actaeon through a play on the words "cerf" and "serf" (stag, servant; 3.629–30). Thus verbal triggers produce a doubling of the deity, in which the different genders of the base text's characters are subsumed into the male Christ.

As we saw repeatedly, instances of problematic sexuality frequently seem to generate a moment of hermeneutic reflection in the *OM*. Two hierarchizations in Book 9 dramatically oppose a meaning related to depraved sexuality with a spiritual signification. The first is the story of Byblis's incestuous desire for her brother and her eventual metamorphosis into a fountain. Here the "istorial sens" claims that Byblis was a too-beautiful and not very virtuous young woman who loved her brother "de putage" (like a whore; 9.2102). When he rejects her she becomes a prostitute, who gives herself, like a fountain, to all men (9.2531–49). The fountain also provides the point of comparison for the allegory that is called "mieudre et plus saine" (better and healthier; 9.2550), which equates Byblis in that shape with Jesus (9.2660) (for whom that image is, of course, a traditional one). "Putage" and Christ's charity are hierarchized, yet the one does not cancel out the other. Rather, they provide a model for a moral transformation.

The next example opposes a shocking "historial sens" to the "meillour sentence" of the allegory. We have already encountered Iphis, the young woman changed into a man at the eleventh hour before her wedding.[79] Although the two interpretations of that story (described above) are both negative, they belong to different realms and are therefore not of equal worth. The spiritual interpretation, "la meillour sentence" (9.3158)—positing Iphis as the sinful soul—is still worthier for our poet than the interpretation in which Iphis is a depraved female seducer. Here, the extreme guilt of the historical Iphis cannot be resolved in a saving allegory as it had been for Byblis.

For Myrrha, guilty of incest but not of same-sex seduction, salvation is possible. In this last example of hierarchization I will consider, the interpretation deemed most worthy is not the last but the middle in the series. As it was in the two previous fables, sexual depravity is at the center: this time Myrrha's incestuous love for her father. The interpretation labeled "Mieudre et plus digne de savoir" (better and more worthy of being known; 10.3749) is the one that equates Myrrha with Mary and her son, Adonis, with Jesus (10.3750–97), followed by an equation of Myrrha with the sinful soul. After that, the poet passes to the possibility of real incest and states that true repentance can save a guilty woman. This interpretation is attributed to "li autours" (the author; 10.3880), who represents the literal level of "historical" incest. Here, the last interpretation brings us back full circle to the fable taken literally, and, as for the story of Byblis, the possibility of moral transformation and, finally, salvation is contained in the interpretive movement from one level to the next.

Most frequently (exceptions are the stories of Actaeon and of Ceres in Book 5 [especially ll. 2882–84]) interpretive hierarchization involves stories about what the poet sees as sexual deviance. Whether it is a question of same-sex seduction with mechanical aids or filial or sisterly incest, each time the historical explanation is valued as inferior to the spiritual one, which, through its position at the top of the interpretive hierarchy, positions the sexual threat posed by figures like Myrrha or Iphis in a spiritual framework of salvation and sin. In contrast, in the hundreds of other cases where the poet offers different types of interpretations, he generally does not offer explicit reflection on his hermeneutics through the introduction of interpretive hierarchies.

Interpretation "to the Second Degree"

The interpretations of Ovid found in the *OM* are not always directly related to the fables themselves. In many instances, the poet arrives at an interpretation only after several steps that have taken him away from his base text.[80] Given the richness of the text, I will have to limit myself to a few examples, each illustrating a slightly different technique.

The story of Deucalion's and Pyrrha's survival of the flood in Book 1 (1945–2118) obviously parallels the account of Noah and the Deluge in the Old Testament. The mysterious command given to the couple by the goddess Themis "to throw behind you as you go the bones of your great mother" (*Met* 1.383) is misinterpreted by Pyrrha, who takes it literally and refuses the task. Deucalion, however, recognizes the metaphor as referring to stones and thus manages to repopulate the earth.[81] This fable is a sign, the poet tells us, of baptism and the faith to come, that is, of holy doctrine. How does he arrive at this idea? The interpretive steps involved are the following: the fable is presented, a physiological (sexual) meaning is proposed, and a moral and spiritual interpretation follows. Only if the stones represent human sperm can the equation of sperm and doctrine (based on the phrase "semer doctrine") be established. Because stones have more often than not a negative connotation,[82] the intermediate step of a physiological explanation is necessary. It is this step that provides the basis for any further interpretation.

The story of Phaeton in Book 2 provides another instructive example. In the last of a series of interpretations Phaeton is equated with the Antichrist (2.916). His cousin Cycnus, changed into a swan because of his excessive grief over Phaeton's fiery death, as well as the Heliades, Phaeton's sisters, transformed into trees, represent those people who believe in the Antichrist and then repent. This rather involved interpretive passage draws not so much on the details of the Ovidian text as on the poet's own interpretation of Phaeton as the Antichrist, which was triggered by the idea of usurpation. Just as Phaeton had tried to usurp his father's power, so the Antichrist wants to take over God's functions. Interestingly, the *OM* poet waits almost 300 lines before deriving the interpretation of the Cycnus story from his own view of the fable of Phaeton. At any moment, then, the first layer of interpretation is as available for further interpretation as the fable, or base text, itself.

A variation on interpretation to the second degree is an instance in which the moral interpretation of a story is already present at the level of fable, as in Book 3 for the story of Narcissus. The "cold pride" already attributed to Narcissus by Ovid[83] surfaces both on the literal level ("Narcisus . . . fu tant outrecuidiez / plains d'orgueil et de sens vuidiez" [Narcissus . . . was so presumptuous and was so full of pride and empty of good sense; 3.1504–7]) and on the moral level:

> Qui bien veult ceste fable aprendre,
> Par Narcisus puet l'en entendre
> Les folz musors de sens voidiez,
> Les orgueilleus, les sorcuidiez. (3.1903–6)

Who wants to learn [something from] this fable: by Narcissus one can understand the crazy people, empty of good sense, the proud and the presumptuous ones.

The vocabulary of diegesis and interpretation is almost identical. This similarity shows on the one hand that in some cases there is a logical connection between fable and interpretation and on the other that the interpretation can invade the diegesis. The moral interpretation is thus "to the second degree."

Our next example shows the dependency of the moral on the physical or naturalistic interpretation. In Book 4 the *OM* tells, among others, the story of Juno in hell. Lines 3964–4061 offer first the traditional naturalistic explanation: Juno is the lower air. Consequently, and here the moral begins, she is "of the world" (as opposed to the spirit or cloister, which would be signified by the "higher air") and thus brings riches, which stand for avarice and pride and other negative qualities. Without the initial equation of the lower air and the world, none of the subsequent interpretations would have been possible. This piling up of interpretations characterizes the *OM* poet's techniques. Frequently, one interpretation grows out of the previous one and not out of the fable.

For the story of Niobe, told at length in Book 6 (973–1378), we may ask ourselves how this unfortunate mother comes to represent the contemplative life. The centerpiece in the chain of interpretations is again a stone. This time, however, the meaning of the stone is more positive than that in the Deucalion and Pyrrha story. Latona, the mother of Diana and Apollo, is offended by Niobe's proud account of her fourteen children. She appeals to her divine children, who avenge her by destroying Niobe's offspring. The grieving Niobe is finally metamorphosed into a stone. In the first interpretation, Latona represents religion and Niobe a "l'orgueil dou monde" (worldly pride) that hates religion and despises preaching (6.1381–90). The second proposes that the fact that Niobe was "muee en perre" (transformed into a stone; 6.1432) means that she arrived at a firm humility. Now the phrase "stony grief" already appears in Ovid (*Met* 6.302), but it is the *OM* poet who insists not only on the stone's lack of motion, as Ovid does, but also on its firmness. Clearly, only this quality of the stone—not present in the base text but part of his own interpretation—allows the poet to arrive at the interpretation of Niobe representing the firm humility of the contemplative life.[84]

Our last example of interpretation to the second degree is the story of Hecuba, who goes mad because of the grief over her dead children and changes into a dog (13.1639–2056). Hecuba is repeatedly equated with the personified country Judaea (13.1609 and 2057).[85] Like Hecuba, Judaea reigned as queen, but no longer: for she has lost her children (her subjects) to Christianity. Somewhat later, the story of Memnon is allegorized. Memnon, Aurora's son, had been killed by Achilles in the Trojan War. Mad with grief, his mother begged Jupiter to transform him, and he flew from his funeral pyre as a bird. The allegorization of Memnon's story—God will have pity on Judaea—is predicated on the interpretation of the Hecuba story, for the grieving mother Aurora is never explicitly equated with Judaea. The parallels between Hecuba and Judaea (as women who experienced a loss) exist only for that first story, while the second set of interpretations, that of Memnon and Aurora, is motivated by the allegories of the first and not by the fable of Memnon. If this sounds complicated, it is, for it reflects the *OM*'s extremely intricate interpretive techniques.[86]

This brief analysis of interpretation "to the second degree" gives us a better understanding of how the *OM* poet constructs his text. The interpretive passages are so vast because for them the poet does not always return to his base text, which has, after all, limits set by the Ovidian model. He resorts just as much to his own interpretations, which thus become a second, third, or fourth base text. This kind of self-interpretation generates new texts, which can be seen as another component in the *OM* poet's enterprise of turning himself into a new Ovid.

Intertexts

The vernacular romance tradition obviously left many traces in the *OM*.[87] In fact, the story of Philomena in Book 6 (ll. 2217–3684) is believed by the editor de Boer to be a transcription of Chrétien de Troyes's adaptation of that Ovidian tale.[88] Clearly, the *OM* poet was aware of what his vernacular predecessors had done with Ovid. This is especially visible in the courtly vocabulary used to describe certain love relationships. However, if some passages, such as 11.1674ff. and 11.2200ff., dealing with Venus's powers and the Judgment of Paris, respectively, evoke the *Roman d'Enéas*, this may be the result of the *RE*'s incorporation of many themes and techniques from Ovid. Thus it is extremely difficult to determine when a true intertextual relationship exists between the *OM* and earlier vernacular texts. There is one instance, however, that will allow us to understand how the *OM* poet uses intertextuality as an aid to interpretation: the role the *Roman de la Rose* plays in the interpretations of the fountains of Narcissus and of Salmacis.[89]

The relationship of the Narcissus episode in the *Rose* to Ovid has been studied in great detail with varying results. It is clear that Guillaume de Lorris artfully transposed elements from Ovid, such as Narcissus's eyes, his "twin stars," which reappear as the two crystals in the fountain. On the level of the fable, the *OM* goes back to Ovid for the details of the description of Narcissus's fountain, but for the fable's interpretation the *Roman de la Rose* is used intertextually. Thus the *OM* poet read the *Rose* as a valid interpretation of Ovid; evoking this romance allowed him to add an interpretive dimension to his text that was sanctioned by a long (vernacular) tradition.

The key term alerting us to the *Rose*'s presence is "li mireoirs perillous" (the perilous mirror; 3.1925) repeating line 1569 "C'est li miroers perilleus" of Guillaume de Lorris's text. As did Guillaume (*Rose*, ll. 1569–70), the *OM* poet rhymes "perillous" with "orgueillous" (the proud), who, together with those covetous of wordly glory, had been figured by Narcissus in the mythographic tradition.[90] Thus the interpretation evokes the intertext through the rhyme. The deceiving mirror then comes to stand for the deceptions and vanity of this world. The *OM* adopts the notion of deception in relation to the shining surface of the fountain but does not explicitly follow the *Rose*'s meditations on deceptive love. However, because of the intertextual presence of the *Rose* we can posit a sexual dimension to the poet's tirade against the "folie et forsenage" (craziness and madness; 3.1911) of those who admire themselves in the false mirror of the secular world, a dimension that will be confirmed in the interpretation of Salmacis's fountain. In addition, the whole development of the term "Mireoirs perillous" as the world is a consequence of the *Rose*'s intertextual function: previous traditions had made much of Narcissus's reflection in the fountain but had not elaborated on the surface as a dangerous mirror.

When we turn to the fountain of Salmacis in Book 4, we see that not only the *Rose* but also the passage of the *OM* in Book 3 we just analyzed functions as intertext here. The *OM* refers to Salmacis's fountain as "fontaine perilleuse" (4.2002), which is clearly not a translation of Ovid's term "infamis" (of ill repute; 4.285) but rather an allusion to Narcissus's fountain. This connection confirms a very interesting reading of Ovidian fountains done by Marta Powell Harley in 1986.[91] As the *OM* sees it as well, there is indeed a connection between the two fountains, and that connection is based on the fountains' sexual powers: one ensnares lovers, the other enfeebles them. The *OM*'s first interpretation of Salmacis's fountain is indebted to John of Garland:[92] the fountain represents the uterus with its seven cells (a medieval belief), three on each side and one in the middle; if conception occurs in the middle cell, a hermaphrodite will be the result. In the second interpretation Salmacis herself stands for a woman who loves makeup.

It is in the third interpretation that the connection to Narcissus and especially to the interpretation of the Narcissus fable becomes evident: Salmacis "puet noter le monde" (can signify the world; 4.2284) and its perils. Nothing in the Salmacis and Hermaphroditus story itself would suggest this interpretation. It is intertextually motivated through the connection of the two perilous fountains, a fact which is also visible in the sexual overtones ("lecherie, delit, deduire," and so on) of the interpretation. Thus, the *OM* reads the Narcissus fountain through the *Rose* and the Salmacis fountain through both the *Rose* (which combines the two Ovidian fountains into one as the Narcissus fountain) and Book 3 of the *OM* itself. This sophisticated use of medieval intertextuality allows the interpretations to acquire dimensions that had not been visible in the preceding mythographic traditions.

"Literary Criticism" in the *Ovide Moralisé*

For a fourteenth-century text the term *literary criticism* has a large hermeneutic component.[93] The *OM* poet offers a number of explicit reflections on interpretive techniques and modes of reading that together begin to form definitions of a theoretical approach to the hermeneutics of the *Metamorphoses.*

Interpretive Surplus and Refusal

As we saw in our analysis of the Prologue, the *OM* poet uses the familiar topos of "I cannot tell you everything because that would lengthen my text excessively" (1.47–51). The implication of this statement is obvious: there are even more interpretations available than can be found in the present text. But why is the *OM* incomplete, and who is authorized to uncover this interpretive surplus?

The story of Peleus and Thetis's wedding in Book 11 provides some good examples of refusal and surplus.[94] First of all, the story is not in the *Metamorphoses* and is thus part of a vast "surplus" of mostly Theban and Trojan material the *OM* poet adds to his Ovidian base text.[95] This may be a reason why he does not want to interpret the story as extensively as he could:

> Je m'en passe legierement,
> Si l'espondrai grossetement,
> Au plus briement que je porrai,
> Si que pas tout ne desclorrai
> Quant que la fable signifie. (11.1351–55)

I will pass over this quickly and interpret it summarily, as briefly as I can, so that I will not reveal everything the fable signifies.

The poet then goes on to interpret the story as relating to difficulties of conception and sexual intercourse (some people do it too fast, some too slow, and so forth; 11.1357–88). We saw in the section on interpretive hierarchies that for the *OM* poet sexual interpretations represent a special locus for explicit reflections on interpretation. The same is true here. As for the "summary" interpretation, alas, it goes on for a hundred lines or so. What the poet exposes here are the false fictions offered to people by some poets regarding the multiplicity of gods, specifically, that each body part had its own god.[96] He then goes on to an explanation of the four humors that ends with yet another reflection on interpretation:

> Or vous ai dit à grosse somme
> Quel sens la fable puet avoir.
> Qui plus parfont vaudra savoir,
> Aillours querre et trouver porra
> Qui le sourplus le desclorra.
> Je n'en vueil plus ci avant dire,
> Ains avancerai ma matire
> De Discorde (11.1462–69)

Now I have told you summarily which meaning this fable can have. Whoever wants to know about this in more depth can go elsewhere to look for and find someone who will reveal the surplus to him. I do not want to continue with this, rather I want to get on with my subject matter on Discord.

The poet does not specify who these people in command of further and deeper interpretations might be.[97] In view of his attacks on other interpreters of Ovid in the Prologue, they can hardly be his predecessors, such as Arnulf of Orléans. The question must thus remain unanswered. In addition to the traditional brevity topos, we find a consciousness of the inexhaustibility of meanings.[98] The *OM* as a whole is a monument to the vastness of interpretive possibilities; the passages just cited demonstrate how the poet inscribes himself into this vastness: while offering his readers what they—not he—may consider interpretive excesses, he nevertheless does not offer perfect interpretive plenitude.[99]

Two more cases of the refusal to interpret are of interest here. The first includes a brevity topos; the second is related to the question of believability and thus leads us to our next section.[100]

In a revealing segment of Book 15, which has a great concentration of passages that could be classified as literary criticism, the poet allegorizes the animals that Pythagoras mentions in his teachings. Suddenly he introduces the brevity topos by saying:

> Trop y avroit longue escripture,
> Se tous les secrez de nature
> Voloie mot à mot espondre
> Où sens que l'en i puet espondre. (15.6219–22)
>
> . . .
>
> Ne suis je pas si discrez
> Que tous les natureuz secrez
> Puisse atraire à moralité. (15.6225–27)

This book would get too long if I wanted to interpret all the secrets of nature word by word, according to the meaning one could offer for them. . . . I do not have sufficient discernment to interpret morally all the secrets of nature.

It is significant that this statement comes in Book 15, the last of this enormous text. Earlier the poet had admitted that there were other interpretations that could be found elsewhere; now he admits that he cannot unveil all the secrets of nature that have a moral meaning. On the one hand, this admission could simply be attributed to interpretive exhaustion. But it could also have a deeper meaning: it may represent a moment of doubt concerning the entire enterprise of the *OM*, that is, perhaps not everything *has* a moral meaning. Until now, the poet confidently allegorized any possible detail of a given fable. Now he suggests that some secrets remain impervious to interpretation.[101] Indeed, one could read this passage as an elaboration of an earlier refusal to interpret the story of Pythagoras's feathered men.

In that instance, the poet reacts to a story Ovid has Pythagoras tell to prove that all things are changeable. Pythagoras speaks of some singular men in a region called Hyperborean Pallene "who gain a covering of light feathers for their bodies after they have nine times plunged in Minerva's pool" (*Met* 15.356–58). The *OM* poet translates this passage faithfully, down to Pythagoras's disclaimer "I do not vouch for it" (*Met* 15.359), translated as "mes c'est grief à croire / Que tel chose puisse estre voire" (But it is hard to believe that something like this could be true; 15.951–52). When the moment comes—approximately 5000 lines later—to allegorize this passage, the poet refuses to do so:

> Je ne quier metre alegorie
> En ce que l'auctors ne croit mie
> Qui puisse estre à voir amené:
> Des homes qui sont empené. (15.5917–20)

I do not wish to put an allegory to something the author does not believe can be made true, namely [the story] of the feathered men.

Thus, since in Ovid the narrator of this story expresses doubts as to its authenticity, the *OM* poet refuses to allegorize it. In other words, as unlikely as most of the stories in the *Metamorphoses* may be, as long as they are ostensibly believed by the Ovidian narrator, they can be allegorized; their being seen as unbelievable within the *Metamorphoses* itself precludes allegorization—certainly a tribute to Ovid's authority.[102]

Right and Wrong Interpretations

By imposing Christian meanings on Ovid's *Metamorphoses*, the poet engages in a form of allegoresis that by its very nature cannot be termed right or wrong. Because the *OM* poet's allegoresis works by faith all the interpretations of the fables are "correct." We saw for the story of Myrrha, to cite just one of hundreds of examples, that she can stand for both an incestuous woman and the Virgin Mary. This uniting of extremes is in fact one of the hallmarks of the *OM*.

Nevertheless, the poet is conscious of right and wrong interpretations, but not in his own text, that is, *his* interpretation of Ovid. Rather the distinction between right and wrong is made to bear on more general hermeneutic issues related to the profoundly Christian distinction between the "letter" and the "spirit," frequently figured by the opposition between the synagogue and the Church.

The contrast between the obscurity of the synagogue and the truth of the Church first appears as part of the allegory of the story of Ceres and Proserpina in Book 5. The synagogue is represented by the lizard into which an impertinent boy is transformed for calling the thirsty Ceres greedy when she is searching for her lost daughter. The blind synagogue

> Delesse la voire clarté,
> Si vague en dampnable obscurté,
> Et veult la verité repondre,
> Et pour ce qu'el ne set respondre
> Ne ne deigne otroier la letre,
> Diverse sentence i veult metre,
> Toute contraire à verité. (5.3154–60)

abandons true clarity and moves about in damnable darkness, and wants to cover up the truth, because it does not know how to explain or be in accord with the letter; it wants to impose a different interpretation, contrary to the truth.

"Diverse sentence" is the key term here: it is this interpretation that is opposed to the truth. Thus the poet is conscious that the possibility of an incorrect interpretation exists—but only in the realm of the synagogue, not that of the Church.

For our second example we will return to the story of Hecuba (in Book 13), who had been equated with Judaea. In the context of Judaea, the poet begins to speak of the Roman emperors Titus and Vespasian, who are two of the protagonists in the story of Veronica's veil (from the apocryphal gospels). From an interpretive perspective this story is interesting because it is interpolated in the allegorization of Hecuba and thus represents an "invasion" of sacred history into the interpretive realm.

In addition, one could consider the story of Veronica's veil an interpretive trigger for the poet's reflection on the "letter and the spirit." For, according to Bernard of Clairvaux, for example, the veil is a symbol for the "written letter that brings death [and that] is torn in two at the death of the crucified Word."[103] Thus the veil that features "la sole umbre de Jhesucrist" (the shadow of Jesus Christ; 13.2106) may be seen as a counterpart to the "veil of the letter," that is, the Old Testament *without* the spirit of the New. Veronica's veil thus may be capable of undoing the "veil that brings death." Finally, the covering veil, or integument, is also a central term for the poet's own enterprise of reading Ovid. Just as the veil of the Old Testament had to be removed to make visible the New, so the veil has to be removed from the fable in order to uncover its true—often spiritual—meaning.

Here is what the *OM* poet reflects on within the context of the Veronica story:

Quar cil qui solement s'afferme
Au texte et vainement afferme
Qu'il est en sauf estat de vivre,
Li textes l'ocist, sans revivre.
La letre ocist qui s'i fie,
Mes li misteres vivifie,
Que sainte Yglise garde et tient. (13.2137–43)

For that person who relies solely on the text and vainly affirms that he is leading a saved life, him the text kills, without reviving him. The letter kills those who trust it, but the mystery that the holy Church guards vivifies.[104]

He adds that those who adhere to the mere text are in danger of damnation. And, in a reprise of the image of the blind synagogue, he alerts us to the existence of false glosses offered by the synagogue:

Par la glose le trait à part
Et de verité le depart,
Si vait le texte derrompant
Et la sentence corrompant. (13.2181–84)

By the gloss it [the synagogue] distances and moves him away from the truth. It breaks the text into pieces and corrupts the interpretation.[105]

The false gloss, he continues, plays cruelly with students of the "obscure" text.

We have already encountered a similar interpretive vocabulary in our section of that title, above. Here, this vocabulary appears in a more traditional exegetical context. What is important here is that it shows the poet's consciousness of the existence of false glosses and incorrect interpretations. These, however, exist only in the realm of the synagogue, that is, outside the poet's own text. The false glosses represent the act of interpretation without the grace of the spirit. But since the *OM* poet works within the realm of the spirit, the possibility of error, of a false interpretation on the *OM* poet's part, is excluded. Incomplete interpretation, as we just saw, is possible, however, and is attributable to the poet's inability to achieve interpretive plenitude.

A perfect image for the congruence of text and (correct) gloss is that of Atlas equated with God the Father:

> C'est li maitres de bone escole,
> Qui a toute science enclose
> En soi seul: le texte et la glose. (4.6431–33)

This is the master of the good school who contains in himself alone all knowledge: text and gloss.

So, finally, does (at least in his own estimation) the *OM* poet himself.

How to Read (Benoît de Sainte-Maure and Ovid)

In Book 5 the poet proposes a model for reading and writing correctly. It is true that this model is an extended metaphor for true repentance, which will become manifest at the Last Judgment, but it nevertheless tells us something of the poet's convictions on how to establish a correct text.

The poet proposes an equation between repentance and a corrected reading: just as one must repent and mend one's ways, one must erase and correct a corrupt text. This equation leads to some revealing remarks on methods of reading and writing:

> Li bien doit l'en dou mal eslire,
> Et son livre lire et relire,
> Et cerchier enterinement,
> Et se faute y a, si l'ament. (5.2400–403)
> . . .
> Efface et ament, sans targier,
> Se riens i treuve a corrigier,
> Et escrive diligamment
> Chose qu'il doie apertement
> Lire à la grant desputaison
> Devant le Mestre (5.2418–23)

One must choose the good over the bad and read and reread one's book, and search all through it, and if there is a fault, correct it. . . . He should erase and add without delay, if he finds something to correct, and write diligently those things that he will read openly before the Master at the great disputation.

The book in question here is the book of conscience and, in line with a number of mystical texts, the Last Judgment is seen as the moment of "open" reading: now will be uncovered what was covered then ("descouvert couvert"; 5.2428–29).[106] We have already seen in our analysis of the Prologue that reading "apertement" (without a veil or integument) is what the poet proposes to do in the *OM*. Thus, despite the traditional and metaphorical quality of this passage, we can read it as an exhortation for a correct reading, that is, reading as "uncovering," not only of our life and conscience but of Ovid as well. The passage is at the same time a profession of faith and of technique.

Correct reading is, of course, a necessity for dealing with all preceding texts. But it is especially necessary for those texts that provide the bulk of the *OM*'s subject matter. Benoît de Sainte-Maure, the author of the twelfth-century *Roman de Troie*, and Ovid are the two authors the *OM* poet needs to come to terms with most. Let us first look at Benoît de Sainte-Maure.

We already saw that large portions of the Trojan subject matter did not come from Ovid but from other texts, one of which is the *Roman de Troie*. In Book 12 (1709–54), the *OM* poet provides an explicit critique of the twelfth-century romancer and his text. As Paule Demats has given a close reading of this passage, I would like to highlight only a few details.[107] After an homage to Benoît's writerly talents, the *OM* poet takes issue with the older poet's treatment of Homer. In the prologue to his *Roman de Troie* Benoît had said of Homer:

> Mais ne dist pas sis livres veir,
> Quar bien savons senz nul espeir
> Qu'il ne fu puis de cent anz nez
> Que li granz oz fu assemblez. (ll. 51–54)

But his [Homer's] book does not speak the truth, for we know full well that he had not been born by a hundred years at the moment when the great army was assembled.

Dares and Dictys, on the other hand, the late antique writers who claimed to have been present at the Trojan War, can be trusted, according to Benoît.[108] The *OM* poet accuses Benoît of having misunderstood Homer, that is, he asserts that Benoît rejected the ancient poet because he thought that Homer could not have been an eyewitness to the Trojan War. However, and this is the key phrase, the poet further states that [Homer] "Il parla par metaphore" (12.1733) but that Benoît did not realize that fact and so denigrated Homer's poem. Demats believes that this "par metaphore" only refers to the presence of gods and goddesses in the *Iliad*.[109] It is more likely, though, that the *OM* poet draws a parallel with the *Metamorphoses* and speaks of Homer's text in its entirety. Thus he can contrast himself with Benoît, who did not discover the fundamental quality that, for the *OM* poet, seems to be universal to all ancient texts: their truth is not only historical but is also hidden away in metaphors, and it is the medieval poets' task to uncover and explain these metaphors.

Benoît is also cited as an *auctor*. When the poet declines to recount the fall of Troy in great detail he adds: "Par Beneoit puet on sans faille / Savoir toute l'auctorité" (Through Benoît one can learn without fail all of the authoritative text; 13.1352–53). Both Benoît's romance and his sources may be designated by "auctorité." Thus the polemics the *OM* poet directs against Benoît in Book 12 do not undermine Benoît's authority, although they cast some doubt on his choice of rejecting Homer. The main purpose of the criticism of Benoît clearly was to contrast the *OM* poet's own interpretive method, as applied to Ovid, with that of Benoît and in the process to valorize it.

In the Prologue the *OM* poet makes clear why he dealt with Ovid's fables: because under the fables there lies hidden a worthwhile truth that the poet has to uncover (1.45–46). In Book 15, in the context of allegorizing Pythagoras, he elaborates on these remarks.[110] Lines 2517–57 are essentially a defense of reading the *Metamorphoses* with a Christian purpose. He forestalls criticism by acknowledging that some might condemn Ovid's fables as sorcery and "bogrerie" (15.2520). The latter term, referring to the Bogomil heresy, highlights the religious danger of the *OM* poet's enterprise: he might expose himself to charges of heresy. In truth, the poet continues, those readers who take Ovid "à la letre" (literally; 15.2526) and do not see the profitable teaching that lies under the fable are indeed guilty of heresy ("bogrerie"; 15.2535). However, only those who have good sense can find the hidden meanings. As Saint Augustine taught, if on the literal level the Bible does not conform to charity it cannot be taken literally. For the *OM* poet the Bible seems often as "trouble" (murky) and "obscure" as the *Metamorphoses*. Indeed, it often seems to be a fable! Though echoing Augustine, the poet may also be taking up here some ideas associated with Siger of Brabant (d. 1284) on the possibility that even the literal level of the Bible contains fables and falsehoods.[111] Although propositions of this kind had been condemned in 1277, they continued to be discussed, particularly in the context of commentaries on Aristotle's *Metaphysics*. The *OM* poet demonstrates that he is conscious of these currents when he proposes that those who are so naive ("por non-savoir"; 15.2554) that they do *not* give another meaning to the letter of the Bible (that is, those who read it literally) are in danger of damnation. Similarly, those who read Ovid only literally are on the wrong track. Thus he puts biblical exegesis and the interpretation of the *Metamorphoses* on the same level and concomitantly stresses the correctness of his own method.

What had been initiated in the twelfth century by thinkers like William of Conches in the context of the uses of the integumenta of fiction in the revelation of truth is now fully elaborated. Exegesis and the interpretation of fiction seem to become indistinguishable; consequently Ovid's text is accorded an epistemological status equal to that of the Bible and its interpretation becomes nothing less than the *Bible des poètes*.[112]

What distinguishes the *OM* from other commentaries on Ovid's *Metamorphoses*? How does it work? And what does this text provide for posterity?

The *OM* provides the first French translation of the entire *Metamorphoses*, and it is the first allegorization of that text that systematically assigns Christian interpretations to Ovid's pagan fables. Unlike other commentators, the *OM* poet does not base his interpretations on paraphrases of Ovid's text but on a rather faithful translation, supplemented by details from glosses and other texts.[113] In fact, as the text progresses we see a growing consciousness of Ovidian narrative coherence, or at least a growing respect for Ovidian speakers, such as Orpheus or Pythagoras, whose discourses are not interrupted by interpretations. In the later books of the *OM* there is a movement away from excessive segmentation.

In another interesting move, the *OM* transfers ideas of typology from the biblical sphere to that of fable. The constant equations made between figures like Apollo, Aeneas, and even Glaucus and Jesus make us think of these gods and heroes as prefigurations of the Savior to come. The two systems, that of classical mythology and that of Christian faith, are juxtaposed in such a way that they are connected by countless threads of equivalencies. In many cases these equivalencies are integrated into a hierarchy of meanings, something absent from the mythographic tradition but present in exegesis. The transference of techniques of biblical exegesis to that of fables is a hallmark of the *OM*. The consequence of this transference is a forceful valorization of fable and an expansion of twelfth-century techniques of interpreting fables. The *OM* also introduced an interpretive vocabulary into the French vernacular that hitherto had been reserved for learned, mostly Latin, discussions. From its uses in the *OM* we can discern what these terms meant for a fourteenth-century scholar. Furthermore, the poet highlights moments in which Ovidian sexuality becomes particularly transgressive in a medieval context. He uses these moments for hermeneutic reflections that link sexual and interpretive crises and provide models for rejecting transgression through correct spiritual interpretation.

We also saw that the *OM* poet uses vernacular intertexts, particularly the *Roman de la Rose*, to enrich the signification of the Ovidian stories. Explicit reflections on how to read authors like Ovid and Benoît de Sainte-Maure illuminated the *OM* poet's thoughts on "reading myth."

It is important to remember that the *OM* replaced Ovid as a source for future vernacular writers. When Machaut, Froissart, or Christine de Pizan worked with Ovidian references, they turned to the *OM* much more frequently than to Ovid himself. This also meant that they had a text with built-in interpretations at their disposal and had to decide in each case what to retain, modify, or reject. The *OM* thus provided a virtual storehouse of interpretations as well as new ways of reading Ovid.[114] In many different senses, then, the *OM* poet did become a new Ovid. As I suggested earlier, however, instead of beings, he metamorphoses meanings, and while his meanings might not be as colorful as Ovid's plants, flowers, and animals, they had as much staying power and exercised a lasting hold on the medieval imagination.

Chapter 4

Myth and Fiction in the *Dits* of Machaut and Froissart

In the late fourteenth century Eustache Deschamps (ca. 1344–1404) entitled one of his mythological ballades "balade sur poetrie" and thus highlighted one of the characteristics of fourteenth-century poetics: classical mythology had become one of the major components of poetry.[1] "Poetrie" is fiction, and fiction is for a great part mythology or fable. This state of affairs at the end of the century is largely the result of the vernacularization of Ovid's *Metamorphoses*, the *Ovide moralisé*, which we studied in the last chapter. The poets who followed in the *OM*'s wake made use of the new expanded subject matter and cast their own poetic concerns in an Ovidian mold. Of these poets Guillaume de Machaut (ca. 1300–1377) and Jean Froissart (1337–ca. 1404) were the most sophisticated: for them, classical mythology became a key element for their self-definition as artists and lovers.

The *dit* was the ideal locus for this self-definition. As a genre it dates back to the thirteenth century, where the term usually designated a short first-person nonlyric poem on a limited topic.[2] In the fourteenth century the *dit*'s nature and function changed. At that time, it was usually a longer poem, open to a variety of discourses: love lyrics; narrative passages dealing with political or moral themes; letters; allegorical passages often centering around what Daniel Poirion calls "une image directrice" (a guiding image); and mythological fables. The *dit*'s function is to "communicate a certain wisdom" and to serve as a "comfort" or "remedy."[3] Furthermore, as Jacqueline Cerquiglini points out, the *dit* is characterized by "son jeu au second degré" (its play to the second power) and by the mise-en-scène of the poetic *je*.[4] The metalevel of discourse is thus an essential element of the *dit*, in which the creation of the *dit* itself is frequently thematized.[5] In all these areas of function and definition, mythology plays a crucial role and goes to the very heart of the *dit* as a genre. Myths, both traditional and newly invented, are used to figure the poet's creativity, to problematize the acts of reception and of writing, or to introduce threatening erotic undercurrents barely visible on the text's surface.

In the *dits* of Machaut and Froissart mythological themes and figures are integral parts of thematic patterns centering on love and writing as well as on contemporary history and social relations. For Deschamps, in contrast, mythology was never in the forefront, although mythological figures do surface here and there in his works. The themes that seemed more urgent to him—war, the city, the corruption of the times and of his own body, to name only some of the subjects of his vast fragmented oeuvre—did not open themselves up to classical mythology in the way the themes of Machaut's and Froissart's *dits* did.[6] At first sight Deschamps's choice of topics reflects more dramatically the troubled second half of the fourteenth century. In light of the ravages of the Hundred Years' War, of the Great Plague (evoked vividly, however, in Machaut's *Jugement dou roy de Navarre* of 1349), of the "Babylonian captivity" of the papacy in Avignon, some of the passages on love in the *dits* may seem escapist and perhaps irrelevant to the real preoccupations of the times. Yet, it is here that a new poetic self-consciousness is elaborated and that the concept of poet in a more modern sense is born.[7]

This new poet is a professional, someone who generally writes for a patron with whom he interacts not only in real life but in the fictionalized context of his poetry. He is also someone for whom poetry is but one of many activities. Both Machaut and Froissart were extremely productive in other areas, Machaut as the foremost composer of his time, Froissart as the author of the *Chroniques*, the writing of which spanned many decades. Clerks by formation, both poets interacted with the rulers of their times and traveled throughout Europe in various capacities.[8] Neither of them elaborated an *ars poetica*,[9] but one can extrapolate from their *dits* how they saw their function as poets and their place in the poetic tradition. In this domain their treatment, transformation, and even invention of classical myths provide the most helpful signposts.

Machaut's and Froissart's use of mythology sets itself off from the learned tradition at the time. Fourteenth-century commentators of the classics, such as Nicholas Trévet, Giovanni del Virgilio, and Pierre Bersuire (the last two commented on the *Metamorphoses*), moved in the realm of allegorization.[10] Like the author of the *OM*,[11] they were interested in the different levels of meaning of a text, in the historical, moral, or spiritual significance of mythological figures and stories. But where the *OM* had provided a coherent vernacular text, these commentators wrote in Latin and fragmented the classical texts the same way their predecessors had over centuries.

It is clear that Machaut and Froissart used the *OM* rather than Ovid as a source for mythological stories,[12] and although the *OM* is always present, none of the major spiritual or Christian concerns of that text resurfaced explicitly in their works. Rather, they use myths to problematize different concerns: the relationship of art and love, artistic subjectivity, their relationship to patrons, and finally questions of vernacular glossing and hermeneutics.[13] In this, they also follow in the footsteps of the *Roman de la Rose*, a text that is omnipresent in the *dits* of both poets. As we saw in Chapter 2, myth and interpretation of myth were integral parts of the romance, and although the lessons drawn from the mythological stories applied most directly to the aspects of love taught by the various characters, the myths also fell into a pattern that revealed the connections between art, love, and sexuality or procreation. Yet the subjectivity of the poet did not enter into the mythological texts themselves in the same way; and although the lessons drawn from the myths were often seemingly perverse, such as La Vieille's remarks on table manners in the context of Palinurus's death, generally the details of the myths themselves were preserved with regard to the sources.

In Machaut and particularly in Froissart this changes: myths are combined in new ways, modified, intentionally falsified, and invented out of whole cloth. Since none of these activities can be accidental, given the high sophistication of both authors, they have particular significance for the authors' poetic concerns. Machaut and Froissart question the mythological and mythographic traditions—the validity of mythological exempla, for instance—and offer a new poetics of myth.

The Value and Hermeneutics of Mythological Exempla

When Machaut's benefactors Jean of Luxembourg and his daughter Bonne, wife of the French King Jean Le Bon (reigned 1350–64), died (in 1346 and 1349, respectively), Machaut turned to a new patron, Charles of Navarre, who married Jean Le Bon's daughter Jeanne in 1352. Charles's own sister was married to Philip VI, French king from 1328 to 1350. The two works Machaut dedicated to Charles, the *Jugement dou roy de*

Navarre (= *Navarre*; 1349) and the *Confort d'Ami* (= *Confort*; 1357),[14] mark the limits of Machaut's involvement with this king, who later came to be known as Charles le Mauvais (Charles the Bad or Evil), most likely because of his role in the assassination, in 1354, of the French constable Charles of Spain (who was in possession of the domains that Charles de Navarre laid claim to in the wake of his marriage to Jeanne) and because of his dealings with Jean Le Bon's adversaries (who included Jean's own son).[15] The latter led to Charles's imprisonment for about eighteen months in 1356 and 1357. The *Navarre* was written at Charles's majority and thus predated his troubles. The *Confort*, the last work in which Machaut mentions Charles, was written during his imprisonment for treason. It is in these two texts that Machaut confronts most clearly the value and the hermeneutics of classical mythology in its most traditional medieval form, that of the exemplum.

Both works arise out of a crisis: an evocation of the plague dramatically opens the *Navarre*;[16] Charles's imprisonment calls forth the *Confort*. But there is also a crisis within the fictional oeuvre of Machaut that provokes the composition of the *Navarre*: the *Jugement dou roy de Behaigne* (Judgment of the King of Bohemia), written before 1346 for Jean of Luxembourg. In that poem, Guillaume is a witness and participant in a debate between a lady and a knight.[17] Who suffers more, is the debated question, the lady who enjoys a perfect love relationship but whose lover dies or the knight whose lady love turns out to be unfaithful? When no solution can be found, Guillaume leads the lovers to Jean of Luxembourg's castle, where Jean resolves the question in favor of the knight.[18] This judgment is considered misogynistic by various allegorical ladies, in particular Dame Bonneurté (Happiness). Thus the *Jugement dou roy de Behaigne* ends with a verdict deemed unacceptable (because it is misogynistic) by the female allegorical characters. This fictional crisis needs to be resolved and this is why Dame Bonneurté, a character from the previous text, pounces upon Guillaume at the opening of the *Navarre*. He is called on to rectify the first verdict as he ventures out for the first time after a long period of confinement in his house during which the plague killed half a million people.

The *Navarre* is set up as a trial before the King of Navarre in which both sides have their say. Most of their argumentation consists of exempla and their interpretation.[19] What Machaut stages here is a continuation, revision, and expansion of the earlier *Jugement dou roy de Behaigne*, in which mythological exempla had played no role at all. Part of the expansion is the introduction of the allegorical characters Dame Bonneurté, Pais, Franchise, Doubtance, Souffisance, and others. Significantly it is these figures who try to support their arguments through tales from mythology. Machaut thus highlights the affinity between myth and allegory that goes back to the late antique tradition. Since the character of Guillaume eschews classical mythology and only has recourse to medieval exempla (except at the very end, as we will see), the whole debate takes on the character of a struggle of "ancients versus moderns." Given the authority invested in ancient mythology, and the precedent of the *OM*, whose author found countless secure meanings in each fable, the questioning of the value of myth, evident in the open debates on the appropriateness and exemplary value of mythological stories in the *Navarre*, surprises and amuses the reader. Machaut inscribes his character Guillaume here in the doubting tradition of the second part of the *Roman de la Rose*, but he isolates the problematics of the hermeneutics of myth more clearly by projecting them onto the plane of hermeneutical warfare between the poet figure grounded in medieval exempla and his adversaries, the allegorical ladies, who draw on the mythological tradition.

It soon becomes apparent, however, that in the course of the debate neither side uses its exempla to its best advantage. The question that had been central to the *Behaigne* (who suffers more?) is soon displaced by a discussion on who is more faithful in love, men or women. One should note that this question fits much better into the context of misogyny, the charge brought against Guillaume by Dame Bonneurté. This refocusing of the debate allows for the introduction of the standard repertory of pairs of classical lovers who serve to illustrate mostly men's treachery in love. These lovers bear the weight of tradition, but Guillaume is not impressed. Indeed, he points out that the examples of Theseus and Jason adduced by Franchise have nothing to do with the matter at hand:

> Damoiselle, la traïson
> De Theseüs ne de Jason
> Ne fait riens a nostre matiere, (ll. 2823–25)
> . . .
> Ne je ne donroie .ii. pommes
> De vostre entention prouver
> Par si fais exemples trouver. (ll. 2830–32)

Damsel, the treason of either Theseus or Jason has nothing to do with the issue we're arguing. . . . I wouldn't give two apples for proving your point by the introduction of exempla such as these.

Guillaume thus does not doubt the value of all exempla, just that of the mythological ones. As Jean-Louis Picherit points out, Guillaume here rejects the long moralizing and pedagogical tradition that myth had gained in medieval culture.[20] The poet may also want to criticize the oversaturation in contemporary poetry with mythological tales that are used frivolously and in an inapposite manner. What he pits against the mythological tales are medieval ones, such as that of a clerk of Orléans who dies of his mistress's supposed unfaithfulness, that of the Chatelaine de Vergy, or that of a knight who returns his (married) lady's ring with his finger still attached to it. The examples are not always apt, however.

The same reservation applies, however, to some of the mythological exempla told by the allegorical ladies. When Pais uses Dido's case to comment on the sorrow a woman experiences because of her lover's death (ll. 2095–130), she omits to mention that Aeneas treacherously left Dido but did not die.[21] Nevertheless, Guillaume comes round toward the end when Souffisance tells at length the story of Hero and Leander (ll. 3221–98). Souffisance refrains from drawing a lesson from this tale and only concludes by saying to Guillaume that "cils debat soit en deport; / Car vraiement, vous avez tort" (this debate's a joke; doubtless you are wrong; ll. 3309–10).

But now Guillaume decides to draw a moral from the story that is supposed to help his cause: profiting from the flexibility of the myths' interpretations, he now concludes that Souffisance's tale shows that Leander suffered more for love than Hero, ergo men are better in love, and that his case is proved beyond a doubt (ll. 3323–64). His conversion to the value of classical exempla comes too late, however, for no one takes any notice of it.

The comic open-endedness of Guillaume's interpretive efforts underlines the ineffectiveness of mythological stories as tools of rhetorical persuasion if used in an inapposite way. In light of Machaut's later works we may see here a plea for a more effective and relevant use of myth. Here, in any case, Guillaume's efforts at using mythological tales are simply ignored, for when Mesure refutes his arguments toward the end of the debate she only cites the medieval stories Guillaume had adduced in support of his arguments. Needless to say, these are demolished one by one (ll. 3631–724) and what remains is Guillaume's condemnation by the king and his punishment of having to compose three poems.

Thus the *Navarre* offers a dramatization of medieval modes of argumentation that relied heavily on the use of exempla. It shows a kind of apprenticeship during which Guillaume watches the allegorical ladies argue by means of exempla and commentary. That his final conversion brings him no benefit is no accident: as became clear throughout the debate, the lessons drawn from the classical examples did not always fit the argument. Nevertheless, the ladies, the champions of antiquity, win the debate.

From a poetological perspective, Machaut here examines the efficacy of the classical subject matter that was a staple of fourteenth-century poetry. In the tradition of the *Roman de la Rose* and the *OM*, myth's primary function in Machaut's work is exemplary. The mythological stories and characters are supposed to fit into patterns of parallels and equivalencies, something the *OM* indicates by the hundreds of times it used the terms "est" or "signifie" in order to align Ovid's myths with their moral or spiritual significations. These equivalencies do not quite work out in the *Navarre*. The result is skepticism with regard to the exemplary tradition.

This skepticism may be due to what Cerquiglini calls "the breakdown of the codes in the fourteenth century, undermined by war, treason, this anxiety in face of the collapse of values."[22] Thus, the skeptical attitudes toward myth one finds in the *Navarre* must be read, I believe, in the context of the opening sequence, in which Machaut paints the ravages of the plague and insists—almost in the manner of Thucydides's famous evocation of the plague—on the breakdown of the bonds that hold society together. This moment of crisis seems to vanish when Guillaume rides out into a landscape no longer ravaged by the plague. Yet, the dramatic prologue informs the whole text and points to a crisis not only in society but also a crisis of poetic subject matter and method.

The hermeneutics of myth, as we saw, became one of the central aspects of the text, and this is surely significant, for it leads to the question: Was myth exhausted or could it still play a role in the poetic activity of fourteenth-century artists? The answer to this question is ambiguous, for if the allegorical ladies win the day they do so with not quite convincing exegeses of the myths they tell, and although Guillaume begins in the *Navarre* his own exploration of myth's value with his interpretation of the Hero and Leander story, he reaps no benefits from this hermeneutic activity. Does Machaut have faith that myths can still contribute something to fourteenth-century culture? In order to answer this question we have to turn to the *Confort d'Ami*.

The *Confort* has several distinct parts,[23] offering both consolation and advice to Charles of Navarre. Significantly, the poem was written well into Charles's imprisonment, and R. Barton Palmer speculates that "Machaut was moved to write by Charles' impending release from custody."[24] Indeed, one gets the impression throughout the text that Machaut is aware that a movement to liberate Charles is afoot. Thus Charles will be better off than Boethius, whose *Consolation of Philosophy* underlies the *Confort.* Boethius was awaiting his inevitable execution while Charles's release is only a question of time. The comfort the poem provides is thus not only meant for Charles's imprisonment but also for his life in general, as shown by the last section, which could be called a "handbook for princes." The initial sections are replete with exempla: the first contains a series of tales from the Old Testament (centering on the story of Daniel), the second stories from classical mythology.

All the stories, narrated directly by the poet figure for the benefit of Charles, emphasize that hope sustained and encouraged the protagonists and that consequently Charles himself should not abandon hope. The Old Testament exempla of Susanna and the Elders, the dream of Nebuchadnezzar, and Daniel in the lion's den focus on wrongful accusations and imprisonment as well as deliverance through God's intervention. In the context of King Manasseh's idolatry, Machaut exhorts Charles to examine his conscience to determine whether he has perhaps offended God.[25] In any case, I would agree with Palmer that Machaut does not accuse Charles of any political wrongdoing (p. xlv); therefore his hope is justified from a moral perspective.

The idea of hope resurfaces in the mythological exempla, mostly in the sense that figures like Paris, Orpheus, and Hercules were inspired by hope to perform great deeds. That they ultimately failed is not something Machaut dwells on.[26] What kind of functions and values does Machaut assign to the stories from mythology in the *Confort*? Most of them are figurative representations of various situations that could have moral implications in the areas of sin, repentance, and deliverance. But there is also a poetological dimension that finds its clearest expression in the story of Proserpina, a myth whose significance in the *Confort* critics have not yet explored.[27] When reading this myth through the *OM* we will see that it provides an important commentary on the function of the poet in the context of a Boethian consolation. Machaut thus seems to answer here his own questions posed in the *Navarre* as to the usefulness of mythological exempla. After the playful use of myth in the *Navarre* we now find serious meditations on myth's moral and poetological importance.

The story of Proserpina's rape by Pluto is intercalated in the story of Orpheus. As in Ovid (*Met* 10.46) and the *OM* (10.121) the queen of the underworld is mentioned (though in these two texts she is without a name) in the context of the power of Orpheus's lyre to move the inhabitants of the nether regions. This induces Machaut to "laissier ma matire" (lay aside my theme; l. 2351) and to tell in detail Proserpina's story, based on the *OM* (5.1833–2299). There is more than a thematic connection provided by the underworld, however; for Proserpina's story, in the *OM* referred to as "ditié" (5.1861), is told by Calliope, a muse and Orpheus's mother.

Orpheus's importance to Machaut becomes especially clear in the Prologue to his works, in which he enumerates the gifts Nature has given him: "Retorique, Scens, et Musique" (V.1–2).[28] Here, David and Orpheus are the ideal musicians (echoing the pattern of the *Confort*, which moves from the Old Testament to mythology), and their function is consolation (V.69–146)—music has no business with melancholy, rather it wants to make people laugh and dance. Again, Machaut fails to mention that in the end Orpheus lost Eurydice, insisting instead on the positive power of music. Orpheus is a central figure in Machaut's poetics since Orpheus's music is likened to the poet's own activity.[29]

It is therefore especially interesting that Machaut here inserts into the Orpheus story a fable told by his mother. Jacqueline Cerquiglini traces the feminization of the poet figure occasioned by the Orpheus story in the later *Voir-Dit*.[30] For Plato, she points out, Orpheus was a feminized figure, "amolli, rien d'autre qu'une femme" (softened, nothing but a woman) in the words of Roland Barthes.[31] In the *Confort* itself Machaut insists on Orpheus's "douceur" (l. 2315) that softens stones (l. 2600). I would argue that in contrast to the *Voir-Dit*, in which the poet is feminized in various ways, the *Confort* offers a poetic mother-son pair, Calliope and Orpheus. This pairing would run counter to the myths of the motherless births, the "naissance(s) sans mère," of the *Voir-Dit*.[32] There, these mythological births were "an image of the birth of the poet's writing," which indicated that "Machaut's writing emerges solely from his desire."[33] But this self-sufficient writing does not work in the Boethian project of the *Confort*.

The mother's story, dealing with a desperate mother, Ceres, searching for her daughter—that is, for consolation—here legitimizes the poet's role in the *consolatio*. But the Proserpina story does more than illuminate the emotional perspective of the *Confort*; it also is significant on the poetological level, for right after the fable of Proserpina in the *OM* we find an important meditation on the roles of poets and philosophers.[34] Calliope here appears as the prototype of the philosopher, who is opposed to the vain poets, figured by the Pierides, the nine daughters of King Pierus, who had challenged the muses to a contest and, when defeated, were changed into magpies.[35] These poets

Si cuident philosophier
Et bien profiter en clergie,
Mes de voire philosophie
N'ont il la dois ne la fontaine
Quar lor science est vuide et vaine,
Poi savoreuse et profitable,
Combien qu'ele soit delitable. (5.2673–79)

. . .

Quar de lour sourt poesie,
Qui plus veult plaire et deliter
Qu'ele ne pense à profiter. (5.2683–85)

. . .

cestes (the Pierides) en vaine fiction
Metent lor estude et lor cures.
Cestes ont pour les creatures
Lor Creatour mis en oubli. (5.2689–92)

. . .

Cestes seult apeler ribaudes
Philozophie apertement,
Se li bons Boeces ne ment. (5.2703–5)

They believe they are philosophizing and doing good learned work (*clergie*), but they are not in possession of the fountain of true philosophy, for their learning is empty and vain, not pleasing or profitable, however delectable it may be. . . . For from their [fountain] gushes poetry that wants to please and delight more than it wants to profit. . . . They (the Pierides) devote their study and attention to vain fictions. They have, for the sake of the created beings, forgotten their Creator. . . . Philosophy openly called them ribald, if the good Boethius does not lie.

In a striking reversal of Boethius, who had condemned the muses,[36] the *OM* poet sets up a dichotomy between philosophers and poets, figured by the muses and the Pierides, respectively. But since the philosophers are aligned with the muses, we have to assume that they also produce poetic works, which are, however, not vain fictions, as are the products of the Pierides, but serious works that honor the Creator and not his creatures.[37]

As we just saw, the name of Boethius appears in the section of the *OM* that allegorizes Calliope's reciting of the Proserpina story. Since Machaut used the *OM* as a source for his own version of the fable,[38] we can assume that he realized the significance of this passage for his own work, which relies so clearly on a Boethian project of consolation. The passage provides an argument for serious poetry growing out of mythological fables, for if the Pierides are condemned by the *OM* poet, the muses—just as much a part of the pagan pantheon—are valorized.

In an earlier section of the *Confort* Machaut articulates the threat of idolatry and the making of images through the myth of Pygmalion, significantly the first mention of myth in the *Confort*:

Si ressamble Pymalion
En meurs et en condition,
Qui fist l'image et tant l'ama
Qu'amie et dame la clama. (ll. 1301–4)

And that man [who makes an image and prays to it] is just like Pygmalion in his beliefs and way of thinking, the one who made an image and then loved it so much he called it lady and beloved.

It is that same danger of idolatry that the *OM* stresses in the allegorization of Calliope, which was familiar to Machaut. But Machaut links the mythological tale to the Old Testament: like King Manasseh, who celebrated his false images and idols (ll. 1305–10), someone who makes an image and then "calls it his lord and god" (l. 1292) is nothing but an idolater. Pygmalion fits into this category, for he made an image and then called it his "amie" and "dame." Machaut echoes here the traditional mythographic interpretation of the Pygmalion myth. But it is the congruence of the lessons drawn from the Old Testament and the Ovidian myth that validates the myth as a serious teaching tool. Furthermore, the Pygmalion myth introduces idolatry or false worship as a theme, which we see later in the contrast Machaut establishes between the Pierides, as false philosophers, and the muses, as proclaimers of the true faith. Indeed, the Pierides are called idolaters in Machaut's source, the *OM* (5.2699), a term that provides the thematic link between the idolatrous artist Pygmalion and the vain, idolatrous fiction of the Pierides.

Through his use of a unified system of myth that draws on the Old Testament and Ovid as well as through his specific use of Orpheus and Calliope, then, Machaut reclaims mythology from the realm of mere fiction. Integrated into a Boethian context of philosophical poetry and its power, the mythic constructs serve to validate the role of the poet and his legitimate use of mythology.

Thus the *Confort* is not only a consolation for Charles de Navarre, thus fulfilling one of the essential functions of the *dit* as genre, but it also imparts the wisdom, largely drawn from ancient myth, Poirion sees in this genre.[39] It is a consolation of poetry, just as Boethius's is a consolation of philosophy.

Myth and Poetic Creation

In the *Dit de la Fontaine amoureuse* (ca. 1360–62), also known as *Morpheus*,[40] Machaut uses classical mythology in even more complex ways. This text serves to figure and define the fundamental dynamics of the *dit*: the circumstances of its creation, the relation between poet and patron and between poetry and love, the importance of the *Roman de la Rose* as an intertext, and the interaction between myth and diegesis. It also reflects the different types of discourses to which the *dit* as a genre is open. Indeed, each element of the *dit* uses mythology differently, and thus the *Fontaine* provides a kind of summa of the different uses of myth available to a poet like Machaut. The elements that contain different manifestations and interpretations of myths are the lyric, ekphrastic description, dream narrative, gloss, and finally, in the Lady's poem of comfort, a mythological fable plus moralization. What makes the *Fontaine* so fascinating is that it makes a coherent narrative out of these elements and thus is simultaneously, as Laurence de Looze argues, a mimesis of product as well as of process.[41]

The *Fontaine* recounts—in no fewer than seventeen mini-narratives by de Looze's count[42]—the story of the clerkly narrator who overhears one night a Lover's complaint, centering on the myth of Ceyx and Alcyone, from the neighboring room. He quickly gets his pen and transcribes what he hears. The next morning he meets his neighbor, a pale nobleman modeled on the Duc de Berry, and they stroll together into an enchanting garden that boasts a beautiful fountain as a centerpiece. The Lover tells the story of its creation: it is the amorous fountain. But neither the Lover nor the poet desire to drink from it since they have had their fill of love, defined as unhappy in the case of the Lover. Being overtired from their sleepless night, they both fall asleep and dream the same dream featuring a discourse by Venus on the Judgment of Paris, providing a gloss on the fountain. Venus then lets the Lover have a vision of his lady, who recites a comforting lyric poem. The Lover awakens with a ring from his lady on his finger. Lover and poet realize that they had the same dream—just as one hundred Roman senators once did—and the Lover departs by sea.[43]

Critics agree that this poem is more about the making of poetry than it is about love.[44] Indeed, the very opening sequence is a *mise en abyme* of the creation of love poetry: a Lover suffers and complains (but not so much that he could not think of a hundred different rhymes! [l. 1021]), a writer puts down the words.

The myth of Alcyone and Ceyx (ll. 539–698) forms a central part of the Lover's plaint. It tells of King Ceyx and his wife, Alcyone, who are separated because Ceyx must visit Apollo's temple and oracle at Claros. When he does not return, Alcyone prays to Juno to find out what happened to her husband. Juno orders Iris to send Morpheus, the god of sleep, to Alcyone. He appears to her in the shape of her dead husband, perished in a storm at sea. When the corpse washes up on Alcyone's shore, she leaps into the water to be forever united with him: whereupon both are changed into birds and enjoy halcyon days.

This mythological tale is introduced by the Lover explicitly as "autre voie" (another path) that he must look for if he wants to know how his love will eventually fare:

> Si me couvient autre voie querir,
> Se savoir vueil a quel fin puis venir
> De ceste amour que je vueil maintenir,
>   Qui tout me mine. (ll. 539–42)

I need to look for another path if I want to know what can happen to me as a result of this love that saps my strength.

These lines show the motivation for his plunge into the mythological repertory: hope for an elucidation of his predicament. He begins the fable: "Quant roy Ceïs fist Fortune perir" (when Fortune made King Ceyx perish; l. 543), omitting Ceyx's motivation for his voyage (the visit to the Clarian oracle) as well as Alcyone's premonitions (*OM* 11.3003–108) and instead focusing on Alcyone's prayer to Juno, Iris's mission to the god of sleep, Morpheus's apparition to Alcyone in the shape of the drowned Ceyx, and the final metamorphosis of the two spouses into birds (to l. 698).

The story is identified as a digression by the Lover after he finishes it: "Or me couvient venir a mon propos / Et dire ce dont a parler propos" (now I must come to my theme and speak of that which I intend to tell; ll. 699–700). The "ce" he refers to is not the spiritual significance of the *OM*,[45] but rather the power of Morpheus, one of the sons of the god of sleep (l. 652) to take on any shape he desires and to transmit messages between lovers. What the Lover extracts from the myth, then, is the belief in the power of dreams. As Kevin Brownlee observes: "The story of Ceyx and Alcyone . . . is used not only to invest dreams with authority but serves as a model for [the Lover's] prayer to the god of sleep; [the Lover] asks that Morpheus help him by revealing his love and suffering to his dame in a dream."[46] The reading the Lover gives of the myth is thus conditioned by the needs of the Lover in this specific text; it is as contextual as the readings of myth were in the *Rose*. Here, the story is meant to persuade Morpheus to act for him; the insistence on the truth of dreams points to the further dreams in the *Fontaine*, which occur after the two protagonists contemplate and interpret the fountain of love.[47]

This fountain figures in very intricate ways not only the intertextual relationship between Machaut's text and the *Roman de la Rose* but also functions as a point of intersection between the diegesis and classical myth. It also represents the text itself, appearing at the crucial midpoint of the romance and supplying the text's title.[48] The ekphrastic description of the fountain is a nexus that allows the poet to introduce new figurations of myth. Some of the mythological figures will come alive, others will remain static; some will be glossed, others will receive no explicit interpretation.

The fountain features a carved lifelike figure of Narcissus on its pillar; he seems to embody a danger, for the garden's animals do not drink from it (ll. 1301–12). The fountain itself is decorated with the story of Troy, in particular with the figures of Venus, Paris, Helen, Achilles, Hector, the Sagittaire, Troilus, and Briseide. The description of the fountain features no commentary, except that Venus is called "masquerelle" (pimp; l. 1320), a term belonging to the realm of commentary and moral judgment that casts a negative light on Paris and Helen's love.[49] The commentary proper, or the "ordenance de la fonteinne" (l. 1373), is provided by the Lover, who explains that the garden used to be the habitat of Cupid, Venus, and Jupiter (just as the garden in the first part of the *Rose* was the *same* garden where Narcissus had died) and that Venus commissioned Pygmalion to carve the fountain (ll. 1381–1400).

"Ordenance" is an important term in Machaut's critical vocabulary: it refers to ordering as well as to judgment;[50] here it defines the fountain's form and the function. All the details listed by the Lover evoke the *Roman de la Rose* and its dialectic of narcissistic courtly ideology and procreative artistic energy.[51] The artist-lover Pygmalion, come to life as the garden's master carver, created the figure of the lover Narcissus, who is not allowed to come to life. Venus functions as patron here and completes the *mise en abyme* of the text's creation. Love inspires art that again depicts art. The artist can also be lover, but a lover like Narcissus, whose love remains sterile—he is incapable of creative activity—and who cannot leave his marble pillar. The ekphrasis thus establishes the important theme of the relationship between creativity and love and at the same time opens up the text to commentary, first by the Lover and then by Venus herself. Indeed, commentary itself can be seen as a creative act here.

The ekphrasis generates these possibilities and begins a series of mythological figures that become more and more concrete. That is, the figures move from ekphrastic representations to characters that intervene directly in the narrative proper.[52] In the dream the two protagonists see Venus enter the scene not as depiction on the fountain but as a living, active figure. She is no longer the "masquerelle" but a commentator of her own and others' stories.

After the Lover's explanation of the fountain he asks the poet to produce a "lay" or a "complainte" (l. 1504) for him because the poet has not only a theoretical but also a practical knowledge of love. Machaut specifies here that it was the Lover who had "l'engin si soutil" (l. 1514); *his* subtle mind produced the poetry the poet wrote down. The poet is delighted that he can produce—with a flourish—the transcript of the Lover's plaint he had made the night before. As Brownlee observes:

> This request not only presents an integrated resume of the three major components of the narrator's identity (clerc, lover, and professional court poet), but provides a model, within the context of the story line, of the extratextual situation (the poet/patron relationship) that lies behind the dit as a whole.[53]

This is also exactly the situation figured by the fountain: at Venus's, that is, the patron's, request Pygmalion with the help of Cupid (artist-lover knowledgeable of and helped by L/love) fashioned a fountain on which love and chivalry (incarnated in the Duc de Berry) were portrayed. The equation of Narcissus with the pillar suggests that a certain amount of self-love forms the basis of any love relationship. Thus the Lover's patron provides a gloss on the fountain that in its mythological configuration mirrors the dynamics of the text's production.

The dream is the next step in the concretization of mythological figures. Now Venus appears as a three-dimensional figure and introduces the Apple of Discord, an object that provokes in the poet the desire for a gloss of the inscription on it ("Donnee soit a la plus belle" [may it be given to the most beautiful one; l. 1603]). Venus yields to his desire, presenting her subsequent words explicitly as comfort for the narrator's trouble: through her speech the darkness and torments of his heart will be lifted away from him (ll. 1613–24).

The tale she tells is that of the wedding of Peleus and Thetis, at which Orpheus, Apollo, and Pan played their instruments and became involved in a contest. King Midas preferred Pan's music to Apollo's but the judge Tmolus pronounced himself in Apollo's favor (*Met* 11.146–74).[54] When Discord, piqued at not having been invited to the wedding, throws the Apple of Discord amongst the wedding guests they are at a loss. Venus then elaborates the familiar story of the Judgment of Paris, at the time a shepherd and unaware of his royal origins. Juno and Pallas offer their bribes: riches and learning, respectively. Venus offers love in the shape of Helen.

It is interesting that Paris in choosing Helen initially believes that he opts for "l'estat de chevalerie" (the estate of chivalry; l. 2132) and not passionate love, but he will also be a "fin et loial amant" (a courtly and loyal lover; l. 2136). This double identification as knight and lover makes us see the double nature of the patron, a nature to which the poet—who early on in the poem called himself more cowardly than a rabbit (l. 92)—cannot aspire. It is important to note that Paris rejected not only riches but also "scens et . . . clergie" (understanding and learning; l. 2131). Because Venus addresses this portion of her speech to the poet, Paris's rejection of "clergie" becomes significant in light of his later unhappy fate: the implication is that love and chivalry without the support of learning can lead to disaster. Venus thus seems to validate the Duke's and the poet's partnership since together they possess all the attributes desirable for a life of learning, chivalry, and love.[55] In addition to being a moral mirror for princes, the *Fontaine* is therefore also a mirror of poetic art: both the fountain and the fable of the Judgment figure in mythological terms the principles necessary for the inspiration and creation of a *dit*.

Within the dream, Venus makes the Duke's lady appear to him and offers a lay (ll. 2207–509). Just as Venus comforted the poet through her gloss on the Apple of Discord, the lady will comfort the Lover, and she too will use mythological elements to accomplish her mission. Her use of Ovidian fable encourages us to turn to the *OM* and leads us to some further considerations on the *dit*'s poetics.

In her long poem the lady evokes a number of examples of the ingenuity of Venus, among them the story of Danae, whose father, Acrisius, tried to guard her by locking her in a tower. Jupiter circumvented this guard by appearing to her and impregnating her as a shower of gold; thus Perseus was born. The lady then draws a moral from the fable, which echoes the *OM* (4.5516–19), that is, if women do not guard themselves no one else can. This is a little mythographic set-piece (myth plus moralization) that allows Machaut to introduce one further, thoroughly traditional, use of myth. This moral interpretation makes the reader recall the *OM*, not only Book 4, from which this fable comes, but much more Book 11,[56] for it is here that we find in a cluster the two lengthiest myths of the *Fontaine*: the Judgment of Paris and the story of Alcyone and Ceyx. And, most important, as for the story of Proserpina considered above, we also find in Book 11 an explicit meditation on the interpretation of mythology and the role of poets.

In Book 11, the *OM* poet interprets the wedding of Thetis and Peleus as the creation of humankind and the promise of Christ.[57] He then proceeds to explain human sexuality—as briefly as possible and without "vilonie" (baseness)—listing some of the possible problems in conception (11.1352–88). This brings him to the fictions of the poets who make people believe that every body part had a specific god responsible for it. Echoing Augustine's critique of the pagan gods in the *City of God*, he gives a physical explanation of the gods, only to reject it out of hand as a harmful fiction that deceives people (11.1389–94). We remember that the word *fiction*—rather rare in the *OM*[58]—also appears in the passage on Boethius (5.2689) that allegorized the Proserpina fable used in the *Confort*. Since Machaut adapted most of the *Fontaine*'s fables from the *OM* he undoubtedly read and perhaps meditated on this condemnation of the pagan gods, characters ubiquitous in his own *Fontaine*.

I propose that one could see the growing concretization of myth (sealed by the reality of the ring the Lover finds on his finger after the dream of Venus [l. 2523]) as a commentary on the *OM*'s condemnation of one type of mythological fiction, namely of that which does not lead to faith.[59] Machaut breaks with the moralizing and allegorizing tradition of the *OM* and its predecessors by assigning a positive valuation to fiction as such, that is, without attached allegories. The equation of fiction, *poetrie*, and myth evoked at the opening of this chapter finds its clearest expression in the *Fontaine*, where mythology figures basic poetic principles.

The authentication of dreams, one of the most common elements of allegory, emerges from the Ceyx and Alcyone myth, where Machaut, in a shift from the Ovidian emphasis on perfect love, places the emphasis on the truth of dreams. The symbiotic relationship of poet and patron and of poetry and love is figured in Venus's commission to Pygmalion. The glossing that accompanied myths in the mythographical tradition is replaced here by Venus's narrative. The fact that narration, not moralization, functions as gloss is a clear signal that the myths of Machaut are poetic myths, that they are texts, not pretexts for allegorizations. They produce the crystallization of images that illuminate the text's poetic processes. Thus, in the *Fontaine*, myth and diegesis penetrate each other in such a way that the mythological elements provide a *mise en relief* as well as a *mise en abyme* of the basic poetic constructs of the *Fontaine*.

Myth and the Threat of the Feminine in the *Voir-Dit*

The *Livre du Voir-Dit* (Book of the true tale; 1363–65) is the work in which Machaut foregrounds most clearly the problems involved in poetic creation and in the collaboration between two poets, one male, the other female. One of the first questions asked by the work's early critics was whether the *Voir-Dit* told a true story.[60] The story is certainly unusual: it tells of a love relationship between an aged poet and an admiring young woman, Toute-Belle, who is also a poet. She makes the first move by contacting him with a poem and a flattering letter; they correspond, meet, perhaps make love, are troubled by doubts, separate, and reconcile. All the while, "their" book, the *Voir-Dit*, is being produced through the poet's assemblage of their letters to each other and the poems they send back and forth. This process is chronicled by the poet, who tells in long narrative passages of external events (travels, dangers of various kinds) as well as of the feelings that move them. In some instances they know more about each other than they possibly could were this really a "true" story.[61]

But whether Toute-Belle is a figment of the poet's imagination or a real woman named Peronne d'Armentières is not really relevant to an understanding of the *Voir-Dit*'s poetics. At its heart lies the idea of male-female collaboration not only in love but also in the creation of poetry and ultimately of the book. One knows that Machaut was the first medieval author to be preoccupied with the production or "ordenance" of the manuscripts containing his works.[62] This preoccupation is thematized in many instances in the *Voir-Dit*, notably in the passage in which the poet (whose persona we will refer to as Guillaume) speaks in a letter of the "livre ou je met toutes mes choses" (the book where I assemble all my things). Thus, despite Toute-Belle's collaboration it is the "je" of Guillaume who assembles and finally intends to control the "things" or texts. Throughout the text there is a struggle not only between Guillaume's identities as poet and lover, but also between his male and female sides.[63] I will argue that there is a further struggle: that between male and female poet figures and their creativity, represented by Guillaume and Toute-Belle; this struggle is not explicitly articulated but is figured by mythological women who, in one way or another, threaten male autonomy and creativity.

Brownlee has demonstrated that the more inadequate the lover becomes, the more competent is the poet. Guillaume's self-representation as lover shows him as an elderly, weak, cowardly, unattractive, one-eyed, non-noble clerk. Toute-Belle by contrast is young (around fifteen years old), beautiful, and noble. The only thing that connects them is poetry, and it is by means of a poem joined to an invitation brought by a messenger that Toute-Belle first approaches Guillaume. At that moment he finds himself in a particularly sterile period in which he has simply run out of subjects to write about:

Si que parfondement pensoie
Par quel maniere je feroie
Aucune chose de nouvel,
Pour tenir mon cuer en revel.
Mais je n'avoie vraiement
Sens, matiere ne sentement
De quoy commencier le scéusse,
Ne dont parfiner le péusse. (pp. 2–3)

I was thinking deeply about how I could make something new in order to keep my heart merry. But I truly had neither sense,[64] nor subject matter, nor emotion with which I could start something new or finish it.

Toute-Belle's messenger arrives therefore at the perfect moment. It is interesting to note that one of her attractions is that, besides beauty, youth, and so on, she possesses "sens" (p. 4), exactly what Guillaume lacks at the moment. The poet reads her rondelet with pleasure and evaluates it immediately:

Si me bailla un rondelet
Qui n'estoit pas rudes ne let,
Et en tout cas si bien servoit,
Que nulz amender n'i savoit. (p. 6)

He handed me a rondelet that was neither unpolished nor unsightly; in any case, it was so well made that nobody could have improved on it.

Is this unqualified praise? The accumulation of negations makes us wonder. Did he expect a woman's poem to be "rude" and "let" and to be in need of improvement and is astonished that it is not? His enthusiasm for his new correspondent seems to belie this hypothesis. But the term "amender" will recur several times in the *Voir-Dit* and will help to define the relationship—and tension—between the male and female poets, or perhaps between the male and female sides of the poet.

For Machaut, the androgynous nature of the poet is incarnated in the figure of Orpheus. In the passage by Roland Barthes quoted above Orpheus is even called "nothing but a woman."[65] The sweetness and softness of poetry become apparent in Orpheus's singing, yet he also perished because of women. He is thus both feminized and a victim of feminine force. In Machaut's frequent use of the Orpheus myth, beginning with his Prologue, this tension is laid bare.[66] Yet, Orpheus is absent from the *Voir-Dit*; that is, there is no explicit mention of him, yet an orphic problematic of gender roles persists. And, as we will see, there is in fact a "replacement" for Orpheus in the shape of the female singer Canens.

In the *Voir-Dit* the myth of Pygmalion, rather than Orpheus, dominates; it appears several times, both implicitly and explicitly. The relationship between female and male roles in artistic creation figured by this myth is that of the male as creator fashioning an ideal female object. But in the course of the *Voir-Dit* this myth will be pitted against other mythical stories, such as the ones of Circe and Medusa, that dramatically highlight the power of women.

The Pygmalion myth comes to the fore when Guillaume asks the lady for an "image," which she eventually sends to him.[67] He immediately clothes it, ornaments it, compares it to Venus, and adores it (p. 63). The echoes of the Pygmalion story are unmistakable here. Pygmalion is explicitly mentioned three times: by the narrator, declaring that not even Pygmalion's image could tempt him away from his lady's love (p. 166); in a poem of Toute-Belle (reiterating her love for Guillaume) in which Pygmalion is mistakenly referred to as the father of Adonis (pp. 246–47);

and in a ballade in response to a poem by a certain Thibaut Paien.[68] Guillaume again evokes Pygmalion's image and states that its beauty is inferior to his lady's (p. 275). Thus it is with Pygmalion rather than Orpheus that the poet identifies. Initially he sees himself as the male artist that brings to life the female image.

This myth seems to contradict the active involvement in (literary) creation and the poet's psychological state accorded to Toute-Belle. As we saw, it is she who frees the poet initially from his state of artistic sterility, and further on in the text, this time in person during their second meeting, she does it again:

> Et je, forment la resgardoie,
> Mais nulle chose ne disoie:
> Lors prist doucement à chanter
> . . .
> Je li respondi, sans demeure (p. 92)

And I looked at her intently but said nothing. Then she began to sing sweetly [the first two lines of a rondel]. I answered her at once.

Again it is the lady who prompts the mute poet into composing a rondel. The lady has not only the power to activate the poet's creativity, she even rejuvenates him:

> Si que je puis comparison
> Faire, sanz nulle mesprison,
> De Hebe et de ma dame gente. (pp. 209–10)

I can compare without fault my lady to Hebe.

Hebe, Juno's daughter and Hercules's wife in heaven, rejuvenated Hercules's half brother Iolaus. The reference to Hebe thus evokes rejuvenation. Iolaus is mistakenly identified by Guillaume as the son of Callirhoe: "filz fu Carliore le sage" (p. 210). Callirhoe's sons, however, underwent the opposite process: they were aged prematurely so that they could avenge their father's death. Did Guillaume misread the *OM* here?[69] Rather, Machaut proves to be a creative reader, for the idea of rejuvenation is subtly undermined by mixing the myth of Iolaus with the myth of Callirhoe's sons: the sudden aging contradicts the rejuvenation and thus, despite the poet's protestations, the lady's powers are put into question.[70] The explicit and implicit—or perhaps conscious and unconscious—levels of the text seem to compete here to create the tension that comes to characterize Guillaume's relationship to his lady.[71]

It is right after this passage, signaling doubts concerning the lady, that the poet has a disquieting dream in which the lady's image turns away from him and is suddenly dressed in green (p. 213), here a sign of inconstancy.[72] Still in the dream the poet turns to the "Roi qui ne ment" (the king who does not lie), the name of a popular game often encountered in medieval literature. This king (the dauphin, Charles of Normandy), who, by the rules of the game is obliged to tell the truth, counsels Guillaume, who addresses a lengthy question to him that encompasses remarks on politics, the dire situation in France, correct behavior for kings, and other subjects, interwoven with his problems in love (pp. 215–24). The king, pleased but also somewhat exasperated by this long discourse, thanks Guillaume and begins his own lesson. "Don't believe in dreams and don't be frightened by the mutation of the color in your lady's dress," he advises (pp. 225–26). The king here attacks one of the underpinnings of medieval allegory, the dream and its truthfulness, and then turns to the idea of metamorphosis, which he first illustrates by the example of Lot's wife and second by Polydectes, who doubted Perseus's exploits and was changed into stone through the gaze of the Medusa's head.[73]

Both examples apply to Guillaume, although he did not turn around for a forbidden gaze as did Lot's wife (or Orpheus, for that matter), but rather doubted the veracity of his lady, as Polydectes doubted that of Perseus. As Machaut would have known from a long mythographic tradition, the gaze of the Medusa constitutes a profound threat—that of the feminine eros, which petrifies men.[74] Polydectes, the doubter, here is Medusa's victim and is transformed into stone ("en pierre"; p. 227). Other victims are described in Ovid as "a marble statue" (*Met* 5.183) and as simulacra, or images (5.210); in the *OM*, the terms used for transformed men are "pierre dure" (5.1592) or "dur marbre" (5.595), in each case suggesting not only petrification but the appearance of a statue, of a work of art. In the same way, then, Guillaume is endangered. While earlier he saw himself as Pygmalion, bringing a marble statue to life, he now may imitate Polydectes's fate and be petrified himself. Petrification would signal the end of artistic creativity, the drying up of the stream of poetic output.

In the realm of love, the Medusa represents the lady whose erotic desires have frightened him into a kind of petrification. When he goes on a pilgrimage with Toute-Belle and her cousin Guillemette, perhaps Guillaume's feminine alter ego,[75] the three share a bed, which leads Guilaume to exclaim "On m'efforce" (I am being forced [suggesting a rape?];

p. 146). But, most important, he refers to his attitude in bed as "Car j'estoie comme une souche / Delez ma dame en ceste couche" (I was lying like a tree stump next to my lady in this bed; p. 147). Transformation into a tree is the danger the king mentions along with petrification:

Aussi li Dieu les gens muoient
En quelque forme qu'il voloient,
Et les Déesses ensement:
Car on véoit appertement
Les uns mués en forme d'arbre,
Les autres en pierre de marbre. (p. 227)

Thus the gods transformed people into whatever form they pleased, and so did the goddesses. For one saw clearly some people transformed into trees, others into blocks of marble.

Thus, through the gods'—or the lady's—power a man can become an inanimate object. The king closes this section of his speech by pointing out to Guillaume that these are the really frightening mutations, while the changing of the color of a dress—the event that scared him into seeking advice from the king in the first place—is nothing compared to these (p. 228).

By articulating the threat of the Medusa so clearly, the king undermines the ostensibly comforting meaning of his own discourse. For Guillaume had already been metamorphosed into a tree once through the lady's erotic presence; further metamorphosis—petrification—would thus not be impossible. Although the king ends on a positive note (after listing many sages of antiquity who cannot help Guillaume, he simply tells him to go on loving [p. 232]), the threat has been articulated.

Guillaume is astonished by this dream and decides to look once more at the lady's image. Now, she smiles at him, and he feels reassured; he also is convinced—following the king's advice—of the lies contained in his earlier dream (p. 233). For the time being, then, the lovers' situation has been stabilized, but doubts have been planted.

Guillaume then sends Toute-Belle two letters of reproach, which cause her to experience Ovidian love symptoms (p. 242), and she promptly composes a long lay, for the first time using Ovidian themes. This twelve-strophe poem evokes classical lovers, such as Jason and Medea, Byblis and Caunus, and Helen and Paris, who all loved less than she does (Strophe 2, p. 243). All of these lovers were doomed in one way or another, of course, through infanticide and murder, incestuous love, and the murderous Trojan war. If her love exceeds that of these lovers, Guillaume has indeed something to look forward to. She then compares herself to Ulysses, whose courtly language won him the love of goddesses, but her less skillful words, she claims, can not convince Guillaume of her love (Strophe 4, p. 244). She finally tells the stories of Cephalus and Procris (urging Guillaume to love her again before it is too late) and of Venus and Adonis, who perished because he did not follow Venus's advice against hunting wild boars (pp. 246–47). "Or use dont de mon conseil" (take my advice; p. 247), she implores Guillaume, and love me.

This complaint is by far the lady's longest poem and an Ovidian tour de force. She assumes all kinds of Ovidian roles: that of female lovers, such as Medea and Helen; that of a competitor with Ulysses; that of Procris, mistakenly killed by her husband; and finally that of Venus, giving good but unheeded advice to Adonis. Thus, while earlier in the text, Toute-Belle occupies the place of Pygmalion's statue, brought to life through the superior power of the poet's skill, she now usurps not only the place of Ovidian lovers but of Ovidian poetry. And through the length and elaborateness of her poem, she begins to displace the poet himself. The threat of the lady is no longer the threat of the feminine eros but also of feminine writing. After this episode the tension between masculine and feminine poetic creativity, which has driven the *Voir-Dit* up to that point, will seemingly be resolved in favor of the male poet. For after the long Ovidian lay, the lady composes only two more poems: one right afterward, stressing Guillaume's "seigneurie" over her (p. 251), and one, significantly incomplete, much later on (p. 344).

The most important event that intervenes between the lady's Ovidian complaint and that last incomplete poem is the speech of Guillaume's secretary. Its ostensible function is to dramatize the dangers of the inclement weather, but what it really does is to reiterate the threat of feminine narration and poetic creativity. The connection between the weather and mythological figures may indicate that the secretary has read authors like Fulgentius (whose work indeed appears later as Guillaume's reading matter), who offered physical explanations of the pagan gods. But in his skillful linking of *dangerous* weather and female figures, the secretary shows himself above all to be a creative reader of Ovid. For from the vast text of the *Metamorphoses* the secretary assembles fables into a new narrative program that centers on threatening women. Once the threats have been articulated, the balance of power in the text shifts: in the wake of the secretary's speech, the lady is displaced from the literary production of the *Voir-Dit*.

As Kevin Brownlee has shown, in the course of the *Voir-Dit* Guillaume's identity as lover is gradually replaced by that of "clerc/poete."[76] Jacqueline Cerquiglini, in turn, has demonstrated that classical mythology predominates in the second half of the *Voir-Dit*, where periods of disillusionment alternate with provisional reconciliations.[77] What she calls "the space of unlove" is largely defined through mythological fables.[78] As we have seen, this "unlove" is caused not only by the lady's supposed faithless behavior but also by the increasing threat she poses to the dominance of the male poet's art.[79] After the lovers' climactic meeting—where Venus descends in a cloud and veils their lovemaking (p. 156)—the lady's displacement in the production of the *Voir-Dit* begins to parallel that in Guillaume's heart.

Again, mythology intervenes at a critical juncture in the text. As Guillaume contemplates a long-delayed meeting with Toute-Belle, his secretary tries to persuade him not to go by pointing to the dangers of the foul weather. Not even Circe could protect him, the secretary claims (p. 289), nor could Polyphemus's violence compare with weather that is even more violent than the giant himself. But it is not really the weather he depicts as threats to Guillaume but rather two female figures, Circe and Galatea, an enchantress and a nymph who is also a virtuoso narrator. In each case Ovid tells the story of an amorous triangle where jealousy leads to violent action.

First, the secretary tells at great length the story of Circe and Picus. Picus, son of Saturn and king of Latium, is in love with and wedded to Canens, whose name means "chant en grégois" (song in Greek; p. 288). She has the ability to make rocks move, the trees bow down, and make wild animals stop in their tracks (pp. 288–89). But Circe is in love with Picus and pursues him relentlessly and unsuccessfully. The Ovidian Circe, as Charles Segal has shown, embodies, more than the Homeric or Virgilian Circe, "the malignant and wildly destructive side of female passion." It is this fury of a spurned woman, the "goddess of passion and metamorphosis," who takes revenge for his rejection of her and changes him into a woodpecker.[80] To commemorate this metamorphosis a "snow-white marble statue of a young man with a woodpecker on his head" is carved.[81]

Picus and Canens represent a male-female unit: the male part of this unit is the lover, the female part is clearly portrayed as another Orpheus. As we saw earlier Machaut identifies himself throughout his oeuvre with the androgynous Orpheus figure; in the *Voir-Dit* he also works hard at carving out for himself the role of lover. Circe poses a threat to this lover-poet unit through her own magic singing, her "enchantement" (p. 289). After Circe's vengeful transformation of Picus, Canens, bereft of her husband, the male part of the unit, is left to mourn and finally to vanish into thin air. Her husband, in turn, now is both a woodpecker, a bird whose singing or poetry is of the most unmelodious kind, and a statue, as petrified as the victims of the Medusa's gaze had been.

The secretary's choice of this myth spells out a threat to Guillaume's double identity as lover and poet. Circe, the enchantress, allegorized as the whore of the Apocalypse in the *OM* (14.2567–71), destroys not only Orphic poetry, in the shape of Canens, but also her lover, who, in a cruel reversal of the Pygmalion story, ends up as a marble statue and the most unpoetic of birds. In the *OM*, Picus is not only a Christ figure but is also allegorized as prophets and apostles whose preaching stands for true discourse (14.2957–66), a *voir-dit*.[82]

The Picus and Canens myth thus figures the two dangers Guillaume is exposed to in his relationship with Toute-Belle: petrification through the superior force of the feminine eros and magic and the domination of "enchantement" over the kind of poetry identified with Orpheus. His disenchantment with love allows this danger to surface. This danger, then, more than the weather is the essence of this part of the secretary's speech, whose purpose, after all, is to keep Guillaume from visiting Toute-Belle.

The secretary adduces another story that is supposed to illustrate the violent weather and the danger posed by highway robbers (p. 295): that of Polyphemus, the one-eyed giant in love with Galatea, who in turn is in love with Acis.[83] When Galatea is unmoved by Polyphemus's song, the giant kills Acis out of spite and jealousy. Acis is then transformed into a river of the same name.

There are undeniable parallels between Polyphemus and Guillaume.[84] Like Guillaume he is ugly and one-eyed (letter 13: "vostre borgne vallet" [your one-eyed servant; p. 118]), and he sings to his beloved, completely in her thrall. The beloved, however, loves elsewhere. The secretary's speech, we remember, falls into a period of doubt and suspicion, which are only deepened right afterward with the arrival of the first of several "losengiers," or gossip mongers, who brings news of the lady's supposed infidelity (pp. 303–6). The triangle Polyphemus-Galatea-Acis thus prefigures the scenario described by the "losengiers."

But there are more parallels between Toute-Belle and Galatea. For in Ovid it is Galatea who tells the story; it is she who ridicules and vilifies the poet-lover Polyphemus. Thus the doubts about the lady's fidelity are compounded by doubts about her true views about Guillaume and the sincerity of her discourse. Is she laughing behind his back, as are so many characters in the *Voir-Dit* that it becomes a veritable leitmotiv? Does she in truth depict him as another Polyphemus?

Although these doubts are at one point seemingly laid to rest, they stay with Guillaume. The clearest proof, as we will see, is the last long mythological narrative, that of the raven and the crow, uttered by the lady's image in a dream. But one further element surfaces in the Polyphemus story: that of violence. For if Ovid's scenario were to be played out (Polyphemus kills Acis), Guillaume would take revenge on Toute-Belle's unnamed supposed lover. This type of violence would be completely out of character for Guillaume, who portrays himself as a sickly and cowardly elderly man. Like a dream, this myth may therefore signal also a kind of wish fulfillment: before being vanquished by Ulysses, Polyphemus at least took revenge for what he considered Galatea's betrayal. Guillaume is condemned to listen to the "losengiers," but the imaginary scenario of Acis's murder has already been played out.

In reaction to further reports of the lady's faithlessness Guillaume hides her "ymage" in a coffer (pp. 306–8). Soon he receives a long letter from Toute-Belle in which she complains that his long silence makes her suffer more than Medea did for Jason; she also affirms her faithfulness to him (letter 40, pp. 310–12). Guillaume answers her but does not mention the rumors the "losengiers" have transmitted to him; nor does he speak of his unhappiness. Following this, Guillaume has a dream in which the image offers the last long Ovidian narrative of the *Voir-Dit* (pp. 315–30). The image tells the fable of how the raven turned black.[85]

Eager to tell Apollo of the infidelity of his beloved Coronis, the raven is stopped by the crow, who warns him against being a tale teller. He himself learned that lesson the hard way by reporting to Pallas that Erichthonius, Vulcan's son born from the earth without a mother (engendered from his seed spilled because of his lust for Pallas), had been discovered by the daughters of Cecrops. They revealed the secret of his double nature: he had the feet of a serpent. But the raven is undeterred, files his report with Apollo, who rashly kills Coronis and immediately regrets it. He manages to save their unborn child, Aesculapius, by cutting him out of the dying mother and giving him to a centaur to raise. Aesculapius, "qui sceust plus de surgerie / Que nul homme qui fust en vie" (who knew more of surgery than any other man alive; p. 328), knows how to revive the dead "si com je le truis en mon livre" (as I found it in my book), Guillaume adds.[86] This reference to a written source emphasizes again that the characters in the *Voir-Dit* are readers of myth, that they have at their disposal a literary storehouse of fables from which they choose, interpret, and rewrite.

That this reading can be problematic is shown through the fact that the fable of the crow and the raven is not the most appropriate example the image could have chosen (for both birds speak the truth); but this is of course its significance.[87] The example is meant to plant more doubts into Guillaume's—and the reader's—mind, but it does so in a form that is twice removed from the diegesis: the image speaks in a dream.

That the image should displace Toute-Belle becomes meaningful in the context of the Pygmalion myth, which pervades the *Voir-Dit*. Because of the use of this myth the image can be seen as figuring Pygmalion's statue. The ambiguity of whether the image is a painting or a sculpture (it seems to be both at different times in the narrative)[88] adds to its multivalence. It comes from the lady, it represents her, but it also is the artist's creation and thus finally Guillaume's own. Thus the "truth" spoken in the dream is finally Guillaume's own truth about Toute-Belle's behavior. Any reconciliation that follows upon this moment of truth can only be incomplete.

Two important elements in the fable that are not absolutely necessary for the idea that gossip, whether true or false, can lead to disaster are the births without a mother. Their elaboration is thus especially significant. As Jacqueline Cerquiglini has demonstrated, Erichthonius and Aesculapius stand for the kind of writing that can do without "mothers," without the female presence.[89] Having loved is inspiration enough for the poet; the woman can now disappear.

This writing out of the mother parallels what is happening in the course of the *Voir-Dit*. Toute-Belle's poetic contribution to the creation of the text is more and more reduced: in fact, after her long letter complaining of Guillaume's silence, she contributes exactly one poem, and that is incomplete (p. 344). Her lyric words are thus cut in midsentence, as it were. This gradual suppression of the female poetic voice progresses as the erotic threats (figured in the myths of Circe and Medusa) posed by the lady are articulated by the two male "mentors." The extreme productivity that earlier resulted in such compositions as a series of paired ballads has come to an end. After the king's evocation of the Medusa, the lady is accorded one Ovidian complaint (whose length and complexity point to the growing virtuosity of the lady), and one ballade; after the secretary's narration of the fables of Circe and of Polyphemus, the lady's lyric voice peters out.

Significantly, at the end of its discourse the image itself articulates the threat of metamorphosis into stasis and debasement:

> Plust à Dieu que ceuls qui ce font,
> Et qui amour ainsi deffont
> Par faus & par mauvais rappors,
> Devenissent sauvages pors;
> Ou qu'il fussent muez en arbre,
> Ou en noire pierre de marbre. (pp. 329–30)

May it please God that those who do this, those who destroy love through false and evil reports, become wild pigs; or be changed into trees or into black marble stone.

The choice of metamorphic possibilities is telling here for it repeats exactly those metamorphoses that have already "occurred" in the *Voir-Dit*: Circe's victims were changed into pigs, as the *OM* tells "et pors devindrent / Li compaignon" (and [Ulysses's] companions became pigs; 14.2475–76); Guillaume himself became a "souche," a tree stump, in Toute-Belle's erotic presence; and the victims of Medusa's gaze became stony marble statues.

In the face of these threats the lover turns away from the lady and to his clerkly preoccupations: he reads Fulgentius and Livy, describes and glosses the image of Fortune, and is finally persuaded by the lady's confessor that she is an innocent victim of his suspicions. But the poetic collaboration does not resume.

The turning away from the poetic use of myth to a more clerkly treatment of mythological subject matter may signal that at the end of the *Voir-Dit* the aged character of Guillaume opts for philosophy over poetry, a move perhaps adumbrated by the conflict between the muses and the Pierides that surfaced intertextually in the *Confort d'Ami*. The metamorphic has become associated with threatening female erotic figures; what remains are Livy, Fulgentius, and glosses: a safe haven in which the subversive elements of myth can be contained and defused.

But was Guillaume right in feeling so threatened by the lady that he suppressed her lyric contributions to safeguard the male poetic presence of the *Voir-Dit*, that he replaced his identity as lover more and more by that of clerk? One wonders, for in the end it is Toute-Belle who holds on to the *Voir-Dit*:

> Je ne vous envoie pas vostre livre, pour ce que j'ay trop grant doubte qu'il ne fust perdus. Et aussi, c'est tout mon esbatement & que je y vueil aucunes choses amender. (Letter 46, p. 369)

> I am not sending you your book because I fear that it might get lost [on the way]. And also because it is all my joy and because I want to amend [improve, add] certain things in it.[90]

Toute-Belle thus retains the final authority and confirms that the threat of the female poetic voice (and female eros) was only too real.

The innovative poetics of the *Voir-Dit*, the collaboration of lover and beloved, of male and female poet, is a poetics of harmony and complementarity only on the surface. In many different ways male and female identities are exchanged, blurred, and finally opposed. The harmonious surface of a project that defies the traditional gender separation in the production of lyric poetry is shattered by the mythological intertexts. It is here, not in Guillaume's conscious mind, that the threat of the feminine is articulated; and when Toute-Belle retains control of the *Voir-Dit* these threats have come true on the level of the diegesis. Guillaume's power, the power of male discourse, has been undermined, and despite his efforts at silencing the lady's lyric voice, it is she who finally has the last laugh, the laugh of the Medusa.[91]

For Machaut, mythology was not an ornament or a filler as some early critics believed, but rather a means to illuminate his characters' psychology and his plots, to tell a story "selon un autre mode de langage," as Jacqueline Cerquiglini puts it.[92] But it was also a means to articulate his poetics by figuring, through the different fables, the underlying problems of the hermeneutics of myth, of the role of the poet (and of the patron), of the competition between male and female poetic voices and of the creation of the book. The equation of myth and poetry is thus really one of myth and poetics and finds its most profound expression in Machaut's *dits.*

Postlude on Jean Froissart

Froissart, writing a generation after Machaut, continued and expanded the creative use of myth. His major *dits* feature not only the familiar Ovidian myths but also myths of his own making, a kind of bricolage of mythological elements, or "mythemes."[93] These new myths mirror not only the lover's psychology but more often the poetics underlying the text itself. A brief consideration of the *Prison amoureuse* (1372–73) will establish the paradigm of his methods of reading myths and constructing new ones.[94]

The *Prison amoureuse* chronicles the correspondence between a poet, who calls himself Flos, and a nobleman, who uses the pseudonym Rose (representing Wenceslas of Brabant), whose interventions will move the production of the text forward and whose specific requests for mythological fables and glosses will shape the *Prison.*[95] The dynamics of the text thus recall both the *Fontaine amoureuse* and the *Voir-Dit.* Critics seem to agree that "the poetic process is most insistently foregrounded" and that the *Prison* tells the story of its own writing.[96] A crucial element for determining how this poetic process works is the pseudomyth of Pynoteus and Neptisphele invented by Flos at Rose's suggestion.

In Letter 5 Rose asks Flos for

> un petit dittié amoureus, qui se traitast sus aucune nouvelle matere qu'on n'aroit onques veü ne oÿ mise en rime, tele com, par figure, fu jadis de Piramus et de Tysbé, ou de Eneas et de Dido, ou de Tristan et de Yseus, car j'en ai esté requis par pluseurs fois en lieu ou bien me fuissent venu en point, se j'en euïsse esté pourveüs, et feront encor, se je les ai. (p. 82)

> a little amorous tale dealing with some new subject matter that one has not ever seen or put into rhyme before, as figured[97] for example by the tales of Pyramus and Thisbe, or of Aeneas and Dido, or of Tristan and Yseut, for I have been asked several times for something like this at occasions where they would have come in handy, had I had them then, and they will still [prove useful] once I have them.

The task that Rose sets for Flos is thus clearly defined: he wants something new that recalls something traditional (he even gives Flos various examples of the kind of fables he likes), and the tales are to be used for a specific purpose at a given time and place. Flos, of course, obliges with a pseudo-Ovidian myth made to order; he claims to have found it in a "glose" (l. 1295), which contains, as Ovid testifies, the story of Pynoteus (ll. 1296–98).

As many scholars have noticed, the myth itself contains elements of the fables of Pyramus and Thisbe (the two lovers, kept apart, eventually meet at a secluded spot, and Neptisphele is devoured by a lion), of Orpheus (Pynoteus contemplates a visit to Hades, where he would find the same characters that Orpheus had charmed there), of Pygmalion (he fashions a statue of his beloved from soil and water [not stone or silver or wood], and it is brought to life by a prayer to Apollo), and even echoes of Narcissus and Actaeon (his love for hunting and secluded landscapes; ll. 1316–18), and Aesculapius (resuscitation of the dead). The fable is quite long (ll. 1316–988), and an important part of it is Pynoteus's lengthy prayer to Apollo (ll. 1744–918), which contains the story of Phaeton's foolish ride and fall. Flos thus manages to invent a fable that contains something old, something new, and something borrowed from Ovid, or as he puts it: "Car je l'ai fet a mon pooir de la nouvelle matere que j'aie trouvé entre les anchiiennes hystores" (For I have fashioned it of the new subject matter that I found amongst the old stories; p. 103).

In addition to the various figurations of the artist (Pygmalion, Orpheus) that Pynoteus surpasses we have the important address to Apollo, who replaces the Venus of the Pygmalion myth: thus an appeal to love is replaced by an appeal to poetry.[98] The consequences of this change of patron are multiple, as Brownlee observes: "This substitution presents in terms of Ovidian mythology the socioeconomic status of Froissart as writer. For the courtly professional poets at the end of the fourteenth century . . . loving and writing on the subject of love have become two completely separate practices."[99]

Pynoteus starts out like Pyramus, but unlike the despairing lover he turns into an artist, refashioning his beloved and animating her with the help of poetry. Thus, the fictive progression undergone by the professional poet from lover to writer about love is effectively figured in the Pynoteus myth. Pynoteus's prayer to Apollo further highlights the interdependence of poet and patron: Phaeton without Phebus, or the poet without patron, embarks on a dangerous ride; but without the poet and the risks he takes, the patron would remain in obscurity.[100]

In the *Prison*, myth is seen as something flexible or malleable, almost like a kind of modular system that can be put together for various purposes. Certainly Flos's new mythological fable surpasses Rose's expectations since he used Rose's suggestion of the Pyramus and Thisbe fable as nothing but a springboard for an elaborate myth of love and the resuscitating powers of art. Nevertheless, Flos has to wait close to ten months for a reply to his efforts.

When Rose finally replies (letter 7, pp. 112–13) we learn that the little amorous treatise, as he calls it, pleased him immensely because of its new subject matter and that he had a dream that can undoubtedly be blamed ("encouper"; p. 113) on Flos's fable. This dream features an allegorical battle between the various forces of love (with Rose as a prisoner in the prison of love), which in turn figures, as Anthime Fourrier and Claude Thiry have shown, the real battle of Baesweiler on August 22, 1371.[101]

One can see this dream as a commentary on the myth of Pynoteus. The fact that Flos referred to its "mystere" (l. 1997) indicated that some kind of interpretation or commentary was called for. However, here it is not a dream that needs to be glossed but rather a dream functioning *as* gloss, thus reversing the general pattern of dream allegory.

Rose now asks Flos for an explanation of his dream (letter 8, p. 149). The dream as gloss allows for the introduction of a new set of equivalencies in which the pseudo-Ovidian myth is explained in terms of love psychology. That is, Pynoteus stands for Desir, Neptisphele for Plaisance, the lion for Envie, Phebus or Apollo for the god of love, and Jupiter for Franchise.[102] When, as here, one mythological character (Phebus) is glossed as another (the god of love), the different levels of interpretation become blurred. In letter 10 (p. 163) Rose thanks Flos for his interpretations and now considers both the explanation of his dream *and* the *exposicion* (interpretation) of the Pynoteus story as a gloss on his dream. Rose also asks Flos to begin assembling all his poems into a book, which Flos does instantly, baptizing the text *Prison amoureuse* (ll. 3760–819).

But there still are not enough glosses. Rose's lady complains that Flos has neglected to gloss Pynoteus's prayer to Phebus. In letter 12 (pp. 170–75) Flos obliges and glosses the prayer in terms of allegorical figures denoting love psychology: Mercury is Douls Regars, and so forth. A return to reasonable love is finally the meaning of Phaeton's fall (p. 175)—an interpretation that contradicts the preceding mythographic tradition of seeing in Phaeton's ride presumption and pride.[103] This is the last communication between the two friends, and all that remains to be done is to put all the different texts into a coffer provided by Rose; the *Prison* ends with the poem in the hands of a messenger en route to Rose.[104]

The *Prison* thus features a conscious act of mythological bricolage as did other *dits* by Froissart. In the *Paradis d'amour* (1361–62) Froissart had already invented a new mythological personage, Enclinpostair, the son of Morpheus. In the *Espinette amoureuse* (1370), he introduced Papyrus and Idoree, whose experience with mirrors authenticates the lover's own experience. Finally, in the *Joli buisson de jonece* (1373) Froissart invented the myth of Ydrophus and Neptiphoras (ll. 2015–92) to show that eternal youth is an illusion produced by love, as is also proved by the fable of Telephus and Orphane; in the same text the new figures of Cepheus and Hero appear in a rather funny version of "death for love" (Cepheus falls off a laurel tree and dies after a prolonged and futile wait for his beloved), and the myth of Narcissus and Echo is rewritten so that Narcissus continues to love the prematurely dead Echo.[105]

Froissart does not so much present the existing Ovidian fables as inadequate as celebrate the freedom of inventing new "pagan" myths on the model of existing ones. These new myths are tailor-made, as it were, for each text. They stress the power of mirrors, eternal youth, and other themes. At the same time, Froissart refuses to use traditional mythographic exegeses and, in the *Prison*, reshapes the relation between myth, dream, and allegory by using one as gloss for the other(s), effectively dissolving existing limits between text and gloss. Froissart thus added a new dimension to the notion of the fourteenth-century poet by liberating himself not only from the Ovidian text (while remaining in the Ovidian tradition) but also from the interpretive tradition of moralization and gloss. The myths are his own; they define his own poems and figure his own poetic processes. With Froissart the medieval appropriation of myth in the form of poetry reached a new level.

Chapter 5

Christine de Pizan: Mythographer and Mythmaker

The question whether Christine de Pizan was a mythographer or mythmaker goes to the very heart of her conception of herself as a woman and as a writer. Mythography is considered a thoroughly "male" genre, since before Christine de Pizan it was employed exclusively by male clerics. Susan Schibanoff claims that "in the *Othéa*, Christine schooled herself in the art of reading as a man or, more accurately, a patristic exegete."[1] Christine indeed often uses traditional molds for her writing but without always subscribing to their ideology. In the *Othéa* she draws on mythographic models, but, as we will see, she appropriates these models and creates her own authority.

Mythmaking is a less well defined activity than mythography. The term can suggest anything from a creative rewriting of mythological material to a radical shifting of the ideological bases of society. In every case, mythmaking is an original enterprise that can range from the very personal to the overtly political. Alicia Ostriker sees a particular potential for the articulation of feminist ideas in "revisionist mythmaking," the appropriation of myths for "altered ends," which would in fact combine the personal and the political.[2] Christine draws on, appropriates, and renews a wide range of ancient myths, inscribing new meanings, both personal and political, into many, if not all, of them. Her works thus provide fascinating examples of late medieval mythographic and mythmaking activities.

Schibanoff suggests that there is an evolution in Christine's work from "male reader" to "female reader," the latter exemplified by Christine's narrator in *Le Livre de la cité des dames*. When we look at the long list of her works, however, we find no such linear progression but rather repeated meditations (although not necessarily in every work) on the roles of women and men in society, in history, and in literary production. One of the touchstones for Christine's convictions—pertaining both to the functions of the two genders and to that of literature—is her use of ancient myth. In a cluster of texts composed between 1399 and 1405 her use of myth and its interpretations is most revealing.[3] By turns accepting, transforming, or rejecting existent interpretive traditions of mythological figures and fables, Christine builds her own complex mythological edifice. Thus the diverse currents in Christine's thought can be illuminated through analyses of her choice of particular mythological stories and the interpretations she attaches—or refuses to attach—to them.

Her early poems of love and loss (*Cent ballades*) use mythological stories in a personal and yet seemingly rather traditional way. But things change in the *Epistre au dieu d'amours*, her first polemical text. Here we find an explicit awareness of what earlier poets, in particular Jean de Meun, had done with figures like Cupid,[4] which triggers Christine's own process of remythisization. But following the *Epistre* there is no radical break with preceding interpretive traditions, rather a shift of perspective: the *Othéa*, a collection of 100 mythological "story moments," seems at first sight to be not much more than an impressive accumulation of mythographic material.[5] However, the impression of the work as one of traditional "male" writing does not survive even a superficial analysis, for the transformations Christine introduces with respect to her sources adumbrate the radical rewriting of her sources in the *Cité*. In fact, the *Othéa* is a central text for Christine's creative use of myth. The schema of multiple interpretation she adopts there, reminiscent of course of the *Ovide moralisé*, spawns the dominant forms myth takes in her subsequent works. Myths of history, of learning, and of feminine achievement are already present in the *Othéa* and will be worked out in a less schematic form in her subsequent works. Thus we will be able to gauge the great movements visible in Christine's literary production by an analysis of her manipulation of classical myth.

Christine's *horizon d'attente* as a reader and writer of myth was primarily shaped by the *Roman de la Rose*, the *OM*, and the works by Machaut, Deschamps, and Froissart.[6] Thus, while the earliest vernacular romancers confronted "only" the vast intertext of the Latin commentary and mythographic tradition, Christine also faced an intricate and fecund vernacular tradition. The use Machaut and Froissart made of myth centered on issues of love experience, poetic creativity, artistic self-definition, and hermeneutic reflection. Christine takes up some of the same issues but adds that of the role of women in the history of learning and politics. She also has a distinctly personal affinity to certain mythological figures and integrates herself, or rather her poetic persona, into elaborate mythical and allegorical frameworks like those of the *Mutacion*, the *Chemin*, or the *Cité*.

Christine's Personal Myths

Christine's earliest collections of poetry comprise several hundred poems.[7] Only fourteen of these deal with, or at least allude to, classical mythological material.[8] It is therefore all the more interesting to see which figures she privileged by juxtaposing them to her own poetic "I," which establishes itself, in a series of early poems, as a female persona bemoaning in the most moving terms the loss of her husband and the solitude of her widowhood. I would like to highlight four myths here that, in light of her later works, seem to contribute to an establishment of her own personal mythology: the stories of Hero and Leander, Io, the Judgment of Paris, and Circe.[9]

Hero and Leander's story, told in *Cent ballades* 3, is one of true love and sacrifice. Leander crosses the Hellespont "non pas en nef, ne en batel a nage, / Mais tout a nou" (not in a ship or a boat, but swimming; ll. 2–3) in order to see his beautiful Hero. But one night Fortune causes a storm to arise and Leander drowns (ll. 13–18). Hero then throws herself into the water to follow him: "Ainsi pery furent d'un seul courage" (thus they perished as one; l. 21). Yet, the lesson Christine draws from this story of all-consuming love is ambiguous. Her first-person voice appears in the refrain in the form of an imperative: "Voiés comment amours amans ordonne!" (See how love commands [or orders around] lovers; ll. 8, 16, 24, 28). My two possible translations show that Christine's exhortation to her listeners is somewhat equivocal: are Hero and Leander Love's slaves, that is, a negative exemplum to be avoided or are they Love's faithful servants, an example to be emulated?[10]

The envoi continues the ambiguous message. At first sight it seems to say that the story of Hero and Leander represents a celebration of a bygone era of perfect love, that is, people these days do not love like this anymore (ll. 25–26). But then comes the line "mais grant amour fait un fol du plus sage" (but great love turns the wisest man into a fool; l. 27), followed again by the refrain. So the poem ends on a negative note, for wisdom is surely to be preferred to "folie."

The poem bears witness to an interpretive struggle: will the view of passion as a positive emotion win out over the negative tradition of mythography and Ovid commentary? In the end, Christine opts for tradition and makes use of the negative of the two interpretive possibilities offered by the *OM*, where, in the "alegorie" (4.3587), Leander stands for dissolution (4.3590) and Hero for "luxure" (4.3593). Hero's birthplace, Sexte, is interpreted as the feminine sex, which is, of course, equated with "luxure" (4.3595–98).[11] But another exposition is possible, adds the *OM* poet: Hero is divine wisdom (4.3666–68), and Leander is the human race, which crosses the perils of life (such as the "storm of temptation") to rejoin divine wisdom (4.3670–731). Thus rather than valorizing the feminine, as Christine does later, here she concentrates on the ill effects that exaggerated love can have on human beings.[12]

Love, rather than wisdom as in some later works, is also the focus in the story of Io, recounted in Ballade 61. In Ovid and the *OM*, there is a striking and amusing recognition scene, in which Io, metamorphosed into a cow, reveals her identity to her father by tracing her name with her hoof. Like Boccaccio in *Concerning Famous Women*, Christine makes no mention of this achievement. This detail is also missing, as we will see below, in the *Othéa*, where it could have provided the key to the interpretation.[13] In any case, except for this detail Christine follows the familiar story line: Jupiter, who is in love with Io, is surprised by his wife and to disguise his unfaithfulness changes Io into a heifer. Juno asks for the heifer as a gift and Jupiter has to give it to her. The heifer is then watched by Argus with his 100 eyes. But Mercury (sent by Io's father) plays the flute so sweetly that Argus falls asleep and thus Mercury rescues Io.[14]

Christine's comments in the first person ("pour ce je die" [I say this for this reason], l. 31) rejoin exactly the lesson La Vieille in the *Roman de la Rose* draws from the story of Io: even the best guard is worth nothing when the lovers are really determined to be together.[15] Christine's generally negative view of the *Rose* does not prevent her here from adopting the traditional moral attached to the fable.[16] Throughout her works Christine's interests in the story of Io persist, and she will rework it many times, each time changing its focus.

Formally speaking, Christine takes on the role of mythographer here, for the two ballades offer radically shortened versions of the formal arrangement of the *OM*. The mythological story is paraphrased, and then an interpretation or moral in the first-person singular "je" follows. This "je" is quite different from the "je" of, say, Froissart's Ballade 7, in which he says, "A Leander me puis bien comparer" (I can well compare myself to Leander; l. 21). Froissart's "je" is that of the lover/poet, who identifies with Leander on an experiential level; Christine's "je" has, in its moralizing tone, a mythographic tinge to it. She is, in these two poems, not a participant but an interpreter who conveys a message to the audience.

In Poem 7 of *Autres ballades*, in which Christine offers a version of the Judgment of Paris, her self-involvement is different: the personal pronoun "me" appears on the very first line:[17]

> Se de Pallas me peüsse accointier
> Joye et tout bien ne me fauldroit jamais;
> Car par elle je seroie ou sentier
> De reconfort, et de porter le fais
> Que Fortune a pour moy trop chargier fais; (ll. 1–5)

If I can become acquainted with Pallas, I will never lack joy and all good things. For through her I will enter the path of comfort and [I will be capable] of carrying the load that Fortune has made too heavy for me.

The whole first stanza deals only with Christine's relationship to Pallas, Juno (who "hates" Christine), and Fortune. Venus makes no appearance in the first stanza, nor does Paris. From the beginning, Christine appropriates the myth of the Judgment for herself.

It is certainly true, as Margaret Ehrhart states, that in order to understand the poem, the reader has to be aware of the mythographic tradition equating Paris's choice with a choice of three lives: the contemplative (Pallas), the voluptuous (Venus), and the active (Juno). But there is a more personal—less mythographic—tone in this poem. More than anything else, it seems to be Christine's first "oath of allegiance" to Pallas, repeated many times throughout her career. As she will say in the *Livre des faits d'armes et de chevalerie*: "O Minerve . . . je suis comme toy femme ytalienne" (Minerva, like you I am an Italian).[18] Juno's hatred, acknowledged by Paris (ll. 19–20) and by the narrator (ll. 10, 30, and 34) in the refrains connects the two figures (in fact, Christine "enters" the Judgment), yet each chooses a different alternative to Juno. While Paris pursues love, Christine pursues wisdom. That this choice is a permanent one becomes clear at the end of the later *Mutacion* where she declares:

> J'ay choisie pour toute joye
> (Quelqu'aultre l'ait), telle est la moye,
> Paix, solitude voluntaire,
> Et vie astracte [et] solitaire. (ll. 23633–36)

I have chosen as my sole joy—whatever joy others may have, this is mine—peace, voluntary solitude, and a retiring and solitary life.[19]

In *Autres ballades* 7, then, the Judgment of Paris, with its long-established interpretive history, serves the purpose of self-definition. Rather than represent a choice of lives for humankind, it dramatizes Christine's autobiography: when Juno with her riches has proven hostile to Christine, that is, when through the loss of her father and her husband her personal fortunes have changed for the worse, she makes the conscious choice of a solitary life of learning. This first use of the Judgment in her writings signals a long-lasting interest in this myth, but its meaning will shift, depending on the text Christine uses it in. For instance, the story will be reworked several times in the *Othéa* and appear at the end of the *Chemin*. But here, as is fitting for a lyric poem, it is part of the interior life of the lyric "I."

The last mythological story we will consider here, that of Circe in *Autres ballades* 17, will lead us into the *Mutacion*, where it will become one of the three defining myths for Christine's poetic autobiography.

Circe was an enchantress who turned knights into pigs, but Ulysses saved them (ll. 1–4). The poet continues that while this may have been the right thing for Ulysses to do, she herself would hesitate to do such a good turn for some people she knows "qui sont plus que porz vilz et ors" (who are more vile and dirty than pigs; l. 7). She then goes on to describe these people: proud, vain, without prowess, and not inclined to good works. They are *mesdisants*, slanderers, persecuting women and destroying their good reputation. A metamorphosis into pigs would be too good for them, the poet implies, "mieulx que vifs vaulsissent mors" (they'd be worth more dead than alive; l. 23).

The envoi makes this forceful statement:

Je ne mesdi de nullui, fors
D'aucuns qui sont de Judas pire
Et sont de tous mauvais accors,
N'on n'en pourroit assez mesdire. (ll. 25–28)

I am not maligning anyone, except some who are worse than Judas and who are so uniformly bad that one could never say enough bad things about them.

Here the "je" extends the lesson learned in the mythological context. As in the Judgment of Paris, where the "je" occupied the same place as Paris (that is, having to make a choice), in this poem Christine sees herself in the same position as Ulysses, and again she makes a choice that differs from the male mythological protagonist. This choice reflects her awareness of the mythographic tradition, which had indeed seen the pigs as figures for morally inferior people.

This tradition comes to the fore in Christine's source, the *OM*, in which Circe's story forms part of the vast fourteenth book of the *OM*. In it, the poet tells the story of the aftermath of the Trojan War with a focus on Glaucus, who, in *OM* 13.4492, had been likened to Christ. Circe's magic formula, her "sentence obscure" (obscure meaning; 14.150), is based on the forces of nature, that is, her knowledge of plants and herbs (14.2430–31). She is immediately qualified as "la desloiaulz, la treitresse" (the disloyal, treacherous one; 14.2438). And, sure enough, the first interpretation of Circe confirms this image: she is none other than the whore of the Apocalypse (14.2564), and those she enchants are the "pigs": "Pors de glotonie et d'ordure" (gluttonous and filthy pigs; 14.2599). A lengthy anaphoric listing of all the vices of these "pigs" follows:

Pors plains d'ordure et de vilté,
Pors glout et plain d'enfermeté,
Pors qui n'ont ailleurs les beances
Fors en farsir lor gloutes pances,
Pors qui l'aise dou monde absorbe,
Pors qui se soullent en la bourbe. (14.2643–48)

Pigs full of dirt and baseness, gluttonous pigs, full of sickness; pigs who have no other desire than to fill their gluttonous bellies; pigs who are preoccupied with wordly pleasures, pigs who roll in the muck.

Next, in the historical interpretation, Circe takes the place of evil tyrants persecuting the apostles and the martyrs (14.3127–58). Finally, there is a slightly more positive note: Circe warns Ulysses's men of the sea's perils (14.3469). The long allegory that follows has only a loose connection to the story line. The comment "Jesus saves" (14.3509) could refer to either Circe's warning or Ulysses's rescue of his men from Circe's enchantment. Nevertheless, in general, this last positive interpretive effort has no influence on Christine. In the *Othéa*, for example, Circe is a dangerous sorcerer, and even in the *Cité*, as we will see, Christine finds little to say about Circe. It is all the more interesting, then, that Circe's story is one of the three chosen for the opening of the *Mutacion*.

But before turning to the *Mutacion*'s Circe, let us see how *Autres balades* 17 fits in with some of Christine's preoccupations. The theme of the *mesdisants* in the form of the *losengiers* is, of course, a staple of courtly poetry, in which they are the ones threatening to reveal the secret love of the poet and his lady. For Christine, the *mesdisants* are not potential revealers of the truth, but rather malicious slanderers.[20] In many of her works Christine underscores the importance of a woman's guarding her good reputation.[21] The danger is that even if a woman is innocent, the "false tongues" can injure her (ll. 18–21). In the envoi Christine stresses, however, that she herself speaks ill of people occasionally, but only if they merit it.

How does Circe fit into all this? Circe's story here is a signal of Christine's mythographic intent and knowledge. That is, where she occupied Paris's place in the Judgment, she here could play the role of Ulysses if she chose to: she could close her eyes to the fact that some people are swine and retransform them into humans. But she chooses not to do so, preferring rather to reveal these people's true character to the world, thus showing greater judgment than Ulysses. This purpose of showing the true character of men fits into the programmatic refutation of the false courtly ideals she sees everywhere around her. The use of the Circe story here illustrates one of the many possible uses of myth: it gives a moral slant to this ballade and transforms Christine's voice into that of a moralizing mythographer.

The personal, the moral, and the mythographic thus intersect in these four myths and their interpretations from the *Cent ballades* and *Autres ballades*. What is still missing is the larger vision of history and politics that Christine offers us in works like the *Mutacion* and in the feminist vision of the *Cité*, grounded in myth and history. Yet, the vast vision of history in the *Mutacion* begins on a personal note: the Mutacion "is a universal history framed by a personal history."[22]

The four informing mythological stories of the *Mutacion* are those of Circe, Tiresias, Iphis, and Alcyone and Ceyx. The first three are grouped together, since they all deal with the transformation of gender or form, an important theme in the opening of the *Mutacion*.[23] The last one, a heartbreaking story of love beyond death, is related to the dominant image of this part of the *Mutacion*, that of Christine's marriage as a sea voyage ending in shipwreck with her husband swept overboard to his death.

Christine prefaces her telling of the *Metamorphoses* stories by stating that here we will learn "comment de femme homme devins" (how from a woman I turned into a man; l. 1029). This, she adds, is neither "mençonge" nor "fable" (lie nor fable; l. 1032), but rather "parler selon methafore" (speaking metaphorically; l. 1033). Her experiences offer an illustration of the powers of Fortune. What she then goes on to tell are of course Ovidian fables, thus highlighting the complex meaning of the term *fable*. In the *OM* the term was almost always used as a reference to the Ovidian base text, which was "false" yet true in many different ways. It was false from a doctrinal perspective, and it was false because it was fiction; yet it became true through the poet's ingenuity. The fables' hidden meaning was as orthodox as could be desired. Christine, then, by using the terms *fable* and *metaphor* in this context signals her awareness of the interpretive problematics inherent in the use of Ovid's fables. The theoretical allegiance here is not so much to Ovid as to the *OM*.[24] There, multiple interpretations, the removal of the integument, had turned fable into truth. Here, her story is authenticated not only by her mastery of metaphor but by her personal experience. Thus her mastery of literary technique combines with her authentic experience to create a new kind of story that is indebted to Ovidian fable and its interpretations yet independent from it.

Let us now turn to the stories introducing—and prefiguring—Christine's own metamorphosis. Unlike *Autres ballades* 17, in which the focal point is Ulysses's power to give back human shape to his men, the *Mutacion* focuses on Circe's (and Fortune's) ability to metamorphose humans. Interestingly, Christine first mentions that Fortune has transformed "bestes en seigneurs" (beasts into knights; l. 1038) and only second that she can also metamorphose "chevaliers en bestes" (knights into beasts; l. 1041). Thus the introduction to the Circe story acknowledges the possibility of a two-way transformation (although in a strange order), but the narration of the story features only the transformation into pigs, leaving out Ulysses's rescue mission. The metamorphosis is described as:

> en faisant semblant d'amer
> A ses chevaliers on tendi
> Buvrage, qui les estendi
> a la terre comme chetis,
> Et en pors furent convertis. (ll. 1046–50)

by pretending to be in love with them, one gave his knights a potion that made them stretch out on the ground like sick people, and they were changed into pigs.

Christine thus underlines Fortune's power (for she was the real preparer of the potion [ll. 1051–52]). Circe, so it seems, was nothing but Fortune's instrument.

This transformation of the mythological story serves distinct purposes. First, by restricting the metamorphoses to a one-way transformation (in this passage, the men remain pigs) Christine prepares the reader for her own one-way transformation. Another function is that by referring to the two-way transformation but then not narrating it, Christine demonstrates her knowledge of Ovid while at the same time recalling her own Circe poem, in which she had stated that if it were up to her, certain men would remain pigs. This is the very thing that she has Circe do here; it is as if Circe were following Christine's commands. Also, the reversal of the order of transformations, mentioned in lines 1038–41, plays on one- and two-way transformations, one of the principal themes of this part of the *Mutacion*. Finally, by setting Fortune's power above that of Circe, Christine highlights the guiding idea of the entire *Mutacion*: Fortune governs history.

In her telling of the next story, that of Tiresias, Christine omits almost as much as she tells. In the *Metamorphoses*, Tiresias's story forms part of a whole series of tales related to the history of Thebes: Cadmus (introducing the serpent theme), his daughter Semele, his grandson Actaeon, and others. The theme of wanting to know too much or of seeing forbidden things ties these stories together. Ovid tells of Tiresias's transformation into a woman and back into a man to explain his qualification as arbiter in a dispute between Jupiter and Juno as to which gender experiences more pleasure during the sexual act (*Met* 3.316–38). Tiresias "knew both sides of love" (3.323), for he once saw two serpents mating, separated them with his staff, and consequently was transformed into a woman.[25] The same action brings back his male shape seven years later. When Tiresias agrees with Jupiter that women have more fun in bed, Juno punishes him by striking him blind. To compensate for this punishment, which he could not undo, Jupiter bestows on Tiresias the gift of prophecy.

Of this extremely brief yet complex passage in Ovid Christine retains only the two incidents with the serpents and the fact of the double metamorphosis. What she adds, however, is quite significant:

> En ce point .VII. ans demoura,
> Ou il fila et laboura
> De tieulx mestiers, que femmes font. (ll. 1079–81)

In this state he remained seven years, during which he spun and did such work as women do.

Thus the entire sexual framework has vanished; the definition of woman is no longer the knowledge of female sexual pleasures but rather the "work that women do." There are no remarks as to the possible usefulness of this knowledge, and there is no reference to the dispute between Jupiter and Juno.

This story, then, expands on the Circe story in that it shows us a two-way transformation: from man to woman to man. Christine follows a similar trajectory in her own works, for in the *Cité* she becomes a "woman" again, defined by "woman's work," which in that case will be writing, not spinning.[26] By focusing on work rather than on sexuality, Christine reinterprets the Tiresias story. It is undoubtedly significant that Christine here accepts none of the multiple interpretive possibilities offered by the *OM*. Treating in a sly way the power of women, this same story inspired the *OM* poet to compose an acerbic attack on domineering women (3.1060–83), which prefaces the physical and the allegorical expositions. In the physical interpretation, which is based on Fulgentius's *Mythologies* 2.5, Tiresias represents the weather; Juno is the lower layer of air, and so forth. In a move not unusual for the *OM*, the allegory transposes the lascivious story into a sacred context: the *OM* poet states that women love God more ardently than men, but links this love to female voluptuousness.

Christine must have been aware of the misogynistic and sexually charged tone of the *OM*'s interpretive passages. But she elaborates neither on women's love of God nor on women's power over men but emphasizes the notion of "woman's work," which ultimately constitutes the definition and the power of Tiresias in his female incarnation.

The third metamorphosis, that of Iphis from a woman into a man, is told at much greater length than the two previous examples (ll. 1094–158). It represents a sort of climax in her meditations on the transformations of gender because it comes closest to the events of Christine's own life as described in the *Mutacion*. What is most striking here is a desexualization of the Ovidian story, similar to that of the Tiresias story. Christine removes the sexual conflicts Iphis experiences when she—still a girl—feels attracted to another girl; she also substitutes the goddess Vesta for Isis as Iphis's mother's "patron saint."[27] Ovid tells the Iphis story in the context of tales of "unnatural love" in *Metamorphoses* 9. For Christine, of course, the metamorphosis occupies center stage.

The first parallels with Christine's own story are the reference to the fact that Iphis's father hated women so much that he ordered his wife to kill the baby she was expecting if it turned out to be a girl. Less radical, but nevertheless similar, is what Christine said about her own father:

Mon pere, dont j'ay mencion
Faite cy, ot devocion
Et tres grant voulenté d'avoir
Un filz masle, qui fust son hoir,
Pour succeder a sa richesce,
Qui n'appetisse pour largesse,
Comme il disoit, bien m'en recort;
Lui et ma mere d'un accort
M'engendrerent en celle attente,
Mais il failli a son entente,
Car ma mere, qui ot pouoir
Trop plus que lui, si voult avoir
Femelle a elle ressemblable,
Si fus nee fille, sanz fable. (ll. 379–92)

My father, whom I have mentioned here, had the inclination and great desire to have a male son to be his heir, to inherit the riches that do not diminish through generosity,[28] so he said, I remember it well; he and my mother agreed on this and conceived me in that expectation. But he failed in his intention, for my mother, who was more powerful than he, wanted to have a girl similar to herself; thus in truth I was born a girl.[29]

Although Christine's father eventually accepts Christine's femaleness and wants to share his wealth of learning with her, Iphis's father persists in his cruel design, and her mother is forced to disguise the child as a boy. The name fortunately is an androgynous one. All goes well until the father picks a bride for his "son." In Ovid, Iphis is terribly attracted to the chosen girl; she muses at length that her love is even more unnatural than that of Pasiphae, who, though in love with a bull, at least chose a male (*Met* 9.726–46).[30] The mother, in despair, prays to the goddess Vesta, a chaste goddess as opposed to Ovid's unchaste Isis, and "filz devint, par la soubtille / Deesse Vestis, qui deffit / Son corps de femme et filz le fit" ([she] became a son through the skillful goddess Vesta who undid her woman's body and made her a son; ll. 1156–58). It is significant that Christine does not say "man" here but "son."[31] The story thus points in two directions: backward to the above-cited passage on Christine's birth and forward to her own transformation.

Ovid's *Metamorphoses* functions here as an intertext. For while lines 1156–58 in the *Mutacion* give an all too brief description of Iphis's transformation, Ovid, and to some extent the *OM*, provides a vocabulary that is strikingly similar to that of Christine, who thus calls our attention to the correspondences between her own and Iphis's story. In Ovid we read:

Iphis walked beside her [her/his mother] as she went, but with a longer stride than was her wont. Her face seemed of a darker hue, her strength seemed greater, her very features sharper, and her locks, all unadorned, were shorter than before. She seemed more vigorous than was her girlish wont. (9.786–89)[32]

Here is how Christine describes her own metamorphosis effected by Fortune:

Si me toucha par tout le corps;
Chacun membre, bien m'en recors,
Manÿa et tint a ses mains, (ll. 1327–29)
. . .
Transmuee me senti toute.
Mes membres senti trop plus fors
Qu'ainçois (ll. 1336–38)
. . .
Si me senti trop plus legiere
Que ne souloye et que ma chiere
Estoit muee et enforcie
Et ma voix forment engrossie
Et corps plus dur et plus isnel, (ll. 1347–51)
. . .
Fort et hardi cuer me trouvay,
Dont m'esbahi, mais j'esprouvay
Que vray homme fus devenu. (ll. 1359–61)
. . .
Or fus je vrays homs, n'est pas fable (l. 1391)

She [Fortune] touched my whole body; she fingered and held in her hand every part of my body, I remember it well. . . . I felt completely changed. My limbs felt stronger than before. . . . I felt lighter than I used to and my face was changed, was stronger, and my voice stronger and my body harder and faster. . . . I found my heart to be strong and bold. I was astonished at this, but I felt that I had become a true man. . . . Thus I was a real man, in truth.

Interestingly, the wording of this dramatic transformation into a man reappears in the *Cité* when Christine describes her readiness to begin work on the city: "me sentant . . . trop plus forte et plus legiere" (feeling much stronger and swifter; p. 640). The strength thus remains, but the gender transformation effected in the *Mutacion* is no longer necessary in the *Cité*, and, like Tiresias, Christine has rejoined her original gender.

In her reading of the fable of Iphis Christine offers a literal reading of the Ovidian heroine's gender transformation that she then applies figuratively to herself. She thus reconciles the two apparently contradictory hermeneutic statements I cited earlier (that Christine's turning from a woman into a man is neither "lie nor fable" but "speaking metaphorically" [ll. 1032, 1033]). For Iphis the fable was literally true; for Christine it is metaphorically true.

Given Christine's strong identification with Iphis, we can understand why she omits the unrelievedly negative interpretations (a female seductress of young girls; the sinful soul) of this story in the *OM*.[33] Yet, it is the intertext of the *OM* that defines the myriad reasons why Christine had to turn into a "man." Not only did society require her to act like a man, but through her transformation she could also avoid the negative values associated with women, here figured by Iphis in her pretransformation state.

By framing her own metamorphosis with the Ovidian one, Christine adds a new dimension to her poetic autobiography. Ovid's *Metamorphoses* functions as intertext. This fact is signaled by the use of the Ovidian vocabulary.[34] The *OM*, as well, is an intertext, and here we have the added interest of the *exposicions* (interpretations), assigning negative valences to Iphis as a woman. The intertexts that hover behind Christine's text enhance the richness of the *Mutacion* and add a new dimension to the question of gender. Here, unlike in the *Avision* of 1405, a vast allegory whose third part is largely autobiographical, Christine does not spell out her anxieties and frustrations of being a woman in a male-dominated society; rather, she lets the myths and their interpretations speak. Thus the passage is not only very moving in purely human terms but also part of a web of Ovidian references that go beyond explicit citation.

The three examples of metamorphoses, then, prepare the reader for what is to come in Christine's own life story. They cover the whole spectrum of metamorphosis: a one-way (although potentially two-way) transformation of men into pigs; a two-way gender change of man into woman into man; and finally a transformation of a woman into a man. Christine thus sets the stage not only for her own transformation but for a problematic of gender roles, which she will explore in later works, such as the *Cité*. Circe's story highlights the moral dimension of metamorphosis, while Tiresias's story teaches us that a transformation need not be final, even if at first it appears to be. Thus while Christine starts out in her professional life like Iphis, she leaves the possibility for a retransformation open. The mythological examples are thus far more than mere illustrations of the powers of Fortune. They are essential parts of Christine's self-definition.

The final example of Christine's "personal myths" in the *Mutacion*, which add both emotional and intellectual resonances to her text, is not a gender change but a tale of eternal love. One of the most moving stories in the *Metamorphoses* is that of Alcyone and Ceyx, which takes up a large part of Book 11.[35]

Ceyx, the king of Trachis, leaves on a sea voyage to consult the oracle at Claros. His wife, Alcyone, fears for his life and does not want him to go, or at least she would like to go with him. He reassures her but later perishes in a shipwreck, in one of the most dramatic descriptions of the *Metamorphoses.* During the fierce storm all of Ceyx's thoughts are devoted to Alcyone. She has a dream vision, in a message delivered by Iris, of her husband's fate. She rushes off in search of his body, and when she finds it they are both transformed into birds. One week each year Alcyone "broods upon her nest floating upon the waters. At such a time the waves of the sea are still" (11.745–47). Alcyone and Ceyx are the perfect loving couple, "their affection kept unbroken to the end" (11.750).[36]

Christine's reference to the story occupies no more than three lines, yet it gives great depth of feeling to her text:

Quant sceü le fait, dont me doubtoye,
Dessoubz la pope, ou j'estoye,
Me lieve com femme enragiee,
Hault m'en monte et en mer plungiee
Je me fusse, et ja n'y failisse,
Qui ne me tenist, je y saillisse,
N'onc Alchyonie ne sailli
Plus tost en mer, quant lui failli
Ceÿs, que tant souloit amer,
Que je fusse tumbee en mer,
Qui me laissast, mais fu tenue,
De ma meisgnïe (ll. 1251–62)

When I learned this fact [that her husband is dead] of which I had been afraid, I got up from the poop like a madwoman. I climbed up the poop and would have thrown myself into the sea, and I would not have failed if no one had held me back. Never would Alcyone have jumped more readily into the sea when she lost her husband, Ceyx, whom she loved so much, than I would have jumped, if only one would have let me. But I was held back by the people from my household.

This is only a small part of a truly heartbreaking account. But the presence of the Alcyone and Ceyx story tempers the despair of this passage. For, reading against the Ovidian intertext, we know that eventually the two spouses were united, albeit in a different shape. Christine's answer to the myth of the halcyon days that awaited Alcyone and Ceyx is the myth of Iphis. If she cannot have her man, she must become one. With this transformation she also achieves a certain union with her dead husband: she now plays his role as captain and provider. What the gods did for Alcyone and Iphis, Fortune does for her.[37]

Moreover, the Alcyone and Ceyx story can be read against the tale of Hero and Leander, one of Christine's earliest uses of an Ovidian source. The similarities between the two stories are striking: in each case a distressed woman throws herself into the sea in which her loved one has perished. But the differences are just as great. While Hero and Leander are an example of sensuality, doomed to perish through their foolish love, Alcyone and Ceyx are exemplars of *married* love: they do not die but survive as birds that tenderly raise their young together. The desexualization we observed in the Tiresias and Iphis stories continues here and helps to spell out Christine's deepest convictions on the nature of true love and fidelity. Christine thus completely changes the focus by referring to a story that only on the surface resembles the sad tale from the Ovid's *Heroides*.

The four myths of this part of the *Mutacion* acquire deeper and truer meaning through their position in a "personal" system. Where in the *Cent ballades* and *Autres ballades* mythological stories are dispersed throughout the collection and respond in each case to one of Christine's preoccupations, here the myths form part of a poetic autobiography. Christine's voice in the myths of the *Cent ballades* is primarily that of the moralizer and mythographer, although a personal or autobiographical voice made an appearance in the Judgment of Paris poem. In other poems, her interpretations of the stories range from the flat and not very well motivated, as in the Io poem, to the passionate, as in the Circe poem. Yet, it seems that she does not exploit the full potential of each myth. In part this is due, of course, to the restrictions of the lyric form[38] and in part to the choice of poetic voice. Although the widowhood poems in the same collection employ a deeply emotional register,[39] the mythological ones are more didactic and do not present a complex Christine figure.

In the *Mutacion* Christine makes the myths part of her poetic life. They speak to her and the reader through the qualities that make them eternal: they provide answers, hope, and links to the past. At the same time, Christine uses the myths as structuring principles within the first part of the *Mutacion*: the three metamorphoses of gender and form announce the "miracle" to come, and the Alcyone and Ceyx story evokes the hopeful aspect of the Ovidian tale at just the right moment and thus predicts Christine's future strength. We also see a progression of personal involvement with the myths. While the three stories of gender change are ostensibly exempla (though they acquire a deeply personal meaning along the way), the Alcyone and Ceyx story forms part of a passionate outcry that clearly states Christine's participation: *I*, Christine, am even more ready to throw myself into the sea after my husband than Alcyone was.[40]

In the poems and the *Mutacion*, then, we find the moralizing, mythographic, and personalized uses of myth that together with her later feminist perspective define Christine's exploitation of the classical tradition.

Christine's Original Mythography in the *Epistre d'Othéa*

The *Othéa* addresses two areas important to our understanding of what "reading myth" in the middle ages meant. First, the question of techniques of interpretation, already treated at length in Chapter 3, will become prominent here again; second, the question, not yet explored, of what it means to read as a man or as a woman will lead us toward the *Cité*.

According to Rosemond Tuve "the peculiar usefulness" of the *Othéa* lies in the fact that here Christine shows how she wanted her text to be read;[41] it is a work that contains its own interpretation. Indeed, in the gloss to Texte 1, Christine introduces her interpretive categories. Othéa, who is "sagece de femme" (p. 155), rules over the whole enterprise. "Nous crestiens" indicates the spiritual Christian perspective of one level of interpretation; "ramener a moralite" (to connect to morality) signals the moral level (here the gloss); the reference "en leur temps" indicates a euhemeristic view of the ancient gods and goddesses; and finally, the "temps a venir" (p. 156) points to an anagogical view of mythology.

But is the *Othéa* a work of mythography in the traditional sense? Certainly the segmentation of the mythological stories and the insistent use of allegoresis would suggest that the Othéa is a mythographic text. "Allegoresis . . . thematizes interpretation,"[42] as we saw for the *OM*, and to a certain extent Christine follows in the footsteps of that text here, though mercifully not at such great length. Indeed, two critics recently suggested that the *Othéa* is a "straightforward work of mythography" and that in it Christine reads "as a man, or, more accurately, a patristic exegete."[43] Two other critics, on the other hand, see distinctly feminist traits in the

Othéa.[44] The heading of this section suggests my position. I believe that both the form and the content attest to Christine's original use of myth.

Were there any models for a text like the *Othéa*? Formally, each chapter consists of the *texte*,[45] gloss, and allegory. The *texte* is usually four lines in length (except for the first few chapters) and contains a brief interpretation of a mythological story couched in the imperative. Thus, the *texte* is not a capsule narrative of a given myth, as has been claimed by most critics, but a preliminary interpretation. Then follows the gloss, which frequently provides a historical interpretation or explanation and always supplies a moral lesson for the knight, another imperative, often supplemented by a quote from an ancient philosopher. The allegory offers a spiritual interpretation and exhorts the knight to lead a pious life. It usually closes with a quote from the Bible or a Church Father. As has been already pointed out by Tuve, the order of the texts is determined by the allegories, which offer such series as the seven deadly sins, the twelve articles of the creed and the Ten Commandments.[46] Thus it seems that the myths are subservient to the spiritual interpretations. Christine establishes a new sequence, determined by the interpretations, and thus distinguishes herself clearly from the *OM*, in which the texte was taken from Ovid, in a more or less faithful translation, presented in the order in which the fables appeared in the *Metamorphoses*. Moreover, Christine here is the author of all three elements and thus essentially offers a self-exegesis, which functions also as a commentary on the mythographic tradition.[47]

Returning to the question about possible models, we see that there certainly were texts that suggested the form of the *Othéa*. Examples include the *OM* but also the *Ovidius moralizatus* of Pierre Bersuire, in which the fables "might best be understood as 'interpretable segments,' " and in which "many of the moralizations or allegorizations end with a quotation from the Bible."[48] Tuve suggests that summas, such as the *Somme le roi*, are predecessors of the *Othéa*.[49] What makes the *Othéa* different, however, is the triple imperative of texte, gloss, and allegory. By couching the texte in that form Christine effectively removes the texte from its historical and even its traditional interpretive framework and makes it her own.[50] A typical texte reads like this:

> A Phebé ne ressembles mie;
> Trop est muable et ennemie
> A constance et a fort courage,
> Merencolieuse et lunage. (texte 10, p. 173)

Do not resemble Phoebe. She is too changeable and hostile to constancy and a steady heart; she is melancholic and lunatic.

or

> Se bien aimes chiens et oyseaulx,
> D'Antheon, li gent damoiseaulx,
> Qui serf devint, bien te souviengne,
> Et gard qu'autant ne t'en aviengne. (texte 69, p. 246)

If you like dogs and birds, remember Actaeon, the noble young man, who became a stag, and beware that the same thing does not happen to you.

The function of the imperative is *conative*, and, according to Roman Jakobson, it differs from other nominal and verbal categories because unlike the declarative mood it cannot be subjected to "a truth test"; that is, an imperative cannot provoke the question Is it true or false?[51] Rather, if there is any truth in an imperative it derives from the authority of the speaker. Christine usurps the authority in the texte through the direct connection between speaker and listener that is created by the imperative and that needs no external referent. The initial distillation of the myth in the texte is, formally speaking, not part of the exemplary tradition, which is generally characterized by phrases like "as Ovid recounts" or "as we find in Ovid" (or another *auctor*).

By segmenting the text the way she does and by using the imperative (which already *is* an interpretation) Christine offers a summa not so much of interpretations as of interpretive methods. Unlike the *OM* poet, who constantly evokes Ovid, the narrator of the *Othéa* studiously avoids the naming of her *auctor*. Thus liberated—and thus having established herself *as* an authority—she proceeds to her tendentious rewriting of myth, an interpretive method we will encounter again in the *Cité*. At the same time, by citing philosophical and scriptural authorities in gloss and allegory, she aligns the voice of the texte, that is, her own, with these authorities. Thus by choosing a form that makes her look like a patristic exegete, Christine actually creates great interpretive freedom for herself. The whole apparatus of philosophical and biblical citations that surrounds her own (or Othéa's) voice in fact lends support to her own view of myth.[52]

Let us first see how Christine herself defines her project in the *Othéa*. The Prologue is rather traditional, emphasizing the lineage of her patron (Louis of Orléans) and of Christine: the former is of Trojan stock (denoting warfare), the latter from Bologna, the home of learning. Her work contains "matiere nouvelle" (new subject matter; l. 11; p. 151), although her own learning is deficient—mere crumbs fallen from her father's table.[53] After imploring her patron's good will, Christine adds a prose passage explaining that the images of the gods and goddesses are "in clouds" to show that they are "spiritual things and elevated above the earth" (Prologue, ll. 25–27; pp. 152–53), so that those who are neither clerks nor poets can understand the meaning of the stories in this book (Prologue, ll. 20–21; p. 152). Christine thus controls every aspect of her production: text, image, and interpretation.

She then goes on to her first texte, in which she describes Othéa, the goddess of Prudence who addresses herself to Hector of Troy. At one point, Othéa says: "Et comme deesse je sçay, / Par science non par essay, / Les choses qui sont a venir" (and as a goddess I know through science, and not through experience, the things that are to come; chap. 1, texte; p. 154). This is an important statement, especially in light of the gloss, which tells us that Othéa stands for the wisdom of woman (chap. 1, gloss; p. 155). Wisdom, science, and knowledge (that is, book learning), not experience, provide the basis for what is to come.[54] But in addition to relying on the ancient authors, Christine creates her own authority figure. First, through her original use of texte, which, as I suggested earlier, does not contain bits of Ovid or even the *OM* but rather a "pre-interpreted" command, only loosely based on any tradition; and second, through the use of the goddess Othéa, unknown in classical mythology.[55]

In the gloss of Chapter 1 Othéa proposes the kinds of interpretation already known from the mythographic tradition: the euhemeristic, the moral, and the spiritual (which she explains in the allegory of Chapter 1 as the application of "la Sainte Escripture a noz dis" [Holy Scripture to our stories; p. 157]). And she gives an example of the moral interpretation by stating that in fact "par Othea nous prendrons la vertu de prudence et sagece, dont lui mesmes fu aournez" (by Othéa we mean the virtue of prudence and wisdom with which he himself [Hector] was adorned; p. 156). Thus, morally, Othéa is actually part of Hector. This "disappearance" of Othéa within Hector in a sense parallels Ovid's "disappearance" in the imperative of the texte. Christine usurps the voice not only of Ovid but of Ovid's interpreter Othéa. Christine inscribes herself again in a myth, only this time the myth is her own creation.

How does she interpret her textes? It is in the glosses that we find the most explicit methodological reflections, whose vocabulary suggests a rather orthodox mythographic approach. In Chapter 3 of the *Othéa*, on Hercules, the gloss explains that he was a great traveler and that his marvelous prowess induced the poets to say that he descended into the underworld. The poets said this "soubz couverture et en maniere de fable" (under a covering and in the manner of fable; chap. 3, gloss; p. 162). This vocabulary is already familiar; the idea that secular poetry is valuable because it contains hidden truths dates back to late antiquity. Christine uses variations of this terminology. In Chapter 4, for example, she interprets the fable of Minos by saying: "Et a parler moralement, dirons une fable a ce propos selon la couverture des poetes" (and to speak morally, we will tell a fable for this purpose according to the covering of the poets; chap. 4, gloss; p. 164).

Chapter 4 is a good example of the complexity of Christine's method. The texte here consists of eight lines, exhorting the knight to resemble Minos, who, although part of the underworld, was a wise judge. In the gloss, after the sentence cited above, Christine tells the story of Minos's activities, likening the underworld to hell, where God's justice reigns. Then she presents the euhemeristic interpretation that Minos was a Cretan king known for his "grant rigueur de justice" (great judicial rigor; p. 164). The gloss closes with a quote from Aristotle that states that justice is a measure established by God to "limiter les choses" (to be a limit to things; p. 164), the function earlier attributed to Othéa's sister, Attemprance (chap. 2, allegory; p. 159). The allegory of the Minos story urges the knight to cultivate justice as a path toward God. Quotes from Saint Bernard and Solomon to this effect follow. This brief summary shows that the division between the different functions of texte, gloss, and allegory is not as rigid as one might think: the texte already contains elements that one would expect in the gloss.[56]

The clearest expression of Christine's views on fables can be found in the gloss on Chapter 82, on Hermaphroditus:

Ceste fable peut estre entendue en assez de manieres, et comme les clercs soubtilz philosophes ayent muciez leur grans secres soubz couverture de fable, y peut estre entendue sentence appartenant a la science d'astronomie, et autressi d'arquemie, si comme dient les maistres. Et pour ce que la matiere d'amours est plus delitable a ouyr que d'autre, firent communement leurs ficcions sus amours pour estre plus delitables mesmement aux rudes, qui n'y prennent fors l'escorce, et plus agreable aux soubtilz, qui en succent la liqueur. (chap. 82, gloss; pp. 265–66)

This fable may be understood in many manners, and because learned subtle philosophers have hidden their great secrets under cover of fable, one can understand by this meanings pertaining to astronomy and also to alchemy, as the masters say. And because matters of love are more pleasant to hear than others, especially for the unlearned who only take the rind, and more agreeable to the learned who suck the juice, [the clerks] commonly wrote fictions of love in order to delight the simple people.[57]

Theoretically Christine subscribes here to the tenets of the mythographic tradition: there are many expositions possible for a given fable;[58] there are two kinds of audiences, the unlearned and the learned; both of them enjoy matters of love more than others, yet they get different things out of the fables. While the unlearned remain on the surface, the learned penetrate to the true inner meaning, the meaning under the surface. This last comment remains a purely theoretical statement, though, because neither astronomy nor alchemy are applied to the fable in question. Christine displays her knowledge of interpretive traditions only to reject them.

Further, Christine does not adopt any of the interpretive possibilities of the *OM*. For the *OM* poet, Salmacis's fountain stands for the uterus, divided into seven cells in which human generation was taking place. The female, we are told, is conceived on the left side, the male on the right. If, however, the semen enters the central cell, a hermaphroditic being is conceived (4.2224–49). Or Salmacis is a woman who likes makeup in order to entrap men (4.2250–81); or Salmacis represents the world, where vanity abounds, while Hermaphroditus is a lapsed religious who has a double nature, religious and secular (4. 2282–389). Thus, except for the fantastic biological interpretation, for the *OM* poet the female nymph Salmacis always represents something evil.

In contrast, Christine's interpretation of the myth, that one should not hesitate to grant something that can cause no harm, was already apparent in the texte of Chapter 82:

> Ne soyes dur a ottroyer
> Ce que tu peus bien emploier.
> A Hermafrodicus te mire,
> A qui mal prist pour escondire. (p. 265)

Do not be hard in granting that which you may use well. Reflect on Hermaphroditus who was harmed for refusing.

The same lessons reappear in the gloss and allegory.[59] Thus despite the tripartite division, highlighted in the layout of at least one manuscript as an imitation of a traditional glossed text, the distinction between the lessons of the texte, gloss, and allegory is not always clear-cut.[60] Each lesson takes the side of Salmacis, who was rejected by Hermaphroditus. While in the *OM* every interpretation of the Salmacis figure is negative, here she is the innocent victim of the man's arrogance.[61]

Chapter 82, then, can serve as a distillation of Christine's methods and intentions. Theoretically, she demonstrates her knowledge of the techniques advocated by the mythographers. However, the very interpretive possibilities she lists, the astronomical and the alchemist, she does not use here.[62] Moreover, as she did for the Iphis story in the *Mutacion*, Christine resolutely rejects the sexual ambiguities the myth had in both Ovid and the *OM*.

This chapter of the *Othéa* shows especially clearly how the imperative in the texte subsumes the lessons of gloss and allegory, thus displacing both Ovid and the *OM*. This displacement is consistent with the linguistic properties of the imperative analyzed above. Already the texte, unlike the fables in the *OM*, is subject to Christine's intentionality. It is not only a moral imperative but a hermeneutic imperative, in the sense that "allegoresis proposes to save the text by preempting it and substituting itself as dynamic intentionality which acts not on the text but through it."[63] Allegoresis is used here truly as a means of text production.[64] By incorporating the interpretation into the level of texte and framing it in an imperative, Christine defines her project as something different from traditional exegeses of Ovid. She *is* both Ovid and his interpreters. The *Othéa* is thus not only an appropriation and rewriting of Ovid and the *OM* but of the whole methodology of the allegorization of fable. Christine's originality certainly consists in her rewriting of some of the myths and their interpretations, but even more so, I believe, in her usurpation of the methodological bases of mythography.[65] Having established her authority in a traditionally "male" genre, Christine can go on to other uses of myth, concentrating on the areas of learning (especially that of women), political unrest, and the lessons of history.

Myths of Learning and History

In *Autres ballades* 7 Christine participates in the Judgment of Paris by choosing Pallas, and not Venus, as Paris did. This ballade adumbrates her self-inscription into myth and dramatizes her choice of a life of learning over one of love. It is this life of learning, inserted into an elaborate allegorical/mythical framework, that provides the subject matter for the *Chemin*.[66] In the *Chemin*, inspired by Boethius and Dante, Christine recounts a vision she had after anxious ruminations on the evils of this world.[67] The Sibyl of Cumae appears to her and takes her on a journey that begins on earth and ends in the heavens. A large part of the text is taken up with a debate between the four queens governing the world: Richesse, Sapience, Noblesse, and Chevalerie. In the middle of these queens sits Reason, surrounded by the Virtues. They are debating a letter Earth has written to Reason, complaining that things were going badly on earth, a fact for which the four queens blame one another. Finally the participants in the debate conclude that covetousness is the principal vice of the inhabitants of the earth. The solution will be to find a perfect knight—his qualities are expounded at length based on a long list of *auctores*—who will restore order. Where can he be found? In France, of course, and it is Christine who will be sent there as a messenger of the heavenly powers. Christine, meanwhile, has written down everything the queens and Reason have told her and is ready to carry out her mission, but before she can set out for France the allegory breaks off: Christine is awakened by her mother.[68]

The most important innovation of the *Chemin* compared to Christine's previous uses of myth is its transposition of classical mythology to the diegetic level. She eschews the moralizing and didactic voice of some of the ballades and the *Othéa* and adopts that of an allegorical dreamer who travels through a mythical universe. She thus becomes a personage in her own mythic creation, at the same time living and describing what it means to lead a life of learning. In the mythic construct of the *Chemin*, Christine avoids the mythographic tradition. Interestingly, the only way this tradition appears in the *Chemin* is in the shape of Fulgentius, who is cited as an *auctor* (l. 5239). Therefore, although she cites one of the foremost mythographers, she does not employ his methods. She acknowledges Fulgentius's *Mythologies* and even paraphrases a passage from it, but here his work is not a model for multiple interpretations. Rather, Fulgentius is part of the repertory of *auctores* listed by the learned character Christine. In many ways, then, she distances herself from received ways of looking at myth and instead constructs her own mythic world, dominated by wise women, such as her guide, the Sibyl of Cumae, and Reason. Christine herself is, of course, a central figure in this universe: she is not only a visionary and a traveler, but also the narrator. And, as we will see, at the end she adopts the function of no less a mythological personage than Mercury, the heavenly messenger.

As she does so often in her works, in the *Chemin* Christine contrasts her own text with the *Roman de la Rose.* While Amant's vision was motivated by nothing else but his youth and springtime, Christine's is the result of her deep thinking and, most important, of her reading of Boethius. Boethius's *Consolation of Philosophy* provides the impetus and framework for the appearance of the Sibyl.[69] The Sibyl identifies herself by telling her story: how Apollo pursued her; how she finally received the gift of a life lasting 1000 years; how she led Aeneas in the underworld; how Virgil spoke of her (ll. 506–658). Her origins, then, are steeped in classical mythology, but not only that, her origin is also linked to Christine's own works, for she was the voice of wisdom in the last chapter of the *Othéa.* Thus Christine is led not only by a known mythological character but also by one of her own poetic creations.[70] Casting the Sibyl, who had previously led Aeneas and had been written about by Virgil, as her leader allows Christine to adopt the dual role of successor to the founder of Rome and successor to the poet who had celebrated him. Thus equipped—and this authorial equipment is at least as important as the scarf and belt she takes along to bind up her skirt—Christine follows the Sibyl to a *locus amoenus.*

Again, we hear distinct echoes of the *Rose,* but this enchanted place is not a place of love but of learning, and the fountain in the garden is not that of Narcissus but that of wisdom. Another allusion to the *Rose* is the *chapiaux jolis* (pretty hats) of line 1060, recalling Amant's flower-bedecked hat in the *Rose.* Here, however, the hats signify the talents given by the muses to poets like Homer, Ovid, Horace, and Orpheus. This move from love to poetry is characteristic for the fourteenth and fifteenth centuries, or, as Jacqueline Cerquiglini puts it, in the late middle ages "the love of the Rose is replaced by the love of the *Roman de la Rose.*"[71] Although Christine is not exactly a lover of the *Rose,* she certainly is a lover of texts and thus is firmly anchored in this late medieval trend.

The transposition of the locus of love into one of learning—where Christine also redirects the vocabulary of desire from love to learning—is achieved by her reorganization of diverse materials from Books 3 to 5 of the *OM.*[72] She describes the mountain of knowledge (a kind of fusion of Parnassus and Mount Helicon) and the fountain of wisdom and learning ("de sapience et de clergie"); the latter is surrounded by the nine muses, and the winged horse Pegasus hovers above.[73] This fountain is also the fountain where Cadmus tamed the serpent (ll. 1075–80). In the *OM,* Cadmus was presented as a wise and subtle clerk with companions who tired quickly of studying philosophy. Following the *OM,* in the *Othéa*

(Chapter 28), the serpent came to stand for learning and Cadmus's taming it for his mastery of philosophy. In this landscape, then, Christine is allowed to live her choice of *Autres ballades* 7, for this is also Pallas's dwelling place (l. 1095).[74] It was also the place of Aristotle, Socrates, Plato, and others. Christine's father, as well, knew the way to this fountain.

The mention of her father signals Christine's personal history, which, as in the *Mutacion*, provides a framework for the mythical construct. Still grieving for the death of her husband thirteen years earlier (ll. 120–33), Christine is a recluse when the Sibyl appears to her. The allegorical voyage, then, opens up Christine's closed universe. Similarly, her views of mythology undergo an expansion. Christine, in fact, practices what is known in modern myth criticism as bricolage, using a variety of mythical elements to construct her own universe. I would suggest that the *Chemin* can be read as a dramatization of the role classical learning should play in medieval culture. Such learning should not only provide the background for any education but also open itself up, in an exemplary manner, to analysis relevant to the political conflicts of the day. What Christine had prescribed and had Othéa practice in the *Othéa*—a wise woman teaching moral conduct to a ruler, basing herself on ancient mythology—is now dramatized and integrated into the mythic framework of the allegorical voyage in the *Chemin*.[75]

This dramatization also touches on the inadequacy of Christine's learning, which does not allow her to reach the highest level of scholarship, and explains via the Sibyl that this was the result of the late start of her education (ll. 1670–80). For this reason, Christine is somewhat fearful as they approach the fourth heaven. Using a mythological referent, Christine fears that she will fall like Icarus (ll. 1721–32), but the Sibyl reassures her "comme Ycarus ne cherras mie" (you will not fall like Icarus; l. 1741), for Christine's wings are not attached with wax. Not presumption but a genuine desire for learning led Christine to the heavens, the Sibyl argues, so nothing will harm her. It is significant that right after the Sibyl mentions Christine's somewhat inferior learning, a fault for which she cannot be blamed, however (ll. 1678–80),[76] Christine refers to the story of Icarus, thus demonstrating her learning at the very moment when it is doubted. Christine the protagonist thus approaches the level of learning of Christine the author, whose learning, in fact, turns out to be vast, if we go by the list of the authors cited in the *Chemin*. Vegetius, Plutarch, Fulgentius, John of Salisbury, Valerius Maximus, Suetonius, and of course Boethius and Dante make many appearances. At one point, Christine underlines the breadth of her learning by saying in the context of exemplars of perfect knighthood "infinis exemples pourroie / Dire au propos" (I could list an infinite number of examples for this point; ll. 6057–58).

Christine presents the reader with a vast tableau of traditional book learning as well as with images that stress the importance of processes of interpretation or glossing. When the Sibyl and her companion arrive in the heavens, Christine is allowed to contemplate the evils of this world. She thus repeats *within* the vision what had triggered the vision in the first place. But now she is granted full knowledge of various causes, such as the appearance of the comet of 1401. She twice uses the word "appertement" (openly; ll. 2175, 2179) to describe how knowledge was granted her. We saw that this term was part of the interpretive vocabulary of poets such as Jean de Meun and the *OM* poet, as well as of mythographers. Like these writers, Christine is allowed to look beneath the surface of the "text" that is this world. This view of the events of this world as "open" texts is supported by a passage on the sibyls and Merlin. Having been granted visions of future comets as well as of solar and lunar eclipses that announce great evils to come, Christine is also granted an interpretation of these omens:

> Des dix sebilles qui tant sceurent,
> De Merlin et de ceulx qui furent
> Le temps futur prophetisans,
> L'effect, ou, comment et les ans
> Me fu la du tout exposé,
> Tout ne fust leur texte glosé. (ll. 2193–98)[77]

By the ten sibyls who knew so much, by Merlin and by those who prophesy the future, all this was explained to me although their text was not glossed: the effect [of these portents], where, how, and the years [when they would appear].

The future is thus seen as a text that requires interpreting but has no gloss: the insights transmitted to Christine are more illuminations than learning. Christine's relative lack of learning is thus no obstacle: she can become an apprentice in this process, instructed by the sibyls, Merlin, and other prophets. Christine insists here that she will be allowed to participate in the privileged business of prophecy, something that will become important at the end of the *Chemin*, when her political mission is defined.

Meanwhile, the debate between the four queens and Reason commences. The letter from Earth, which triggers the debate, is replete with mythological allusions. Earth complains that Proserpina was taken from her, that Phaeton "par son oultrage" (outrageously; l. 2655) burned her with the sun's chariot; but all this is nothing compared with the grief that humans are inflicting on her. This whole passage recalls, of course, Alan of Lille's *De planctu Naturae*, in which Nature complains to Genius that humans are not following her precepts of propagating the species. Christine, however, anchors Earth's complaint and the revelations granted the character Christine firmly in contemporary history. The comet, she mentions, for example, is the comet of 1401; the travels she relates recall contemporary travel accounts. Thus Christine skillfully establishes a parallel between outrages committed by mythological figures and those committed by humans, highlighting again the close connection between the themes of mythology—the world of learning—and pressing contemporary concerns. One unbroken line leads from the mythological past to current calamities.[78]

This genealogy finds its counterpart in the genealogy defining Noblesse's candidate for the perfect knight who will be chosen as an arbiter and savior (who in the Prologue is already identified as Charles VI). In approximately a hundred lines (ll. 3521–625) Christine enumerates the survivors of the Trojan war who went forth to found empires elsewhere: Alexander (presented as a descendant of Helenus); Aeneas; Francus, founder of France; Romulus and Remus; and Brutus, founder of Britain. This is the historicized version of myth we found in the *romans antiques* and the *Histoire ancienne*, complete with the function it had in these early texts: to provide a link to contemporary politics. Christine moves easily from myths of learning to those of history and in fact demonstrates that they illuminate each other. Just as the *Othéa* had offered a summa of interpretations of myth applicable to the knight's moral and spiritual life, the *Chemin* offers an overview of personal and political uses of myth.

The importance of Christine's function is highlighted by her role in the Judgment of Paris at the end of the *Chemin*, which is related to the great debate on the fate of the world. This time, as we will see, she does not play the role of Paris but that of Mercury. Margaret Ehrhart has analyzed the different versions of the Judgment in Christine's works and found that there is a distinct connection between the Judgment of the *Othéa* and that of the *Chemin* in that Christine emphasizes the political choices a ruler must make in both works.[79] The choice of Venus, that is of love, is never presented as a possibility. Ehrhart also shows that the gifts offered to Paris by the three goddesses (except for Venus's), which are not otherwise mentioned, appear in the *Chemin* as the properties of the four goddesses involved in the debate, who, she argues, represent psychological forces. While I essentially agree with this view I would suggest that the forces are less psychological than social. Let us now focus on the way Christine inserts the Judgment in the *Chemin* and on the manner in which she inscribes herself into this scene.

Just as the path of learning is identified as the one Dante had tread before her (l. 1128), so the place of the debate is *identical* to that of Paris's Judgment, as we are told by "un vaillant docteur et sage" (a valiant doctor and sage; l. 6133), later identified as "maistre Avis" (Master Opinion; l. 6221). It is this same wise man who later tells the story of the Judgment. His insistence on the geographical congruence is very important, for it equates the place of the debate with the mythological universe of the wedding of Thetis and Peleus where the Judgment had its origin. Christine is present not only in the heavens but at the very site of a central mythological event, one that has already surfaced several times in her writings. The Judgment is inserted, then, as a *story* told by an unidentified wise man and as an *event* that happened at the very same spot many years earlier.

The complexity of the mythological heritage in medieval culture could not be dramatized more effectively. Myth is a learned story, and it is an event that can be repeated but, and this is crucial, with a new significance[80] and in a new place. For while the debate has taken place on the site of the Judgment, the arbiter will be found—in an extratextual future—in France, which is described as the endpoint of the movement of *clergie* from Athens to Rome (the famous description of the *translatio studii* topos, familiar from the *Roman de Troie* and Chrétien de Troyes's *Cligés*). Again, myth is bound up with learning: Mercury's trajectory is now replaced by that of Christine herself as she will reenact the movement of letters from classical times to the present.

That this movement implies change is clear from Christine's reworking of the Judgment story. For, as we can see, Paris's choice of love is downplayed in her version: "A Venus la pomme donna / Qui de l'avoir moult se pena" (He gave the apple to Venus who went to great trouble to get it; ll. 6191–92). Yet Venus's "bribe," Helen, goes unmentioned, as do the disastrous consequences of Paris's choice. Christine's rewriting of the Judgment thus also implies a correction. Moreover, the bribes or gifts offered by the goddesses appear not in the story line of the Judgment but rather, as mentioned above, as the qualities the four allegorical queens represent. They are thus no longer "bribes" but values central to

Christine's own culture. Thus the *Chemin*'s story line acts out one of the important aspects of the traditional Judgment story, illustrating another way that Christine appropriates myth.

Equally important is the role Christine assigns herself in this mythological construct. While in the ballade featuring the Judgment she had played the role of a corrected Paris, she here takes over the function of Mercury, or eloquence.[81] For it is Christine who, like Mercury in the Judgment, is sent off to find an arbiter to resolve the debate. Her eloquence is what qualifies her to undertake this mission that focuses on a political goal, that of ending civil strife on earth. The fact that Christine here adopts the role of a male god is interesting in the context of the *Mutacion*, which she interrupted to write the *Chemin*. In the *Mutacion* she turns into a man at the beginning of the text, in the *Chemin* she slips into a male role at the end. Thus from a man, she turns into a kind of hybrid figure woman/man (Mercury).[82] That she is woken by her mother before accomplishing her mission does not diminish the mission's importance, although it perhaps signals Christine's doubts as to her readiness or ability to take part in the political events of her time.[83]

The *Chemin* employs ancient myths in extremely complex ways: as part of the allegorical landscape, as brief reference (Icarus), as a story told by a learned clerk, and finally as an event that can be reenacted in the present. But one use is glaringly absent: mythography. I suggested that Fulgentius's appearance as an *auctor* rather than as a model that supplies a method signals Christine's distancing herself and her work from the mythographic tradition. In the same way, the Judgment of Paris is not allegorized; rather it is made *part* of the allegory, yet removed from the diegetic level, for it appears *as* an exemplary story, one of the major functions myths fulfilled in medieval culture. However, Christine alters its significance by highlighting the political aspects of the story at the expense of the mythographic tradition, which saw in the Judgment a choice of three lives.

The *Chemin* thus also advocates the rewriting of myths. Just as Leonard Barkan suggests that metamorphosis could be seen as a vast metaphor for the fate of classical culture in the medieval West,[84] I suggest that the *Chemin* illustrates the many ways in which myth can be made part of that culture. Rather than offering us a theoretical treatise on these possibilities, Christine practices what she preaches, as it were. The acquisition of learning, presented in mythical terms, finally culminates in the ways this learning can be put to political use. At the same time, the *Chemin* functions as a kind of catalog of the many ways myth can be integrated into medieval culture and can be made relevant to the present.

Christine inscribes herself into the mythic and historical universe of the *Mutacion* in a way quite different from that of the *Chemin*.[85] The autobiographical passages in Book 1 are much more elaborate than those in the *Chemin*, but on the whole Christine presents herself much more as a spectator than as a participant. The *Mutacion*, with its over 23,000 lines, is conceived on a grander scale than the *Chemin*, and the bulk of the work is much less original than the *Othéa* or the *Chemin*; yet, as we will see, there are a few extremely interesting rewritings of myth. On the whole Christine rather faithfully follows such sources as the *Histoire ancienne*, the *Grandes Chroniques*, and the *Historia de preliis* (for the parts on Alexander the Great). The sheer scope of the work seems to overwhelm the narrator, who offers frequent comments about how much is still to be done. The topos of *abbreviatio*, as well, makes many appearances.

In brief, the setup is that Christine is visiting the castle of Fortune, a windy place in constant motion.[86] It is there that Fortune dwells with her two brothers, Heur and Meseur (Luck and Bad Luck). In the palace are paintings on the walls depicting the historical events that were the results of Fortune's actions. Christine, in conveying this history to us in an ekphrastic manner, is thus both witness (though one step removed from the actual events), transcriber, and interpreter of the events.

The overriding concept and unifying principle of the *Mutacion* is the power of Fortune. Christine sees her own life and the entire history of the world as subject to that power. Christine's retelling of the myth of Actaeon can serve as a paradigmatic example of her treatment of myth in the *Mutacion*. Here it is no longer Diana who is responsible for Actaeon's unfortunate metamorphosis into a stag but rather Fortune:

> Mais n'avint pas, ce m'est advis,
> Par Dyane aviser ou vis,
> Ains fu par Meseur et ma dame,
> Qui maint lieu met a feu et flame. (ll. 4851–54)[87]

But this did not happen because of [his] looking Diana in the face, but it happened through Bad Luck and my lady who burns down many a place.

Noticeably absent is also any attempt at interpretation in the manner of the *OM* (where a wordplay on "serf" and "cerf" [servant, stag] allowed the equation of Actaeon and Christ; 3.604–69) or of the *Othéa* (chap. 69, where Actaeon was an exemplar against wasting time by hunting and, spiritually, came to stand for the penitent who has vanquished the flesh). Rather, the myth is used in the extremely interesting context of a diatribe against the (contemporary) English as a kind of commentary on the story of Brutus, the founder of Britain, and his descendants. Christine points out that she will not tell all about Britain except to say that King Arthur no longer reigns there and that the later inhabitants of Britain do not have much to do with their glorious past (ll. 4832–39). It is true that in fictions they claim to be sweet, full of faith, and loyal (ll. 4840–42), but in reality they are hateful and treacherous. Christine surely had in mind the English king whose refusal to be Charles VI's vassal contributed to the outbreak of the Hundred Years' War. Thus the story of Actaeon's dogs, who, incited by Actaeon's men, turned against him and eventually killed him, should warn any disloyal subjects against attacking their master, and although in the fable the dogs are not explicitly punished, Christine is certain that Fortune will redress the wrong done to the ruler and punish the rebellious subjects.

Thus, by focusing on an element of the Actaeon story (the hunters and the dogs) that is usually not considered important, Christine completely reorients the myth toward the political.[88] In her sorrow about the ravages of the Hundred Years' War, she cries out against the English, who are cast here in the role of the hunters who pursue their lord and master to his death. Significantly, she uses the first person singular to introduce this interpretation: "Je me doubt bien que mal l'atourne / Car de mal faire mal avient" (I well believe that this will turn out badly, for from doing evil comes evil; ll. 4860–61).

Another diatribe, equally passionate in tone, is directed against the noblemen who indulge in too much wine and entertainment:

Je ne puis penser dont il vient
A chevaliers et nobles gens
D'estre ore si tres diligens
De grans delices pour leur corps
Avoir! Et, certes, j'ay recors
Que tous les anciens escrips,
Qui des bons ont esté escrips,
Dient que les bons n'estoient
Delicatifs, ainçois hantoient
Rudes viandes et durs lis,
n'il ne leur chaloit des delis (ll. 5190–200)

I cannot imagine where knights and nobles these days get the idea of being so preoccupied with obtaining pleasures for their bodies! I certainly remember that all the ancient writings, written by good people, say that the good [nobles] were not delicate; rather, they ate plain food and slept in hard beds; they did not care about pleasures.

It is here that Ulysses appears as an exemplar of temperance (ll. 5179–82). For it is true, Christine states, Ulysses taught his knights to drink when they were resting, albeit in moderation.[89] Again, Christine uses "je" in expressions such as "je croy" (l. 5178) and "je ne puis" (l. 5190), highlighting her personal stake in this story and its moral. She posits Ulysses as a positive ancient example whose lessons in moderation are not heeded by nobles today. The consequences of this decadence of the nobility are, of course, tangible in the French's inability to chase the English from their territory. Again, a lesson from ancient myth is bound up with a political and social reality of Christine's own time.

Complementing historico-political uses of myth is the presentation of the feats of Cadmus as a metaphor for learning. Cadmus makes an appearance on the third of the four paths leading up to Fortune's castle. This is the path of "Grant Science" (l. 3237) that those who vanquish the great serpent that lies on the path will be able to tread:

Qu'un fier serpent moult orgueilleux
. . .
Couvient dompter, a trop grant peine.
(Cellui dompta, a la fonteine,
Jadis, a Thebes, Cadmus) (ll. 3187–91)

One has to tame a wild and proud serpent, with much effort. (This same one Cadmus tamed long ago at the fountain in Thebes.)

Christine then goes on to describe the marvelous landscape of learning as a kind of paradise with beautiful fountains and streams, in other words, the enchanted place we already know from the *Chemin*. The interpretation of the serpent as the pains of scholarship goes back to the *OM* and Christine's own *Othéa* (chap. 28) and *Chemin*. (Cadmus, of course, had also made an important appearance as one of the founders of civilization in Genius's sermon in the *Roman de la Rose*, but without an explicit mythographic interpretation.) The use of Cadmus, then, is an example not only of Christine's recycling of material in a variety of works but also of skillful integration of the mythographic tradition into the allegory of Fortune's castle.

Nevertheless, the predominant use of myth in the *Mutacion* is historical, and there are numerous examples of euhemerism. I will mention only three: the stories of Io (Isis), Minerva, and Hercules.[90]

In the context of Greek history in Part 5 of the *Mutacion* Christine tells of Ynacus's daughter Io, who went to Egypt and taught the Egyptians agriculture. After her death, the Egyptians prayed to their benefactress as to a goddess and erected images to her. Christine passionately condemns this idolatry by calling the Egyptians "gent / folle, incredule et non sachant" (crazy, unbelieving, and ignorant people; ll. 11,907–8). What is missing here is the story of Io's metamorphosis,[91] as well as the extravagant praise Io receives in the *Cité*. Rather, Christine speaks as a Christian historian here who condemns the errors of the pagans.

Minerva appears shortly after Io (in a Greek lake, as Christine indicates; l. 11,983) as a lady full of wisdom. She was an expert in the production of armor, and because of this expertise Minerva, also called Pallas after the island where she was born, was venerated as the goddess of chivalry (l. 11,997). She was also learned in other arts, such as letters and spinning. Because of this, she was called "Pallas, deesse de savoir" (Pallas, the goddess of knowledge; l. 12,016). It is interesting that here Christine does not cry out against the pagan deification of a human. This certainly has something to do with the special status Pallas had in Christine's life and writings.[92] From her early choice of Pallas in *Autres ballades* 7 to the praise of Pallas and the elaborate ekphrastic description of her statue in the *Cité* (see below), Christine presents the goddess almost as her "patron saint." Consequently she refrains from condemning those who adored her.

In Part 6 of the *Mutacion* Christine presents the Amazons and the Trojan War. She introduces the story of Hercules by a reference to the wall she contemplates and from which her memory draws its inspiration.[93] Because of his superhuman exploits he was called a son of Jupiter, and because he conquered strange monsters, people said of him that he went down to hell. Poets, Christine tells us, wrote down his deeds in their works. Ovid, who speaks of true history according to metaphor, also wrote about him (ll. 13,900–917).

This passage allows us a glimpse into Christine's thinking about mythical heroes. She rationally explains why some people may have interpreted Hercules's deeds as those of a son of the highest pagan god. Her mention of Ovid is very revealing and betrays a familiarity with the *OM*, whose author was intent on reconciling true history with fable. This could be achieved if one read the fable metaphorically, as covering a deeper truth. Christine does not go into a theory of fable here, but she clearly shows that she knew about the principal ways of interpreting stories like the one of Hercules.

In the vast historical tableaux of the *Mutacion*, then, we find in addition to "straight history," reproduced more or less faithfully from various sources, a variety of rewritings and interpretations of myths. From denunciations of the errors of the pagans to the exemplary use of mythological figures, Christine masters all the interpretive methods available at the time. But here she does not emphasize the reading and interpretation of myth as she does in the *Othéa*; rather, she integrates her interpretations into the flow of a universal history and thus creates perhaps not a radically new vision of history but a new version: that witnessed and recorded by a woman whose own professional history began with her transformation into a man.

Myths of Feminine Achievement in the *Cité des Dames*

In the *Cité* the new vision of myth gives way to a new vision of history that represents a culmination of Christine's efforts to rehabilitate women's role in history and society, begun in 1399 with the *Epistre au dieu d'amours*. It is this framework that determines the interpretation of the many mythological figures in the *Cité*.[94] Boccaccio's *Concerning Famous Women*, one of Christine's major sources, does not contain an overriding ideological system that determined the interpretation of his famous women. In contrast, Christine's women all have the exemplary value of demonstrating women's achievement. The uniformity of this positive message levels the differences of origin between mythological, pagan, and Christian women. The means to achieve this leveling is euhemerism. Thus the dominant mode of interpretation of mythological figures in the *Cité* is the historical. That is, myth is turned into history, and history takes on an exemplary value. Furthermore, this privileging of the literal level for the exempla shifts the focus to the allegorical frame while passing over the allegorical functions myths had acquired over the centuries.[95]

Through this manipulation of myth Christine achieves what one could call mythmaking. Ancient mythology is now subservient to the new myth of a society founded and determined by feminine achievement. If a myth answers such fundamental questions as "Where do we come from? How did we become what we are today?"[96] then the *Cité* is indeed a powerful myth since it repositions the bases of Christine's culture. Myths define how a society thinks about itself. By creating her new mythical *Cité*, Christine wants her society—including both its male and female members—to rethink itself. Her mythmaking is so successful in part because she builds on uses of myth that she herself had already offered in her previous works. This continuity, together with her astute use of traditional learned sources, provides her with a powerful authorization for her enterprise.[97]

In the opening scene of the *Cité* Christine plays with motifs from both the *Chemin* and the *Mutacion*. Just as a book, that of Boethius, provided the impetus for the composition of the *Chemin*, so a book, that of the misogynist Matheolus, makes Christine think about the status of women and finally write the *Cité*. But while Boethius's was a book that gave Christine consolation and inspired her in a positive way, Matheolus's diatribe against women plunges Christine into a profound depression before it calls forth a refutation not only of that particular book but of the entire misogynistic tradition.[98] This refutation will take the shape of a reorganization and rewriting of mostly traditional sources, such as Boccaccio's *Concerning Famous Women*, several tales from the *Decameron*, Jean Le Fèvre's *Livre de Leesce* (Book of Joy), and Vincent de Beauvais's *Miroir historial*, which is the source for most of the saints' lives of Part 3.[99] The appearance of the three allegorical ladies Reason, Rectitude, and Justice, who encourage her to reevaluate these sources, enables Christine to come up with countless examples of women's worthiness and to construct from them a fortified city that provides an alternative model to male-dominated history.

What makes the *Cité* so different from Boccaccio's model and from the *Mutacion* is its focus on virtuous women only and its nonchronological organization. Men do make an appearance but mostly as negative foils for women's positive exploits or as those responsible for women's suffering. It is women's achievements that give shape to the *Cité*, for each book has a thematic organization based on female talents and accomplishments such as political and military shrewdness, learning, prophecy, filial piety, marital love, chastity, constancy, honesty, and generosity.[100]

While Boccaccio excludes saints from his book and mentions very few Christian women, Christine integrates Christian and pagan women and devotes her entire Book 3 to female saints. Thus women from mythology appear on the same level as women from more recent history or even women Christine has known. Yet, mythological characters do play a slightly different role because they are the only ones who already have a long interpretive history. Women mentioned in chronicles, female saints, and contemporary women did not form part of the misogynistic tradition in quite the same way as did women from mythology. While the first group had been maligned in more general terms *as* women, the last group, though not all of them, of course, had a long tradition of negative interpretations attached to them.[101] It is therefore the mythological characters in the *Cité* who are most subject to remarks dealing with questions of interpretation and who consequently best represent Christine's methods of rewriting and reinterpreting the misogynistic tradition.

Since the *Cité* is a privileged place populated only by women of some intellectual or moral achievement, the same standards are applied to mythological, historical, and contemporary women. The framework is that of a universal history, in which mythical, biblical, and ancient history are integrated to form a common chronology. Texts like the *Histoire ancienne*, one of Christine's important sources for the *Mutacion*, and the *Mutacion* itself had already demonstrated the essential unity of history. Christine had also shown the usefulness of ancient myth for understanding contemporary mores in the *Othéa*. The basis for the *Cité*'s project was thus firmly established. In order to fulfill her own imperative of praising women, Christine has to apply certain principles of selection with regard to her mythological sources. In the process, she refocuses many stories, flattens some of them, and, most important, cleanses them of negative aspects, in particular of the erotic threats so many of the women traditionally represented.

The story of Arachne is one example of Christine's many transformations. We saw that in the *Mutacion* the notion of "woman's work" defined Tiresias in his female incarnation. The words that Christine uses there, "to spin and labor" (l. 1080), become more problematic in the *Cité*, where they are used, on the one hand, in Rectitude's accusations of Christine's mother that she kept her from learning and instead insisted on Christine's occupying herself with "filasses selonc l'usaige commun des femmes" (spinning, which is the usual occupation of women; p. 875);[102] and, on the other hand, in the story of Arachne, the master spinner, who is cited by Boccaccio mostly as an example of female vanity (chap. 17), and who is in the *Cité* nothing less than the person responsible for humans' emergence from the dark age before agriculture and civilization.[103]

The two instances of the evaluation of spinning highlight the importance of the context Christine creates for the mythological fable: while for Arachne spinning was a prerequisite for her contributions to civilization (in the form of nets used for hunting), for Christine spinning was supposed to replace the learning she so much desired. Unlike in Boccaccio, in the *Cité* Arachne is placed into the context of the Golden Age, which Christine proceeds to debunk: people were not better off "quand la gent ne vivoyent fors de cenelles et de glans, et ne vestoyent ne mes les piaulx des bestes" (p. 754; when [they] lived only from haws and acorns and wore nothing more than animal skins, p. 82). She does add, though, that she utters her opinion "sauve sa grace" (with all due respect, p. 82) to Boccaccio and other authors. Interestingly, Boccaccio discusses the merits of a simpler age versus civilization not in his chapter on Arachne but in that on Ceres (chap. 5), while his focus in the Arachne story is on the foolishness and vanity of those people who believe that they surpass others (p. 39).

Given this context, we can see why Christine may want to take issue with her *auctor* here and address questions of interpreting the mythological topos of the Golden Age. Like Arachne, she may actually surpass her model, and she does this by highlighting Arachne's contribution to civilization while downplaying the weaving contest with Pallas and the negative aspects of the mythographic tradition that had inspired Boccaccio. Therefore she does not mention Arachne's suicide, nor does she indicate that the metamorphosis into a spider may have been a punishment meted out by Pallas. Given Pallas's importance for Christine, she could hardly emphasize Pallas's pettiness and envy. Christine completely displaces the center of the story by focusing on Arachne's role in civilization instead of on the contest and the metamorphosis. Thus Arachne is part of a whole program dealing with the founders of human culture, such as Carmentis, inventor of the alphabet, Ceres, inventor of agriculture and other arts, and Isis (Io), cultivator of gardens and bringer of laws to the Egyptians.

Io's story will provide another example of how mythological figures are adapted and rewritten for the *Cité*. As we saw earlier, Christine showed interest in Io in her lyric poetry and in the *Othéa*. In fact, in the *Cité*'s part on Io Christine has Reason cite the *Othéa*: "si que toy meismes as touchié en ton *Livre de Othea*" (just as you yourself have touched upon in your *Epistre d'Othéa*; p. 745, p. 76). Io invented a form of shorthand, brought laws to the Egyptians as well as skills, such as planting gardens and grafting. Everyone showed her the greatest reverence and temples were erected in her honor. Her husband was supposed to have been the son of Jupiter and Niobe but only "selonc l'erreur des payens" (according to the error of the pagans; p. 746, p. 77). Thus, Christine rejects the deification accorded to Io's husband through an erroneous tradition, while hinting that the adoration Io received in her form as the goddess Isis was justified. "Divinity," it seems, has to be earned through achievements of the highest order and not just claimed by ancient poets.

Interestingly, in the chapter on Io we find one of several references to Christine's own writings.[104] Autocitation replaces here the citing of an *auctor*. The reference to her own *Othéa* reminds her audience of what she says about Io there:

> Elle devint vache, car si comme la vache donne laict, le quel est doulx et nourrissant, elle donne par les letres que elle trouva doulce nourriture a l'entendement. (p. 197)

> She was transformed into a cow, for as a cow gives milk, which is sweet and nourishing, she gave through the letters she invented sweet nourishment to our understanding.

This interpretation of the Io story is Christine's own, and it fits into the context of Christine's describing creativity and the dissemination of learning in terms of lactation, proper to women.[105] Thus, the reference to her own *Othéa* in the context of Io calls attention to Christine's previous rewriting of the Io story and the existence of a new interpretation invented by her.[106] By implication, Christine may be another Io, that is, a woman who distributes her learning as generously as Io had done.

In many other examples of Christine's rewriting of myth, the stories are pressed into the service of Christine's revisionist project and in the process leave behind many of the connotations they had acquired in the tradition. Circe, for example, who threatens the poet in Machaut's *Voir-Dit*, as we saw in Chapter 4, and who in Boccaccio is a seductress whose name has come to stand for women who change men into beasts "by their lustfulness and their vices" (p. 78), is simply a learned magician in the *Cité*. Christine makes no reference to her virtue (or lack thereof) and merely indicates that she metamorphosed Ulysses's men. She does add an extenuating circumstance, however, when she says of Circe that she was "thinking they were her enemies" (p. 70), thus alluding to the anxieties a female ruler may feel when strange men invade her island. We find another example in Medea, who is "the most cruel example of ancient wickedness" in Boccaccio (p. 35) but is "moult belle, de corsaige haulte et droitte" (p. 732; beautiful, with a noble and upright heart, p. 69) in the *Cité* and knowledgeable about the forces of nature. In a different section of the *Cité*, illustrating the faithfulness of women in love, Medea is an example of a woman spurned undeservedly by her faithless lover.[107] Dido is the only other woman to have such a divided history: while in Part 1, she is cited as the skillful founder of Carthage and a manly woman (p. 775), in Part 2 she falls into the same category as Medea, a woman deserted by a false lover. Christine thus divides up the traditional elements of well-known stories to serve her own purposes. This freedom of interpretation signals a refutation of preceding interpretive traditions that is more implicit but no less effective than the overt rejection of the misogynists.

The last mythological figure I would like to consider in some detail is Minerva/Pallas, Christine's chosen patron goddess, who forms the center of an intricate mythographic set piece. We have seen that Christine modifies her role in the Arachne story because Pallas's role had always been a negative one there. All the more elaborate is the treatment accorded to Pallas in her own story, which follows Boccaccio's *Concerning Famous Women* (chap. 6) more faithfully than many other stories. In fact, the interpretive possibilities listed there do not appear elsewhere in the *Cité* and do not correspond to her overriding scheme of euhemeristic interpretation. In most instances Christine rewrites and rearranges her source material so that it will fit into the literal and historical scheme of the *Cité*. Yet, for her favorite figure, Pallas, she closely follows Boccaccio. Why?

Following Boccaccio is nothing negative in itself. For the story on Carmentis, inventor of the Latin alphabet, for example, Christine cites Boccaccio very positively: "Ce sont les propres parolles de Bocace, desquelles la verité est notoire et magniffeste" (they are Boccaccio's own words, and his credibility is well known and evident; p. 748, p. 78). It is likely that her faithfulness to Boccaccio in the Pallas story is due to his bringing together almost all of the interpretive methods and concerns that are dispersed in the mythographic tradition and some of Christine's own works: the euhemeristic, the moral, and the ekphrastic (popularized in texts on the images of the gods, such as Pierre Bersuire's Book 1 of his *Ovidius moralizatus*). But, and this is important, although her chapter on Pallas is almost an exact translation of Boccaccio's, Christine weaves another autocitation into the very first sentence. Thus she makes all that follows her own.

The euhemeristic interpretation, prominent in other stories of the *Cité*, such as that of the goddess Ops or her daughter Juno,[108] appears first:

> Minerve, si que toy meismes en a ailleurs escript, fu une pucelle de Grece et fu surnommee Pallas. Ceste pucelle fu de tant grant excellence en engin que la folle gent de lors, pour ce que ilz ne savoyent pas bien de quelz parens elle estoit et lui veoyent faire des choses qui oncques n'avoyent esté en usaige, disdrent qu'elle estoit deesse venue du ciel. (p. 739)

> Minerva, just as you have written elsewhere, was a maiden of Greece and surnamed Pallas. This maiden was of such excellence of mind that the foolish people of that time, because they did not know who her parents were and saw her doing things which had never been done before, said she was a goddess descended from heaven. (p. 73)

Right after that Christine adds "si que dit Bocace" (as Boccaccio says; p. 739).[109] The euhemeristic explanation of Pallas's divinity is thus framed by references to two *auctores*, one of whom is Christine herself.

After listing Pallas's accomplishments in inventing weaving and the making of armor, Christine offers a moral interpretation of parts of her story:

> Et pour la grant chasteté dont elle estoit, disdrent les pouettes en leurs ficcions que Vulcan, le dieu du feu, avoit longuement luitié a elle, et que fynallement elle vainqui et le surmonta: qui estoit a dire que'elle surmonta l'ardeur et concupiscence de la char, qui donne grant assault en jeunesce. (p. 741)

> Because of her outstanding chastity, the poets claimed in their fictions that Vulcan, the god of fire, wrestled with her for a long time and that finally she won and overcame him, which is to say that she overcame the ardor and lusts of the flesh which so strongly assail the young. (p. 74)[110]

Finally, the ekphrastic section explains all the attributes of the statue of Pallas. These objects and their interpretation (the coat of mail, which "stood for the power of the estate of chivalry"; a spear, "which meant that the knight must always be a rod of justice"; a shield, "which meant that the knight must always be alert and oversee everywhere the defense of his country"; and the head of the serpent on her shield, "which teaches that the knight must always be wary and watchful" [p. 75]) recall very clearly the *Othéa*, especially so since Christine substitutes the word "chevalier" (knight) for Boccaccio's "wise man."

What Christine is doing here is framing the most elaborate series of multiple interpretations in the *Cité* with an autocitation and a conscious modification that links the ekphrasis and its moral lessons to her own previous text, the *Othéa*. And it is surely no accident that Pallas is at the center of this interpretive tour de force. Pallas, Christine's own choice in the Judgment of Paris, becomes a kind of patron of interpretation here. With Pallas, Christine demonstrates her extraordinary mastery of previous interpretive traditions as well as her skill at rewriting these traditions, making them her own, and finally integrating them into her *Cité.* Classical mythology, then, affords Christine the opportunity to demonstrate her particular mastery of learning, which will allow her to do what she set out to do at the beginning of the *Cité.* First, following the maxim of her *auctor* Boethius, who says in the *Consolation of Philosophy*: "Whoever wants to sow in virgin soil / First frees the fields of undergrowth and brush" (3m1), she clears a site of the misogynists' "underbrush" and then, by rewriting her many other *auctores,* she goes on to construct a new city built on the authority of women.

From her early lyric poetry to the *Cité* Christine weaves the stories of women and men from classical mythology into the fabric of her own texts. From the emotional and autobiographical connotations of the figures in the ballades and the first part of the *Mutacion* to the virtuoso display of learning in the *Othéa,* the rest of the *Mutacion,* the *Chemin,* and the *Cité,* Christine draws on a familiar repertory of myths that features humans in all their diversity. That the myths have profound resonances in every one of Christine's works is due not only to a skillful exploitation of her own learnedness but also to the realization that these women and men are eternal and that each re-creation can bring forth new myths. The most powerful new myth Christine helps shape at the end of her life is that of Joan of Arc, the heroine of her *Ditié de Jehanne d'Arc,* written at the height of Joan's fame in 1429.[111] Throughout her career and to the end of her life Christine was thus both a mythographer and a mythmaker, dramatizing in her own works that in order to be a maker of myths you first have to be a reader of myths.

Conclusion

In its move from the twelfth to the fifteenth centuries this study has focused on particular moments of reading, reflection, and interpretation. Each moment has marked innovations, points when something new was happening in vernacular literature: the translation and adaptation of Latin epics; love allegories expanded to encyclopedic proportions; the vernacularization and Christianization of Ovid's *Metamorphoses*; a new poetic consciousness and reflectiveness; and finally the emergence of a learned woman writer who both perpetuated and questioned tradition.

Interestingly, the mythographic interest in the gods and their attributes did not really come to the forefront in the earlier vernacular texts. The gloss on the *Echecs amoureux*, composed around 1400, is the first example of a truly mythographic approach in French.[1] We saw that the *Ovide moralisé* does not include the "images of the gods" that the Latin version of Bersuire's *Ovidius moralizatus* lists prominently. Of course, interest in the mythographic approach never waned, and there is certainly a connection between the composite portraits of the gods and their allegorized qualities one finds, say, in Ridewall's *Fulgentius metaforalis* and in the portrait of the French king Francis I as an antique god, looking peculiarly androgynous while sporting attributes of Mars, Minerva, Mercury, and others.[2] But this is only one branch of the survival and redeployment of classical myth.

The reading and interpreting of myth that has preoccupied us in this book is centered around other interests: the vernacular texts we examined stress the use of myth as narrative, whether as an adaptation of ancient epics, an extended Ovidian *récit* of strange metamorphoses, or a brief exemplary evocation of a mythological story. We found that throughout the medieval period myth was seen as a privileged place for the reflection on problems of language and interpretive issues as well as on dangers lurking in the background of apparently well-ordered political or moral systems. Indeed, almost all of the medieval and Renaissance uses of myth can be found in the texts chosen for this study: political legitimation, moral authorization, erotic aspirations, and artistic figurations.

The twelfth century saw the arrival on French and English soil of the great founding myth of Rome, the Trojan myth of conflict and the creation of new realms, and of the Theban myth of fratricide and destruction in medievalized versions. These stories were infused with Ovidian mythology, which added a further dimension of passion, danger, and mutability to these great epics. We saw that already in these early texts the interpretation of myth was thematized. At times, characters within these texts interpret mythological examples in the service of self-reflection: thus Achilles's awakening to his situation is bound up with his interpretation of the Narcissus myth, and the Thebans' terrible fate takes on added poignancy through the discourse on the mythic past of Thebes. This interpretation of myths within poetic texts themselves is a constant in all the texts we have analyzed. That this practice should be an activity for the poet figure is a major theme in Machaut's *dits*, for example, and the dialogue between the Sibyl and the figure of Christine de Pizan explores the re-creation and meaning of myth in the *Chemin*.

Jean de Meun's late-thirteenth-century *Roman de la Rose* brought a vast expansion of myth into signifying systems, centering on sexuality, language, and art. This is clear, for example, in Raison's discourse where she tests her interpretive methodology on the myth of Saturn's castration, and in the Pygmalion myth, which dramatizes the intersection of eros and art. Also in this work, myths appear in new configurations and interact with other types of discourse to take on new meanings. The triptych structures of Ami's and La Vieille's discourses, for example, introduce the misogynist Le Jaloux and La Vieille's defense of free love in order to recondition the interpretation of the myths of the Golden Age and of Mars and Venus.

The scope of new meanings of Ovidian myths was pushed to the limit by the *Ovide moralisé*, whose spiritual and New Testament grid of interpretation preserved, reunified, and renewed the Ovidian myths scattered throughout the preceding vernacular texts. The *OM* poet restates and reconsiders doctrinal questions on truth and falsehood, on damnation and salvation, in the context of the disordered world of Ovid's *Metamorphoses*. The multiplicity of meanings proposed by the *OM* vastly expanded the mythographic model of interpretation.

Machaut and Froissart drew on the *Ovide moralisé* but refocused its message: they reflected on the usefulness of ancient myth, on its exemplary function not only in the realm of morals but particularly in that of poetic creation. Froissart's bricolage of old into new myths dramatized the creative and interpretive liberties fourteenth-century poets saw as their right.

Christine de Pizan brought together almost all the interpretive and signifying possibilities of mythology, and thus she can be our guide for a final look at the question of the nature and function of ancient myth.

The earliest Christian interpreters had faced the threat of pagan religion embodied in the ancient myths and thus felt compelled to justify their use of it. Christine's *Epistre d'Othéa* illustrated, in the wake of the *Ovide moralisé*, how the Church Fathers had adapted and used the myths for moral instruction. The *Othéa*, with its fragmentary use of myth, also provided a counterpoint to the *OM*, whose long Ovidian narratives became the mythological storehouse for fourteenth- and fifteenth-century poets. In the *OM* the defusion of transgressive and threatening modes of human behavior significantly took place on the allegorical level, thus preserving the integrity of the Ovidian text to an astonishing degree. The *OM* also provided a wealth of interpretive vocabulary in the vernacular, something Christine and others made good use of.

Christine also had a political take on the ancient myths, as we saw, for example, in the *Mutacion de Fortune*. Her insistence on the Trojan origin of the French rulers takes us back to the twelfth century, where these connections were first articulated in French after existing in Latin chronicles for many centuries. The political legitimation based on myth we find in Renaissance festivities, such as processions and tableaux, was particularly visible in the miniatures of Christine's *Epistre d'Othéa*, where rulers were figured as mythological personages.[3]

Christine's use of erotic myths differed significantly from the way these myths were used in the *Roman d'Enéas* or the *Roman de la Rose*. While in the *Enéas* Ovidian passionate women articulate threats to the established feudal order of legitimate marriage and succession, and in the *Rose* Narcissus and Pygmalion figure different attitudes toward passion and creativity, Christine's mythological women in the *Cité des dames* are grounded in history. In the earlier works, most of the female characters' erotic entanglements are subsumed into lessons on women's patience, endurance, and ingenuity. But in Christine's lyric and autobiographical texts she taps myth's emotional potential. Whether she sees herself as Alcyone attempting to follow Ceyx to his watery grave, contemplates the folly of passion in the example of the Hero and Leander story, or sees her life derailed by Juno's wrath, Christine always inscribes herself into a given myth, thereby becoming part of it. She thus continued the long line of fictionalized autobiographical self-inscription into ancient myths that began in the twelfth century with poets like Bernard de Ventadour and continued long past the middle ages into the Renaissance and beyond.

Christine also became part of the learned mythological universes she created, as she did, for example, in the *Chemin de long estude*. Drawing on the Ovidian landscapes the *OM* had made available to her, she shows herself as a wanderer and seeker of wisdom figured by Mount Parnassus, Pegasus, and the fountain of wisdom. The Cadmus of the *Roman de Thèbes* reappears as the founder of written culture. In the later *Cité*, Christine assigns this role to Carmentis, thus insisting on the female contribution to the founding of civilization. Thus the *Cité* represents a new founding myth, that of a culture constructed and perfected by women.

In Christine's works myth is everywhere, and this is true for medieval culture as a whole. Long ago, the idea that the Renaissance had rediscovered antiquity was abandoned in favor of studies like those by Panofsky on renascences or the many thematic studies that showed the ubiquitousness in medieval texts of figures such as Orpheus, Paris, Daphne, Pygmalion, and many others. Each of the medieval texts studied here represents a specific reading of a model text or exhibits a particular choice of classical elements for the making of new myths. This book has tried to show how the many medieval readers of myth turned their reading into creative acts, how they came to terms with long-standing interpretive traditions, and how they fashioned new mythic constructs.

These activities gained special significance in the context of ancient mythology because this subject matter was considered inherently wise (we can think here of Jean Bodel's "matter of Rome"), and it thus conferred wisdom on vernacular poetic activities. The medievalization of classical subject matter allowed poets to encode their own political and poetic concerns "via a displacement to the past."[4] Myth thus became an ideal site for a reflection on a nation's origins and the dangers it faced. In many cases, though, the myths preserved their alterity and were marked as such by formal criteria. This alterity, coupled with their "wisdom," made them into poetic subject matter par excellence (as Eustache Deschamps indicates when he equates *poetrie* and mythological fables) and produced the extraordinary crystallization of profoundly medieval concerns around the ancient myths.

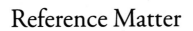

Reference Matter

Notes

All translations are my own unless otherwise indicated.

Introduction

1. The classic work on the different ways of reading mythological texts is still Seznec, *The Survival of the Pagan Gods* (1940). See also Bezold, *Das Fortleben der antiken Götter im mittelalterlichen Humanismus*; and Panofsky, *Renaissance and Renascences in Western Art*. Pépin, *Mythe et allégorie*, traces responses to ancient myth from the Stoics to medieval Christians. See also Ellspermann, *The Attitude of Early Christian Latin Writers toward Pagan Literature and Learning*, which covers writers from Minucius Felix to Saint Augustine. For the role the classics played in medieval culture and education, see Curtius, *European Literature and the Latin Middle Ages*; Haskins, *The Renaissance of the Twelfth Century*; Le Goff, *Les Intellectuels au moyen âge*; Glauche, *Schullektüre im Mittelalter*; and Scaglione, "The Classics in Medieval Education." The transmission of classical texts has been traced in Reynolds and Wilson, *Scribes and Scholars*, while a survey of mythography up to 1177 can be found in Chance, *Medieval Mythography*, vol. 1.

2. See Demats, *Fabula*, pp. 39–40, for references to the sources of these images.

3. Ellspermann, *Attitude of Early Christian Latin Writers*, p. 9.

4. Rabanus Maurus, *De clericorum institutione*, 3.18.

5. Even "Tertullian, by temperament inexorable, recognized that to forbid Christians to become acquainted with profane learning was to reduce them to an intellectual and practical helplessness well-nigh complete" (Ellspermann, *Attitude of Early Christian Latin Writers*, pp. 35–36, quoting De Labriolle, *Histoire de la littérature latine chrétienne*, 3d ed. [Paris, 1940], p. 31).

6. See the table in Munk Olsen, "La Popularité des textes classiques entre le IXe et le XIIe siècle," p. 177. Of the ninth-century *Aeneid* manuscripts 28 are still extant; from the twelfth century there are 65. One manuscript each of the

Metamorphoses and the *Thebaid* dates from the ninth century, while 27 and 51, respectively, survive from the twelfth.

7. Gadamer's observation, in *Wahrheit und Methode,* is also relevant here: "Understanding is 'not merely a reproductive, but always a productive attitude as well' " (as quoted in Jauss, *Toward an Aesthetic of Reception,* p. 31).

8. See Wittig, "The Aeneas-Dido Allusion in Chrétien's *Erec et Enide,*" esp. pp. 246–47. On medieval ways of reading and writing and their interaction, see also Gellrich, *The Idea of the Book in the Middle Ages.*

9. Except at the beginning of Chapter 5, I will focus more on narrative than on lyric poetry. In lyric poetry the use of myth is generally more allusive, and the "built-in" interpretations that interest me most in the context of this study are thus absent.

10. See, for example, Comparetti, *Vergil in the Middle Ages*; Courcelle and Courcelle, *Lecteurs païens et lecteurs chrétiens de l'Enéide*; Curtius, *European Literature*; Hexter, *Ovid and Medieval Schooling*; Munk Olsen, *L'Etude des auteurs classiques latins aux XIe et XIIe siècles*; and Rand, *Ovid and His Influence.*

11. To give just a few examples of this type of study: Barkan, "Diana and Actaeon: The Myth as Synthesis"; Dinter, *Der Pygmalion-Stoff in der europäischen Literatur*; Ehrhart, *The Judgment of the Trojan Prince Paris in Medieval Literature*; Friedman, *Orpheus in the Middle Ages*; Giraud, *La Fable de Daphné*; Heitmann, "Orpheus im Mittelalter"; Lavin, "Cephalus and Procris: Transformations of an Ovidian Myth"; Rudd, "Daedalus and Icarus (I)"; Trousson, *Le Thème de Prométhée dans la littérature européenne*; Vinge, *The Narcissus Theme in Western European Literature up to the Early Nineteenth Century*; and Warden, ed., *Orpheus: The Metamorphoses of a Myth.*

12. For the theory of reception, see Jauss, *Toward an Aesthetic of Reception.* On questions of intertextuality, see *Intertextualités médiévales,* a special issue of *Littérature* 41 (1981). In this volume, Kelly, "Les Inventions ovidiennes de Froissart," analyzes Froissart's creative use of myth; and Regalado, " 'Des contraires choses,' " touches on mythological exempla in the *Roman de la Rose*; see also Riffaterre, "L'Intertexte inconnu" in the same volume. For textual indexes of interpretation (explicit signals calling for interpretation), see Todorov, *Symbolism and Interpretation,* pp. 30–32. The allegory/allegoresis debate has seen an extremely interesting *mise au point* in the recent article by Copeland and Melville, "Allegory and Allegoresis, Rhetoric and Hermeneutics."

13. Although there is no systematic study of ekphrasis for the medieval period, some interesting remarks on ekphrasis in the *Iliad* and the *Aeneid* can be found in Meltzer, *Salome and the Dance of Writing.* In "The Image of History in Christine de Pizan's *Livre de la Mutacion de Fortune,*" Brownlee studies the historical wall paintings referred to in Christine's text; see also Patterson, " 'Rapt with Pleasaunce': Vision and Narration in the Epic." On *mise en abyme,* see Dällenbach, *The Mirror in the Text.*

14. See Freeman, "Problems in Romance Composition: Ovid, Chrétien de Troyes, and the *Romance of the Rose*," esp. pp. 158–59; quote on p. 159.

15. Jean Bodel, *Chanson de Saisnes*, ll. 6–10, in Menzel and Stengel, eds., *Jean Bodel's Saxenlied.*

16. Listed according to Minnis, "The Influence of Academic Prologues on the Prologues and Literary Attitudes of Late-Medieval English Writers," pp. 345–46. The definitions that follow are also listed there. See also Quain, "The Medieval Accessus ad Auctores."

17. For a consideration of the *modus tractandi*, see Minnis, "Literary Theory in Discussions of *Formae Tractandi* by Medieval Theologians."

18. See the appendix "Creative Etymology" to my *Not of Woman Born: Representations of Caesarean Birth in Medieval and Renaissance Culture.*

19. Minnis, "The Influence," p. 346.

20. The four causes were the *causa efficiens*, the *causa materialis*, the *causa formalis*, and the *causa finalis*. For definitions see Minnis, "The Influence," pp. 350–51.

21. See Quain, "The Medieval Accessus ad Auctores," pp. 219–20, for an extensive quote from an *accessus* to Ovid's *Heroides*. Quain rightly concludes here that "the anonymous author's main interest, as is evident, lay in the moral aspects of the work of Ovid" (p. 220).

22. See Krill, "The *Vatican Mythographers*." For a quick introduction to the mythographers, see Chance's introduction to *The Mythographic Art: Classical Fable and the Rise of the Vernacular in Early France and Britain*; pp. 33–34 present a handy list of the major mythographers.

23. Comparetti (*Vergil in the Middle Ages*, p. 112) says of Fulgentius: "But the process of Fulgentius is so violent and incoherent, it disregards every law of common sense in such a patent and well-nigh brutal manner, that it is hard to conceive how any sane man can seriously have undertaken such a work, and harder still to believe that other sane men should have accepted it as an object for serious consideration."

24. Macrobius, *Commentary on the Dream of Scipio*, pp. 84–87. On Macrobius, see Demats, *Fabula: Trois études de mythographie antique et médiévale*, pp. 16–26; and Dronke, *Fabula: Explorations of the Uses of Myth in Medieval Platonism*, chap. 1. Stock, *Myth and Science in the Twelfth Century*, devotes his first chapter to an examination of the concept of *narratio fabulosa*, a fictional discourse using fables.

25. *The Mythologies* (Whitbread, trans.), p. 45. Fulgentius's commentaries deal of course with Roman texts, but the gods were a legacy from the Greeks.

26. Stock, *Myth and Science*, p. 32.

27. See Brinkmann, "Verhüllung ('Integumentum') als literarische Darstellungsform im Mittelalter," pp. 320–22. See also M.-D. Chenu, "'*Involucrum*': Le Mythe selon les théologiens médiévaux."

28. For William of Conches, see Jeauneau, "L'Usage de la notion d'*integumentum* à travers les gloses de Guillaume de Conches"; Dronke, *Fabula*; and Wetherbee, *Platonism and Poetry in the Twelfth Century*, esp. pp. 29–48. Already Theodolphus of Orléans "believed that under a false exterior there lay hidden truths" (Born, "Ovid and Allegory," p. 363). He used the word *tegmen* to describe the covering: "In quorum dictis quamquam sint frivola multa, plurima sunt falso tegmine vera latet" (*PL* 105, col. 331, quoted by Born, p. 363).

29. Tuve, *Allegorical Imagery*, chap. 4.

30. Exceptions are Virgil's *Eclogues*, which were believed to have announced the coming of Christ, and some texts of Ovid. There were efforts to see in Ovid a kind of platonic prophet who had an intuition of the truth, that is, Christianity; see Demats, *Fabula*, pp. 131–33.

31. Hexter, "Medieval Articulations of Ovid's *Metamorphoses*," p. 63. See also his extremely insightful article "The *Allegari* of Pierre Bersuire," in which he describes the preconditions for interpretation. We will return to the questions raised here in Chapter 3.

32. See McLeod, *Virtue and Venom: Catalogs of Women from Antiquity to the Renaissance*. For an earlier period, see West, *The Hesiodic Catalogue of Women*.

33. P. 63; p. 69. The Latin words used to signal these equivalencies are *est* and *designat*. In this type of equation there is no room for the literal level.

34. For the two examples just cited from John of Garland, Arnulf tells only the story without appending any moral interpretation. For more on John and Arnulf, see Chapter 3.

35. See, for example, the manuscript Bodleian Digby 104, described by Ghisalberti in "Arnolfo d'Orléans: Un cultore d'Ovidio nel secolo XII," p. 190. There, he speaks of a "fusion" of text and commentaries.

36. See Hexter, "Medieval Articulations," for a good description of this type of gloss and a comparison with Arnulf's commentary. Hexter also reproduces some manuscript pages that show how closely hemmed in the Ovidian text was by its commentaries.

37. The image of the chains is, of course, that of Jauss ("Allégorie, 'remythisation' et nouveau mythe"), who refers to the allegorized existence of myth as a Babylonian captivity. The quote is from Herzog, "Metapher—Exegese—Mythos," p. 163. Another term used by Herzog to describe the survival of mythology is also interesting in this respect: *überwintern* (to winter). This term, of course, implies a new spring or flowering; that this flowering also took place in the vernacular tradition is something that Herzog does not consider. Lewis, in *The Allegory of Love*, also used rather picturesque language in the same context: "The gods must be, as it were, disinfected of belief" (by allegory) and "such a sleeping-place was provided for the gods by allegory" (p. 83).

38. Herzog, "Metapher," p. 167. *Remythisierung* is the term used by Jauss in his "Allégorie, 'remythisation' et nouveau mythe." *Bricolage*, as used by Lévi-

Strauss, implies a segmentation similar to that of the classical texts mentioned above (*La Pensée sauvage*, p. 31).

39. See Stierle, "Mythos als 'Bricolage' und zwei Endstufen des Prometheus-mythos," p. 458. Stierle points out that a history of myth is only possible when *signifiant* (signifier) and *signifié* (signified) no longer coincide. And he adds, "an understanding of myth that is directed toward 'the origin of myth' would have to speak here of *abusio* or a deviation of purpose" (p. 458).

40. Blumenberg, *Work on Myth*, p. 35. See the introduction by Edmunds to *Approaches to Greek Myth* for the prevalent contemporary methods for dealing with myth. Edmunds also reflects on modern critics' urge to identify *the* version of a myth as the "authentic" one.

41. See Weinrich, "Structures narratives du mythe," p. 27: "Linguistically speaking, myth therefore has the status of *parole* in the Saussurian sense of the term" (with a note to Barthes's *Mythologies*).

42. See Jauss, *Pour une esthétique de la réception*: "It is therefore necessary to include in this relationship, which links the work and humanity, the relationship between the works themselves, and to situate the historical relationship between the works in the complex of reciprocal relations that exist between production and reception" (p. 39). A good example of this phenomenon is Christine de Pizan's use of myth, which is frequently conditioned by the function of myth in the *Roman de la Rose*. See Brownlee, "Discourses of the Self: Christine de Pizan and the *Rose*."

43. Weinrich, "Structures narratives du mythe."

44. See Todorov, *Symbolism and Interpretation*, the chapter entitled "The Decision to Interpret" (pp. 27–38). The term *diegesis* is Genette's (*Figures III*, p. 72 and n.1). He adapts the term from cinematography to mean story line.

45. Not all critics would agree with this. For useful approaches to this question, see, for example, Mora, "Sources de l'*Enéas*"; and Nolan, "Ovid's *Heroides* Contextualized: Foolish Love and Legitimate Marriage in the *Roman d'Enéas*."

46. Poirion, "De l' 'Enéide' à l' 'Enéas.' "

47. See Weinrich, "Structures narratives du mythe," p. 30.

48. See Angeli, *L'Eneas e i primi romanzi volgari*, and my "Old French Narrative Genres: Towards a Definition of the *Roman antique*."

49. See Cooke, "Euhemerism: A Medieval Interpretation of Classical Paganism," and Pépin, "The Euhemerism of the Christian Authors."

50. See my "Moralization and History: Verse and Prose in the *Histoire ancienne jusqu'à César*," for the formal aspects (verse and prose) and some examples of the moralizations attached to episodes from the *romans antiques*. I mention the *Histoire ancienne* for the sake of completeness and to suggest further areas of research; it will not form part of the bulk of this book. The *Histoire ancienne* still has not been edited. For some remarks on the relationship between the romances of antiquity and the *Histoire ancienne*, see Raynaud de Lage, "Les 'Romans an-

tiques' dans l'Histoire ancienne jusqu'à César"; my "The Traditions of the Old French *Roman de Thèbes*," chap. 4; and Singerman, *Under Clouds of Poesy: Poetry and Truth in French and English Reworkings of the Aeneid, 1160–1513*, chap. 3.

51. The explanation of the existence of the Minotaur as the offspring of Minos's secretary Taurus (conceived by Pasiphae in an adulterous relationship) is probably one of the more hilarious examples. It comes straight from the antique mythographic tradition, as Nestle shows (*Vom Mythos zum Logos*, p. 150). See my "The Scandal of Pasiphae: Narration and Interpretation in the *Ovide moralisé*" for the interpretive history of this story.

52. See, for example, Fleming's *The 'Roman de la Rose': A Study in Allegory and Iconography*.

53. One such pattern, that of petrification, has been brilliantly analyzed by Huot in "The Medusa Interpolation in the *Roman de la Rose*."

54. The only mythological stories told by the narrator in Jean de Meun's part are those of Adonis and Pygmalion. See Brownlee, "Orpheus' Song Re-sung: Jean de Meun's Reworking of *Metamorphoses X*."

55. See Huot, "From *Roman de la Rose* to *Roman de la Poire*," p. 102. See also Weinrich, "Structures narratives du mythe" (p. 31): "The myth, reduced as far as the narrative is concerned and immobilized as an event in the form of a scene, has thus become comparable to the allegory, which was so much prized by the middle ages."

56. See Smalley, *English Friars and Antiquity in the Early Fourteenth Century*, for an excellent description of the intellectual climate of the fourteenth century. A text that equals in its interpretive excesses the *Ovide moralisé* is the *Glose des Echecs amoureux*, composed around 1400 by Evrart de Conty. This text presents the new case of a mythographic commentary on a vernacular text, the *Echecs amoureux*, a descendant of the *Roman de la Rose*. The *Glose* became a vast storehouse of mythography in the vernacular and is preserved in splendid manuscripts that transmitted the iconographic tradition associated with mythography. See Tesson, "La *Glose des Echecs amoureux*," and her dissertation, "La *Glose des Echecs amoureux*: Les Idées et le genre de l'oeuvre d'après le commentaire du verger de Déduit." The illuminations of MS B.N. f.fr. 9197 have been reproduced in Legaré, *Le Livre des Echecs amoureux*. See also the edition of the *Glose* by Roy and Tesson: Evrart de Conty, *Le Livre des eschez amoureux moralisés*. For a study of the text, see Badel, *Le Roman de la Rose au XIVe siècle*, pp. 290–315.

57. See Herzog, "Metapher," pp. 159–63, where he analyzes the absorption of biblical figures into the realm of mythology. This, in Herzog's opinion, is a *Spätphase* (late phase) or even *Schlussphase* (final phase) of a thousand-year reception history (p. 160).

58. See, for example, Ehrhart, *The Judgment*, p. 139: "Since Machaut took the outline of his Judgment from the *Ovide moralisé*, he *must* have been aware

of the moralization there" (my emphasis). But does that mean that he accepts it? Brownlee, in *Poetic Identity in Guillaume de Machaut*, p. 202, makes the opposite point; for him, Machaut demoralizes his source. Is the garden in the *Fonteinne amoureuse* really, like Eden, a "locus for a fall" and love a "choice of damnation" (Ehrhart, *The Judgment*, p. 141)? It seems to me that the "moral" interpretation does not always take into account the polysemy of available interpretations. (Pygmalion in the *Ovide moralisé* would be another good example: first he is an exemplar of idolatry, then he stands for God as Creator.)

Chapter 1

1. Poirion, *Résurgences: Mythe et littérature à l'âge du symbole (XIIe siècle)*, p. 55.

2. The first two romances are anonymous, the third is by Benoît de Sainte-Maure. They are dated 1152–54, 1160, and 1165, respectively, although these dates are mostly conjectural. See Langlois, "Chronologie des Romans de 'Thèbes,' d' 'Enéas' et de 'Troie.'" For a recent *mise au point* and a thorough study of all three romances, see Schöning, *Thebenroman—Eneasroman—Trojaroman*, and Nolan, *Chaucer and the Tradition of the 'Roman Antique,'* chaps. 1–3. In my "Remarques sur songe/mensonge" I show that even the relative chronology of these romances is not clear-cut. Henceforth the titles will be abbreviated as *RTh*, *RE*, and *RTr*. The editions I used are *Le Roman de Thèbes*, ed. Raynaud de Lage; *Le Roman d'Enéas*, ed. Salverda de Grave; and Benoît de Sainte-Maure, *Le Roman de Troie*, ed. Constans. The romances are based on Latin texts: Statius's *Thebaid*; Virgil's *Aeneid*; and the late antique résumés of the history of the Trojan War by Dares and Dictys: *Daretis Phrygii de excidio Troiae Historia* and the *Ephemeridos Belli Troiani Libri* of Dictys. Both works are translated in Frazer, *The Trojan War: The Chronicles of Dictys of Crete and Dares the Phrygian.*

3. On the circulation of manuscripts of classical texts in this period, see Munk Olsen, *L'Etude des auteurs classiques latins.* On the survival of classical texts, see Reynolds and Wilson, *Scribes and Scholars: A Guide to the Transmission of Greek and Latin Literature.*

4. On the first romances and possible political connections in general, see Angeli, *L' 'Enéas' e i primi romanzi volgari.*

5. See Hexter, "Medieval Articulations of Ovid's *Metamorphoses*," for ideas on segmentation and its consequences.

6. Though by no means all, as some critics argue. See Salverda de Grave in his edition of *Le Roman d'Enéas*, 1:xxiii.

7. Barkan, *The Gods Made Flesh: Metamorphosis and the Pursuit of Paganism*, p. 49.

8. Ibid., p. 13.

9. See Beaune, "L'Utilisation politique du mythe des origines troyennes en

France à la fin du moyen âge," p. 332. The earliest texts to feature a more or less coherent version of the Trojan origins of the Franks were the *Pseudo-Fredegarius* and the *Liber historiae Francorum*.

10. On Geoffrey and his predecessors, see Hanning, *The Vision of History in Early Britain*. The *Roman de Brut*, while not a true romance of antiquity (because the text was not translated from a *classical* model), addresses many of the same concerns—the *translatio* (transference) of power, Trojan origins, etc.

11. See Angeli, *L''Eneas' e i primi romanzi volgari*; Bezzola, *Les Origines et la formation de la littérature courtoise en occident*; Patterson, "Virgil and the Historical Consciousness of the Twelfth Century," esp. pp. 179–80; Poirion, "De l''Enéïde' à l''Enéas'" and my "Old French Narrative Genres." Benoît de Sainte-Maure, the only identified author, was most likely also the author of the *Chronique des ducs de Normandie*, in which he flatters Henry. It is believed that he took over this task from the aging Wace, who wrote the same history in his *Roman de Rou*. For remarks on a possible "dedication" (in the form of a discourse of praise) to Eleanor of Aquitaine, see n. 93, below.

12. Guenée, *Histoire et culture historique dans l'occident médiéval*, pp. 334–35; quote from Hanning, *The Vision*, p. 141.

13. *Cronicon Richardi Divisensis de tempore Regis Ricardi Primi*, fol. 25v. Devizes quotes Statius here: "Oedipodae confusa domus" (the confused house of Oedipus; *Thebaid* 1.17). I elaborate the argument on the connection between Henry's troubles and the *RTh* at length in "The Traditions"; "Chrétien de Troyes as a Reader of the *Romans Antiques*"; and "The Gods as Metaphor in the *Roman de Thèbes*." The *RTh*'s two distinct versions could address themselves to different moments in Henry's reign: the troubles leading up to his accession to the throne (pitting Stephen of Blois against Henry's mother, Matilda, relative against relative) and the later armed conflicts between his sons. On the former conflict, see Warren, *Henry II*, chap. 2; on the latter, see chap. 3. Robert of Normandy also compared himself to a Theban character, Polynices, as Orderic Vitalis reports (*Historia ecclesiastica* 5.10; cited by Hanning, *The Vision*, p. 225, n. 26).

14. Dido's epitaph in the *RE* reads, in part, "onques ne fu meillor païene" (there was never a better pagan woman; l. 2141). On questions of the awareness of paganism in this period, see Camille, *The Gothic Idol: Ideology and Image-Making in Medieval Art*, chap. 2 (which includes a discussion of contemporary travelers' accounts of what they saw in Rome).

15. On the School of Chartres, see Wetherbee, *Platonism and Poetry in the Twelfth Century: The Literary Influence of the School of Chartres*; see also Dronke, *Fabula: Explorations of the Use of Myth in Medieval Platonism*. On the intellectual climate of this period, see Chenu, *Nature, Man, and Society in the Twelfth Century*. A figure such as John of Salisbury could be seen as emblematic of the links between the School of Chartres and Anglo-Norman writing. He lived in France

from 1136 to 1148 and studied with William of Conches; his classical culture is evident in the *Policraticus*; and he was secretary to the archbishop of Canterbury, Henry II's friend and, later, enemy. He also had a great interest in translation. On John see Liebeschütz, *Medieval Humanism in the Life and Writings of John of Salisbury*, and Chenu, *Nature, Man, and Society*.

16. See Jauss, "Allégorie, 'remythisation' et nouveau mythe." Strangely, Jauss does not mention the romances of antiquity in this article or in "La Transformation de la forme allégorique entre 1180 et 1240." For the remythisization of the god of Love, see Ruhe, *Le Dieu d'Amours avec son paradis*. For the problem of mythological figures versus personification, see Lewis, *The Allegory of Love*, chap. 2.

17. For the importance of the late antique epithalamium for the preservation of the antique gods (especially Venus and Cupid), see Mora, "Sources de l'Enéas," and Ruhe, *Le Dieu d'Amours*, chap. 1 (called chap. A in the book).

18. See Poirion, "De l' 'Enéïde' à l' 'Enéas,' " and, for the *RTh*, my arguments in "The Gods as Metaphor in the *Roman de Thèbes*."

19. But see Detienne, "The Interpretation of Myths": "In asking for an admission of guilt within the Oedipal configuration, psychoanalysis indeed marks a return to myth and the religious; but in seeing both of them as merely the visible tip of the iceberg of the 'Unconscious' . . . it has condemned mythology to being nothing but the symbolic and obsessive repetition of a few unconscious representations centered on sexuality" (p. 8).

20. Poirion, "Edyppus et l'énigme du roman médiéval."

21. One earlier Latin text that testifies to some interest in the Oedipus legend is the *Mathematicus* (based on a story from Quintilian) by Hildebert of Lavardin (d. 1133). Although a number of plot developments are different (no parricide, for example), it still evokes the Oedipus legend. A later reworking, based on the *RTh* and the *Second Vatican Mythographer*, can be found in the early-thirteenth-century *Histoire ancienne jusqu'à César*. This text reintroduces some mythographic elements. See Raynaud de Lage, "Les 'Romans antiques' dans l'*Histoire ancienne jusqu'à César*"; my "Moralization and History: Verse and Prose in the *Histoire ancienne jusqu'à César*"; and chap. 4 of my "The Traditions of the Old French *Roman de Thèbes*," which is devoted to the *Histoire ancienne*.

22. *Pré-texte* is Huchet's term (*Le Roman médiéval*, p. 187.) Poirion prefers *avant-texte* ("Edyppus").

23. For example, "Already had Oedipus with avenging hand probed deep his sinning eyes and sunk his guilty shame in eternal night, abiding in a long and living death" (*Thebaid* 1.46–48).

24. *Thebaid* 1.56–87.

25. Donovan, *Recherches sur le Roman de Thèbes*.

26. Huchet, *Le Roman médiéval*, pp. 188, 86.

27. See Poirion, *Résurgences*, pp. 56–58.

28. The idea of parricide of the author seems to be implied by Huchet's remarks in *Le Roman médiéval*, p. 11. For an analysis of the three occurrences of Statius's name in the *RTh*, see my "Old French Narrative Genres," pp. 153–54.

29. For example, ll. 127f. "Car li enfes qui en haut pent / avra secours prochainement." For the contest:

> Or verrons nos qui porra plus,
> ou Appolo ou Laÿus:
> se li enfes est decolez,
> dont est li dex a fox provez;
> s'il eschape des mains as trois,
> poor em puet avoir li rois. (ll. 97–102)

Now we will see who is more powerful, Apollo or Laius: if the child is beheaded, the god is proved wrong; if he escapes from the hands of these three, then the king can be afraid of him.

30. The term *couverture* appears in all manuscripts of the *RTh*. For the notion of integument, see Jeauneau, "L'Usage de la notion d'*integumentum* à travers les gloses de Guillaume de Conches."

31. For example, the riddle of the Sphinx solved by Oedipus is not even explicitly stated in the *Thebaid*; all Oedipus says about it is "I solved the riddles of the cruel Sphinx" (ll. 66–67). The details come from the *Second Vatican Mythographer* (*Mythographi Vaticani I et II*, chap. 166, p. 226).

32. I am of course thinking of the pseudo-Fulgentian *Super Thebaiden* (English text in Whitbread, trans., *Fulgentius, the Mythographer*, pp. 239–43). On the twelfth-century dating of this text, see Stock, "A Note on Thebaid Commentaries." The preceding remarks are also valid for the Prologue, in which the poet aligns himself with the ancient authorities Homer, Plato, Virgil, and Cicero—thus authorizing his own enterprise—but does not mention Statius, his true *auctor*.

33. For a detailed comparison between the *Thebaid* and the *RTh*, see Petit, *Naissances du roman: Les Techniques littéraires dans les romans antiques du XIIe siècle*, vol. 1, pp. 21–137; pp. 139–326 deal with the technical aspects of translation and adaptation. For a list of those instances where the gods no longer intervene in the *RTh*, see Schöning, *Thebenroman*, pp. 90–91.

34. Her transformation into a spider is omitted. For her story, see Ovid's *Metamorphoses* 6.1–145; see also the *Vatican Mythographers*, 1.90, 2.88.

35. Semiramis's transformation into a dove and her building of Babylon are mentioned in *Met* 4.47–56. Her story was also transmitted to the middle ages by such historians as Justinus, Valerius Maximus, and Orosius. She was thus considered both a historical and a mythological figure (she was believed to be the daughter of Neptune). A version of her story based on the sources just listed is in Boccaccio's *Concerning Famous Women* (Guarino, trans., pp. 4–7).

36. Barkan, *The Gods Made Flesh*, p. 2.

37. For an analysis of the connection between weaving and poetry, see Macfie, "Ovid, Arachne, and the Poetics of Paradise."

38. See my "The Traditions," chap. 2, for a detailed analysis of this project.

39. Syncretism of this kind is common in medieval texts. The *RTh* poet speaks of churches, nunneries, and bishops, yet never suggests that the Thebans or their enemies were actually Christians. The anachronistic touches were surely intentional and served to underline the story's eternal human appeal. Schöning has shown in his recent study that frequently, especially in the *RTh* and the *RTr*, God and the pagan gods belong to different spheres: the former to the sphere of the poet and his audience, the latter to that of the characters (*Thebenroman*, p. 317). However, this distinction is not completely watertight, for there are instances where the pagan characters themselves invoke God. Grout's "Religion and Mythology in the *Roman de Thèbes*" does not shed much light on these problems: she concentrates on the intermingling of pagan and Christian ritual without really drawing any conclusions. Raynaud de Lage, in "Les Romans antiques et la représentation de la réalité," concludes his analysis of the role of religion in the romances of antiquity by saying: "We notice that sometimes there is a partial but relatively correct knowledge of antiquity, and sometimes a travesty that touches on the burlesque" (p. 286). Basically, Raynaud de Lage takes a disparaging view of the *RTh*'s treatment of religious ritual.

40. The following remarks draw on my "The Gods as Metaphor," p. 6.

41. Other details of the chariot include the nine spheres, the planets, the world, beasts, the sea and its inhabitants, and winds and storms. Ovid and Macrobius are likely sources for this description: see my "The Gods as Metaphor," p. 6, n. 30. Huchet sees in the chariot a metaphor for the romance (*Le Roman médiéval*, p. 208), an argument I made in "The Traditions" (p. 81).

42. On the connection between memory and painted images, see Carruthers, *The Book of Memory: A Study of Memory in Medieval Culture*, pp. 229–41.

43. Holden, ed., ll. 1–4.

44. The Capaneus episode was considered an interpolation by Constans, the first editor of the *RTh*. For a detailed examination of the critical controversy on whether or not this passage is an interpolation, see Petit, "Un Passage controversé du 'Roman de Thèbes': La Capanéïde." His close stylistic and technical analysis demonstrates that the episode must have been an integral part of the short version, MSS B and C (the base manuscript for the more recent edition by Raynaud de Lage).

45. Most of these figures also appear in Ovid's *Met*, Book 4. Amphion appears in *Met* 6.176ff.; his magic powers are emphasized here. Other references in Capaneus's speech can also be found in *Thebaid* 1.6–16 and 10.874–906 (the passage that corresponds to the action of the *RTh* under consideration here).

46. The only goddess who is out of place here is Juno—traditionally anti-Thebes.

47. The *RE* has generated considerably more criticism than the *RTh*, yet much of it does not illuminate any problems related to classical mythology in the romance. Mora-Lebrun's excellent *L'ʻEnéide' médiévale et la naissance du roman* considers the *RE* both as an endpoint of developments begun by Anglo-Norman historians, mythographers, and the thinkers of the School of Chartres and as a new departure for the genre of medieval romance. Other useful studies in this area are Blask, *Geschehen und Geschick im altfranzösischen Eneas-Roman*; Huchet, *Le Roman médiéval*; Mora, "Sources de l'Enéas"; Poirion, "De l' ʻEnéïde' à l' ʻEnéas' "; and Schöning, *Thebenroman*. Comparetti, *Vergil in the Middle Ages*, is still an indispensable general guide. He treats the *RE* on pp. 245–46 but mentions mythology only briefly as "stepping . . . into the background" (p. 245). From now on I will use Enéas to refer to the protagonist of the medieval text, and Aeneas to refer to the Virgilian hero. Analogously, I will use Lavine to indicate the *RE* character and Lavinia to indicate Virgil's character.

48. Fulgentius, *Exposition of the Content of Virgil*, in Whitbread, trans., *Fulgentius the Mythographer*, pp. 105–53.

49. [Bernardus Silvestris], *The Commentary of the First Six Books of the Aeneid of Vergil, Commonly Attributed to Bernardus Silvestris*.

50. Cormier offers a rather cursory examination of this problem in "Laughter and Smiles (and a Few Non-Virgilian Chuckles) in the Old French ʻRoman d'Enéas.' " See also Baswell, *Virgil in Medieval England*, for an examination of these problems in greater detail. Wittig, "The Aeneas-Dido Allusion in Chrétien's *Erec et Enide*," sees the influence of Fulgentius's and Bernardus's commentaries on the *RE*. Yet Wittig ultimately casts this influence in very general psychological terms that do not necessarily stem from these commentaries. Nolan in "Ovid's *Heroides* Contextualized: Foolish Love and Legitimate Marriage in the *Roman d'Enéas*," argues for the distinction between the two kinds of love made in *Heroides* commentaries as applicable to the *RE*. This argument seems to be more reasonable than looking for the six ages of man in the *RE*. Singerman, *Under Clouds of Poesy: Poetry and Truth in French and English Reworkings of the Aeneid, 1160–1513*, sees a kind of commentary on the commentary tradition in the fact that the *RE* gives twice as much space to Virgil's Books 7–12 as to Books 1–6, while Bernardus, for example, omits Books 7–12 altogether (p. 38). Zink, "Héritage rhétorique et nouveauté littéraire dans le ʻRoman antique' en France au Moyen Age," sees in the *RE* "a point of view which is diametrically opposed to that of commentators on Virgil who write in Latin" (p. 261). Cormier takes a similar position in *One Heart, One Mind: The Rebirth of Virgil's Hero in Medieval French Romance*, pp. 184–86 (where he calls Bernardus's influence negligible). Poirion's point on Pallas in the *RE* would confirm these opinions. Poirion shows

that in William of Conches Pallas stood for wisdom and the contemplative life, while in the *RE* she signifies prowess ("De l' 'Enéïde' à l' 'Enéas,' " p. 215).

51. By now, this is one of the commonplaces of *RE* criticism, which should not blind us to the revolutionary nature of this innovation, however. Faral examines Ovidian influence in his *Recherches sur les sources latines des contes et romans courtois du moyen âge*, pp. 73–157. The *RE* influenced not only medieval romance but also other genres, such as the lyric. See Roncaglia, "Les Troubadours et Virgile," esp. pp. 269, 274.

52. The expression "opening towards the feminine" is Schnapp's ("Dante's Sexual Solecisms: Gender and Genre in the *Commedia*"). See also Ovid, *Heroides and Amores*. As a counterpoint to this reading, see Baswell, "Men in the *Roman d'Enéas*."

53. Although the gods are much more present here than in the *RTh*, their role has been greatly reduced in comparison to the *Aeneid*. Pauphilet, "L'Antiquité et l'Enéas," deals mostly with the suppression of Virgilian mythological elements. The best study on this subject is Blask, *Geschehen und Geschick*. He shows that in general the human sphere is highlighted at the expense of the divine sphere; that in the *RE* there is an important distinction between individual gods, such as Venus, and the gods as a collective force; and that Fortuna has become a more important force than the gods (although I would not agree with Blask's point, p. 169, that the gods are mere "left-overs" from Virgil). For the most part, I will leave aside the question of religion in the *RE*, treated in detail by Schöning and Blask. Both critics distinguish between the level of the pagan gods and of God, and finally that of the only vaguely defined idols as objects carried around by King Latinus and mentioned by King Evander's wife as deities that she will no longer pray to since they have failed to protect her son (ll. 6353–55). These "gods" can also usefully be compared to the idols in medieval saints' lives. The queen's treatment of the idols recalls the beating of the pagan figures in the *Jeu de saint Nicolas* (in turn related to the Christian "humiliation of saints"; see Geary, "Humiliation of Saints"). Latinus's idols also recall the pagan idols of the *chanson de geste*. They do not seem to have much to do with the "mythological" gods.

54. This has been shown most recently by Nolan in "The Judgment of Paris in the *Roman d'Enéas*." Nolan also traces the connections between the versions by Donatus and Hyginus to those of the Vatican mythographers. The second of the mythographers, possibly Remigius of Auxerre, added the Fulgentian interpretation of the three lives (p. 53). Ehrhart, *The Judgment of the Trojan Prince Paris in Medieval Literature*, posits a text related to the *Excidium Troiae* and the *Compendium Historiae Troiae-Romanae* as a source for the *RE* (pp. 37–39).

55. For the Judgment's function of giving shape to the romance, see Freeman, "The 'Roman d'Enéas': Implications of the 'Prologue' "; Huchet, *Le Ro-*

man médiéval, pp. 39–59; Nolan, "The Judgment of Paris"; Poirion, "L'Ecriture épique: Du sublime au symbole," i–xiii, esp. p. xiii; and Rousse, "Le Pouvoir, la prouesse et l'amour dans l'Enéas." Schöning's view of the Judgment as a "persiflage" (*Thebenroman*, p. 238) does not make much sense.

56. Unlike most other medieval romances the *RE* has no explicit prologue.

57. Nolan ("The Judgment of Paris," p. 55) argues that the *RE* poet adds an interpretation to his source by mentioning Paris's "engin" (cunning).

58. One could also argue that the Judgment digression shows that the *RE* poet was well aware of Virgil's *ordo artificialis* and gave his audience his own version of the artificial order by going back to the time of the Judgment.

59. Rousse, "Le Pouvoir."

60. Pallas Athena, for example, is "contained" in both Pallas, Evander's son, and Camille. (On the androgynous aspects of this double presence and the play on names see Huchet, *Le Roman médiéval*, chap. 3.) I would go so far as to argue that this greater flexibility in the *RE* is a commentary on the mythographic tradition. We saw that the medieval poet must have been aware of this tradition for the Judgment. Here he seems to dangle a mythographic possibility before the audience's eyes yet refuses to follow up on it.

61. See Poirion, *Résurgences*, p. 69. More on Enéas's supposed homosexuality below.

62. A further detail that dramatizes the distance between Troy and Rome is that of language. While the golden apple was inscribed "in Greek," Lavine writes her famous letter to Enéas "in Latin." On the depiction of the cultural differences in the *RE* in general, see Eley, "The Myth of Trojan Descent and Perceptions of National Identity."

63. Poirion, "De l' 'Enéide' à l' 'Enéas,' " p. 218. Pauphilet lists some of the instances where pagan mythology is reduced in the *RE* ("L'Antiquité et l'Enéas," esp. pp. 97 and 101). Schöning analyzes the consequences of the elimination of much of the mythological material and shows that new motivations for the characters' actions had to be found (*Thebenroman*, pp. 89–90). Moreover, in the *RE* humans frequently take over from the gods: Ascanius is no longer a transformed Cupid; Dido's story is told by the narrator, not a disguised Venus; a messenger replaces Allecto in inciting Turnus to war; Amata plays the role of Juno, and so on. All the more important, therefore, are the mythological elements the *RE* poet chose to preserve.

64. See Schnapp, "Dante's Sexual Solecisms," p. 219.

65. On this complex problem, see Ruhe, *Le Dieu d'Amours*. Ruhe shows that it was Claudian who in the early fifth century made Cupid the only (divine) son of Venus and that in the ninth century Remigius of Auxerre posited two Venuses: the chaste one (*uxor Vulcani*) and the libidinous one (pp. 30, 50). Cupid always belongs to the (bad) libidinous realm for Remigius (p. 51).

66. In a curious phrase, the poet states that "they returned quickly" (l. 780)

but where exactly Ascanius and his caretakers returned from remains unclear. The gods do not necessarily have to descend from Mount Olympus to intervene in human affairs; rather, the poet points to a mythological domain that is accessible to humans.

67. "Eine spezielle Schicksalsinstanz" (*Geschehen und Geschick*, p. 59; Blask's title could be roughly translated as "plot and destiny.") Blask further states: "In the *Roman d'Enéas* there is no longer a special sphere for the gods. Nonetheless, it seems that the multiplicity of gods (l. 1616) and their efficacy were for the *Enéas* poet an element of his subject matter from a pre-Christian time that he could not do without. As mere agents, 'the gods' are grouped together as a collective force, an almost abstract entity" (p. 85). The gods can be seen as Enéas's personal protective deities (p. 112). The first point is confirmed by n. 66, above; the sphere of the gods has become vague and cannot be specifically localized.

68. On this passage, see the interesting remarks by Pauphilet, "L'Antiquité et l'Enéas," p. 103.

69. *Micro-récit* is Huchet's term (*Le Roman médiéval*, p. 190). For Huchet, the *micro-récit* introduces "an extended and mythic span of time."

70. Huchet considers this episode on pp. 191–202 of *Le Roman médiéval.* Blask sees in this episode primarily a conjunction of the mythological and the *merveilleux* (*Geschehen und Geschick*, pp. 129–31). In chap. 5 of his *Virgil in Medieval England*, Baswell views the connection between the Mars and Venus digression and the Judgment of Paris as an instance of "the power of feminine erotics."

71. *Met* 4.176–89; *Amores* 1.9.39–40; *Ars amatoria* 2.561–92 (in *The Art of Love and Other Poems*, 2d ed. rev. Goold).

72. Patterson, "Virgil and the Historical Consciousness of the Twelfth Century," sees the two digressions as "metaphoric illustrations—thematic exemplifications—rather than historical sources." He uses the phrase "thematic antitype" in connection with the Ovidian subtexts in the Lavine episode (p. 172). On the possibilities of Virgil's "unwritten or potential texts" (centering on Juno and Dido), see Spence, *Rhetorics of Reason and Desire: Vergil, Augustine, and the Troubadours*, part 1.

73. *Met* 4.188. The laughter of the gods was a well-known detail in the middle ages. Jean de Meun, for example, repeats it in his version of this story in part 2 of the *Roman de la Rose*: "les dex i fist venir en heste / qui mout ristrent et firent feste / quant en ce point les aperçurent" (he made the gods come there in haste; they laughed and carried on when they saw them in this situation; ll. 13, 823–25.

74. See Huchet, *Le Roman médiéval*, p. 193: "Is it possible that the Christian ideology of an indissoluble marriage could contaminate the antique myth of man in the grip of desire because of a woman?" But one does not have to posit a Christian concept of marriage here. Nolan traces the distinction between

foolish and wise love (marriage) to the commentaries on Ovid's *Heroides.* She makes a good case for the influence of these texts on the *RE* ("Ovid's *Heroides*"). Neither critic, however, considers the question of union and discord in the two digressions.

75. Huchet argues for an equation between the anonymous poet, who does not overtly sign his work, and Vulcan, who does (see my "The Traditions," p. 68). Huchet adds some interesting remarks on the net as a work of composition and on the implications of the conjunction of artistry and sexuality (*Le Roman médiéval*, pp. 196–99).

76. Baswell also sees the integration of Arachne's pennon into Enéas's military equipment as "the containment of subversive feminine power" (*Virgil in Medieval England*, p. 181).

77. Toward the end of the romance, at the moment when he accepts Enéas's offer of single combat, Turnus acknowledges:

Li deu ne vollent, ce m'est vis,
qu'aie la terre et lo pais,
al Troien l'ont tot doné,
vos an seroiz deseritez.
Asez an i a mort por moi;
li deu ne vollent, ge lo croi,
que nus de vos an face plus,
mais tuit vos estez loing ansus. (ll. 9657–64)

It seems to me that the gods do not want me to have the land and the country. They have given everything to the Trojan, and you will be disinherited. Enough people have died for me. I do not believe that the gods would want any one of you to do more. You should rather be far from here.

Turnus reiterates here what King Latinus, Lavine's father, had been saying all along; the gods are on Enéas's side (e.g., ll. 6611, 7794).

78. For exact references see the notes to these lines in the Salverda de Grave edition and Faral, *Recherches sur les sources latines*, pp. 109–54. Most of the vocabulary comes from the *Ars amatoria* and the *Remedia amoris.*

79. Cadden, *Meanings of Sex Difference in the Middle Ages*, p. 223. Auerbach, *Literary Language and Its Public in Late Latin Antiquity and in the Middle Ages*, deals with the story of Scylla (*Met* 8.1–151) as an Ovidian intertext on pp. 210–15. His principal point is that the *RE* destroys the beauty and harmony of Ovid's text. Auerbach's conclusion is ambiguous: the transposition of Ovidian love casuistry into the new context of the *RE* seems "out of place" to him, yet "the elevation of love to a theme worthy of the sublime style" (in troubadour lyric, which the *RE* influenced) is "one of the most important developments in the history of European literature" (p. 215). Patterson briefly mentions Scylla's and Myrrha's stories as Ovidian subtexts that provide a "thematic antitype" (a

point with which I agree). Unaccountably, Patterson names Byblis as the *father* of Myrrha (his name was Cynaras: see "Virgil and the Historical Consciousness of the Twelfth Century," p. 172). Byblis was a young woman incestuously in love with her brother (*Met* 9.454–665). For Myrrha's story, see *Met* 10.298–518. For a different reading of some of these intertexts, see Huchet, *Le Roman médiéval*, chap. 5.

80. Lavine's knowledge of mythology seems quite impressive here. For the story of Ganymede (a Trojan like Enéas), see *Met* 10.155–61. Cormier deals with Lavine's mother's accusation against Enéas on pp. 216–28 of his *One Heart, One Mind*. See also Levy, "L'Allusion à la sodomie dans *Enéas*." For more nuanced analyses, see Burgwinkle, "Knighting the Classical Hero: Homo/Hetero Affectivity in 'Enéas,' "; and Gaunt, "From Epic to Romance: Gender and Sexuality in the *Roman d'Enéas*." See also Baswell, "Men in the *Roman d'Enéas*," pp. 162–63.

81. The problem of incest can also be read in the context of changing rules of marriage in the eleventh and twelfth centuries. Consanguinity or "incest" became more and more important and led to the dissolution of a number of aristocratic marriages. In fact, it became a tool in the power politics of the twelfth century. Louis VII divorced Eleanor of Aquitaine by claims of consanguinity. Thus Henry II's increase of his holdings through his marriage to Eleanor was a direct result of the rules governing supposedly "incestuous" marriages. On these questions, see Duby, *Medieval Marriage*, and Brundage, *Law, Sex, and Christian Society in Medieval Europe*. Nolan sees in Lavine's writing of the letter an allusion to the *Heroides*'s depiction of illegitimate love as well (*Chaucer*, pp. 79 and 92).

82. I would not agree, however, with the statement that Enéas has liberated himself "de l'emprise de Venus" ("De l' 'Enéïde' à l' 'Enéas,' " p. 229).

83. This is one of the criteria Lewis uses in his distinction between mythological figures and personifications (*The Allegory of Love*, pp. 50–56).

84. On the attributes of Love and his description (and the Ovidian sources), see Faral, *Recherches sur les sources latines*, pp. 143–46. See also Ruhe's important study, *Le Dieu d'Amours*; a reference to the *RE*'s temple image is on p. 65.

85. Marchello-Nizia, "De l'*Enéide* à l'*Enéas*: Les Attributs du fondateur," esp. p. 265.

86. Quoted above, p. 33.

87. *Ovide moralisé* 12.1733. For a close reading of this passage in the *Ovide moralisé*, see Chapter 3 of this text. See also Demats's reading of the passage in her *Fabula: Trois études de mythographie antique et médiévale*, pp. 96–99.

88. The most interesting recent work on the *RTr* is in Nolan, *Chaucer*. For a detailed comparison between the texts by Dares and Dictys and the *RTr*, see Petit, *Naissances du roman*, 2.1213–17.

89. For a close reading of the Prologue, see my "Old French Narrative Genres," pp. 151–52, and Nolan, *Chaucer*, pp. 15–25.

90. See Schönings's remarks on the gods in the *RTr*: "In the *RTr* mythology belongs to the domain of the characters" (*Thebenroman*, p. 249). This analysis summarizes Schöning's observations throughout his book that the gods most often form part of the world of the characters while references to God point to the world of the poet and of the audience (though not always).

91. Frazer, *The Trojan War*, p. 146. Dares calls these duties simply "res divinas," divine things (*De excidio Troiae*, p. 19).

92. On the love stories (Jason and Medea; Paris and Helen; Troilus and Briseide, and Diomedes and Briseide; Achilles and Polyxene) in the *RTr*, see Lumiansky, "Structural Unity in Benoît's *Roman de Troie*," and Nolan, *Chaucer*, pp. 96–117. Another love story, somewhat exaggeratedly portrayed by Hatzantonis in "Circe, redenta d'amore nel *Roman de Troie*" as a story of true and even redemptive love, is that of Odysseus and Circe at the end of the romance. However, there is no Ovidian vocabulary, nor is Amors present here. The offspring from this love, Telegonus, eventually kills his father by mistake. Thus, the cycle of the *romans antiques* begins and ends with a parricide.

93. This passage is followed by the praise of a woman who is quite different: the beautiful "riche dame de riche roi" (l. 13,468) in whom "tote science abonde" (l. 13,465). This woman is most likely Eleanor of Aquitaine, the wife of Henry II, and the lines in question can be read as a dedication of the romance to Eleanor. The story of Briseide and Troilus and then Diomedes was also the basis for Chaucer's *Troilus*.

94. In keeping with his sources, Benoît portrays Enéas as an evil traitor, almost on the same level as Antenor. The narrator calls Antenor a Judas (ll. 25,841 and 26,135); Hecuba refers to Enéas as Satanas (l. 26,164).

95. For the story of Narcissus, see *Met* 3.339–510; for Hero and Leander, *Heroides* 18 and 19.

96. The Narcissus reference was mentioned by Adler in "*Militia et Amor* in the *Roman de Troie*," p. 22. He briefly considers the problem of Achilles's supposed homosexuality in this context and adds: "Is it not odd that Achilles, desperately in love with a beautiful princess, should compare himself with Narcissus, in love with himself? Is Achilles a narcissist in the modern clinical sense?" Adler then goes on to claim that homosexuality, often associated with narcissism, is really a nostalgic search for a man's lost childhood. For the connection between Narcissus and the topoi of courtly love poetry, see Goldin, *The Mirror of Narcissus in Courtly Love Lyric*. Dares's text simply says: "Achilles . . . being struck by Polyxena's beauty fell madly in love. The burning power of love took all the joy out of love" (Frazer, *The Trojan War*, p. 154).

97. *Chaucer*, p. 92 (for Achilles and Polyxene, see pp. 102–4); "Ovid's *Heroides*," p. 157 (Nolan's emphasis).

98. See Hexter, *Ovid and Medieval Schooling*, p. 201 (for an analysis of the

commentary contained in the Munich MS clm 19475), and pp. 289–96 (for the edition dealing with letters 18 and 19).

99. The word *drut* comes from Gallic *druto* (strong). It can also refer to a friend. But its frequent use as "beloved" both in lyric poetry and in the *Roman d'Enéas*, for example, together with Hector's earlier explicit accusation, seems to suggest that it is used here in the sense of "beloved." The semantic field studied in von Wartburg's *Französisches Etymologisches Wörterbuch*, vol. 3, refers almost exclusively to love and passion.

100. For another example where characters in a romance "read" and interpret exemplary stories, see Chrétien de Troyes's *Cligés*. I show in "Chrétien de Troyes as a Reader of the *Romans Antiques*" how both the *RTh* and the *RE* appear in *Cligés* and are used by the characters either to avert impending doom or to celebrate the values of their own world.

101. This acceptance of the gods' functions contrasts sharply with the criticism found in the long (later) version of the *RTh* represented by manuscripts A and P:

> Encor n'erent pas crestiien,
> Mais por le siecle tot paiien:
> L'un aouroient Tervagan,
> L'autre Mahom et Apolan;
> L'un les estoiles et les signes,
> Et li auquant les ymagines;
> . . .
> Et li dius lor donnast repons:
> Ce n'ert par voirs, ains estoit fable,
> Car cou erent li vif diable
> Qui les respons a els donoient
> Et les caitis en decevoient (ll. 65–80 [Constans's edition])

They were not yet Christians, but lived in a pagan world: some adored Tervagan, others Mohammed and Apollo; some the stars and signs, and others also images; . . . And the god gave them an answer. This was not true; rather, it was just a fable, for those who gave them the answer were living devils and thus deceived these miserable people.

This view of pagan religion is completely different from that of the short version of the *RTh* and that of the *RE*. Note especially the reference to the pagan gods generally associated with the epic (Tervagan, Mahom as a god) and the idea that the gods are devils who deceive humans. For the demonic current in the interpretation of pagan mythology, see Bezold, *Das Fortleben der antiken Götter im mittelalterlichen Humanismus*, especially the opening pages.

102. On the nature of the narrators in different genres, see Uitti, *Story, Myth, and Celebration in Old French Narrative Poetry 1050–1200*.

Chapter 2

1. I will refer to Guillaume de Lorris's part of the *Roman de la Rose* as *Rose I* and to Jean de Meun's as *Rose II*. All references are to the Lecoy edition. Translations are my own.

2. On the two jars or tons of good and evil, see Boethius, *The Consolation of Philosophy*, p. 58 (in reference to *Iliad* 24.527ff.).

3. For the growing popularity of, for example, the story of Narcissus in the lyric, see Goldin, *The Mirror of Narcissus in Courtly Love Lyric*.

4. In particular of Jupiter, who seems to play the role of godfather here. As Kauke points out, the positive image of Jupiter bears some resemblance to Jean de Meun himself ("Jupiter et Saturne chez Jeun de Meun," pp. 260, 263). Kauke shows that throughout the romance Jupiter is an ambiguous figure, standing alternately for the end of the Golden Age (following the mythographic tradition) and for the reign of pleasure (in the astrological tradition). He thus figures the multiple interpretive traditions Jean de Meun works into his text.

5. See the Introduction and the first sections of Chapter 3 for a brief history of these processes. Fleming rightly claims that Jean de Meun "actually takes as a principal poetic theme the moral and poetic relationship of the pagan past with the Christian present" ("Jean de Meun and the Ancient Poets," p. 85).

6. "Instead of being glossed, they [the mythological exempla] function as glosses for the story" (*La Rose, le Renart et le Graal: La Littérature allégorique en France au XIIIe siècle*, p. 222).

7. On the idea of new myths, see the pathbreaking article by Jauss, "Allégorie, 'remythisation,' et nouveau mythe," and the last section of this chapter.

8. "The Medusa Interpolation in the *Roman de la Rose*."

9. *Le Roman de la Rose*, p. 25.

10. See Jauss, "Allégorie, 'remythisation,' et nouveau mythe." Jauss's argument has to be modified somewhat. As I showed in Chapter 1, he omits an important link between Venus as mere personification and the remythologized Venus of the *Rose*: the *Roman d'Enéas*.

11. It was also important to give these characters a past. This is especially interesting for the case of La Vieille, admittedly a nonmythological figure, who is given a prehistory in the *Rose*. See Beltrán, "La Vieille's Past." References to a character's prehistory are for Lewis an important criterion for the distinction between mythological figure and personification (*The Allegory of Love: A Study in Tradition*, chap. 2).

12. There are, of course, differences between these places: Venus's habitat is part of the diegesis (however far removed), as is Nature's forge; the other two are parts of the discourses of Raison and Nature, respectively. More about these problems below.

13. Strubel defines Jean's model: "Jean's model is based on the interpretation of preexisting texts with an obscure or hidden meaning, the truth of which

comes forth through the gloss" (*Le Roman de la Rose*, p. 72). But these glosses, as we will see, are not necessarily the traditional mythographic ones.

14. One should not forget that the *Rose* acquired a kind of summa function, providing a storehouse of themes and of mythological subject matter. See Badel, *Le Roman de la Rose au XIVe siècle.*

15. The Narcissus episode has been the subject of a large number of studies. The most useful in our context are Hult, *Self-fulfilling Prophecies: Readership and Authority in the First Roman de la Rose*, chap. 4; Huot, *From Song to Book: The Poetics of Writing in Old French Lyric and Lyrical Narrative Poetry*, pp. 86–90; Poirion, "Narcisse et Pygmalion dans le *Roman de la Rose*"; Rychner, "Le Mythe de la fontaine de Narcisse dans le *Roman de la Rose* de Guillaume de Lorris"; and Thut, "Narcisse versus Pygmalion." Hillman, "Another Look into the Mirror Perilous: The Role of the Crystals in the *Roman de la Rose*," provides a good bibliography. An extremely interesting analysis of the formal aspects of the integration of exempla can be found in Bermejo, "Notas sobre las modalidades retóricas de inserción de anecdotas en el 'Roman de la Rose de Jean de Meun.' "

16. See Goldin, *The Mirror of Narcissus.*

17. See Hult, *Self-fulfilling Prophecies*, chap. 3.

18. For the possible significance of the pine tree, see Harley, "Narcissus, Hermaphroditus, and Attis."

19. For the importance of the textual nature of the story, see Huot, *From Song to Book*, p. 89.

20. Hult points out that Narcissus and Echo belong to the "shadowy past" of the garden (*Self-fulfilling Prophecies*, p. 265).

21. "Dames, cest essample aprenez, / qui vers vos amis mesprenez; / car se vos les leesiez morir, / Dex le vos savra bien merir" (Ladies who are angry at your boyfriends, learn from this example: if you let them die, God will make you pay for it; ll. 1505–8).

22. There are actually two accounts of Narcissus's death: l. 1493 and l. 1501 say more or less the same thing. Interestingly, in the Poirion edition of the *Rose* Narcissus's "deaths" are connected by the line "Ce est la somme de la glose" (This is the sum of the gloss; l. 1495). In Lecoy's edition the line reads "C'est la some de ceste chose" (This is the sum of the matter; l. 1494). The myth—and not its moral—is thus identified as a gloss, which would support Strubel's contention cited in n. 13.

23. *Allegoriae super Ovidii Metamorphosin.* On Arnulf and the *Rose,* see Knoespel, *Narcissus and the Invention of Personal History.*

24. One thinks, of course, of Zumthor's apt term "la circularité du chant," a concept worked out in *Essai de poétique médiévale.* Cf. Huot, *From Song to Book*, pp. 86–90, and Hult, *Self-fulfilling Prophecies*, chap. 3.

25. It is extremely important to remember that the Narcissus story cannot

be abstracted or pried loose from its poetic framework. The *Rose* is not a purely didactic treatise like Arnulf of Orleans's, for example.

26. See Jauss, "Allégorie, 'remythisation,' et nouveau mythe," p. 477, for examples from Prudentius's *Psychomachia* and Alain de Lille's *Anticlaudianus*. Both Jauss and Ruhe (*Le Dieu d'Amours avec son paradis*) show that the late antique epithalamium was instrumental in reducing Venus to a personification of *luxuria*. See also Schreiber, "Venus in the Medieval Mythographic Tradition."

27. See Kay, "The Birth of Venus in the *Romance of the Rose*." See also Kauke, "Jupiter et Saturne chez Jean de Meun," for a *mise au point* of Jean de Meun's sources. In the antique tradition, it was Chronos who had castrated his father, Uranus. For details, see Fritz, "Du dieu émasculateur au roi émasculé: Métamorphoses de Saturne au moyen âge." On the implications of the story of Jupiter and Saturn in general, see Hult, "Language and Dismemberment: Abelard, Origen, and the *Romance of the Rose*."

28. The story is told in Ovid's *Metamorphoses* 4.167–89 and *Ars amatoria* 2.561–92 (the advice here is that lovers should not engage in the same games of detection as husbands).

29. Ll. 13,810–43. Here, our focus is on Venus. See the section on interpreters of myth for a closer analysis of La Vieille's techniques.

30. Ll. 14,131–56. On the significance of the rhyme "ouvert" and "couvert" (ll. 14,141–42) both for the strategy of sexual conquest and that of interpretation, see my "*Overt* and *Covert*: Amorous and Interpretive Strategies in the *Roman de la Rose*."

31. See the section later in this chapter on "Myth Criticism and Some New Myths."

32. L. 15,726. "Estoire" is ambiguous here: it could mean both story and history. This ambiguity underlines the ambiguity of the message, which clearly must be read in conjunction with the explicit moral drawn from the Narcissus story (addressed to "dames").

33. This vague temporality also plays with the parameters of *Metamorphoses* 10. For brief remarks on the status of the Adonis story in *Rose II*, see Brownlee, "Orpheus' Song Re-Sung: Jean de Meun's Reworking of *Metamorphoses* X." Brownlee rightly insists on the fact that the Adonis and Pygmalion stories are the only ones to be told directly by the narrator in *Rose II* (while in Ovid they form part of the song of Orpheus). Technically, this passage could be called a *paralepse*, that is, information that constitutes a surplus in the framework of a given focalization (Genette, *Figures III*, pp. 211–13).

34. See in particular Poirion, "Narcisse et Pygmalion"; Dragonetti, "Pygmalion ou les pièges de la fiction dans le *Roman de la Rose*"; Huot, *From Song to Book*; and Brownlee, "Orpheus' Song Re-Sung." Huot, "Poetics of Pygmalion" (*From Song to Book*, pp. 96–99), sees Pygmalion as a "counterpart to the protagonist" (p. 98); Brownlee sees in Pygmalion a "general artist figure" (p. 204).

Camille, in *The Gothic Idol: Ideology and Image-Making in Medieval Art*, considers Pygmalion's relationship to idolatry and concludes that he is not guilty of that sin (p. 332). See also the important study by Huot, "The Medusa Interpolation." This interpolation appears right before the Pygmalion story in several manuscripts and is part of an intricate web of mythological exempla. See n. 15, above, for further references to criticism dealing with Pygmalion.

35. "Quant par queur la chançon savez / que tant oï chanter m'avez, / si con joer nous alion, / de l'ymage Pimalion" (When you know by heart the song of Pygmalion's statue that you have heard sung so much when we used to go and play; ll. 13,055–58). In his notes to these lines Lecoy suggests that perhaps Jean de Meun had earlier composed the Pygmalion episode and then inserted it into *Rose II*. La Vieille would thus be making a sly reference to Jean's own production.

36. See Dinter, *Der Pygmalion-Stoff in der europäischen Literatur*, chaps. 1–2.

37. On this question, see the excellent article by Dragonetti, "Le 'Singe de nature' dans le *Roman de la Rose*."

38. See Chapter 1, pp. 46–49.

39. This is a point made most explicitly by Thut, "Narcisse versus Pygmalion."

40. Dällenbach, *The Mirror in the Text*, p. 8. See this text in general on *mise en abyme*; on the use of myth, see p. 59.

41. Heinrichs rightly insists on the importance of identifying the speaker for each mythological exemplum (*The Myths of Love: Classical Lovers in Medieval Literature*, chap. 3). Her general remarks on the interpretation of mythological allusions and exempla in medieval texts (chap. 1) provide useful signposts.

42. The relevant lines are 6898–7200. My discussion here is indebted to Jung, "Jean de Meun et l'allégorie," and particularly to Poirion, "De la signification selon Jean de Meun." See also Quilligan, "Words and Sex: The Language of Allegory in the *De planctu naturae*, the *Roman de la Rose*, and Book III of the *Faerie Queene*." Most recently, see Hult's excellent discussion in "Language and Dismemberment."

43. Poirion rightly sees in this argumentation an attack against realism ("De la signification," p. 174) in the discussion on the relationship between words and things, going back to Plato's *Cratylus*. The nominalists considered names a pure convention; the realists believed in an essential and "real" relationship between words and things (p. 173).

44. This is also true for the *Ovide moralisé*. See in particular my "The Scandal of Pasiphae: Narration and Interpretation in the *Ovide moralisé*."

45. On Amant's (and Jean's) glossing, see Regalado, "The Medieval Construction of the Modern Reader: Solomon's Ship and the Birth of Jean de Meun."

46. Regalado, " 'Des contraires choses': La Fonction poétique de la citation et des *exempla* dans le 'Roman de la Rose' de Jean de Meun," pp. 76–77.

47. Fritz, "Du dieu émasculateur," p. 53.

48. Hult, "Language and Dismemberment," p. 112; and Poirion, "De la signification," pp. 177–78. None of the mythographic interpretations is thus applicable here. For another view, see Hill, who stresses the Augustinian reading of the end of the Golden Age as equivalent to the fall ("Narcissus, Pygmalion, and the Castration of Saturn"). For the mythographic texts, see Hill, "Narcissus," pp. 418–19, and Fleming, *Reason and the Lover*, which supplies a wealth of background material on this problem.

49. "Language and Dismemberment," p. 111.

50. On the different interpretations of the Golden Age, see in particular George, "Jean de Meung and the Myth of the Golden Age," and Pelen, *Latin Poetic Irony in the 'Roman de la Rose'*, pp. 8–15. On La Vieille's digression, see Hill, "La Vieille's Digression on Free Love." Hill does not consider the second half of the Mars and Venus story, which appears after the digression.

51. See Allen, *The Art of Love: Amatory Fiction from Ovid to the Romance of the Rose*, chap. 4. Bouché lists no fewer than 32 borrowings from Ovid's *Art of Love* in Ami's discourse ("Ovide et Jean de Meun," p. 86). See Hill, "Narcissus," on Ami and La Vieille's failures (pp. 422–23).

52. See George, "Jean de Meun," p. 37.

53. See Wilson and Makowski for an analysis of the different misogynist traditions and on *Rose II*'s use of them (*Wykked Wyves and the Woes of Marriage: Misogamous Literature from Juvenal to Chaucer*, esp. pp. 132–39).

54. The misogynist Matheolus, in the late thirteenth century, attributes the poisons used to kill stepdaughters to Trotula's art. See *Les Lamentations de Matheolus et le Livre de Leesce de Jehan Le Fèvre de Ressons*, 2.3519–24.

55. On the technique of *emboîtement* (interlocking, encasing) in Ami's discourse in general, see Poirion, *Le Roman de la Rose*, p. 125. On the rearrangement of the discourse by Gui de Mori, "replacing Jean's digressive ring structure with a linear order," see Huot, "Authors, Scribes, Remanieurs," p. 215. In another manuscript the Jaloux has vanished completely (ibid., p. 221).

56. Arnulf of Orléans interprets Io as a virgin loved by God who then lost her virginity. Her transformation into a cow figures her bestiality (*Allegoriae*, p. 203). The Vatican mythographers offered no particular interpretation of the story.

57. This context resurfaces in the literal interpretation given to the myth in the *Ovide moralisé* 4.1538–629.

58. Fulgentius, *The Mythologies*, p. 73 (Whitbread, ed.). See Heinrichs, *The Myths of Love*, for other treatments of the story (esp. pp. 59–60); on La Vieille's use of myth, see pp. 116–19. Generally, in the mythographic tradition the story was not seen as representing a typical love triangle. Astrological and physical allegories were more common. For the moral interpretation as it occurs, for ex-

ample, in Bernardus Silvestris (which can be found in *Mythographi Vaticani I et II*, chap. 144, Kulcsár, ed., p. 206), see Wetherbee, *Platonism and Poetry in the Twelfth Century*: "Mars is . . . a good man corrupted by Venus, and the capture of the pair is made to show 'how the fire of concupiscence fetters virtue with the unbreakable bond of habit' " (p. 117). See also Hill, "La Vieille's Digression." However, Hill misrepresents La Vieille's awareness of the dangers of free love when he claims that La Vieille "shows herself utterly unaware of the existence of bondage implicit in unrestrained sensuality" (p. 115). But La Vieille expounds at length on the dire consequences (such as war) of unrestrained sensuality (ll. 13,893–905).

59. The use of animal exempla recalls the Jaloux's comparisons of women and horses (horses can be tested before one buys them [ll. 8637–47]), a bit of rhetoric common to the misogynistic tradition.

60. See Ovid, *Ars amatoria* (and also n. 28, above).

61. *The Commentary on the First Six Books of the Aeneid of Vergil, Commonly Attributed to Bernardus Silvestris*, p. 30. My paraphrase is based on the translation by Schreiber and Maresca, *Commentary on the First Six Books of Virgil's Aeneid by Bernardus Silvestris*, p. 33.

62. Heinrichs, *The Myths of Love*, p. 114. See also Minnis, *Chaucer and Pagan Antiquity*, pp. 16–17.

63. See Heinrichs, *The Myths of Love*, chap. 2; McLeod, *Virtue and Venom: Catalogs of Women from Antiquity to the Renaissance*; Quilligan, "Words and Sex," p. 207; and Minnis, *Chaucer and Pagan Antiquity*, pp. 16–17. Fleming, in "Jean de Meun and the Ancient Poets" (see also n. 5, above), discusses Hercules in the *Rose* on pp. 93–99 (but he does not consider the Jaloux's evocation of Hercules). He rightly calls Jean de Meun "a poet of contexts" (p. 92). For the many meanings of Hercules, see Panofsky, *Herkules am Scheidewege und andere antike Bildstoffe in der neueren Kunst*, and Jung, *Le Mythe d'Hercule dans la littérature française du XVIe siècle*. For Boethius, Hercules is the *vir sapiens*: see *The Consolation of Philosophy*, 4p7 (pp. 144–45).

64. For this story, see Virgil's *Aeneid* 8.193–267.

65. This implicit prediction of evil things to come would thus tie in with Amant's regret over having fallen into love's snares voiced in *Rose I* (ll. 1606–12).

66. Fleming, "Jean de Meun and the Ancient Poets," pp. 92, 95.

67. "Allégorie, 'remythisation' et nouveau mythe," p. 489; my translation from the French.

68. See Jauss's remarks on Amor and Venus who, conditioned by the late antique epithalamium, became the driving forces in the establishment of this new myth: "It is at the end of the twelfth and at the beginning of the thirteenth century that the antique myths, of Amor and Venus in particular, become a nucleus around which courtly love crystallizes in a ritual manner and elaborates

its new mythology. . . . André le Chapelain establishes his codification of courtly love by taking into account—in the background—the new myth constituted by the Beyond of the earthly kingdom of Amor" (Ibid., p. 470).

69. See Ruhe, *Le Dieu d'Amours.*

70. See Quilligan, "Words and Sex" (p. 206): "The inescapable eroticism of the metaphors is, however, precisely the point of the episode; with it Jean demonstrates the necessarily unallegorical results of a strict adherence to courtly euphemism."

71. On this midpoint passage, see especially Allen, *The Art of Love,* pp. 81–83; Brownlee, "Jean de Meun and the Limits of Romance," esp. pp. 115–16; and Uitti, "From 'Clerc' to 'Poète.' "

72. Allen, *The Art of Love,* p. 82, says of this rhyme: "The link between 'porriz' and 'Lorriz' makes it clear that Guillaume is already in a state of decay."

73. On the complexity of the "I" in the *Rose,* see especially Vitz, "The *I* of the *Roman de la Rose.*" Despite the many borrowings from Ovid (conveniently tabulated by Bouché in "Ovide et Jean de Meun"), Jean refers to Ovid as both an unsuccessful teacher and an unsuccessful lover. As Allen points out, "Jean mentions Ovid only five times, and these references are, without exception, deprecatory" (*The Art of Love,* p. 81).

74. This is also clear from the sheer mass of lines quoted from the dozens of authors Jean used: 12,000 of a total of 17,500 in Langlois's estimate (*Origines et sources du Roman de la Rose,* pp. 95, 102).

75. Allen's *The Art of Love* persuasively argues that the art of love was actually the art of writing about love, which already existed in Ovid's time.

76. On the idea of the "miroer," see Eberle, "The Lovers' Glass: Nature's Discourse on Optics and the Optical Design of the *Romance of the Rose,*" and especially Jónsson, *Le Miroir: Naissance d'un genre littéraire.*

77. Jauss, "Allégorie, 'remythisation,' et nouveau mythe," pp. 479–83.

78. On Genius in the *Rose,* see Nitzsche, *The Genius Figure in Antiquity and the Middle Ages,* pp. 116–25; Economou, *The Goddess Natura in Medieval Literature,* pp. 104–24; and Quilligan, "Words and Sex," pp. 204–7. On the relationship between Alan of Lille's Genius and Jean de Meun's, see Wetherbee, *Platonism and Poetry,* esp. pp. 257–66, and his "The Theme of Imagination in Medieval Poetry and the Allegorical Figure 'Genius,' " pp. 56–61. On the park, see Piehler, *The Visionary Landscape: A Study in Medieval Allegory,* pp. 105–10. I disagree with Piehler's views that in the park fecundity stands for "general virtue" (p. 108) and that "the Park of the Good Shepherd stands finally in no clear relation to the Rose Garden" (p. 109). See also Lynch, *The High Medieval Dream Vision,* who sees Genius as "imaginative failure" and heretical (pp. 135–36); Smith, "In Search of the Ideal Landscape: From 'Locus Amoenus' to 'Parc du Champ Joli' in the 'Roman de la Rose' " (Smith for some reason posits Genius's speech as the end of the romance: "The novel then ends . . . with a

supreme authority: as the *locus amoenus* has yielded to the *locus amoenissimus*, so nature has given way to God" [p. 242]); Strubel, *Le Roman de la Rose*, pp. 105–7; and especially Brownlee, "Jean de Meun and the Limits of Romance."

79. As Brownlee points out, the two registers of language that are necessarily excluded from Guillaume's courtly world—the sexual and the spiritual—are the principal components of Genius's speech ("Jean de Meun and the Limits of Romance," p. 120).

80. For Jean's relation to and subversion of Chartrian cosmological allegory, see Wetherbee, *Platonism and Poetry*, chap. 7, part 2.

81. "Jean de Meun and the Limits of Romance," pp. 122–32.

82. For a close reading of the *excusacion* (apology), see Brownlee, "Reflections in the *Miroer aus Amoreus*."

83. For definitions of the term *allegory*, see Whitman, *Allegory: The Dynamics of an Ancient and Medieval Technique*, pp. 263–68.

84. On this terminology throughout the *Rose*, see my "*Overt* and *Covert*."

85. For a step-by-step comparison of the two fountains, see Brownlee, "Jean de Meun and the Limits of Romance."

86. Dahlberg's translation "in order not to know themselves at all" (p. 335) is not convincing here. "Por ce" is frequently used causally. See also Nature's references to self-knowledge in ll. 17,544 and 17,761–62, where she points out that only those who know themselves "antierement" (fully) can love "sagement" (wisely).

87. On the negative associations of the pine tree, see Harley, "Narcissus, Hermaphroditus, and Attis."

88. Respectively, Quilligan, "Words and Sex," p. 205; Smith "In Search of the Ideal Landscape," p. 243; and Wetherbee, "The Theme of Imagination," p. 60.

89. See Hult, "Language and Dismemberment." Hult does not deal with this specific passage, however.

90. Another eighteen lines are added in the edition by Poirion.

91. This is the argument of my "*Overt* and *Covert*."

Chapter 3

1. The term is Todorov's, not in reference to the *OM*, however. See Todorov, *Symbolism and Interpretation*, p. 38. Paris aptly described the feeling one has when finishing the *OM*: (the author) "finally finishes his work and the relief one feels in closing the book undoubtedly gives us some idea of the relief [the author] felt after writing his 72,000 verses" ("Chrétien Legouais et autres traducteurs ou imitateurs d'Ovide," p. 522). I refer to the de Boer edition of the *Ovide moralisé*. Translations are my own.

2. For a general introduction to the *OM*, see Paris, "Chrétien Legouais," esp. pp. 502–25. Paris's attribution to Chrétien Legouais has been refuted by Engels,

Etudes sur l'Ovide moralisé, who concludes that "the *Ovide moralisé* was written by an anonymous minor friar" (p. 62).

3. Indeed, as Leube demonstrates convincingly, in the sixteenth century the *OM* was still used as a source for the Ovidian fables instead of Ovid's *Metamorphoses* (*Fortuna in Karthago*, p. 48).

4. Demats's excellent *Fabula: Trois études de mythographie antique et médiévale* remains the only study exclusively devoted to the *OM*. See my Introduction for examples of the thematic studies of specific myths that made use of the *OM*. Smit, *Contribution à l'étude de la connaissance de l'antiquité au moyen âge*, has some interesting but very brief remarks on techniques of translation in the *OM* (see esp. pp. 74–126, which deal with a French translation of Seneca's *Moralium dogma philosophorum* and the *OM*). Most recently, Levine has considered some techniques of the *OM* in comparison with Bersuire in "Exploiting Ovid: Medieval Allegorizations of the *Metamorphoses*." See also the excellent remarks focusing on translation and hermeneutics in the *OM* in Copeland, *Rhetoric, Hermeneutics, and Translation in the Middle Ages*, pp. 107–26. She also observes that "as a critical performance the text has remained largely invisible" (p. 108).

5. For the notion of segmentation in Ovid "exegesis," see Hexter, "Medieval Articulations of Ovid's *Metamorphoses*."

6. I am using the term *allegoresis* as distinct from *allegory* because Ovid's fables were not composed as allegories but had allegorical interpretations imposed on them. "Imposed allegory" is Tuve's term (see *Allegorical Imagery: Some Medieval Books and Their Posterity*, chap. 4).

7. See Moss, *Poetry and Fable: Studies in Mythological Narrative in Sixteenth-Century France*, p. 7.

8. This works even though not *all* Ovidian fables receive a euhemeristic explanation. For Lubac, see his *Exégèse médiévale*, vol. 1, chap. 2; "Mythe et allégorie." Unlike some other medieval writers the *OM* poet did not ascribe a Christian intention to Ovid and did not claim that Ovid was a Christian. See Demats, *Fabula*, pp. 113–36, on "Ovide chrétien."

9. *Hygini fabulae*, p. 47.

10. *The Mythologies*, chap. 8: "and as the father struck at the tree with his sword, Adonis was born" (p. 92).

11. *The Mythologies*, p. 92.

12. For some interesting remarks on Fulgentius's method, see Edwards, "The Heritage of Fulgentius," in *The Classics in the Middle Ages*, esp. pp. 142–43, as well as his "Fulgentius and the Collapse of Meaning."

13. *Mythographi Vaticani I et II*, #197 (p. 77), #45 (p. 129).

14. *Scriptores rerum mythicarum latini tres Romae nuper reperti*, no. 11 (p. 239).

15. For the idea of the catalog of women and/or lovers, see West, *The Hesiodic Catalogue of Women*; McLeod, *Virtue and Venom: Catalogs of Women from Antiquity to the Renaissance*; and Heinrichs, *The Myths of Love: Classical Lovers in Medieval Literature*.

16. Alan of Lille, *Plaint of Nature*, pp. 135–36. Myrrha reappears in Meter 5 in the definition of Love by contraries (p. 152).

17. Ghisalberti calls Arnulf's theoretical musings part of a *Vita Ovidii* ("Arnolfo d'Orléans: Un cultore d'Ovidio nel secolo XII," p. 180). My questions paraphrase Demats, *Fabula*, p. 108.

18. The paraphrase is Demats's (*Fabula*, p. 109). For the Latin text, see Ghisalberti, "Arnolfo," p. 181.

19. For some other Christian interpretations in Arnulf, see Giraud, *La Fable de Daphné*, pp. 96–97. For Orpheus as a Christ figure, see Irwin, "The Song of Orpheus and the New Song of Christ," and Vicari, "*Sparagmos*: Orpheus among the Christians."

20. As Hexter observes, although "Ovid's poetry had gathered about it school commentaries like clouds of glory, . . . medieval Ovid commentaries were not by nature allegorizing and moralizing" ("Medieval Articulations," p. 77).

21. Ghisalberti, ed., p. 201.

22. Ghisalberti, ed., I.5, p. 35.

23. "Rem miram mirare novam Mirram per amorem / In mirram verti quam dat amarus amor" (Marvel at the wondrous thing, at strange Myrrha whom bitter love granted to be changed into a myrrh tree out of love; 10.413–14 [p. 68]; I would like to thank my colleague Dennis Looney for help with this translation). Ghisalberti points out that *amarus amor* is a "gioco di parole proverbiale" (a proverbial play on words; p. 68, note to l. 414). The same play on words existed in Old French with the word "amer," meaning both "bitter" and "to love."

24. Pp. 69 and 65, respectively.

25. This was, however, not the first vernacular translation of the *Metamorphoses*: Albrecht of Halberstadt translated it into German in 1210. See Bartsch, *Albrecht von Halberstadt und Ovid im Mittelalter.*

26. Not all books have the same structure. There is quite a wide variety in the distribution between story line and interpretations. See the section on "Interpretive Structures," later in this chapter, for further analyses.

27. This technique is also used by commentators. See Hexter, "Medieval Articulations," p. 69, for examples from Arnulf of Orléans. Similarly, commentators tried to facilitate the reading by placing a list of all the *mutationes* (metamorphoses) at the beginning of each book.

28. I will not go into every detail here. See Friedman, *Orpheus in the Middle Ages*, chap. 4, and Heitmann, "Orpheus im Mittelalter" and "Typen der Deformierung antiker Mythen im Mittelalter: Am Beispiel der Orpheussage," for medieval interpretations of Orpheus, including the *OM.*

29. But sometimes it refers to the *OM* itself or to someone else's subject matter, as in the critique of Benoît de Sainte-Maure in Book 12 (12.1736). For a detailed analysis of the interpretive vocabulary, see the section by that name later in this chapter.

30. Augustine, *On Christian Doctrine*, 3.12 (p. 90). On opposites producing meaning, see Gellrich, *The Idea of the Book*, p. 133.

31. It is interesting in this context to think of Christine de Pizan's *Débat sur le Roman de la Rose*, in which she rejects exactly this argument made by Pierre Col in favor of the *Rose*. Christine argues that no one has ever learned anything from negative exempla; rather, they give people wrong ideas in the first place (pp. 133–34).

32. "Qui sages est nel doit celer, / Ainz doit por ce son senz moutrer / que quant il ert du siecle alez / touz jors en soit mes ramenbrez" (Whoever is wise should not hide it. He should rather show his good sense so that, once he is dead, he will always be remembered; *Le Roman de Thèbes*, Raynaud de Lage, ed., ll. 1–4).

33. See Marie de France's *Lais*: "Pur ceo començai a penser / D'aukune bone estoire faire / E de latin en romaunz traire" (For this reason I began to think of writing some good story and to translate it from Latin into French; Rychner, ed., ll. 28–30). Marie, however, does not go on to translate but rather chooses tales that did not come from the learned tradition. For an analysis of the *OM* prologue, see Copeland, *Rhetoric, Hermeneutics, and Translation*, pp. 107–26. She shows how the translator-exegete becomes an *auctor* himself who "has thoroughly substituted his own text for that of the *auctor*" (p. 126).

34. This may be an allusion to Matt. 11.25 and Luke 10.21, where Christ speaks of secrets revealed to "babes."

35. At the end of the 72,000-line text readers may well ask themselves what exactly the poet understood by "briefment" (l. 56).

36. This criticism refers to what Arnulf says in his *Vita Ovidii* (Ghisalberti's term) as a commentary on *Metamorphoses* 1.1–4. See Ghisalberti's introduction to "Arnolfo," p. 181. Arnulf claims that Ovid wrote "Formas mutatas in nova corpora" (forms changed into new bodies).

37. But Ovid had in fact written "In nova fert animus mutatas dicere formas / corpora," which translates as "of bodies changed into new forms" (*Metamorphoses*, Loeb ed., 1.1–2).

38. For the use of this vocabulary in the *Roman de la Rose*, see my "*Overt* and *Covert*: Amorous and Interpretive Strategies in the *Roman de la Rose*."

39. When it comes to translating Ovid's plural "dei," however, the poet translates the term as both "Dieus" and "Dieu." Ovid's "dei" thus yields both the pagan gods and the Christian God.

40. Barkan, *The Gods Made Flesh*, pp. 113–14; quotes on p. 113 and p. 114, respectively.

41. At least this is one of the focal points of this extremely rich study. See also Allen, *The Friar as Critic*.

42. See Allen's remarks on Ridewall's *Fulgentius metaforalis*: "Allegorization is the assertion of a parallelism between organized systems, rather than the elu-

cidation of some referentially symbolic meaning" ("Commentary as Criticism," p. 32).

43. Nestle, *Vom Mythos zum Logos*, p. 126.

44. Demats, *Fabula*, pp. 61, 63. See Barkan, *The Gods Made Flesh*, p. 95, on the fusion of commentary and primary text.

45. See Demats, *Fabula*, chap. 1; Dronke, *Fabula*, chap. 1; and my remarks in the Introduction.

46. "Typologische Figuren aus Natur und Mythos," p. 140; my translation from the German. Ohly also points out that an equal typological treatment of texts such as the Old Testament and the *Metamorphoses* was facilitated through their chronological range from the Creation to Augustus (p. 141). Ohly then gives a brief analysis of the Orpheus story in the *OM* (pp. 141–43).

47. "But one mocked at their credulity, a scoffer at the gods, one reckless in spirit, Ixion's son, Pirithous. 'These are but fairy-tales, you tell, Achelous,' he said" (8.611–14). This passage, in which Pirithous first questions and then is convinced of the veracity of metamorphosis, occurs at a privileged point: the exact midpoint of the *Metamorphoses*. See Solodow, *The World of Ovid's Metamorphoses*, p. 15.

48. On the intersecting of interpretive and other types of vocabulary (such as the diegetic), see my "*Overt* and *Covert*," which also deals with the problem of covering and uncovering the truth.

49. A brief history of the term can be found in an appendix to Whitman's *Allegory: The Dynamics of an Ancient and Medieval Technique*. For the distinction between *allegoria in factis* (allegory of deeds) and *in verbis* (of words), see Strubel, " 'Allegoria in factis' et 'Allegoria in verbis.' " See also Tuve, *Allegorical Imagery*; Fletcher, *Allegory: The Theory of a Symbolic Mode*; and the articles in Haug, ed., *Formen und Funktionen der Allegorie*. For a useful distinction between allegory and allegoresis, see, most recently, Copeland and Melville, "Allegory and Allegoresis, Rhetoric and Hermeneutics." On the distinction between allegory and *figura* and the interplay between scriptural and secular exegesis, see Auerbach's important study "Figura."

50. "Zu Walter Benjamins Begriff der Allegorie," p. 670; my translation from the German.

51. The four levels can be memorized in these handy verses: "Littera gesta docet, quid credas allegoria, / Moralis quid agas, qui tendas anagogia" (The literal level teaches us about the things that happened, the allegorical level about what we should believe. The moral level teaches us what we should do, and the anagogical about the future). Cited by Mâle, *L'Art religieux du XIIIe siècle en France*, 2:82, n. 28. For opposing views on the relationship between Pauline allegory and allegories of profane texts, see Pépin, *Mythe et allégorie*, and Lubac, *Exégèse médiévale*, vol. 1, chap. 2, "Mythe et allégorie." For Lubac the two views are incompatible: "These are two contrary methods, coming from two contrary

doctrines and inspirations" (p. 396). But even if the two methods may be doctrinally opposed, *methodologically* they are very similar. This is the crucial point for the *OM*.

52. There are, of course, many more examples one could cite. Some are couched in formulas such as "Mes or tornons à autre fueil / Ceste fable, et par autre estoire / Veons comment la fable est voire" (But now let us look at this fable from another side and see, by means of another story, how this fable is true, 1.3830–32). This other story claims that Inacus was the first king of Greece and that this is the true historical explanation.

53. With slight variations also in 4.1176–77, 4.6342–43, 6.1379–80, 7.709–10, 9.1839–40, 11.2706–7, and 14.971–72, as well as many other instances.

54. Or as in 12.2881–82: "Or vous vueil faire aparisable / Le mistere de ceste fable" (Now I want to make clear to you the mystery of the fable). The "mistere" is that Jesus wanted to "marry" human nature. This is consistent with medieval usage. Lubac has shown that it is a Pauline term and practically synonymous with allegory: "Esprit, mystère, allégorie: tels sont donc les trois vocables majeurs, pratiquement synonymes" (Spirit, mystery, allegory; these are the three principal terms, practically synonymous; *Exégèse médiévale*, vol. 1, chap. 2, p. 403).

55. For more details on the Iphis story from *Metamorphoses* 9, see Chapter 5, the section "Christine's Personal Myths."

56. Nor does Bersuire, who to a certain extent modeled the second redaction of his *Ovidius moralizatus* on the *OM*.

57. We saw in Chapter 1 that in the *Roman de Thèbes* the city also symbolizes culture, albeit classical and not "divine" culture.

58. The story of Narcissus and Echo will be considered once more in the section on intertexts, to follow.

59. There is also a play on Bacchus's other name: Liber = the Deliverer (3.2819).

60. For a thorough analysis of the Cephalus and Procris story in the *OM* and other texts, see Lavin, "Cephalus and Procris."

61. Some of the observations that follow were already made in the section on Myrrha. Since they are pertinent here as well, I ask the reader to bear with me if I repeat myself.

62. For the parallels between Orpheus and Christ see Friedman, *Orpheus in the Middle Ages*, esp. chap. 3, and Heitmann, "Typen der Deformierung" and "Orpheus im Mittelalter," as well as the articles listed in n. 19. For de Mézières's text see *Le Livre de la vertu du sacrement de mariage* (Williamson, ed.). Here, the objects for meditation are jewels and the dishes, listed in great detail, at a spiritual wedding feast.

63. On Ganymede, see Kempter, *Ganymed: Studien zur Typologie, Ikonographie und Ikonologie*. On medieval attitudes toward homosexuality, see Boswell,

Christianity, Social Tolerance, and Homosexuality. In chaps. 10 and 11 Boswell analyzes the rise of intolerance to homosexuality in the later middle ages.

64. "Commentary as Criticism," pp. 33, 34. Seznec, *The Survival of the Pagan Gods*, assigns Ridewall to the mid-fifteenth century (p. 94). Allen rightly sees him active around 1331 (p. 29). On some of the difficulties of this type of allegory, see Minnis, ed., *Medieval Literary Theory and Criticism c. 1100–1375*, p. 320 (in reference to William of Aragon's interpretation of the Orpheus myth).

65. *Passagenwerk*, p. 122. Cited by Steinhagen, "Zu Walter Benjamins Begriff der Allegorie," p. 677; my translation from the German.

66. Ovid, *Met* 1.383. For more on this story as an example of interpretation "to the second degree," see the section by that name, to follow.

67. See the equation of "laicus" (lay person) and "lapis" (stone) made by Johannes Balbus in his *Catholicon* (ca. 1285): the lay person is hard and impervious to knowledge, that is, stupid (cited by Vauchez, "Lay People's Sanctity in Western Europe," p. 24, n. 8).

68. Barkan, in *The Gods Made Flesh*, sees in the story of Deucalion and Pyrrha a drama of interpretation that leads to creation (p. 31). See also Huot, "The Medusa Interpolation in the *Roman de la Rose*," esp. p. 875, and Freccero, "Medusa: The Letter and the Spirit," on the relation between petrification and interpretation.

69. In Ovid, the story is mentioned by Scylla in her tirade against Nisus in *Met* 8.132–37 and in Iphis's lament, in which she calls her own love for a girl even more unnatural than Pasiphae's love for a bull, who was at least a male (*Met* 9.735–37). Ovid's *Ars amatoria* 1.295–326 gives more details. Fuller versions of the story were also available in Hyginus's *Fabulae* (n. 40) and the *Vatican Mythographers* (esp. 1.43). I deal with this story and its interpretation as well as with the question of bestiality in the middle ages in "The Scandal of Pasiphae: Narration and Interpretation in the *Ovide moralisé*."

70. For Fulgentius, see *The Mythologies* (Whitbread, trans.), p. 73. For the second Vatican mythographer, see *Mythographi Vaticani I et II* (Kulcsár, ed.), #149 (p. 210).

71. See Bersuire's *Ovidius moralizatus*, which makes this equation explicit (Reynolds, *The 'Ovidius Moralizatus' of Petrus Berchorius*, p. 303). Altogether, the interpretation is different here. Bersuire says, for example, "Minos, that is a prelate. . . . A wife, that is the church" (p. 303). Bersuire, unlike the *OM* poet, interprets every character and many specific details of the story.

72. Since the *OM* poet begins telling Pasiphae's story with great distaste ("Ja ne cuncheriai ma bouche / Pour si vilain blasme retraire" [I will not soil my mouth by recounting such villainous accusations, 8.686–87] or "Donc le dirai je sans aloigne, / Mes honte m'est et grant vergoigne" [Thus I will tell it without too much detail, but I feel greatly ashamed, 8.715–16]), perhaps it is not too sur-

prising that he avoids interpreting precise narrative details. On the other hand, the story is so elaborate with regard to its sources that one cannot help but believe that the poet enjoyed telling it. I investigate this paradox in "The Scandal of Pasiphae." Another example in which the poet omits an unpleasant narrative element from the allegory is the story of Philomena in Book 6 (the rape is not allegorized).

73. *The Exposition of the Content of Virgil*, p. 131. In Hyginus's *Fabulae* she is one of the victims of suicide listed in fable #243.

74. *The Commentary of the First Six Books of the Aeneid of Vergil, Commonly Attributed to Bernardus Silvestris* (Jones and Jones, eds.), p. 25, ll. 18–21; or *Commentary on the First Six Books of Virgil's Aeneid by Bernardus Silvestris* (Schreiber and Maresca, trans.), p. 27. Dido's love also served as an example of "amor stultus" in medieval commentaries on the *Heroides*. See Nolan, "Ovid's *Heroides* Contextualized: Foolish Love and Legitimate Marriage in the *Roman d'Enéas*." On Dido in the *OM*, see also Leube, *Fortuna in Karthago*, pp. 41–45. Leube, who concentrates on the sources and on the function of the gods in this passage, states that the strange ("eigentümliche") interpretation of the story in the *OM* need not be considered in any detail (p. 44).

75. This interpretation already appeared in 13.3660 and 3667 ("Scilla puet noter signagogue").

76. This analysis cannot be made in these pages. In fact, almost every one of the hundreds of stories displays a slightly different pattern, some more interesting than others, of course. The allegorizations of the animals in Pythagoras's discourse of Book 15, such as the cranes whose long legs stand for earthly desires, would provide any number of entertaining examples.

77. For some theoretical remarks on this topic, see Todorov, *Symbolism and Interpretation*, pp. 52–59 ("The Hierarchy of Meanings").

78. Nestle, *Vom Mythos zum Logos*, p. 150.

79. See pp. 108–9. We will encounter her/him again in Chapter 5.

80. See Hexter's remarks in "The *Allegari* of Pierre Bersuire: Interpretation and the *Reductorium Morale*," pp. 51–84, on the fact that most commentators do not comment directly on the base text but on a paraphrase thereof (p. 57). In the *OM*, however, paraphrase does not play an important role since the fables are translated directly from Ovid. Of course, most of them are modified, expanded, and so forth.

81. See n. 66, above.

82. See n. 67, above.

83. *Met* 3.354; "dura superbia" literally means "hard pride." "Cold pride" is Miller's translation.

84. The next interpretation sees in Niobe "convoitise" (desire) and equates her seven sons with the Seven Deadly Sins and then continues for another 150 lines or so on this topic.

85. The first equation is made in passing, before her story is told in full.

86. There are some other examples of this "piling up" of interpretations. Remarks on the good housekeeping habits of Mineas's daughters in Book 4 lead to an allegorization involving a "spiritual house" (although in another set of interpretations they stand for all kinds of sins). The fable of Ixion in the same book is inscribed into an allegorization of Juno, so that the borderlines between fable and interpretation are blurred completely. In Book 7 Medea is equated ("iert" [was] is the term used here) with the Golden Fleece (7.692), which in turn stands for virginity. By this route, Medea comes to represent virginity.

87. Hexter, "The *Allegari*," analyzes the use of biblical intertexts in Bersuire's *Ovidius moralizatus*. Since the focus of my study is the vernacular tradition in the interpretation of myth (and not of the Bible), I will concentrate on vernacular intertexts.

88. For a recent analysis of the Philomena story in the *OM*, see Azzam, "Le Printemps de la littérature: La 'Translation' dans 'Philomena' de Chrestiiens li Gois."

89. For a bibliography, see chap. 2, n. 15. There is another passage, a tirade against "baillif, bedel, prevost et maire" (bailiffs, beadles, provosts, and mayors), that seems inspired by the *Roman de la Rose* (1.1583–614), as de Boer points out in a note. Copeland also points to an intertextual relationship between Boethius (and Jean de Meun's translation of the *Consolation of Philosophy*), the *Rose*, and the depiction of the Golden Age in Book 1 of the *OM* (*Rhetoric, Hermeneutics, and Translation*, pp. 120–22).

90. See, for example, John of Garland, *Integumenta Ovidii*, p. 49, ll. 164–65.

91. "Narcissus, Hermaphroditus, and Attis."

92. As usual, the *OM* vastly expands John's two lines: "Cellula matricis fons fertur Salmacis in qua / Infans conceptus hermafroditus erit" (The fountain of Salmacis is interpreted as the cell of the uterus in which the conceived fetus will be a hermaphrodite). The *OM* poet omits the notion of transformation ("fertur") and the future tense ("erit"): *Integumenta Ovidii*, p. 52, ll. 193–94.

93. For literary criticism in this period, see the useful anthologies by Minnis, *Medieval Literary Theory and Criticism*, and Hardison et al., *Medieval Literary Criticism: Translations and Interpretations*. The preface of the former (p. viii) contains some useful remarks on defining the term *literary criticism* for the medieval period.

94. The refusal to interpret or to describe something is, of course, a traditional topos. What is different here is the combination of this topos with that of interpretive surplus.

95. See Ehrhart, *The Judgment of the Trojan Prince Paris in Medieval Literature*, p. 86 (and notes to that page), on the possible sources of the *OM*. Ehrhart posits versions of the *Excidium Troiae* or the *Compendium Historiae Troianae-Romanae*.

96. This recalls Augustine's remarks in the *City of God*: "Then what about those functions assigned to the gods, portioned out in minute penny packets, with instructions that each of those divinities should be supplicated for his special responsibility?" (Bettenson, trans., pp. 243–44). A residue of the belief that gods are responsible for parts of the body can be found in medieval medicine, where the signs of the zodiac were assigned to different body parts and astrology determined propitious and unpropitious days for medical interventions.

97. There is another instance in which the poet is defensive about his text and invites others to write it differently. He discusses the different words for spleen and finally says that he does not care what people call it and further that he is content with his simple rhyme scheme (which he uses to "save time"!) for his enormous subject matter. He goes on to say that if others feel differently, however, they are free to rewrite the verse in "leonine" rhyme (15.4192–212).

98. Although Bersuire's *Ovidius moralizatus* is much shorter, it contains a similar consciousness. Hexter refers to "the inexhaustible text" ("The *Allegari*," p. 69).

99. Another, rather curious, meaning of the term *surplus* can be found in Book 2 for the fable of Chiron, who is a "wise and reasonable man." The passage ends "Ensi puet la fable estre voire. / Tout l'autre surplus est histoire" (Thus the fable can be true. The entire other surplus is history; 2.3131–32). My inelegant translation is meant to highlight the obscurity of the passage, which seems to mean that those details that do not form part of the moral-spiritual interpretation remain in the realm of history.

100. In Book 2 the poet also expresses doubt when he says in relation to the complaint of Earth: "Moult volentiers, si com moi samble, / Se plainsist a Dieu, s'el poist, / Et tel complainte li fiest" (she would gladly, it seems to me, complain to God, if she could. Here is the complaint she made; 2.538–40). But although he says "she would if she could" the poet then goes on to translate this very complaint from Ovid. His doubts clearly did not prevent him from following Ovid.

101. Cf. Saint Bonaventure, who argues that not everything can have an allegorical or mystical sense (Minnis, ed., *Medieval Literary Theory and Criticism*, p. 237).

102. We should keep this analysis in mind for the section on reading Ovid, to follow. This type of disbelief is different from the one in the Myrrha story, in which the poet exhorts his female listeners not to believe the story. The implication there is that, although the story is so horrible that it *should* not be true, it nevertheless is.

103. *Sermones super cantica canticorum* 14.4; cited by Damrosch in "*Non alia sed aliter*: The Hermeneutics of Gender in Bernard of Clairvaux," p. 193.

104. See 2 Cor. 3:6: "[God] Who also hath made us able ministers of the

new testament; not of the letter, but of the spirit: for the letter killeth, but the spirit giveth life." Hugh of Saint Victor comments as follows: "because it is certainly necessary that the student of the Scripture adhere staunchly to the truth of the spiritual meaning and that the high points of the literal meaning, which itself can sometimes be wrongly understood too, should not lead him away from the central concern in any way whatever. Why was that former people who received the Law of life reproved except that they followed the death-dealing letter in such a way that they did not have the life-giving Spirit?" (*Didascalion* 6.4., in Minnis, ed., *Medieval Literary Theory and Criticism*, p. 81). The letter represents the Old Testament, the Spirit the New. For poetic images attached to the letter/spirit distinction, see Freccero, "Medusa: The Letter and the Spirit."

105. Again, the notion of movement is important here. We saw earlier that allegory moves the text toward the truth; here, we have the verbs "traire" and "departir," used to give a spatial dimension to the harmful function of false glosses. They literally move their victims away from the realm of truth.

106. One is also reminded of Jean-Jacques Rousseau, of course, who, in his *Confessions*, sees himself at the Last Judgment with his book in his hand, ready for inspection by the judge (*Les Confessions*, ed. B. Gagnebin and M. Raymond [Paris, 1959], p. 5).

107. Cf. Demats's reading of this passage and 12.4580–610 on pp. 96–101 of her *Fabula*.

108. See Chapter 1 for a detailed reading of Benoît's prologue. We can also recall that my principal argument, that the *romans antiques* reject allegorizations of mythology, holds true: the *OM* poet recognized that Benoît refused to allow Homer any allegorical intent.

109. *Fabula*, p. 98.

110. See Demats, *Fabula*, pp. 112–13, who analyzes this passage in order to show that the *OM* poet never thought that Ovid could have intended the meanings that he (the *OM* poet) finds in the *Metamorphoses*. Rather, Ovid was motivated by politics, that is, gaining Augustus's favor (15.7153).

111. For Augustine, see *On Christian Doctrine*, bk. 3. This view certainly goes against exegetical traditions, which insisted that the historical (i.e., literal) level of the Bible is as true as all the other levels. We should recall here my earlier observations on the truth of the Ovidian base text: when the base text was considered patently false, that is, considered false by the Ovidian narrator, the *OM* poet refuses to allegorize the story. Yet for the Bible the poet sees no such problem: there even the literal level can be false. These remarks can be seen in the context of the "condemnation of 1277," in which certain propositions concerning the use of myth and fable in religion and philosophy as well as on theological teaching were condemned by the bishop of Paris, Stephen Tempier. Several of these condemned ideas were associated—whether rightly or wrongly—with

Siger of Brabant. See the balanced article by Maurer, "Siger of Brabant on Fables and Falsehoods in Religion." For a general view of this problem, see Lubac, "Importance de la lettre," pp. 425–39 in *Exégèse médiévale*, vol. 1, chap. 2.

112. This is the title given to a prose version of the *OM* (often associated with Colard Mansion) by the Parisian printer Vérard for his 1493 edition. See Paris, "Chrétien Legouais," p. 524, and Moss, *Poetry and Fable*, p. 6. A more detailed treatment of the question can be found in Leube, *Fortuna in Karthago*, pp. 46–47 and n. 47. Cf. Hexter, "The *Allegari*," n. 4, in which the author disentangles the different *OM* texts and the correct and incorrect attributions to various authors. In the context of the title *Bible des poètes*, one could also rethink Herzog's remarks concerning an "antik-biblische Einheitsmythologie" (antique-biblical unified mythology) in "Metapher—Exegese—Mythos," p. 184.

113. See Giovanni del Virgilio's *Allegorie*, based on Fulgentius, the Vatican mythographers, John of Garland, and Arnulf of Orléans, where Ovid appears only in paraphrase (as Ovid does in the works just cited as del Virgilio's sources). See Minnis, ed., *Medieval Literary Theory and Criticism*, p. 322.

114. Obviously, not all writers would be interested in the Christian interpretations offered by the *OM*. In fact, in the manuscript illuminations of *OM*, there is a trend away from depicting the allegorical meanings and a growing preference for showing only the literal level. See Lord, "Three Manuscripts of the *Ovide moralisé*." She shows that in the earliest manuscript of the *OM* (Rouen MS 0.4; 1315–25) about 20 percent of the illustrations were devoted to allegorical images. This figure drops to 10 percent in MS Arsenal 5069 (second quarter of fourteenth century), and in the later-fourteenth-century Lyon MS 742, owned by Jean duc de Berry, only two images are pious (p. 169).

Chapter 4

1. See Jung, "Poetria: Zur Dichtungstheorie des ausgehenden Mittelalters," p. 58. The ballade in question is no. 129 in *Oeuvres complètes* (Marquis de Queux de Saint-Hilaire and Raynaud, eds.), vol. 1, pp. 251–52.

2. See Cerquiglini, "Le Clerc et l'écriture: Le *Voir dit* de Guillaume de Machaut et la définition du *dit*," p. 159.

3. Poirion, "Traditions et fonctions du *dit poétique* au XIVe et XVe siècle," pp. 148–49.

4. Cerquiglini, "Le Clerc et l'écriture," pp. 158–62.

5. Waugh, in *Metafiction: The Theory and Practice of Self-Conscious Fiction*, defines the characteristics of metafiction as "a celebration of the power of the creative imagination together with an uncertainty about the validity of its representations; an extreme self-consciousness about language, literary form and the act of writing fictions; a pervasive insecurity about the relationship of fiction to reality; a parodic, playful, excessive or deceptively naive style of writing"

(p. 2). Although Waugh adduces these characteristics for modern texts, they may equally well apply to the *dits*.

6. Cerquiglini-Toulet highlights the crisis of subject matter in the fourteenth century in *La Couleur de la mélancolie*.

7. On this concept, see Brownlee, *Poetic Identity in Guillaume de Machaut*, chap. 1.

8. On the life of Machaut, see Hoepffner's introduction in vol. 1 of his *Oeuvres de Guillaume de Machaut*; Poirion, *Le poète et le prince*, pp. 192–205; and Palmer's summary of his life in his edition of *The Judgment of the King of Navarre*, pp. xi–xvii, based on Machabey's *Guillaume de Machaut, 130?–1377*. On Froissart's life, see especially Bastin, *Froissart: Chroniqueur, romancier et poète*; Poirion, *Le Poète et le prince*, p. 218; and Dembowski, *Jean Froissart and His 'Meliador.'*

9. Deschamps did, and his 1392 *Art de ditier* (in *Oeuvres*, vol. 7) is largely a treatise on the different forms of poetry. The *Arts de seconde rhétorique*, edited by Langlois in *Recueil d'Arts de seconde rhétorique*, contain guides to versification, alphabetical lists of words and glosses, lists of rhyme words, etc. The second (anonymous) treatise, based on B. N. n.acq.fr. 4237 and dating from the first third of the fifteenth century, also contains a kind of mythological handbook (with some Old Testament figures thrown in), which is meant to provide accurate materials for the composition of "diz, lays ou ballades ou rommans" (p. 39), indicating that more than one genre could profitably draw on classical mythology. Other treatises contain remarks about the pagan gods in such contexts as alphabetical lists.

10. On these authors, see Minnis and Scott, eds. (with the assistance of Wallace), *Medieval Literary Theory and Criticism c. 1100–c. 1375*, chap. 8.

11. *OM* (de Boer, ed.).

12. See Thomas, "Guillaume de Machaut et L'*Ovide moralisé*," and de Boer, "Guillaume de Machaut et L'*Ovide moralisé*."

13. They do not go so far as to gloss their own works explicitly, as Dante had done in the *Vita nuova*, for example. As we will see, the glossing takes place within the context of the fiction.

14. In Hoepffner, ed., *Oeuvres*, vols. 1 and 3. I use the editions and translations by Palmer, *The Judgement of the King of Navarre* and *Le Confort d'Ami*.

15. For the details of Charles's life, see Pietri, *Chronique de Charles le Mauvais*. Palmer, in his introduction to *Le Confort d'Ami*, gives a detailed account of the events of the time.

16. On the different ways the plague is evoked in contemporary texts, see Zink, "The Time of the Plague and the Order of Writing."

17. "Guillaume" will refer to the character, "Machaut" to the author. For the taxonomy of Machaut's poetic self-representation to which I refer here, see Brownlee, *Poetic Identity*.

18. For detailed analyses of this text, see Calin, *A Poet at the Fountain*, chap. 2; Brownlee, *Poetic Identity*, pp. 157–71; Imbs, *Le Voir-Dit de Guillaume de Machaut*, pp. 110–16; and Palmer's introduction.

19. For a close reading of the exempla, see Picherit, "Les *Exemples* dans le *Jugement dou Roy de Navarre*," and Heinrichs, *The Myths of Love: Classical Lovers in Medieval Literature*, pp. 189–96.

20. "Les *Exemples*," p. 110.

21. For more inapposite examples and interpretations, see Heinrichs, *The Myths of Love*, pp. 192–96.

22. "Le Clerc et l'écriture," p. 168. (Cerquiglini does not speak specifically of the *Navarre* here.)

23. Three, according to Hoepffner's introduction (*Oeuvres*, vol. 3, p. ii); four according to Ehrhart, *The Judgment of the Trojan Prince Paris in Medieval Literature*, p. 192, and Wallen, "Biblical and Mythological Typology in Machaut's *Confort d'Ami*," p. 191.

24. See p. xxix in his edition and translation of *Le Confort d'Ami*.

25. See Palmer's introduction, pp. xxxvi–xlv, for detailed analysis of the parallels between Charles's situation and the biblical exempla. See also Wallen, "Biblical and Mythological Typology."

26. Cf. Kelly, *Medieval Imagination: Rhetoric and the Poetry of Courtly Love*, p. 125: "But in each case Machaut ignores the misfortune to stress the immediate advantages of hope."

27. See Palmer, *Le Confort d'Ami*, p. xxix, and Wallen, "Biblical and Mythological Typology," for detailed analyses of the lessons and parallels of the other mythological exempla (although there are some slight differences of opinion between the two).

28. Hoepffner, ed., *Oeuvres*, vol. 1, p. 6. For an analysis of this terminology, see Lukitsch, "The Poetics of the *Prologue*," and Cerquiglini, *"Un engin si soutil": Guillaume de Machaut et l'écriture au XIVe siècle*, pp. 15–21. See also Ferrand, "Regards sur le *Prologue* de Guillaume de Machaut," and Brownlee, *Poetic Identity*, pp. 16–20.

29. See Huot, *From Song to Book: The Poetics of Writing in Old French Lyric and Lyrical Narrative Poetry*, esp. pp. 287–92 (focusing on the *Dit de la harpe*).

30. Cerquiglini, "*Un engin si soutil*," pp. 147–48.

31. *Fragments d'un discours amoureux* (Paris, 1977), p. 268. (Quoted by Cerquiglini, "*Un engin si soutil*," p. 147.)

32. See Cerquiglini, "*Un engin si soutil*," esp. pp. 153–55.

33. Cerquiglini, "*Un engin si soutil*," p. 154.

34. See Chapter 3, p. 130, for an analysis of parts of this passage in another context.

35. Ovid, *Metamorphoses* (Loeb ed.), bk. 5.

36. Boethius, in fact, referred to the muses, not the Pierides, as "hysterical sluts" (*The Consolation of Philosophy*, Watts, trans., p. 36.)

37. Machaut later refers to his own *Voir-Dit* as fiction: "les belles et subtives fictions" (the beautiful and subtle fictions; *Le Livre du Voir-Dit*, Paris, ed. p. 262). For the *OM* passage, compare Augustine's remarks on the "theological" poets (*The City of God* 18.14, Bettenson, trans., pp. 778–79).

38. For the exact references to the numerous correspondences, see Palmer, *Confort*, pp. lxxi–lxxii.

39. "Traditions et fonctions," pp. 148–49.

40. This is how Machaut refers to this text in the *Voir-Dit* (Paris, ed., pp. 53, 69, 241). On p. 331 of the same text he refers to his poem as *L'amoureuse fonteine*. All quotes are from *La Fontaine amoureuse*, ed. and trans. Cerquiglini-Toulet.

41. "Guillaume de Machaut and the Writerly Process," p. 152.

42. "Guillaume de Machaut," pp. 148–50.

43. For a close reading of the entire *Fontaine*, see Brownlee, *Poetic Identity*, pp. 188–207.

44. See de Looze, "Guillaume de Machaut," and Brownlee, *Poetic Identity*. Calin, in *A Poet at the Fountain*, insists more on the love psychology figured in the myths but also says that "the theme of art and artist is central to a tale, where the two protagonists are poets, which describes highly prized works of art in its plot, and itself ranks as a most elegantly finished aesthetic whole" (p. 165). Compare his "*La Fonteinne amoureuse* de Machaut." See also the important study of Huot in *From Song to Book*, pp. 293–301.

45. There, Ceyx's voyage is an attempt to flee earthly delights, represented by Alcyone; his ship is the Church; and the storms are the princes and barons that trouble the Church (11.2996–4147).

46. *Poetic Identity*, p. 194.

47. See, by contrast, Christine de Pizan's use of this myth as a signal of hope in the *Mutacion de Fortune*, which is analyzed in Chapter 5, pp. 185–87.

48. Brownlee sees the fountain as an "emblem not only of the poetic text which it figures (yielding a kind of structured circularity) but of the literary processes (intertextuality, generic transformation, etc.) which have produced the text" (*Poetic Identity*, p. 198).

49. Ehrhart sees the function of the Troy story, and in particular the Judgment of Paris Venus recounts later on in the text, as a criticism of the nobility's involvement with love (*The Judgment*, pp. 130–41). Cf. my reservations to this thesis in my review in *Speculum* 64 (1989): 409–12.

50. On Machaut's use of the term "ordenance" as applied to his own works, see Cerquiglini, "*Un engin si soutil*," p. 15. She defines the two aspects of "ordonner" as both a formal and moral-judicial ordering.

51. For a detailed analysis of the *Fontaine*'s debt to the *Rose*, see Huot, from

Song to Book, esp. pp. 296–97, and her *The Romance of the Rose and Its Medieval Readers*, pp. 242–49. I would also like to acknowledge the contributions of the students in my seminar "Classical Mythology in the French Middle Ages" (Columbia University, fall 1992), in particular the paper by Promita Chatterji, "The Re-figuration of Myth: Narrative and Figurative Language in the *Roman d'Enéas* and *La Fonteinne Amoureuse*."

52. This concretization has been analyzed by Chatterji in the paper mentioned in the previous note.

53. *Poetic Identity*, p. 199. On the poet-patron relationship in the *Fontaine*, see also Kelly, "The Genius of the Patron," esp. p. 79.

54. On the significance of Machaut's use of the judgment of Midas in relation to the *Roman de la Rose*, see Huot, *The Romance of the Rose*, pp. 247–48.

55. In this I neither agree completely with Brownlee, who claims that Machaut purposefully "demoralized" his source (*Poetic Identity*, p. 202), nor with Ehrhart, who sees an entirely negative depiction of love (*The Judgment*, pp. 131–41).

56. In the *Metamorphoses* Danae is also mentioned in Book 11 (in the context of Midas's changing everything he touches into gold; 11.117).

57. On the details of this interpretation, see Ehrhart, *The Judgment*, pp. 89–90.

58. By my count it appears fewer than a dozen times in the text's 72,000 lines, while *fable*, for example, appears 300 times.

59. For the *OM* as a whole, this condemnation of course indicates that the poet condemns the belief in the reality of the gods, not the use of myth as a pretext for allegory.

60. For detailed analyses of the *Voir-Dit*, see Brownlee, *Poetic Identity*, pp. 94–156; Cerquiglini, "*Un engin si soutil*"; and Imbs, *Le Voir-Dit*. The edition by Paris is not very successful, since he omits a number of passages and changes the order of some of the letters. On the details, see Cerquiglini-Toulet, "Le 'Voir Dit' mis à nu par ses éditeurs, même." There is also a 600-line error in the numbering of the verses starting at p. 273. I will therefore indicate only page numbers in citations.

61. See Calin, *A Poet at the Fountain*, pp. 168–71, for details concerning critical opinions on the truth of the story. For arguments of Toute-Belle's fictional nature he follows the arguments by Hanf, "Ueber Guillaume de Machauts Voir Dit." See also Brownlee, *Poetic Identity*, p. 97, n. 9.

62. On Péronne d'Armentières, see *Le Voir-Dit*, Paris, ed., pp. i–ix, and Brownlee, *Poetic Identity*, p.239, n. 25. On Machaut's authorial role, see Williams, "An Author's Role in Fourteenth-Century Book Production"; her "Machaut's Self-Awareness as Author and Producer"; and Huot, *From Song to Book*, chaps. 8 and 9.

63. The first was analyzed in detail by Brownlee, *Poetic Identity*, chap. 3; the second by Cerquiglini, "*Un engin si soutil*," esp. pp. 143–55.

64. "Sens" is of course one of the things given by Nature to Machaut in his Prologue (V, 1.2). (Hoepffner, ed., *Oeuvres*, vol. 1, p. 6).

65. See n. 31, above.

66. The Prologue serves as a preface to his narrative works but was written later.

67. Whether this image is a portrait or a statue remains ambiguous. See Cerquiglini's detailed analysis of the allusions to Pygmalion, "*Un engin si soutil*," pp. 203–10.

68. Whether this poem is by Thibaut or not is debatable since it appears in *Guillaume de Machaut: Poésies lyriques* (Chichmaref, ed.) as Ballade 39 (pp. 561–69). Pygmalion is also the subject of Ballade 115 in *La Louange des dames by Guillaume de Machaut* (Wilkins, ed.) and in *Guillaume de Machaut*, pp. 183–84. In Ballade 115 Machaut compares his lady to Pygmalion's unresponsive statue, but while Pygmalion succeeded in bringing his statue to life, he does not. What he brings to life instead, of course, is the poem.

69. Ovid, *Met* 9.394–401; *OM* 9.1382–401. The allegory sees in the story the rejuvenation (= conversion) of those who leave behind "la vielle pelice / De felonie et de malice" (the old skin of felony and malice; 9.1415–16) through the intervention of the Church (= Hebe). For Callirhoe, see *Met* 9.432, and *OM* 9.1442–50. De Boer points out that the *OM* poet gives Callirhoe only one son ("Guillaume de Machaut," p. 340). In his edition of the *OM*, however, the line reads "aus enfans de Callyroe" (14.1449), obviously indicating a plural. In addition, the stories of Iolaus and Callirhoe's children are clearly distinguished in the *OM*, so even if Machaut read a version that contained "au filz" instead of "aus enfans" he would have seen the demarcation between the two fables. The scene of Hebe and the Elders was illustrated in two of the early manuscripts (Rouen 0.4, fol. 238r and Arsenal 5069, fol. 126v).

70. Another "mistake," this time of the lady, makes Pygmalion the father of Adonis. Rather, he is via his "wife" (the former statue), Paphus (their son), Cinyras, and Myrrha a more remote ancestor of Adonis. Because Adonis was born from the incestuous union of Myrrha and her father, Cinyras, the generations are blurred already. This "mistake" may also point to the generational gap between Guillaume and Toute-Belle.

71. On the revelations the mythological intertexts can bring to a text such as Petrarch's *Rime sparse*, see Vickers, "Diana Described." Vickers observes: "As a privileged mode of signifying, the recounting of a mythical tale within a literary text reveals concerns, whether conscious or unconscious, which are basic to that text" (p. 97).

72. The color green could have a positive or a negative meaning, as Cerquiglini shows in "*Un engin si soutil*," pp. 168–71.

73. Ovid, *Met* 5.242–49; *OM* 5.1585–93. In the allegory, Polydectes signifies the "Multitude ou pluralité / De vilonie et de vilté" (many and varied cases of villainy and vileness; 5.1632–33) of the sinners whose lack of humility and charity makes them hard as stones.

74. This was a common interpretation in the allegorical and mythographic traditions. Huot, "The Medusa Interpolation in the *Roman de la Rose*," p. 874, n. 9, details the different interpretations of this figure. In Dante, the meaning of the Medusa is more complex, as Freccero has shown in "Medusa: The Letter and the Spirit." Both Dante and Machaut may have known the Medusa interpolation in the *Roman de la Rose* (ibid., pp. 126–28; Huot, *The Romance of the Rose*, pp. 264–65).

75. This is suggested by Cerquiglini in "*Un engin si soutil*," p. 148.

76. *Poetic Identity*, chap. 3.

77. On the side of unlove, the stages codified by courtly lyric are less numerous. There are essentially two: the intervention of the slanderers, betrayal. Here the writing emerges from another place: mythology ("*Un engin si soutil*," p. 34).

78. Ibid., p. 166; my translation.

79. Significantly, the theme of poetic competition is introduced on pp. 274–75 with the two ballades of Thibaut and G. de Machaut (as the superscript in MS A reads; this is the only time Machaut's name appears in the *Voir-Dit*, as Brownlee points out [*Poetic Identity*, p. 140]). As I indicated in n. 68, Thibaut's poem appears in Machaut's lyric oeuvre. This competition may thus mirror a poetic contest between two manifestations of "Machaut," just as Toute-Belle's and his own contributions to the *Voir-Dit* ultimately compete.

80. Ovid, *Met* 14.320–434; *OM* 14.2675–956. In these two texts, the story is told by one of Circe's women to Macareus, one of Ulysses's companions, who then retells it. On the different images of Circe, see Segal, "Circean Temptations: Homer, Vergil, and Ovid," pp. 438 and 442.

81. Ovid, *Met* 14.313–14. The *OM* also mentions the statue and describes it as "ymage d'un roi tres bele / Qui de marbre entaillé estoit" (the statue of a very beautiful king, carved from marble; 14.2688–89). In the secretary's speech this detail is missing, but since Machaut used the *OM* it forms part of the story as he read it.

82. The interpretive passage ends with "Ensi s'accorde au voir la fable" (Thus the fable agrees with the truth; 14.3266). Although this formula occurs many times in the *OM*, this is by my count the first time that an allegorical passage ends with this appeal to truth ("voir").

83. Part of this passage, the song of Polyphemus, was omitted in Paris's edition. It was edited by Thomas in "Guillaume de Machaut." The story can be found in Ovid, *Met* 13.738–897; *OM* 13.3689–4147. Polyphemus is interpreted as the devil (13.4175); his flute playing as temptation, fraud, and deception

(13.4252–62); Galatea as divine wisdom (13.4153); and Acis as human nature (13.4159).

84. See Cerquiglini, "*Un engin si soutil*," pp. 166–68, and Calin, *A Poet at the Fountain*, pp. 180–81.

85. Ovid, *Met* 2.535–632; *OM* 2.2121–454.

86. This is the only Ovidian narrative in the *Voir-Dit* that is expanded by comparison with the *Ovide moralisé* (de Boer, "Guillaume de Machaut," p. 351). It is interesting to note that in the commentary on the Aeneid attributed to Bernardus Silvestris, Circe, along with Aesculapius (both children of Apollo), is credited with the invention of surgery (*Commentary of the First Six Books of the Aeneid of Virgil, Commonly Attributed to Bernardus Silvestris*, Jones and Jones, eds., p. 35). This idea is linked to the etymology of her name given by Fulgentius, *Mythologies* 2.7: "Circe, for touch, that is, as if one said in Greek *cironcrine*, which in Latin we call judgment of the hands" (Whitbread, trans., p. 73).

87. Brownlee calls the use of the exemplum "playfully ambiguous, if not deeply ironic" (*Poetic Identity*, p. 147). Sturges feels that the fact "that the crow's story was true is irrelevant, as is the 'truth,' whatever it may be, about Toute-belle's fidelity" (*Medieval Interpretation*, p. 123) and that "fiction may be preferable to the truth" (p. 124) because it allows Guillaume to continue loving.

88. See Cerquiglini, "*Un engin si soutil*," pp. 203–5.

89. Ibid., pp. 152–55.

90. Brownlee translates this phrase as "I want to have certain passages revised" (*Poetic Identity*, p. 154). But the verb is clearly in the active mode, underlining that it is she herself who wants to do the revising.

91. The term is Hélène Cixous's: see "The Laugh of the Medusa," *Signs* 1 (1976): 875–99.

92. "Ethique de la totalisation et esthétique de la rupture dans le *Voir-Dit* de Guillaume de Machaut," p. 261.

93. Cf. Stierle, "Mythos als 'Bricolage' und zwei Endstufen des Prometheusmythos." His definition of bricolage partly applies to Froissart: "The guiding concept, which Lévi-Strauss in *La Pensée sauvage* relates to mythic thought, is that of bricolage, that is, the activity of taking the old, which has become useless, out of its original contexts and to make it serve a new intention through original new combinations" (p. 457). Froissart's *dits* have been published in the following editions: *Le Paradis d'amour [and] L'Orloge amoureus*, ed. Dembowski; *L'Espinette amoureuse*, ed. Fourrier; *La Prison amoureuse*, ed. Fourrier; *Le Joli Buisson de jonece*, ed. Fourrier.

94. In recent years, there has been a veritable explosion of interest in Froissart's myths. A general introduction to Froissart as poet can be found in Poirion, *Le Poète et le prince*, pp. 205–17, and in Dembowski, "La Position de Froissart-poète dans l'histoire littéraire." The first article to address Froissart's use of my-

thology (Graham, "Froissart's Use of Classical Allusion in His Poems") saw it in a rather negative light as tedious and irrelevant. More interesting recent studies include Bennett, "The Mirage of Fiction: Narration, Narrator, and Narratee in Froissart's Lyrico-Narrative *Dits*"; Bradley-Cromey, "Mythological Typology in Froissart's *Espinette amoureuse*"; Brownlee, "Ovide et le Moi poétique 'moderne' à la fin du moyen âge: Jean Froissart et Christine de Pizan"; Cerquiglini-Toulet, "Fullness and Emptiness: Shortages and Storehouses of Lyric Treasure in the Fourteenth and Fifteenth Centuries"; Ehrhart, *The Judgment*, pp. 141–50; Freeman, "Froissart's *Le Joli Buisson de Jonece*"; Heinrichs, *The Myths of Love*, pp. 196–207; Huot, *From Song to Book*, chap. 10, and "The Daisy and the Laurel: Myths of Desire and Creativity in the Poetry of Jean Froissart"; Kelly, "The Genius of the Patron," "Les Inventions ovidiennes de Froissart," and *Medieval Imagination*, chap. 7; Kibler, "Self-Delusion in Froissart's *Espinette amoureuse*"; Nouvet, "Pour une économie de la dé-limitation: La *Prison amoureuse* de Jean Froissart"; Picherit, "Le Rôle des éléments mythologiques dans le *Joli Buisson de jonece* de Jean Froissart"; Ribémont, "Froissart, le mythe et la marguerite"; Thiry, "Allégorie et histoire dans la 'Prison amoureuse' de Froissart"; and Zink, "Froissart et la nuit du chasseur."

95. For a detailed study of the historical reality underlying the allegory, see Thiry, "Allégorie et histoire." On the fictionalized relationship of poet and patron, see Nouvet, "Pour une économie."

96. Quote from Huot, *From Song to Book*, p. 314; Cerquiglini-Toulet, "Fullness and Emptiness," p. 225.

97. "Par figure" does not refer to any figurative sense here but must be seen in the context of the mythological handbook mentioned in n. 9, whose introduction reads: "Pour avoir cognoissance d'aucuns poetes et de pluseurs pars de melodie et d'aucunes (sic) sont mises leurs figure(s) ainsi qu'il s'enssuit, afin de mettre et attribuer leurs fait(s) a aultres, et pour faire diz, lays ou ballades ou rommans" (In order to gain knowledge of some poets and of some parts of the melody and some [lacuna in text] we have put here their figures as follows, so that we can attribute their deeds to others and so that we can compose *dits*, lays or ballades or romances; p. 39). (The passage that follows is an unbelievably garbled—to the modern reader—account of classical mythology.) "Figure(s)" here seems simply to refer to the summary account of the fable, and that is the sense I would attribute to the term in Rose's letter.

98. The most complete analyses of this myth are in Huot, *From Song to Book*, pp. 311–16, and Brownlee, "Ovide et le Moi poétique 'moderne,'" pp. 157–61, in which he identifies the three Ovidian models and the importance of Apollo (also highlighted by Huot in "The Daisy and the Laurel," pp. 243–46); see Fourrier's introduction to the *Prison*, pp. 17–20, and Ribémont, "Froissart, le mythe et la marguerite," esp. p. 131.

99. "Ovide et le Moi poétique 'moderne,'" p. 161; my translation from the French.

100. Kelly, "The Genius of the Patron," p. 96.

101. Fourrier, introduction to the *Prison*, pp. 20–28; Thiry, "Allégorie et histoire." See also Kibler, "Poet and Patron: Froissart's *Prison Amoureuse*."

102. At the same time, the allegorical figures such as Orgueil, Outrage, and Desir stand for historical figures *and* for elements of love psychology. Thus Hardement, for example, "is" Gui de Luxembourg but stands as well for encouragement to a life of love. Thiry (pp. 24–25) has devised some handy charts that disentangle all these equations.

103. For example, in Arnulf of Orléans's *Allegoriae super Ovidii Metamorphosin* (ed. Ghisalberti), p. 204, paragraph 1.; or in the *OM* 2.689–1012, where Phaeton figures not only pride but even the Antichrist. On Flos's "perverse mythographic exegesis" of this fable, see Heinrichs, *The Myths of Love*, pp. 197–202, whose interpretation ("Flos is saying that Rose can continue to enjoy love if he rejects the truth," p. 210) is too narrow in my view.

104. On the importance of various containers of the text, see Cerquiglini-Toulet, "Fullness and Emptiness," pp. 230–34.

105. Ll. 3154–372. For an interpretation of Froissart's rewriting of the Narcissus myth as an enforcement of "compulsory heterosexuality," see Baskins, "Echoing Narcissus in Alberti's *Della Pittura*," p. 29.

Chapter 5

1. Schibanoff, "Taking the Gold out of Egypt: The Art of Reading as a Woman," p. 91.

2. See Ostriker, "The Thieves of Language," p. 72.

3. The principal texts I will consider in this chapter are *Cent ballades* (1390's) and *Autres ballades* (ca. 1395–1405) in *Oeuvres poétiques de Christine de Pisan*, ed. Roy, vol. 1; *L'Epistre au dieu d'amours* (1399) in *Oeuvres poétiques*, vol. 2 (Schibanoff mistranslates the title as "The Letter to the God of Love," not "from the God of Love" [p. 92]); *L'Epistre d'Othéa* (= *Othéa*; ca. 1400), ed. Loukopoulos; *Le Débat sur le Roman de la Rose* (= *Débat*; 1401–2), ed. Hicks; *Le Livre du chemin de long estude* (= *Chemin*; 1402–3), ed. Püschel; *Le Livre de la mutacion de Fortune* (= *Mutacion*; 1403), ed. Solente; and "The *Livre de la cité des dames* of Christine de Pisan, A Critical Edition" (= *Cité*; 1404–5), ed. Curnow.

4. Brownlee, "Discourses of the Self: Christine de Pizan and The *Rose*," sees in the *Epistre* a "corrective rewriting of the famous speech of Jean de Meun's Dieu d'Amours at the structural center of the conjoined *Rose* text" (p. 206). *L'Avision Christine* (ed. Towner) contains only a few elements from classical mythology. For an analysis of the opening section featuring a kind of creation myth, see my "Das Konzept von Frau und Mann bei Hildegard von Bingen und Christine de Pizan," pp. 174–75.

5. The term *story moment* to describe the *texte* in Christine's schema is Tuve's, in *Allegorical Imagery*, p. 34.

6. Christine also used the historical events described in *Histoire ancienne jusqu'à César* as a source for some stories in the *Othéa* and for vast stretches of text in the *Mutacion* without including much of the mythographic material available in the *Histoire*.

7. These are the *Cent ballades*, the *Virelais*, the *Ballades d'estrange façon*, the *Lais*, the *Rondeaux*, *Jeux a vendre*, *Autres ballades*, *Encore autres ballades*, and *Complaintes amoureuses*.

8. *Cent ballades* nos. 3, 4, 42, 45, 52, 61, 83, 86, 90, 92 and *Autres ballades* nos. 7, 11, 14, 17. I do not count those poems that evoke the figure of Fortune, one of the most enduring concepts in Christine's writings (e.g., nos. 7, 8, 10, 12). See Loukopoulos, "Classical Mythology in the Works of Christine de Pisan," chap. 2, on Christine's courtly poetry (which is more a list than an analysis). For a sensitive reading of Christine's *Cent Ballades* in light of Petrarcha, see Walters, "Chivalry and the (En)Gendered Poetic Self: Petrarchan Models in the 'Cent Balades.' "

9. For Hero and Leander, see Ovid's *Heroides*, letter 19; *OM* 4.3150–584; and Machaut's *Jugement dou roy de Navarre*. For Io, Ovid's *Metamorphoses*, 1.611–750; *Mythographus Vaticanus I*, chap. 18, and *Mythographus Vaticanus II*, chap. 7; *Histoire ancienne jusqu'à César*, B.N. fr. 20,125; *OM* 1.3450–796; and Boccaccio, *Concerning Famous Women*, trans. Guarino, pp. 18–19 (the chapter entitled "Isis, Queen and Goddess of Egypt"). For the interpretive history of the Judgment of Paris, see Ehrhart, *The Judgment of the Trojan Prince Paris in Medieval Literature*, and for the Judgment in the works of Christine de Pizan, see Ehrhart, "Christine de Pizan and the Judgment of Paris." For Circe, see Virgil's *Aeneid* 3; Boethius, *Consolation of Philosophy* 4m3; Hyginus, *Fabulae*, no. 125; Fulgentius, *Mythologies* 2.86; and *OM* 14.2363–3509. All of these stories reappear in Christine's later writings.

10. For some of the same ambiguities in Boccaccio's *opere minori*, see Hollander, *Boccaccio's Two Venuses*. The negative interpretation would follow medieval commentaries on the *Heroides*. See Nolan, "Ovid's *Heroides* Contextualized: Foolish Love and Legitimate Marriage in the *Roman d'Enéas*."

11. "Toute femeline luxure / Naist en sexte, membre de feme" (All feminine voluptuousness is born in *Sexte*, the woman's organ; 4.3597–98).

12. In the *Cité* (pp. 936–37 [Richards, trans., pp. 192–93]) Hero is an example of "faithful women" who perished through loving too much. (Page numbers to quotes from the *Cité* in English refer to the Richards translation.)

13. Hyginus Fable 145, which was a source for Boccaccio, also omits the detail of Io tracing her name.

14. The fact that Io then became the Egyptian goddess Isis is also missing

here. We will consider the interpretations offered by the *OM* below in the context of the *Othéa.*

15. La Vieille states, "Nus ne peut metre en fame garde, / s'ele meïsmes ne se garde" (Nobody can watch over a woman, unless she watches herself; ll. 14,351–52) and then proceeds to tell the story of Io.

16. For Christine's condemnation of the *Rose*, see *Le Débat sur le Roman de la Rose* and stanza 57 of the *Enseigenmens moraux*, addressed to her son Jean de Castel: "Se bien veulx et chastement vivre, / De la Rose ne lis le livre / Ne Ovide de l'Art d'amer, / Dont l'exemple fait a blasmer" (If you want to live well and chastely, do not read the book of the Rose, nor the Art of Love of Ovid, which sets blameworthy examples; *Oeuvres poétiques*, vol. 3, p. 39).

17. See Ehrhart, *The Judgment*, pp. 184–85, for one possible interpretation of this poem. While I do not contradict Ehrhart's views, I feel there is more to the poem than a "complaint to the poet's purse" (p. 185).

18. MS B.N. f.fr. 603, fol. 2v., cited by Cerquiglini in "L'Etrangère," p. 240.

19. Willard offers a charming, if less accurate, translation: "I've chosen now for all my joy / My life in study to employ. / With peace and chosen solitude, / A studious world makes my life good" (*Christine de Pizan: Her Life and Works*, p. 113).

20. I am touching here on a complex problem, that of Christine's criticism of courtly conventions. (Note that in courtly poetry the "losengiers" may also be called slanderers, although, of course, there they generally speak the truth.) Christine confronts the problem in the later *Cent ballades d'amant et de dame* (1409–10) and particularly in the earlier letter addressed to a young noblewoman by her duenna in the *Livre des trois vertus* (1405; Willard and Hicks, eds., pp. 110–20; the same letter forms part of Christine's *Le livre du Duc des vrais amants*). There is as yet no systematic study of Christine's attitude toward the courtly tradition, although Brownlee remarks upon it in "Discourses of the Self" (with regard to the *Rose*). See also Willard, "Lovers' Dialogues in Christine de Pizan's Lyric Poetry from the *Cent Ballades* to the *Cent Ballades d'Amant et de Dame*."

21. This is the gist of the letter mentioned in the previous note.

22. Brownlee, "The Image of History in Christine de Pizan's *Livre de la Mutacion de Fortune*," p. 44.

23. The rubric reads "Ci dit d'aucuns miracles, que Ovide raconte de ses dieux" (Here she tells of some miracles that Ovid recounts of his gods, *Mutacion* 1.41). See Brownlee, "Ovide et le moi poétique 'moderne' à la fin du moyen âge: Jean Froissart et Christine de Pizan," esp. pp. 162–69, which focus on Christine's use of the Ovidian stories in the *Mutacion*. The juxtaposition of Circe and Tiresias may have been suggested by such collections as the *Mythographus Vaticanus I*, where Circe's story is Fable 15 and Tiresias's Fable 16.

24. In this, my argument differs slightly from Brownlee's in "Ovide et le

moi poétique," which concentrates on Christine's "good" and "bad" Ovid, an important distinction in her reception of Ovid's works. In the somewhat later *Avision* Christine explicitly addresses questions of the multiple interpretations of fables. For her tripartite scheme of interpreting her own *Avision*, see Reno, "The Preface to the *Avision-Christine* in ex-Phillipps 128."

25. On this transformation, see also Margolis, "Christine de Pizan: The Poetess as Historian," esp. pp. 368–69.

26. See Phillippy, "Establishing Authority: Boccaccio's *De Claris Mulieribus* and Christine de Pizan's *Le Livre de la Cité des Dames*," p. 178, n. 2, on Boccaccio's denigration of "woman's work" in a number of stories of his *Concerning Famous Women*. More on this question with regard to the *Cité* in the section "Myths of Feminine Achievement."

27. The spelling of the name in Christine is "Yplis"; I cite it according to Ovid as Iphis. The story follows upon the incestuous tale of Byblis. For some medieval uses of the Byblis story, see Leclanche, "Biblis: Métamorphose médiévale d'un conte ovidien." For some remarks on the deeroticization of the *Mutacion* version of the Iphis story and the substitution of Vesta for Isis, see Brownlee, "Ovide et le moi poétique," p. 167, n. 20. For another interesting reworking of the Iphis story in the romance *Yde et Olive*, see Durling, "Rewriting Gender: *Yde et Olive* and Ovidian Myth."

28. That is, learning. The text deals with the "tresor" of wisdom her father has accumulated.

29. The term "sanz fable" anticipates her transformation. On Christine's depiction of her complex relationship with her mother, see my "Christine de Pizan and the Misogynistic Tradition," pp. 285–89. The text continues with Christine's observation that although in gender she resembles her mother, in intellect she is her father's likeness—a "son," after all!

30. The story of Pasiphae is not one that would fit into any of Christine's thematics. Jean Le Fèvre de Ressons mentions the story in his *Livre de Leesce* (ll. 2469–86). Since his book was ostensibly written in defense of women, Jean tries to rehabilitate Pasiphae by saying, "Certes, vecy grant fanfelue! / Ce ne puet estre vray, c'est fable, / Mais ce fu euvre de deable" (Certainly, this is great nonsense; this cannot be true, it's a fable. But this was the work of the devil; ll. 2474–76). The noble female gender could not allow something as perverse as Pasiphae's actions, he says. Yet he does describe the perversity in rather crude terms. I examine the ambiguous ways in which Jean attempts to defend women's honor (especially against the accusations of Matheolus) in my "Jean Le Fèvre's *Livre de Leesce*: Praise or Blame of Women?"

31. In Ovid we read "femina nuper eras, puer es!" (you who lately were a girl now are a boy! 9.791), while the *OM* has "Everyone learned that the daughter / girl [fille] Yphis became a son [filz]" (9.3101–2). In light of Christine's views of

her mother and father in ll. 379–92 I would still see a significance in Christine's choice of "son" over "man."

32. In the *OM*:

Hyphis, sa fille, la sivoit
A plus grant pas qu'el ne seult faire,
S'a mains de blanchour ou viaire
Qu'elle n'y avoit ains eue.
Force et fierté li est creue,
Et si chevoul sont abregié.
Tout son cors seult estre alegié,
Si fu plus viguereuse assez
Qu'el n'iert esté au temps passez
Et que feme ne peüst estre.
Tout ot son estat et son estre
Et sa nature femeline
Chanciée, et prise masculine. (9.3082–94)

Iphis, his daughter, followed him, with longer strides than she used to. Her face is less white than before. Strength and pride have grown within her, and her hair is shorter. Her entire body, which used to be so light, is now more vigorous than it was in times past. She can no longer be a woman. Her entire condition and being, her female nature, are changed and have become male.

33. Esp. *OM* 9.3143–260. See Chapter 3 for details.

34. Note that there is no explicit reference to Ovid in this passage.

35. It is also one of the longer stories in the *OM* (11.3003–787, plus a long allegorization of the sea voyage). On the myth in the *Mutacion*, see Walters, "Chivalry and the (En)Gendered Poetic Self," pp. 47–51.

36. The *OM* poet shows no particular sensitivity for this beautiful love story and glosses the birds as the voluptuous; in another gloss Ceyx is a pilgrim who does not want to return to earthly delights (= Alcyone).

37. The story also ties in with Christine's early interest in the Hero and Leander story, where a storm at sea destroys love. Her view of that story is illuminated, retrospectively, as it were, by her treatment in the *Mutacion* of her husband's death as the result of drowning. (He really died in an epidemic.) Also, we might see the danger of loving someone too much.

38. The mythological stories appear only in the ballades, not in the rondeaux or virelays. This suggests that Christine was looking for some narrative coherence even in her earliest use of myth and did not rely on the purely allusive power of simply naming a mythological figure.

39. Of course, one should not confuse the emotional with the "real," as Lacy cautions in "Villon in His Work: The *Testament* and the Problem of Personal Poetry." But one should point out that there is a big difference between the poem

by Gace Brulé that Lacy cites as an example of the use of the courtly conventional "je" and Christine's widowhood poems, which, Lacy claims, are not substantially different in their use of the lyric "je" (p. 62). For the former there were plenty of models and conventions; for the latter, practically none. Thus, while the widowhood poems may not be pure autobiography, they are more personal than Gace Brulé's laments.

40. The difference between a poem and the narrative *Mutacion* is also formal, of course. The technique of saying "Ovide raconte que . . ." is typical of a more didactic voice, while Christine's brief comparison of herself to Alcyone evokes the more allusive use of myth in the lyric. Christine weaves the two forms together.

41. *Allegorical Imagery*, pp. 34, 40. Earlier critical opinions of the *Othéa* tended to be negative. Campbell (*L'Epître d'Othéa: Etude sur les sources de Christine de Pisan*) finds few redeeming features. Ignatius, the first critic to draw attention to the formal complexities of this text, cites Robineau, who in 1882 described the *Othéa* as "a peculiar work . . . in line with the still barbaric taste of that era" ("Christine de Pizan's *Epistre d'Othéa*: An Experiment in Literary Form," p. 127). In the past, the *Othéa* generally interested art historians more than literary critics. Most of the surviving 43 manuscripts are splendid, and the fact that some of them were illuminated under Christine's supervision makes them important documents. Recently, literary interest in the *Othéa* has grown. Studies by Reno ("Feminist Aspects of Christine de Pizan's 'Epistre d'Othéa à Hector' ") and Kellogg ("Christine de Pizan as Chivalric Mythographer: *L'Epistre d'Othéa*") have begun to analyze Christine's originality. Ehrhart focuses on the *Othéa* on pp. 132–44 of her "Christine de Pizan and the Judgment of Paris." This article does not differ much (in its argumentation and conclusions) from the pages on Christine in Ehrhart's *The Judgment*. Hindman's excellent *Christine de Pizan's "Epistre d'Othéa"* covers a wide range of problems surrounding this text, from its political intent to specific literary and art historical questions.

42. Copeland and Melville, "Allegory and Allegoresis, Rhetoric and Hermeneutics," p. 164. The authors do not refer to the *Othéa* here.

43. Kellogg, "Christine de Pizan and Boccaccio," esp. pp. 128–29, and Schibanoff, "Taking the Gold out of Egypt," p. 91. Kellogg changed her mind somewhat in "Christine de Pizan as Chivalric Mythographer."

44. Reno, "Feminist Aspects," and Chance, "Christine's Minerva" (an interpretive essay of her translation of the *Othéa*).

45. I will use the term *texte* to denote these poems to avoid confusion with *text*, which can indicate any part of the written work.

46. See Chance's introduction to her translation of the *Othéa* for more details.

47. She does the same thing in the preface to the *Avision* (see n. 24 to this chapter).

48. Hexter, "The *Allegari* of Pierre Bersuire: Interpretation and the *Reductorium Morale*," pp. 57–58. Bersuire's text is quite different from Christine's and also from the *OM* in that in it Bersuire chooses just a few lines from each of Ovid's books for interpretation, but these he quotes verbatim. The brevity of Bersuire (as opposed to the *OM*) resembles Christine's *Othéa.*

49. *Allegorical Imagery*, p. 286. The *Somme le Roi* was written by the Dominican friar Laurent for Philip III in 1279. It was a manual of moral and religious instruction for kings.

50. The "je" of the lyric poems or of the *Mutacion* has no place here. She directs text and interpretation immediately to the addressee, Hector, who, of course, is a mythological character. In this circular movement Christine does not name herself (the letter is, after all, being written by Othéa, the goddess of prudence) and does not overtly appear as the interpreter.

51. Jakobson, *Essais de linguistique générale*, pp. 214–20; quote on p. 216.

52. In this I agree with Noakes, *Timely Reading: Between Exegesis and Interpretation*, pp. 123–26. Her reading of the *Othéa* focuses on the reader and the temporality of reading. For the feminist rewriting of some of the figures I refer the reader to previous studies. Reno ("Feminist Aspects") analyzes Daphne, Diana, Penthesilea, Io, Cassandra, and Helen. She alludes to Tomyris, Ino, Medusa, and Andromache. Chance ("Christine's Minerva") concentrates on Minerva (Pallas). Kellogg ("Christine de Pizan as Chivalric Mythographer") treats the "trinity" of Ceres, Diana, and Iris. More generally, for the Judgment of Paris, see Ehrhart, *The Judgment*, pp. 117–21. All quotes from the *Othéa* are taken from the edition of Loukopoulos, appended to her "Classical Mythology." Unfortunately, Loukopoulos's line numbering is not very useful since she begins each new page (and not each chapter) with line 1. I will therefore indicate the chapter number (and whether the quote is part of the texte, gloss, or allegory) and the page number. Translations are my own.

53. For further remarks on this image, see my "Christine de Pizan and the Misogynistic Tradition," p. 281 and n. 3.

54. The notion of experience governs the opening of the *Cité.* See my "Christine de Pizan and the Misogynistic Tradition," pp. 289–92 (the section "Books and Experience").

55. On the name Othéa, see Hindman, *Christine de Pizan's "Epistre d'Othéa,"* p. 23, and Mombello, "Recherches sur l'origine du nom de la Déesse Othéa."

56. Another instance of the use of the term *couverture* can be found in chap. 8, gloss; p. 171 (the story of Saturn).

57. The image of a fruit was commonly used to describe the working of allegory.

58. Significantly, Christine first addresses the possibility of multiple interpretations in Chapter 22, which features the quintessential artist figure Pyg-

malion, described as "soutil" (subtle; p. 189). For more statements on multiple interpretations, see pp. 190, 221, and 231.

59. The gloss also contains the story as such, drawn from Ovid or the *OM*.

60. MS Paris, B.N. fr. 848 is the most interesting one from the point of view of layout. Ignatius described it in "Christine de Pizan's *Epistre d'Othéa*," as inviting "a non-linear, contemplative style of reading" (p. 133). She concludes that "indeed, Christine's structure is only superficially tripartite: if we include the miniatures and analyze the components of the glosses and allegories, we actually find a structure based on seven levels: image, poetic text, narrative or gloss, philosophical text, allegory, patristic text and finally scriptural text" (p. 139). MS B.N. fr. 848 is indeed striking. The first impression is that of a traditional glossed manuscript. The rubrics, indicating gloss, allegory, etc., are written in red. Gloss and allegory are written in much smaller letters than the texte. But most important, gloss and allegory surround the texte and miniatures. This layout, then, highlights Christine's usurpation of a time-honored technique with one decisive difference: she is the author of *all* the elements; she comments on her *own* text. (In other manuscripts I examined, such as B.N. fr. 606, the layout is traditional, in two columns.) Boccaccio is the only other vernacular author to do something similar. His autograph text of his *Teseida* is also surrounded by glosses written by Boccaccio himself but in a different script than that of the text. See Carruthers, *The Book of Memory: A Study of Memory in Medieval Culture*, p. 218. A page of the MS is reproduced as Carruthers's Figure 7.

61. This fits in with other profemale rewritings discussed in some of the articles I listed in n. 52.

62. The astrological makes an appearance in other chapters, though, especially, of course, in the chapters on the planets (7–12), where the planets are linked to chivalric virtues.

63. Copeland and Melville, "Allegory and Allegoresis," p. 172.

64. Ibid., p. 173.

65. An analysis of her interpretations reveals that more often than not they are totally inconsistent with any preceding traditions. That the purpose of this reinterpretation was in part political has been demonstrated admirably by Hindman in *Christine de Pizan's "Epistre d'Othéa."*

66. The *Chemin* has so far elicited few critical analyses. But see Gompertz, "Le Voyage allégorique chez Christine de Pizan," and Sasaki, "Le Poète et Pallas dans le '*Chemin de long estude.*'" Ehrhart analyzes the Judgment of Paris in the *Chemin* in *The Judgment*, pp. 189–91, and in "Christine de Pizan and the Judgment of Paris," pp. 144–49. See also Willard, *Christine de Pizan*, pp. 100–106.

67. See Gompertz ("Le Voyage allégorique"), who argues that in the *Chemin* personal poetry is in retreat and that instead the social function of the poet is highlighted. There is also a political aspect: "Christine discovers a new nature for

herself, that of a messenger" (p. 202). See also the excellent article by Blanchard, "Christine de Pizan: Les Raisons de l'histoire."

68. On the function of the mother in the *Chemin* (at the end of the allegory) and the *Cité* (at the beginning of the allegory), see my "Christine de Pizan and the Misogynistic Tradition," pp. 285–89. The *Chemin* signals Christine's new involvement in French politics. On the *Chemin* and Dante, see Brownlee, "Literary Genealogy and the Problem of the Father: Christine de Pizan and Dante."

69. Boethius provides many ideas for the *Chemin*, including the description of the "ladders" of speculation and contemplation (*Chemin*, ll. 1569–780).

70. On the importance of the sibyls in Christine's works, see Brownlee, "Structures of Authority in Christine de Pizan's *Ditié de Jehanne d'Arc*," esp. pp. 140–43.

71. In *La Couleur de la mélancolie*, p. 58.

72. See Sasaki, "Le Poète et Pallas," for details. The term "fontaine de clergie" appears in *OM* 3.209. See also ll. 236–37, in which the image of the serpent and that of the fountain seem to be conflated: "il ot la fontaine conquise, / C'est a dire l'art de clergie" (he conquered the fountain, that is, the art of scholarship).

73. Christine evidently does not share Philosophy's opinion in Boethius's *Consolation of Philosophy*, who calls the muses "hysterical sluts" (p. 36). An illustration of this scene can be found in Brussels, Bibliothèque Royale, MS 10982, fol. 13 verso, reproduced in Willard, *Christine de Pizan* (p. 90). As Willard points out, the illumination recalls similar ones from the *OM* in which Pallas watches the muses (p. 102).

74. Christine's choice of Pallas (= learning) is dramatized in the illumination mentioned in the preceding note by Christine and the Sibyl occupying Pallas's place in the pictorial composition.

75. Other connections to the *Othéa* and to the first part of the *Mutacion* include references to her father's learning and images of her own insufficient learning. On Christine's political thought, see especially Mombello, "Quelques aspects de la pensée politique de Christine de Pisan d'après ses oeuvres publiées," and the articles in *Politics, Gender, and Genre: The Political Thought of Christine de Pizan*, ed. Brabant.

76. It was Christine's mother who was the obstacle to her early education. See *Cité*, p. 875.

77. The intermingling of the sibyls and Merlin shows an attempt at integrating ancient and medieval times: this is a genealogy of prophecy.

78. In the *Mutacion* myth and contemporary history are also linked when, in the last part, an unbroken line connecting ancient history and events of Christine's own time is presented. A good evaluation of Christine's method can be found in Margolis, "Christine de Pizan: The Poetess as Historian."

79. "Christine de Pizan and the Judgment of Paris," p. 146.

80. This view would in part contradict Eliade's claim that "mythical events are not commemorated; they are repeated, reiterated" ("Toward a Definition of Myth"). Eliade completely passes over the learned transmission of myth and insists only on its ritual aspects.

81. As a central "character" in Martianus Capella's *The Marriage of Philology and Mercury*, Mercury was a well-known representation of eloquence.

82. It is only in the *Cité* that she fully accepts her womanhood and writes as a (learned) woman.

83. On the other hand, her dedication of the *Chemin* to the French king Charles VI indicates her desire to play a role in contemporary politics. The *Othéa*, of course, had already addressed a variety of political issues of the time.

84. *The Gods Made Flesh: Metamorphosis and the Pursuit of Paganism.*

85. Several of the most interesting features of the *Mutacion* have been studied by Brownlee in "The Image of History" and in "Ovide et le moi poétique." A chapter of Brownlee's forthcoming book is devoted to the *Mutacion.*

86. The source for this description is Nicole de Margival's *Panthere d'Amours* and Jean de Meun's *Roman de la Rose*. See Solente's excellent notes and study of sources in her edition of the *Mutacion.*

87. Note also that Christine does not say that Actaeon was punished because he saw Diana naked but rather because he looked her in the face.

88. In Ovid's *Metamorphoses* 3, the Actaeon story ties in with that of Narcissus as men who gaze on forbidden things and are punished for their trespass. In the moral interpretations, the motif of hunting as a waste of time was a favorite and could already be found in the writings of Palaiphatos (fourth century B.C.), as Nestle shows in *Vom Mythos zum Logos*, p. 150. For recent readings of this myth, see my "Christine de Pizan and Classical Mythology: Some Examples from the 'Mutacion de Fortune,'" pp. 11–12, and Cerquiglini-Toulet, "Sexualité et politique: Le Mythe d'Actéon chez Christine de Pizan."

89. In the *Othéa* (chap. 83) Ulysses is shown as an inventor of games, such as chess, which, when played in moderation, are an asset to the knight's education.

90. There are other interesting applications of myth such as the intermingling of the personal-emotional and the political in Christine's depiction of Hector and Penthesilea. This aspect has been treated in depth by Brownlee in "Hector and Penthesilea in the *Livre de la Mutacion de Fortune.*" Some mythological figures are simply omitted. Pasiphae, for example, who certainly appears in Christine's source, the *Histoire ancienne*, is not mentioned here. In the *Histoire* (B.N. fr. 20125, fols. 158v–159r) the birth of the Minotaur is rationalized (following Greek traditions) by having Pasiphae conduct an affair with her husband's secretary named Taurus, who thus participates in the conception of twins (with Minos being the father of one of them). For more details, see my "The Scandal of Pasiphae: Narration and Interpretation in the *Ovide moralisé.*"

91. Told in Christine's Ballade 66 and in the *Othéa*, Chapter 30, where Io's milk (while she is a cow) is likened to the learning she gladly distributed to others.

92. See Chance's essay "Christine's Minerva."

93. I cannot go into the details of the description of Christine's technique here. But she always claims that she delves into her memory of the histories as she had "seen" them on the wall in order to write the histories as they appear in the *Mutacion*.

94. On the *Cité* as a "refutation of myth," see Stecopoulos and Uitti, "Christine de Pizan's *Livre de la Cité des Dames*," p. 48. For the framework provided by the idea of compilation, see Blanchard, "Compilation and Legitimation in the Fifteenth Century: *Le Livre de la Cité des Dames*." Since the chapter divisions in the Curnow edition and the Richards translation are different I will only give page numbers. If two page numbers are given in parenthesis, the first refers to the Curnow edition, the second to the Richards translation.

The term "city of ladies" or "city of women" reappears in a number of different contexts, a fact that attests to its mythical power. See Fellini's 1981 film "Città delle donne," which offers a satire of men's behavior toward women, and Christine Stansell's *City of Women: Sex and Class in New York 1789–1860* (New York, 1982). Uitti (with Freeman) uses the term as a kind of metaphor for the courtly treatment of ladies in "Christine de Pisan and Chrétien de Troyes: Poetic Fidelity and the City of Ladies."

95. This return to the literal can also be considered in the context of Bloch's remarks on the negative connotations of the links between veiled discourse and rhetorical ornament. See "Medieval Misogyny."

96. Eliade, "Toward a Definition of Myth," p. 4. For the idea of a feminist myth, see Kellogg, "*Le Livre de la Cité des Dames*: Feminist Myth and Community."

97. See Quilligan's *The Allegory of Female Authority: Christine de Pizan's Cité des Dames* and her "Allegory and the Textual Body: Female Authority in Christine de Pizan's *Livre de la cité des dames*." An interesting evaluation of Christine's debt to and departure from Boccaccio is in Phillippy, "Establishing Authority." Dulac, in "Un Mythe didactique chez Christine de Pizan," focuses on the rewriting of the story of Semiramis.

98. Matheolus's *Lamentations*, an almost 10,000-line diatribe against women in general and his wife in particular, was translated by Jean Le Fèvre de Ressons in 1370. Shortly thereafter Jean composed the *Livre de Leesce* (Book of Joy), designed to refute Matheolus and defend women. Christine never acknowledges Jean as a source, but Curnow has shown in her introduction and notes that Christine knew and used the *Leesce*. For a close reading of the opening scene as well as analyses of the concept of the natural woman and the roles of books and experience, see my "Christine de Pizan and the Misogynistic Tradition."

99. See Jeanroy, "Boccace et Christine de Pisan: Le *De claris mulieribus*

principale source du *Livre de la cité des dames*," and Phillippy, "Establishing Authority." For an evaluation of Christine's rewriting of the Saint Christine story, see Quilligan, "Authority and the Textual Body," pp. 236–40, and Brownlee, "Martyrdom and the Female Voice: Saint Christine in the *Cité des dames*," pp. 115–35. There is as yet no systematic study of Christine's adaptation of Vincent's *Miroir Historial*. I consider some of the stories in relation to Vincent in " 'Femme de corps et femme par sens': Christine de Pizan's Saintly Women."

100. Richards's translation of the *Cité* provides a good overview of its organization on pp. xxxix and xl of the excellent introduction. Kellogg, in "Christine de Pizan and Boccaccio," suggests that the *Cité* might have a tripartite interpretive schema similar to that of the *Othéa*: "Reason presents the text, the literal story. . . . Rectitude glosses women morally. . . . Justice reveals women's potential for salvation" (p. 129). But Kellogg just hints at this possibility and does not really work it out. This seems an intriguing idea but is not supported by the totality of the text.

101. In the mythographic tradition, Arachne, for example, was mostly known for her vanity, and Medusa represented the dangers of feminine eros (see Huot, "The Medusa Interpolation in the *Roman de la Rose*: Mythographic Program and Ovidian Intertext"). Medea was a representation of the "danger of the eyes," in the *Othéa* (chap. 58); the gloss explains that Medea stands for "miscarriage of the senses" ("Ne laisses ton sens avorter / A fol delit" [Do not let your sense be miscarried toward foolish delight]). Even the positive traditional interpretations of women were often intermingled with negative remarks. Christine simply omits these.

102. My translation. Richards's translation, "spinning and silly girlishness" (p. 155), is too much of an interpretation.

103. See Stecopoulos and Uitti, "Christine de Pizan's *Livre de la Cité des Dames*," pp. 52–53. See also Brown-Grant, "Décadence ou progrès? Christine de Pizan, Boccace et la question de 'l'Age d'Or,' " and Phillippy, "Establishing Authority," p. 192.

104. The other references are to the *Débat* in the early discussion of the unjustness of the misogynists; to the *Mutacion* and the *Othéa* in the context of the Amazons (women especially important for Christine's purposes in the *Cité*); to the *Epistre au dieu d'amours* in the discussion on female constancy; and to the *Débat* and the *Epistre* (with a reference to Ovid) in the context of female faithfulness.

105. The more traditional metaphors had been phallic terms such as using one's stylus, ploughing a field, and so on. On the questions of Christine's use of female imagery as a counterpoint to Jean de Meun's phallic imagery, see Huot, "Seduction and Sublimation: Christine de Pizan, Jean de Meun, and Dante," pp. 364–67. In the *OM* Io is depicted as a "femme commune," a woman for everyone's use (a term Christine takes issue with), who gives herself to everyone. See Reno, "Feminist Aspects," pp. 273–74.

106. As we saw earlier, Christine omits the detail of Io's writing her name with her hoof. While present in the *OM*, the detail is also missing in Boccaccio (chap. 8).

107. On Dido, see Desmond, *Reading Dido: Gender, Textuality, and the Medieval Aeneid*, chap. 6.

108. For Ops we read: "During her lifetime she acquired such a great reputation through the knowledge and authority of her children that foolish people called her a goddess and mother of the gods, . . . Like fools they maintained this belief for a long time" (p. 96). In reality, though, Christine informs us, she was a wise queen of Crete. Juno "was Jupiter's sister and married to him. Since he was proclaimed as the supreme god and because she lived luxuriating in such incredible wealth and good fortune, she was reputed to be the goddess of riches" (p. 203).

109. Richards's translation omits this phrase.

110. The story of the "combat" between Vulcan and Pallas comes from Hyginus's fables (no. 165). Another moral interpretation can be found in the story of the sibyl Almathea: "This lady . . . remained a virgin all her life, and because of her great wisdom, several poets claimed that she was loved by Phoebus . . . and that through this same Phoebus's gift, she acquired such great learning and lived so long. This should be taken to mean that because of her virginity and purity she was loved by God, the sun of wisdom, who illuminated her with . . . prophetic brilliance" (p. 103). Christine already told her story in the *Chemin*.

111. A consideration of the *Ditié* lies beyond the scope of this chapter. For an analysis of Christine's mythmaking in that text, see Brownlee, "Structures of Authority in Christine de Pizan's *Ditié de Jehanne d'Arc*."

Conclusion

1. See n. 56 of the Introduction for details on this text.

2. For an example see the portrait of Juno as *memoria*, Ill. 30 (p. 95) in Seznec, *The Survival of the Pagan Gods: The Mythological Tradition and Its Place in Renaissance Humanism and Art*. The portrait of Francis I is reproduced in Schneider, *The Art of the Portrait*, p. 95.

3. See Hindman, *Christine de Pizan's "Epistre d'Othéa": Painting and Politics at the Court of Charles VI*, and, more generally, Beaune, *The Birth of an Ideology: Myths and Symbols of Nation in Late-Medieval France*, chap. 8.

4. For an analysis of this encoding in thirteenth-century historiography, see Spiegel, *Romancing the Past* (quote on p. 8).

Bibliography

Primary Sources

Alan of Lille. *Plaint of Nature*. Trans. James J. Sheridan. Toronto, 1980.

Arnulf of Orléans. *Allegoriae super Ovidii Metamorphosin*. Ed. Fausto Ghisalberti in "Arnolfo d'Orléans: Un cultore d'Ovidio nel secolo XII." *Memorie del reale istituto lombardo di scienze e lettere* 24 (1932): 157–234.

Augustine, Saint. *The City of God*. Trans. Henry Bettenson. Harmondsworth, Eng., 1972; repr., 1984.

———. *On Christian Doctrine*. Trans. D. W. Robertson, Jr. New York, 1958.

Benoît de Sainte-Maure. *Le Roman de Troie*. 6 vols. Ed. Léopold Constans. Société des anciens textes français. Paris, 1904–12.

[Bernardus Silvestris.] *The Commentary of the First Six Books of the Aeneid of Vergil, Commonly Attributed to Bernardus Silvestris*. Ed. Julian Ward Jones and Elizabeth Frances Jones. Lincoln, Nebr., 1977.

[———]. *Commentary on the First Six Books of Virgil's Aeneid by Bernardus Silvestris*. Trans. Earl G. Schreiber and Thomas E. Maresca. Lincoln, Nebr., 1979.

Bersuire, Pierre. *The 'Ovidius Moralizatus' of Petrus Berchorius: An Introduction and Translation*. Trans. William Donald Reynolds. Diss., University of Illinois at Champaign-Urbana, 1971.

———. *Reductorium morale* (bk. 15 of the *Ovidius moralizatus*). Ed. Joseph Engels. Utrecht, 1962.

Boccaccio, Giovanni. *Concerning Famous Women*. Trans. Guido A. Guarino. New Brunswick, N.J., 1963.

Bodel, Jean. *Jean Bodel's Saxenlied*. Ed. F. Menzel and E. Stengel. Marburg, 1906–9.

Boethius. *The Consolation of Philosophy*. Trans. V. E. Watts. London, 1969; repr., 1988.

Dares. *Daretis Phrygii de excidio Troiae Historia*. Ed. Ferdinand Meister. Leipzig, 1873.

Deschamps, Eustache. *Oeuvres complètes.* 11 vols. Ed. Marquis de Queux de Saint-Hilaire and Guy Raynaud. Paris, 1878–1903.

Devizes, Richard of. *Cronicon Richardi Divisensis de tempore Regis Ricardi Primi.* Ed. John T. Appleby. London, 1963.

Dictys Cretensis. *Ephemeridos Belli Troiani Libri.* Ed. Werner Eisenhut. Leipzig, 1973.

Evrart de Conty. *Le Livre des eschez amoureux moralisés.* Ed. Françoise Guichard Tesson and Bruno Roy. Montreal, 1993.

Frazer, R. M., trans. *The Trojan War: The Chronicles of Dictys of Crete and Dares the Phrygian.* Bloomington, Ind., 1966.

Froissart, Jean. *Ballades et rondeaux.* Ed. Rae S. Baudouin. Paris and Geneva, 1978.

———. *L'Espinette amoureuse.* Ed. Anthime Fourrier. Paris, 1963; rev. ed. 1972.

———. *Le Joli Buisson de jonece.* Ed. Anthime Fourrier. Geneva, 1975.

———. *Le paradis d'amour [and] L'Orloge amoureus.* Ed. Peter F. Dembowski. Geneva, 1986.

———. *La Prison amoureuse.* Ed. Anthime Fourrier. Paris, 1974.

Fulgentius. *Expositio virgilianae continentiae.* Ed. and trans. Tullio Agozzino and Ferrucino Zanlucchi. Padua, 1972.

———. *The Exposition of the Content of Virgil.* Trans. Leslie G. Whitbread. In *Fulgentius the Mythographer,* pp. 105–53. Columbus, Ohio, 1971.

———. *The Mythologies.* Trans. Leslie G. Whitbread. In *Fulgentius the Mythographer,* pp. 13–102. Columbus, Ohio, 1971.

———. *On the Thebaid.* Trans. Leslie G. Whitbread. In *Fulgentius the Mythographer,* pp. 235–44. Columbus, Ohio, 1971.

Guillaume de Lorris and Jean de Meun. *Le Roman de la Rose.* 3 vols. Ed. Félix Lecoy. Classiques français du moyen âge. Paris, 1965–70.

———. *The Romance of the Rose.* Trans. Charles Dahlberg. Princeton, 1971; repr. Hanover, N.H., 1983.

Hyginus. *Hygyni fabulae.* Ed. H. J. Rose. 1934; repr., Leyden, 1963.

———. *The Myths of Hyginus.* Trans. Mary Grant. Lawrence, Kans., 1960.

Jean de Meun. *See* Guillaume de Lorris.

John of Garland. *Integumenta Ovidii.* Ed. Fausto Ghisalberti. Milan, 1933.

John of Salisbury, *Metalogicon.* Ed. C. C. J. Webb. Oxford, 1929.

Le Fèvre de Ressons, Jean. *See* Matheolus.

Liebeschütz, H. *Fulgentius metaforalis (John Ridewall): Ein Beitrag zur Geschichte der antiken Mythologie im Mittelalter.* Leipzig and Berlin, 1926.

Machaut, Guillaume de. *Le Confort d'Ami.* Ed. and trans. Richard Barton Palmer. New York, 1992.

———. *La Fontaine amoreuse.* Ed. and trans. Jacqueline Cerquiglini-Toulet. Paris, 1993.

———. *Guillaume de Machaut: Poésies lyriques.* 2 vols. Ed. Vladimir Chichmaref. Paris, 1909.

———. *The Judgment of the King of Navarre.* Ed. and trans. Richard Barton Palmer. New York, 1988.

———. *Le Livre du Voir-Dit.* Ed. Paulin Paris. 1875; repr., Geneva, 1969.

———. *'La Louange des dames' by Guillaume de Machaut.* Ed. Nigel Wilkins. Edinburgh, 1972.

———. *Oeuvres de Guillaume de Machaut.* 3 vols. Ed. Ernest Hoepffner. Société des anciens textes français. Paris, 1908–21.

Macrobius, *Commentary on the Dream of Scipio.* Trans. W. H. Stahl. New York, 1952.

Marie de France. *Lais.* Ed. Jean Rychner. Paris, 1973.

Martianus Capella. *The Marriage of Philology and Mercury.* Vol. 2 of William Harris Stahl and Richard Johnson with E. L. Burge, *Martianus Capella and the Seven Liberal Arts.* 2 vols. New York, 1971, 1977.

Matheolus. *Les Lamentations de Matheolus et le Livre de Leesce de Jehan Le Fèvre de Ressons.* Ed. Anton-Gérard van Hamel. 2 vols. Paris, 1892–1905.

Mézières, Philippe de. *Le Livre de la vertu du sacrement de mariage.* Ed. Joan B. Williamson. Washington, D.C., 1993.

Mythographi Vaticani I et II. Ed. Peter Kulcsár. Corpus Christianorum, series latina XCIc. Turnholt, Belgium, 1987.

Ovid. *Ars amatoria.* In *The Art of Love and Other Poems,* 2d ed. rev. G. P. Goold. English trans. J. H. Mozley. Loeb Classical Library. Cambridge, Mass., 1979.

———. *Heroides and Amores.* 2d ed. rev. G. P. Gould. English trans. Grant Showerman. Loeb Classical Library. Cambridge, Mass., 1986.

———. *Metamorphoses.* 2 vols. English trans. Frank Justus Miller. Loeb Classical Library. Cambridge, Mass., 1916.

Ovide moralisé. Ed. Cornelis de Boer. *Verhandelingen der Koninklijke Akademie van Wetenschapen te Amsterdam: Afdeeling Letterkunde.* Vols. 15, 21, 30, 36–37, 43. Amsterdam, 1915–38.

Pizan, Christine de. *L'Avision Christine.* Ed. Mary Louise Towner. Washington, D.C., 1932.

———. *The Book of the City of Ladies.* Trans. Earl Jeffrey Richards. New York, 1982.

———. *Cent ballades d'amant et de dame.* Ed. Jacqueline Cerquiglini. Paris, 1982.

———. *Christine de Pizan's Letter of Othea to Hector.* Trans. Jane Chance. Newburyport, Mass., 1990.

———. *Le Débat sur le Roman de la Rose.* Ed. Eric Hicks. Paris, 1977.

———. *L'Epistre d'Othéa.* In Halina D. Loukopoulos, "Classical Mythology in the Works of Christine de Pizan, with an Edition of *L'Epistre d'Othéa* from the MS Harley 4431." Diss., Wayne State University, 1977.

———. "The *Livre de la cité des dames* of Christine de Pizan: A Critical Edition." 2 vols. Ed. Maureen Curnow. Diss., Vanderbilt University, 1975.

———. *Le Livre de la mutacion de Fortune.* 4 vols. Ed. Suzanne Solente. Paris, 1959–66.

———. *Le Livre des trois vertus.* Ed. Charity Cannon Willard and Eric Hicks. Paris, 1989.

———. *Le Livre du chemin de long estude.* Ed. Robert Püschel. Berlin, 1881.

———. *Oeuvres poétiques de Christine de Pisan.* 3 vols. Ed. Maurice Roy. Paris, 1886–96.

Rabanus Maurus. *De clericorum institutione.* Patrologiae latinae 107. Paris, 1864.

Ridewall, John. *See* Liebeschütz.

Le Roman d'Enéas. 2 vols. Ed. J.-J. Salverda de Grave. Classiques français du moyen âge. Paris, 1968, 1973.

Le Roman de la Rose. See Guillaume de Lorris and Jean de Meun.

Le Roman de Thèbes. 2 vols. Ed. Léopold Constans. Société des anciens textes français. Paris, 1890.

Le Roman de Thèbes. 2 vols. Ed. Guy Raynaud de Lage. Classiques français du moyen âge. Paris, 1968, 1969.

Scriptores rerum mythicarum latini tres Romae nuper reperti. Ed. Georg Bode. Celle, Germany, 1834.

Servius. *Servii grammatici qui feruntur in Virgilii carmina commentarii.* Ed. G. Thilo and H. Hagen. Leipzig, 1880–1902.

Statius. *The Thebaid.* 2 vols. English trans. J. H. Mozley. Loeb Classical Library. Cambridge, Mass., 1988.

Virgil. *The Aeneid.* 2 vols. Rev. ed. English trans. H. R. Fairclough. Loeb Classical Library. Cambridge, Mass., 1935.

Wace. *Roman de Rou.* 2 vols. Ed. A. J. Holden. Paris, 1970.

Walsingham, Thomas. *De Archana deorum.* Ed. R. A. van Kluyve. Durham, N.C., 1968.

Secondary Sources

Adler, Alfred. "*Militia et Amor* in the *Roman de Troie.*" *Romanische Forschungen* 72 (1960): 14–29.

Albouy, Pierre. *Mythes et mythologies dans la littérature française.* Paris, 1969.

Allen, Judson Boyce. "Commentary as Criticism: The Text, Influence and Literary Theory of the Fulgentius Metaphored of John Ridewall." In P. Tuynman, G. C. Kuiper, and E. Kessler, eds., *Acta conventus neo-latini amstelodamensis* (Proceedings of the Second International Congress of Neo-Latin Studies, Amsterdam, August 19–24, 1973), pp. 25–47. Munich, 1979.

———. *The Friar as Critic: Literary Attitudes in the Later Middle Ages.* Nashville, Tenn., 1971.

Allen, Peter L. *The Art of Love: Amatory Fiction from Ovid to the Romance of the Rose*. Philadelphia, 1992.

Angeli, Giovanna. *L' 'Eneas' e i primi romanzi volgari*. Milan, 1971.

Auerbach, Erich. "Figura." In *Scenes from the Drama of European Literature*, pp. 11–76. Minneapolis, 1984.

———. *Literary Language and Its Public in Late Latin Antiquity and in the Middle Ages*. Trans. Ralph Manheim. Princeton, 1965.

Azzam, Wagih. "Le Printemps de la littérature: La 'Translation' dans 'Philomena' de Crestiiens li Gois." *Littérature* 74 (1989): 47–62.

Badel, Pierre-Yves. *Le Roman de la Rose au XIVe siècle: Etude de la réception de l'oeuvre*. Geneva, 1980.

Barkan, Leonard. "Diana and Actaeon: The Myth as Synthesis." *English Literary Renaissance* 10 (1980): 317–59.

———. *The Gods Made Flesh: Metamorphosis and the Pursuit of Paganism*. New Haven, Conn., 1986.

Barnwell, H. T. *The Classical Tradition in French Literature: Essays Presented to R. C. Knight*. Ed. A. H. Diverres, G. F. Evans, F. W. A. George, and Vivienne Mylne. Edinburgh, 1977.

Bartsch, Karl. *Albrecht von Halberstadt und Ovid im Mittelalter*. Quedlinburg, Germany, 1861.

Baskins, Cristelle. "Echoing Narcissus in Alberti's *Della Pittura*." *Oxford Art Journal* 16 (1993): 25–33.

Bastin, Julia. *Froissart: Chroniqueur, romancier et poète*. Brussels, 1942.

Baswell, Christopher. "Men in the *Roman d'Enéas*: The Construction of Empire." In Clare Lees, ed., *Medieval Masculinities: Regarding Men in the Middle Ages*, pp. 149–68. Minneapolis, 1994.

———. *Virgil in Medieval England: Figuring the 'Aeneid' from the Twelfth Century to Chaucer*. Cambridge, Eng., 1995.

Beaune, Colette. *The Birth of an Ideology: Myths and Symbols of Nation in Late-Medieval France*. Trans. Susan Ross Huston. Ed. Fredric L. Cheyette. Berkeley, 1991.

———. "L'Utilisation politique du mythe des origines troyennes en France à la fin du moyen âge." In *Lectures médiévales de Virgile*, pp. 331–55. Rome, 1985.

Beltrán, Luis. "La Vieille's Past." *Romanische Forschungen* 84 (1972): 77–96.

Bennett, Philip E. "The Mirage of Fiction: Narration, Narrator, and Narratee in Froissart's Lyrico-Narrative *Dits*." *Modern Language Review* 86 (1991): 285–97.

Bermejo, Esperanza. "Notas sobre las modalidades retóricas de inserción de anecdotas en el 'Roman de la Rose de Jean de Meun.' " In Carmona and Flores, eds., *La lengua y la literatura en tiempos de Alfonso X*, pp. 91–108.

Bernardo, Aldo S., and Saul Levin, eds. *The Classics in the Middle Ages*. Binghamton, N.Y., 1990.

Bezold, Friedrich von. *Das Fortleben der antiken Götter im mittelalterlichen Humanismus.* Bonn and Leipzig, 1922.

Bezzola, Reto R. *Les Origines et la formation de la littérature courtoise en occident.* Part 3, vol. 1. Paris, 1967.

Blanchard, Joel. "Christine de Pizan: Les Raisons de l'histoire." *Le Moyen Age* 92 (1986): 417–36.

———. "Compilation and Legitimation in the Fifteenth Century: *Le Livre de la Cité des Dames.*" In Richards, ed., *Reinterpreting Christine de Pizan,* pp. 228–49.

Blask, Dirk Jürgen. *Geschehen und Geschick im altfranzösischen Eneas-Roman.* Tübingen, 1984.

Bloch, R. Howard. "Medieval Misogyny." *Representations* 20 (1987): 1–24.

Bloomfield, Morton, ed. *Allegory, Myth and Symbol.* Cambridge, Mass., 1981.

Blumenberg, Hans. *Work on Myth.* Trans. Robert M. Wallace. Cambridge, Mass., 1985.

Blumenfeld-Kosinski, Renate. "Chrétien de Troyes as a Reader of the *Romans Antiques.*" *Philological Quarterly* 64 (1985): 398–405.

———. "Christine de Pizan and Classical Mythology: Some Examples from the *Mutacion de Fortune.*" In Margarete Zimmermann and Dina De Rentiis, eds., *The City of Scholars: New Approaches to Christine de Pizan,* pp. 3–14. Berlin and New York, 1994.

———. "Christine de Pizan and the Misogynistic Tradition." *Romanic Review* 81 (1990): 279–92.

———. "The Earliest Developments of the French Novel: The *Roman de Thèbes* in Verse and Prose." In *The French Novel: Theory and Practice.* French Literature Series 11 (1984): 1–10.

———. " 'Femme de corps et femme par sens': Christine de Pizan's Saintly Women." *Romanic Review* 87 (1996): 157–75.

———. "The Gods as Metaphor in the *Roman de Thèbes.*" *Modern Philology* 83 (1985): 1–11.

———. "Jean Le Fèvre's *Livre de Leesce*: Praise or Blame of Women?" *Speculum* 69 (1994): 705–25.

———. "Das Konzept von Frau und Mann bei Hildegard von Bingen und Christine de Pizan." In Margot Schmidt, ed., *Tiefe des Gotteswissens, Schönheit der Sprachgestalt bei Hildegard von Bingen,* pp. 167–79. Stuttgart, 1995.

———. "Moralization and History: Verse and Prose in the *Histoire ancienne jusqu'à César* (B.N. fr. 20125)." *Zeitschrift für Romanische Philologie* 97 (1981): 41–46.

———. *Not of Woman Born: Representations of Caesarean Birth in Medieval and Renaissance Culture.* Ithaca, N.Y., 1990.

———. "Old French Narrative Genres: Towards a Definition of the *Roman antique.*" *Romance Philology* 34 (1980–81): 143–59.

———. "*Overt* and *Covert*: Amorous and Interpretive Strategies in the *Roman de la Rose*." *Romania* 111 (1990): 432–53.

———. "Praying and Reading in the *Couronnement de Louis*." *French Studies* 40 (1986): 385–92.

———. "Remarques sur songe/mensonge." *Romania* 101 (1980): 385–90.

———. Review of M. Ehrhart, *The Judgment of the Trojan Prince Paris in Medieval Literature*. *Speculum* 64 (1989): 409–12.

———. "The Scandal of Pasiphae: Narration and Interpretation in the *Ovide moralisé*." *Modern Philology* 93 (1996): 307–26.

———. "The Traditions of the Old French *Roman de Thèbes*: A Poetico-Historical Analysis." Diss., Princeton University, 1980.

Blumenfeld-Kosinski, Renate, and Timea Szell, eds. *Images of Sainthood in Medieval Europe*. Ithaca, N.Y., 1991.

Bonnefoy, Yves, ed. *Mythologies*. A restructured translation of the *Dictionnaire des religions, des sociétés traditionnelles et du monde antique*, under the direction of Wendy Doniger. Trans. Gerald Honigsblum et al. 2 vols. Chicago, 1991.

Born, Lester. "Ovid and Allegory." *Speculum* 9 (1934): 362–79.

Bornstein, Diane, ed. *Ideals for Women in the Works of Christine de Pizan*. Detroit, 1981.

Boswell, John. *Christianity, Social Tolerance, and Homosexuality: Gay People in Western Europe from the Beginning of the Christian Era to the Fourteenth Century*. Chicago, 1980.

Bouché, Thérèse. "Ovide et Jean de Meun." *Le Moyen Age* 83 (1977): 71–87.

Brabant, Margaret, ed. *Politics, Gender, and Genre: The Political Thought of Christine de Pizan*. Boulder, Colo., 1992.

Bradley-Cromey, Nancy. "Mythological Typology in Froissart's *Espinette amoureuse*." *Res publica litterarum* 3 (1980): 207–21.

Brinkmann, Hennig. *Mittelalterliche Hermeneutik*. Tübingen, 1980.

———. "Verhüllung ('*Integumentum*') als literarische Darstellungsform im Mittelalter." *Miscellania medievalia* 8 (1971): 314–39.

Brown-Grant, Rosalind. "Décadence ou progrès? Christine de Pizan, Boccace et la question de 'l'Age d'Or.'" *Revue des langues romanes* 92 (1988): 295–306.

Brownlee, Kevin. *Discourses of the Self: Autobiography and Literary Models in Christine de Pizan*. Forthcoming from Stanford University Press.

———. "Discourses of the Self: Christine de Pizan and the *Rose*." *Romanic Review* 79 (1988): 199–221.

———. "Hector and Penthesilea in the *Livre de la Mutacion de Fortune*: Christine de Pizan and the Politics of Myth." In Dulac and Ribémont, eds., *Une Femme de lettres au moyen âge*, pp. 69–82.

———. "The Image of History in Christine de Pizan's *Livre de la Mutacion de Fortune*." In Poirion and Regalado, eds., *Contexts: Style and Values in Medieval Art and Literature*, pp. 44–56.

———. "Jean de Meun and the Limits of Romance: Genius as Rewriter of Guillaume de Lorris." In Kevin Brownlee and Marina Scordilis Brownlee, eds., *Romance: Generic Transformation from Chrétien de Troyes to Cervantes,* pp. 114–34. Hanover and London, 1985.

———. "Literary Genealogy and the Problem of the Father: Christine de Pizan and Dante." *Journal of Medieval and Renaissance Studies* 23 (1993): 365–87.

———. "Martyrdom and the Female Voice: Saint Christine in the *Cité des dames.*" In Blumenfeld-Kosinski and Szell, eds., *Images of Sainthood in Medieval Europe,* pp. 115–35.

———. "Orpheus' Song Re-Sung: Jean de Meun's Reworking of *Metamorphoses X.*" *Romance Philology* 36 (1982): 201–9.

———. "Ovide et le moi poétique 'moderne' à la fin du moyen âge: Jean Froissart et Christine de Pizan." In Brigitte Cazelles and Charles Méla, eds., *Modernité au moyen âge: Le Défi du passé,* pp. 153–73. Recherches et Rencontres 1. Geneva, 1990.

———. *Poetic Identity in Guillaume de Machaut.* Madison, Wisc., 1984.

———. "Reflections in the *Miroer aus Amoreus*: The Inscribed Reader in Jean de Meun's *Roman de la Rose.*" In John D. Lyons and Stephen G. Nichols, eds., *Mimesis: From Mirror to Method, Augustine to Descartes,* pp. 60–70. Hanover and London, 1982.

———. "Structures of Authority in Christine de Pizan's *Ditié de Jehanne d'Arc.*" In Kevin Brownlee and Walter Stephens, eds., *Discourses of Authority in Medieval and Renaissance Literature,* pp. 131–50. Hanover and London, 1989.

Brownlee, Kevin, and Sylvia Huot, eds. *Rethinking the Romance of the Rose.* Philadelphia, 1992.

Brundage, James A. *Law, Sex, and Christian Society in Medieval Europe.* Chicago, 1987.

Burgwinkle, William. "Knighting the Classical Hero: Homo/Hetero Affectivity in 'Eneas.' " *Exemplaria* 5 (1993): 1–43.

Cadden, Joan. *Meanings of Sex Difference in the Middle Ages: Medicine, Science, and Culture.* Cambridge, Eng., 1993.

Calin, William. "*La Fonteinne amoureuse* de Machaut: Son or, ses oeuvres d'art, ses mises en abyme." In *L'Or au moyen âge,* Sénéfiance 12, pp. 75–87. Aix-en-Provence, 1983.

———. *A Poet at the Fountain: Essays on the Narrative Verse of Guillaume de Machaut.* Lexington, Ky., 1974.

Camille, Michael. *The Gothic Idol: Ideology and Image-Making in Medieval Art.* Cambridge, Eng., 1989.

Campbell, P. G. C. *L'Epître d'Othéa: Etude sur les sources de Christine de Pisan.* Paris, 1924.

Carmona, Fernando, and Francisco J. Flores, eds. *La lengua y la literatura en tiempos de Alfonso X.* Actas del congreso international, March 5–10, 1984. Murcia, Spain, 1985.

Carruthers, Mary J. *The Book of Memory: A Study of Memory in Medieval Culture.* Cambridge, Eng., 1990.

Cerquiglini, Jacqueline. "Le Clerc et l'écriture: Le *Voir Dit* de Guillaume de Machaut et la définition du *dit.*" In Gumbrecht, ed., *Literatur in der Gesellschaft des Spätmittelalters,* vol. 1, pp. 151–68.

———. *"Un engin si soutil": Guillaume de Machaut et l'écriture au XIVe siècle.* Geneva, 1985.

———. "Ethique de la totalisation et esthétique de la rupture dans le *Voir-Dit* de Guillaume de Machaut." In *Guillaume de Machaut: Poète et Compositeur,* pp. 253–62. Paris, 1982.

———. "L'Etrangère." *Revue des langues romanes* 92 (1988): 237–51.

Cerquiglini-Toulet, Jacqueline. *La Couleur de la mélancolie: La Fréquentation des livres au XIVe siècle, 1300–1415.* Paris, 1993.

———. "Fullness and Emptiness: Shortages and Storehouses of Lyric Treasure in the Fourteenth and Fifteenth Centuries." In Poirion and Regalado, eds., *Contexts: Style and Values in Medieval Art and Literature,* pp. 224–39.

———. "Sexualité et politique: Le Mythe d'Actéon chez Christine de Pizan." In Dulac and Ribémont, eds., *Une Femme de lettres au moyen âge,* pp. 83–90.

———. "Le 'Voir Dit' mis à nu par ses éditeurs, même: Etude de la réception d'un texte à travers ses éditions." In Frank Wanning, ed., *Mittelalter-Rezeption.* Begleitreihe zum Grundriss der romanischen Literaturen des Mittelalters, vol. 2, pp. 337–80. Heidelberg, 1991.

Chance, Jane. "Christine's Minerva: The Mother Valorized." In Christine de Pizan, *Christine de Pizan's Letter of Othea to Hector,* trans. Chance, pp. 121–33.

———. *Medieval Mythography.* Vol. 1. Gainesville, Fla., 1994.

———, ed. *The Mythographic Art: Classical Fable and the Rise of the Vernacular in Early France and England.* Gainesville, Fl., 1990.

Chenu, M.-D. " 'Involucrum': Le Mythe selon les théologiens médiévaux." *Archives d'histoire doctrinale et littéraire du moyen âge* 30 (1955): 75–79.

———. *Nature, Man, and Society in the Twelfth Century.* Ed. and trans. Jerome Taylor and Lester K. Little. Chicago, 1968.

Clanchy, M. T. *From Memory to Written Record: England 1066–1307.* Cambridge, Mass., 1979.

Comparetti, D. *Vergil in the Middle Ages.* Trans. E. F. M. Benecke. 2d ed., 1908; repr., Hamden, Conn., 1966.

Cooke, J. D. "Euhemerism: A Medieval Interpretation of Classical Paganism." *Speculum* 2 (1927): 396–410.

Copeland, Rita. *Rhetoric, Hermeneutics, and Translation in the Middle Ages: Academic Traditions and Vernacular Texts.* Cambridge, Eng., 1991.

Copeland, Rita, and Stephen Melville. "Allegory and Allegoresis, Rhetoric and Hermeneutics." *Exemplaria* 3 (1991): 159–87.

Cormier, Raymond. "Laughter and Smiles (and a Few Non-Virgilian Chuckles) in the Old French 'Roman d'Eneas.'" In Dufournet, ed., *Relire le 'Roman d'Enéas,'* pp. 7–23.

———. *One Heart, One Mind: The Rebirth of Virgil's Hero in Medieval French Romance*. University of Mississippi, Romance Monographs series 3. University, Miss., 1973.

Cosman, Madeleine Pelner, and Bruce Chandler, eds. *Machaut's World: Science and Art in the Fourteenth Century*. New York, 1978.

Coulson, Frank T. "The *Vulgate* Commentary on Ovid's *Metamorphoses*." *Mediaevalia* 13 (1989 for 1987): 29–61.

Courcelle, Pierre, and Jeanne Courcelle. *Lecteurs païens et lecteurs chrétiens de l'Enéide*. 2 vols. Paris, 1984.

Curtius, Ernst Robert. *European Literature and the Latin Middle Ages*. Trans. Willard A. Trask. Princeton, 1973.

Dällenbach, Lucien. *The Mirror in the Text*. Trans. Jeremy Whiteley with Emma Hughes. Chicago, 1989.

Damon, Philip. "Allegory and Invention: Levels of Meaning in Ancient and Medieval Rhetoric." In Bernardo and Levin, eds. *The Classics in the Middle Ages*, pp. 113–27.

Damrosch, David. "*Non alia sed aliter*: The Hermeneutics of Gender in Bernard of Clairvaux." In Blumenfeld-Kosinski and Szell, eds., *Images of Sainthood in Medieval Europe*, pp. 181–95.

de Boer, Cornelis. "Guillaume de Machaut et L'*Ovide moralisé*." *Romania* 43 (1914): 335–52.

Delany, Sheila. "The Naked Text: Chaucer's 'Thisbe,' the *Ovide Moralisé*, and the Problem of *Translatio Studii* in the *Legend of Good Women*." *Mediaevalia* 13 (1989 for 1987): 275–94.

de Looze, Laurence. "Guillaume de Machaut and the Writerly Process." *French Forum* 9 (1984): 145–61.

Demats, Paule. *Fabula: Trois études de mythographie antique et médiévale*. Geneva, 1973.

Dembowski, Peter. *Jean Froissart and his 'Meliador': Context, Craft, and Sense*. Lexington, Ky., 1983.

———. "La Position de Froissart-poète dans l'histoire littéraire: Bilan provisoire." In *Mélanges Jean Rychner*. Travaux de linguistique et de littérature XVI, 1, pp. 131–47. Strasbourg, 1978.

Desmond, Marilynn. *Reading Dido: Gender, Textuality, and the Medieval Aeneid*. Minneapolis, 1994.

Detienne, Marcel. "The Interpretation of Myths: Nineteenth- and Twentieth-Century Theories." In Bonnefoy, ed., *Mythologies*, vol. 1, pp. 5–10.

———. *L'Invention de la mythologie*. Paris, 1981.

Dinter, Annegret. *Der Pygmalion-Stoff in der europäischen Literatur: Rezeptionsgeschichte einer Ovid-Fabel.* Heidelberg, 1979.

Donovan, L. G. *Recherches sur le Roman de Thèbes*. Paris, 1975.

Dragonetti, Roger. "Pygmalion ou les pièges de la fiction dans le *Roman de la Rose*." In Georges Güntert, Marc-René Jung, and Kurt Ringger, eds., *Orbis medievalis, Mélanges R. R. Bezzola*, pp. 89–111. Bern, 1978.

———. "Le 'Singe de nature' dans le *Roman de la Rose*." In *La Musique et les lettres: Etudes de littérature médiévale*, pp. 149–60.

Dronke, Peter. *Fabula: Explorations of the Uses of Myth in Medieval Platonism*. Leiden and Cologne, 1974.

Duby, Georges. *Medieval Marriage: Two Models from Twelfth-Century France*. Trans. Elborg Forster. Baltimore, 1978.

Dufournet, Jean, ed. *Relire le 'Roman d'Enéas.'* Geneva and Paris, 1985.

Dulac, Liliane. "Un Mythe didactique chez Christine de Pizan: Sémiramis ou la veuve heroïque." In *Mélanges Charles Camproux*, vol. 1, pp. 315–40. Montpellier, 1978.

Dulac, Liliane, and Bernard Ribémont, eds. *Une Femme de lettres au moyen âge: Etudes autour de Christine de Pizan*. Orléans, 1995.

Durling, Nancy Vine. "Rewriting Gender: *Yde et Olive* and Ovidian Myth." *Romance Languages Annual* 1 (1990): 256–62.

Eberle, Patricia J. "The Lovers' Glass: Nature's Discourse on Optics and the Optical Design of the *Romance of the Rose*." *University of Toronto Quarterly* 46 (1977): 241–62.

Economou, George. *The Goddess Natura in Medieval Literature*. Cambridge, Mass., 1972.

Edmunds, Lowell. *Approaches to Greek Myth*. Baltimore, 1989.

Edwards, Robert. "Fulgentius and the Collapse of Meaning." *Helios* n.s. 4 (1976): 17–35.

———. "The Heritage of Fulgentius." In Bernardo and Levin, eds., *The Classics in the Middle Ages*, pp. 141–51.

Ehrhart, Margaret J. "Christine de Pizan and the Judgment of Paris." In Chance, ed., *The Mythographic Art*, pp. 125–56.

———. *The Judgment of the Trojan Prince Paris in Medieval Literature*. Philadelphia, 1987.

Eley, Penny. "The Myth of Trojan Descent and Perceptions of National Identity: The Case of *Enéas* and the *Roman de Troie*." *Nottingham Medieval Studies* 35 (1991): 27–40.

Eliade, Mircea. "Toward a Definition of Myth." In Bonnefoy, ed. *Mythologies*, vol. 1, pp. 1–5.

Ellspermann, Gerard L. *The Attitude of Early Christian Latin Writers toward Pagan Literature and Learning*. Washington, D.C., 1949.

Engels, Joseph. *Etudes sur l'Ovide moralisé*. Groningen, 1943.

Ezquerra, Julian M. "Tecnicas retóricas y producción del sentido en el episodio de Pigmalion del Roman de la Rose." In Carmona and Flores, eds., *La lengua y la literatura en tiempos de Alfonso X*, pp. 373–92.

Faral, Edmond. *Recherches sur les sources latines des contes et romans courtois du moyen âge*. Paris, 1913.

Feimer, Joel N. "Medea in Ovid's *Metamorphoses* and the *Ovide moralisé*: Translation as Transmission." *Florilegium* 8 (1986): 40–55.

Ferrand, Françoise. "Regards sur le *Prologue* de Guillaume de Machaut." In *Guillaume de Machaut: Poète et compositeur*, pp. 235–39. Paris, 1982.

Fleming, John V. "Jean de Meun and the Ancient Poets." In Brownlee and Huot, eds., *Rethinking the Romance of the Rose*, pp. 81–100.

———. *Reason and the Lover*. Princeton, 1984.

———. *The 'Roman de la Rose': A Study in Allegory and Iconography*. Princeton, 1969.

Fletcher, Angus. *Allegory: The Theory of a Symbolic Mode*. Ithaca, N.Y., 1964.

Fourrier, Anthime, ed. *L'Humanisme médiéval dans les littératures romanes du XIIe au XIVe siècle*. Paris, 1964.

Frappier, Jean. "Remarques sur la peinture de la vie et des héros antiques dans la littérature française du XIIe et du XIIIe siècle." In A. Fournier, ed., *L'Humanisme médiéval*, pp. 13–51.

———. "Variations sur le thème du miroir de Bernard de Ventadour à Maurice Scève." *Cahiers de l'association internationale des études françaises* 11 (1959): 134–58.

Freccero, John. "Medusa: The Letter and the Spirit." In *Dante and the Poetics of Conversion*, edited with an introduction by Rachel Jacoff, pp. 119–35. Cambridge, Mass., 1986.

Freeman, Michelle A. "Froissart's *Le Joli Buisson de Jonece*: A Farewell to Poetry?" In Cosman and Chandler, eds., *Machaut's World: Science and Art in the Fourteenth Century*, pp. 235–47.

———. "Problems in Romance Composition: Ovid, Chrétien de Troyes, and the *Romance of the Rose*." *Romance Philology* 30 (1976): 158–68.

———. "The 'Roman d'Enéas': Implications of the 'Prologue.'" *Medioevo Romanzo* 8 (1981–83): 37–45.

Frenzel, Elisabeth. *Stoffe der Weltliteratur*. Stuttgart, 1962.

Frey-Sallmann, Alma. *Aus dem Nachleben antiker Göttergestalten: Die antiken Gottheiten in der Bildbeschreibung des Mittelalters und der italienischen Frührenaissance*. Das Erbe der Alten 2, Reihe 19. Leipzig, 1931.

Friedman, John B. *Orpheus in the Middle Ages*. Cambridge, Mass. 1970.

Fritz, Jean-Marie. "Du dieu émasculateur au roi émasculé: Métamorphoses de Saturne au moyen âge." In Harf-Lancner and Boutet, eds., *Pour une mythologie du moyen âge*, pp. 43–60.

Fuhrmann, Manfred, ed. *Terror und Spiel: Studien zur Mythenrezeption im Mittelalter*. Munich, 1971.

Gaunt, Simon. "From Epic to Romance: Gender and Sexuality in the *Roman d'Enéas*." *Romanic Review* 83 (1992): 1–27.

Geary, Patrick. "Humiliation of Saints." In Stephen Wilson, ed., *Saints and Their Cults: Studies in Religious Sociology, Folklore, and History*, pp. 123–40. Cambridge, Eng., 1983.

Gellrich, Jesse M. *The Idea of the Book in the Middle Ages: Language, Theory, Mythology, and Fiction*. Ithaca, N.Y., 1985.

Genette, Gérard. *Figures III*. Paris, 1972.

George, F. W. A. "Jean de Meung and the Myth of the Golden Age." In Barnwell et al., eds., *The Classical Tradition in French Literature*, pp. 31–39.

Ghisalberti, Fausto. "Arnolfo d'Orléans: Un cultore d'Ovidio nel secolo XII." *Memorie del reale istituto lombardo di scienze e lettere* 24 (1932): 157–234.

———. "L'Ovidius moralizatus de Pierre Bersuire." *Società filologica romana, studi romanzi* 23 (1933): 5–136.

Giraud, Yves F.-A. *La Fable de Daphné: Essai sur un type de métamorphose végétale dans la littérature et dans les arts jusqu'à la fin du XVIIe siècle*. Geneva, 1968.

Glauche, Günther. *Schullektüre im Mittelalter: Entstehung und Wandelungen des Lektürekanons bis 1200 nach den Quellen dargestellt*. Münchener Beiträge zur Mediävistik und Renaissance-Forschung 5. Munich, 1970.

Goldin, Frederick. *The Mirror of Narcissus in Courtly Love Lyric*. Ithaca, N.Y., 1967.

Gompertz, Stéphane. "Le Voyage allégorique chez Christine de Pizan." In *Voyage, quête, pèlerinage dans la littérature et la civilisation médiévales*, Sénéfiance 2, pp. 195–208. Aix-en-Provence, 1976.

Graham, Audrey. "Froissart's Use of Classical Allusion in His Poems." *Medium Aevum* 32 (1963): 24–33.

Gregory, R. "Reading as Narcissism: The *Roman de la Rose*." *SubStance* 39 (1983): 37–48.

Grout, Patricia. "Religion and Mythology in the *Roman de Thèbes*." In Barnwell et al., eds., *The Classical Tradition in French Literature*, pp. 23–30.

Guenée, Bernard. *Histoire et culture historique dans l'occident médiéval*. Paris, 1980.

Guichard-Tesson, Françoise. *See* Tesson.

Gumbrecht, Hans-Ulrich, ed. *Literatur in der Gesellschaft des Spätmittelalters*. Begleitreihe zum Grundriss der romanischen Literaturen des Mittelalters. Vol. 1. Heidelberg, 1980.

Hanf, Georg. "Ueber Guillaume de Machauts *Voir Dit*." *Zeitschrift für romanische Philologie* 22 (1898): 145–96.

Hanning, Robert. *The Vision of History in Early Britain: From Gildas to Geoffrey of Monmouth*. New York, 1966.

Hardison, O. B., Jr., Alex Preminger, Kevin Kerrane, Leon Golden, eds. *Medieval Literary Criticism: Translations and Interpretations*. New York, 1974.

Harf-Lancner, Laurence, and Dominique Boutet, eds. *Pour une mythologie du moyen âge*, Paris, 1988.

Harley, Marta Powell. "Narcissus, Hermaphroditus, and Attis: Ovidian Lovers at the Fontaine d'Amors in Guillaume de Lorris's *Roman de la Rose*." *PMLA* 101 (1986): 324–35.

Haskins, Charles Homer. *The Renaissance of the Twelfth Century*. Cambridge, Mass., 1927.

Hatzantonis, E. S. "Circe, redenta d'amore nel *Roman de Troie*." *Romania* 94 (1973): 91–102.

Haug, Walter, ed. *Formen und Funktionen der Allegorie* (Proceedings of the Wolfenbüttel Symposium, 1978). Stuttgart, 1979.

Heinrichs, Katherine. *The Myths of Love: Classical Lovers in Medieval Literature*. University Park, Penn., 1990.

Heitmann, Klaus. "Orpheus im Mittelalter." *Archiv für Kulturgeschichte* 45 (1963): 253–94.

———. "Typen der Deformierung antiker Mythen im Mittelalter: Am Beispiel der Orpheussage." *Romanistisches Jahrbuch* 14 (1963): 45–77.

Herd, E. W. "Myth Criticism: Limitations and Possibilities." *Mosaic* 2 (1969): 69–77.

Herzog, Reinhart. "Metapher—Exegese—Mythos: Interpretationen zur Entstehung eines biblischen Mythos in der Literatur der Spätantike." In Fuhrmann, ed., *Terror und Spiel*, pp. 157–85.

Hexter, Ralph. "The *Allegari* of Pierre Bersuire: Interpretation and the Reductorium Morale." *Allegorica* 10 (1989): 51–84.

———. "Medieval Articulations of Ovid's *Metamorphoses*: From Lactantian Segmentation to Arnulfian Allegory." *Mediaevalia* 13 (1989 for 1987): 63–82.

———. *Ovid and Medieval Schooling: Studies in Medieval School Commentaries on Ovid's 'Ars amatoria,' 'Epistulae ex Ponto,' and 'Epistulae Heroidum'*. Münchener Beiträge zur Mediävistik und Renaissance-Forschung 38. Munich, 1986.

Hill, Thomas D. "Narcissus, Pygmalion, and the Castration of Saturn: Two Mythographical Themes in the *Roman de la Rose*." *Studies in Philology* 71 (1974): 404–26.

———. "La Vieille's Digression on Free Love: A Note on the Rhetorical Structure in the *Romance of the Rose*." *Romance Notes* 8 (1966): 113–15.

Hillman, Larry H. "Another Look into the Mirror Perilous: The Role of the Crystals in the *Roman de la Rose*." *Romania* 101 (1980): 225–38.

Hindman, Sandra. *Christine de Pizan's "Epistre d'Othéa": Painting and Politics at the Court of Charles VI*. Toronto, 1986.

Hollander, Robert. *Boccaccio's Two Venuses*. New York, 1977.

Honig, E. *Dark Conceit: The Making of Allegory*. Evanston, Ill., 1959.

Huchet, Jean-Charles. *Le Roman médiéval*. Paris, 1984.

Hult, David. "The Allegorical Fountain: Narcissus in the *Roman de la Rose*." *Romanic Review* 72 (1981): 125–48.

———. "Language and Dismemberment: Abelard, Origen, and the *Romance of the Rose*." In Brownlee and Huot, eds., *Rethinking the Romance of the Rose*, pp. 101–30.

———. *Self-fulfilling Prophecies: Readership and Authority in the First Roman de la Rose*. Cambridge, Eng., 1986.

Huot, Sylvia. "Authors, Scribes, Remanieurs: A Note on the Textual History of the *Romance of the Rose*." In Brownlee and Huot, eds., *Rethinking the Romance of the Rose*, pp. 203–33.

———. "The Daisy and the Laurel: Myths of Desire and Creativity in the Poetry of Jean Froissart." In Poirion and Regalado, eds., *Contexts: Style and Value in Medieval Art and Literature*, pp. 240–51.

———. "From *Roman de la Rose* to *Roman de la Poire*: The Ovidian Tradition and the Poetics of Courtly Literature." *Mediaevalia et Humanistica* n.s. 13 (1985): 95–111.

———. *From Song to Book: The Poetics of Writing in Old French Lyric and Lyrical Narrative Poetry*. Ithaca, N.Y., 1987.

———. "The Medusa Interpolation in the *Roman de la Rose*: Mythographic Program and Ovidian Intertext." *Speculum* 62 (1987): 865–77.

———. *The Romance of the Rose and Its Medieval Readers: Interpretation, Reception, Manuscript Transmission*. Cambridge, Eng., 1993.

———. "Seduction and Sublimation: Christine de Pizan, Jean de Meun, and Dante." *Romance Notes* 25 (1985): 361–73.

Ignatius, Mary Ann. "Christine de Pizan's *Epistre d'Othéa*: An Experiment in Literary Form." *Medievalia et Humanistica* n.s. 9 (1979): 127–42.

Imbs, Paul. *Le Voir-Dit de Guillaume de Machaut: Etude littéraire*. Paris, 1991.

Irwin, Eleanor. "The Song of Orpheus and the New Song of Christ." In Warden, ed., *Orpheus: The Metamorphoses of a Myth*, pp. 51–62.

Jakobson, Roman. *Essais de linguistique générale*. Paris, 1963.

Jauss, Hans Robert. "Allégorie, 'remythisation' et nouveau mythe: Réflexions sur la captivité chrétienne de la mythologie au moyen âge." In *Mélanges d'histoire littéraire, de linguistique et de philologie romane offerts à Charles Rostaing*, pp. 469–99. Liège, 1974.

———. *Pour une esthétique de la réception*. Trans. Claude Maillard. Paris, 1978.

———. *Toward an Aesthetic of Reception*. Trans. Timothy Bahti. Minneapolis, 1982.

———. "La Transformation de la forme allégorique entre 1180 et 1240: D'Alain de Lille à Guillaume de Lorris." In Fourrier, ed., *L'Humanisme médiéval*, pp. 107–46.

Jeanroy, Alfred. "Boccace et Christine de Pisan: Le *De Claris Mulieribus* principale source du *Livre de la cité des dames.*" *Romania* 48 (1922): 147–54.

Jeauneau, Edouard. "L'Usage de la notion d'*integumentum* à travers les gloses de Guillaume de Conches." *Archives d'histoire doctrinale et littéraire du moyen âge* 32 (1957): 35–100.

Jodogne, Omer. "Le Caractère des oeuvres 'antiques' dans la littérature française du XIIe et du XIIIe siècle." In Fourrier, ed., *L'Humanisme médiéval*, pp. 55–83.

Jones, J. W. "Allegorical Interpretation in Servius." *Classical Journal* 56 (1961): 217–26.

Jónsson, Einar Már. *Le Miroir: Naissance d'un genre littéraire*. Paris, 1995.

Jung, Marc-René. *Etudes sur le poème allégorique en France au moyen âge*. Bern, 1971.

———. "Jean de Meun et l'allégorie." *Cahiers de l'association internationale des études françaises* 28 (1976): 21–36.

———. *Le Mythe d'Hercule dans la littérature française du XVIe siècle: De l'Hercule courtois à l'Hercule baroque*. Geneva, 1966.

———. "Poetria: Zur Dichtungstheorie des ausgehenden Mittelalters." *Vox Romanica* 30 (1971): 44–64.

Kauke, Rainer. "Jupiter et Saturne chez Jean de Meun." *Romanistische Zeitschrift für Literaturgeschichte* 2 (1978): 258–63.

Kay, Sarah. "The Birth of Venus in the *Romance of the Rose*." *Exemplaria* 9 (1997): 7–37.

Kellogg, Judith L. "Christine de Pizan and Boccaccio: Rewriting the Classical Mythic Tradition." In Cornelia N. Moore and Raymond A. Moody, eds., *Comparative Literature East and West: Traditions and Trends*, pp. 124–31. Manoa, University of Hawaii, 1989.

———. "Christine de Pizan as Chivalric Mythographer: L'*Epistre d'Othéa*." In Chance, ed., *The Mythographic Art*, pp. 100–124.

———. "*Le Livre de la Cité des Dames*: Feminist Myth and Community." *Essays in Arts and Sciences* 18 (1989): 1–15.

Kelly, Douglas. "The Genius of the Patron: The Prince, the Poet, and Fourteenth-Century Invention." *Studies in the Literary Imagination* 20 (1987): 77–97.

———. "Les Inventions ovidiennes de Froissart: Réflexions intertextuelles comme imagination." *Littérature* 41 (1981): 82–92.

———. *Medieval Imagination: Rhetoric and the Poetry of Courtly Love*. Madison, Wisc., 1978.

Kempter, Gerda. *Ganymed: Studien zur Typologie, Ikonographie und Ikonologie*. Cologne and Vienna, 1980.

Kessler, Joan. "La Quête amoureuse et poétique: La Fontaine de Narcisse dans le *Roman de la Rose*." *Romanic Review* 73 (1982): 133–46.

Kibler, William. "Poet and Patron: Froissart's *Prison Amoureuse*." *L'Esprit créateur* 18 (1978): 32–46.

———. "Self-Delusion in Froissart's *Espinette Amoureuse*." *Romania* 97 (1976): 77–98.

Knoespel, Kenneth J. *Narcissus and the Invention of Personal History*. New York, 1985.

Köhler, Erich. "Narcisse, la Fontaine d'Amour et Guillaume de Lorris." In Fourrier, ed., *L'Humanisme médiéval*, pp. 147–64.

Krill, Richard M. "The *Vatican Mythographers*: Their Place in Ancient Mythography." *Manuscripta* 23 (1979): 173–77.

Lacy, Norris. "Villon in His Work: The *Testament* and the Problem of Personal Poetry." *L'Esprit créateur* 18 (1978): 60–69.

Langlois, Ernest. "Chronologie des Romans de 'Thèbes,' d' 'Enéas,' et de 'Troie.' " *Bibliothèque de l'Ecole des Chartes* 66 (1905): 107–20.

———. *Origines et sources du Roman de la Rose*. Paris, 1891.

———, ed. *Recueil d'Arts de seconde rhétorique*. Paris, 1902.

Lavin, Irving. "Cephalus and Procris: Transformations of an Ovidian Myth." *Journal of the Warburg and Courtauld Institutes* 17 (1954): 260–87.

Leclanche, Jean-Luc. "Biblis: Métamorphose médiévale d'un conte ovidien." In *Mélanges Alice Planche*. 2 vols.; vol. 2, pp. 287–97. Nice, 1984.

Legaré, Anne-Marie, with the collaboration of Françoise Guichard Tesson and Bruno Roy. *Le Livre des Echecs amoureux*. Paris, 1991.

Le Goff, Jacques. *Les Intellectuels au moyen âge*. Paris, 1957.

Lehmann, P. *Pseudo-antike Literatur des Mittelalters*. Studien der Bibliothek Warburg 13. Berlin and Leipzig, 1927.

Leube, Eberhard. *Fortuna in Karthago: Die Aeneas-Dido-Mythe Vergils in den romanischen Literaturen vom 14. bis zum 16. Jahrhundert*. Heidelberg, 1969.

Levine, Robert. "Exploiting Ovid: Medieval Allegorizations of the *Metamorphoses*." *Medioevo Romanzo* 14 (1989): 197–213.

Lévi-Strauss, Claude. *La Pensée sauvage*. Paris, 1962.

Levy, Raphael. "L'Allusion à la sodomie dans *Enéas*." *Philological Quarterly* 27 (1948): 372–76.

Lewis, C. S. *The Allegory of Love: A Study in Medieval Tradition*. Oxford, 1936; repr. 1973.

Liebeschütz, Hans. *Medieval Humanism in the Life and Writings of John of Salisbury*. London, 1950.

Lord, Carla. "Three Manuscripts of the *Ovide moralisé*." *Art Bulletin* 57 (1975): 161–75.

Loukopoulos, Halina D. "Classical Mythology in the Works of Christine de Pizan, with an Edition of *L'Epistre d'Othéa* from MS Harley 4431." Diss., Wayne State University, 1977.

Lubac, Henri de. *Exégèse médiévale: Les Quatre sens de l'écriture.* 4 vols. Paris, 1959–64.
Lukitsch, Shirley. "The Poetics of the *Prologue*: Machaut's Conception of the Purpose of His Art." *Medium Aevum* 52 (1983): 258–71.
Lumiansky, R. M. "Structural Unity in Benoît's *Roman de Troie.*" *Romania* 79 (1958): 410–24.
Lynch, Kathryn L. *The High Medieval Dream Vision: Poetry, Philosophy and Literary Form.* Stanford, 1988.
Macfie, Pamela Royston. "Ovid, Arachne, and the Poetics of Paradise." In Rachel Jacoff and Jeffrey Schnapp, eds., *The Poetry of Allusion: Virgil and Ovid in Dante's 'Commedia,'* pp. 159–72. Stanford, 1991.
McLeod, Glenda. *Virtue and Venom: Catalogs of Women from Antiquity to the Renaissance.* Ann Arbor, Mich., 1991.
Macnabey, Armand. *Guillaume de Machaut, 130?–1377: La Vie et l'oeuvre musicale.* 2 vols. Paris, 1955.
Mâle, Emile. *L'Art religieux du XIIIe siècle en France.* 1898. 8th ed., 2 vols. Paris, 1958.
Marchello-Nizia, Christiane. "De l'*Enéïde* à l'*Enéas*: Les Attributs du fondateur." In *Lectures médiévales de Virgile*, pp. 251–66. Rome, 1985.
Margolis, Nadia. "Christine de Pizan: The Poetess as Historian." *Journal of the History of Ideas* 47 (1986): 361–75.
Maurer, Armand. "Siger of Brabant on Fables and Falsehoods in Religion." *Mediaeval Studies* 43 (1981): 513–30.
Meltzer, Françoise. *Salome and the Dance of Writing.* Chicago, 1987.
Meyer, Paul. "Les Premières Compilations françaises d'histoire ancienne." *Romania* 14 (1885): 1–81.
Milan, Paul B. "The Golden Age and the Political Theory of Jean de Meun: A Myth in *Rose* Scholarship." *Symposium* 23 (1969): 137–49.
Minnis, Alistair J. *Chaucer and Pagan Antiquity.* Cambridge, Eng., 1982.
———. "The Influence of Academic Prologues on the Prologues and Literary Attitudes of Late-Medieval English Writers." *Mediaeval Studies* 43 (1981): 342–83.
———. "Literary Theory in Discussions of *Formae Tractandi* by Medieval Theologians." *New Literary History* 11 (1979): 133–45.
———. *Medieval Theory of Authorship.* 2d ed. Philadelphia, 1988.
Minnis, Alistair J., and A. B. Scott, eds., with the assistance of David Wallace. *Medieval Literary Theory and Criticism c. 1100–c. 1375: The Commentary Tradition.* Rev. ed. Oxford, 1991.
Mombello, Gianni. "Quelques aspects de la pensée politique de Christine de Pisan d'après ses oeuvres publiées." In Franco Simone, ed., *Culture et politique en France à l'époque de l'humanisme et de la Renaissance*, pp. 43–153. Turin, 1974.

———. "Recherches sur l'origine du nom de la Déesse Othéa." *Atti della Accademia delle scienze di Torino, Classe di scienze morali, storiche e filologiche* 103 (1968–69): 343–75.

Mora, Francine. "Sources de l'*Enéas*: La Tradition exégétique et le modèle épique latin." In Dufournet, ed., *Relire le 'Roman d'Enéas'*, pp. 83–104.

Mora-Lebrun, Francine. *L'Enéide' médiévale et la naissance du roman*. Paris, 1994.

Moss, Ann. *Poetry and Fable: Studies in Mythological Narrative in Sixteenth-Century France*. Cambridge, Eng., 1984.

Munk Olsen, Birger. "Les Classiques latins dans les florilèges médiévaux antérieurs au treizième siècle." *Revue d'histoire des textes* 9 (1979): 47–121.

———. *L'Etude des auteurs classiques latins aux XIe et XIIe siècles*. 4 vols. Paris, 1982–87.

———. "La Popularité des textes classiques entre le IXe et le XIIe siècle." *Revue d'histoire des textes* 14–15 (1984–85): 169–81.

Nestle, Wilhelm. *Vom Mythos zum Logos*. 2d ed., 1942; repr., New York, 1978.

Nitzsche, Jane Chance. *The Genius Figure in Antiquity and the Middle Ages*. New York, 1975.

Noakes, Susan. *Timely Reading: Between Exegesis and Interpretation*. Ithaca, N.Y., 1988.

Nolan, Barbara. *Chaucer and the Tradition of the 'Roman Antique.'* Cambridge, Eng., 1992.

———. "The Judgment of Paris in the *Roman d'Enéas*: A New Look at Sources and Significance." *Classical Bulletin* 56 (1980): 52–56.

———. "Ovid's *Heroides* Contextualized: Foolish Love and Legitimate Marriage in the *Roman d'Enéas*." *Mediaevalia* 13 (1989 for 1987): 157–87.

Nouvet, Claire. "Pour une économie de la dé-limitation: *La Prison amoureuse* de Jean Froissart." *Neophilologus* 70 (1986): 341–56.

Ohly, Friedrich. "Typologische Figuren aus Natur und Mythos." In Haug, ed., *Formen und Funktionen der Allegorie*, pp. 126–66.

Ostriker, Alicia. "The Thieves of Language: Women Poets and Revisionist Mythmaking." *Signs* 8 (1982): 68–90.

Ott, Karl-August. "Neuere Untersuchungen zum Rosenroman." *Zeitschrift für Romanische Philologie* 104 (1988): 80–95.

Panofsky, Erwin. *Herkules am Scheidewege und andere antike Bildstoffe in der neueren Kunst*. Berlin and Leipzig, 1930.

———. *Renaissance and Renascences in Western Art*. Stockholm, 1960.

Panofsky, Erwin, and Fritz Saxl, "Classical Mythology in Mediaeval Art." *Metropolitan Museum Studies* 4 (1932–33): 228–80.

Paris, Gaston. "Chrétien Legouais et autres traducteurs ou imitateurs d'Ovide." *Histoire littéraire de la France* 29 (1885): 455–525.

Patterson, Lee. "'Rapt with Pleasaunce': Vision and Narration in the Epic." *English Literary History* 48 (1981): 455–75.

———. "Virgil and the Historical Consciousness of the Twelfth Century: The *Roman d'Enéas* and *Erec et Enide*." In *Negotiating the Past: The Historical Understanding of Medieval Literature*, pp. 157–95. Madison, Wisc., 1987.

Pauphilet, Albert. "L'Antiquité et l'Enéas." In *Le Legs du moyen âge*, pp. 91–106. Melun, France. 1950.

Pelen, Marc M. *Latin Poetic Irony in the 'Roman de la Rose.'* Liverpool, 1987.

Pépin, J. "The Euhemerism of the Christian Authors." In Bonnefoy, ed., *Mythologies*, vol. 2, pp. 666–71.

———. *Mythe et allégorie: Les Origines grecques et les contestations judéo-chrétiennes*. Paris, 1958.

Petit, Aimé. "Aspects de l'influence d'Ovide sur les romans antiques du XIIe siècle." In R. Chevallier, ed., *Colloque Présence d'Ovide*, pp. 219–40. Paris, 1982.

———. *Naissances du roman: Les Techniques littéraires dans les romans antiques du XIIe siècle*. 2 vols. Paris and Geneva, 1985.

———. "Un Passage controversé du 'Roman de Thèbes': La Capanéïde." *Marche Romane* 31 (1981): 43–61.

Phillippy, Patricia. "Establishing Authority: Boccaccio's *De Claris Mulieribus* and Christine de Pizan's *Le Livre de la Cité des Dames*." *Romanic Review* 77 (1986): 167–94.

Picherit, Jean Louis. "Les *Exemples* dans le Jugement dou Roy de Navarre." *Les Lettres romanes* 36 (1982): 103–16.

———. "Le Rôle des éléments mythologiques dans le *Joli Buisson de jonece* de Jean Froissart." *Neophilologus* 63 (1979): 498–508.

Piehler, Paul. *The Visionary Landscape: A Study in Medieval Allegory*. London, 1971.

Pietri, François. *Chronique de Charles le Mauvais*. Paris, 1963.

Poirion, Daniel. "De l' 'Enéïde' à l' 'Enéas': Mythologie et moralisation." *Cahiers de civilisation médiévale* 19 (1976): 213–29.

———. "De la signification selon Jean de Meun." In Lucie Brind'Amour and Eugene Vance, eds., *Archéologie du signe*, pp. 165–85. Toronto, 1982.

———. "L'Ecriture épique: Du sublime au symbole." In Dufournet, ed., *Relire le 'Roman d'Enéas,'* pp. i–xiii.

———. "Edyppus et l'énigme du roman médiéval." In *L'Enfant au moyen âge*, Sénéfiance 9, pp. 287–99. Aix-en-Provence, 1980.

———. "Narcisse et Pygmalion dans le *Roman de la Rose*." In Urban T. Holmes and Raymond Cormier, eds., *Essays in Honor of Francis Solano*, pp. 153–65. Chapel Hill, N.C., 1970.

———. *Le Poète et le prince: L'Evolution du lyrisme courtois de Guillaume de Machaut à Charles d'Orléans*. Paris, 1965.

———. *Résurgences: Mythe et littérature à l'âge du symbole (XIIe siècle).* Paris, 1986.

———. "Traditions et fonctions du *dit poétique* au XIVe et XVe siècle." In Gumbrecht, ed., *Literatur in der Gesellschaft des Spätmittelalters*, vol. 1, pp. 147–50.

———, ed. *Le Roman de la Rose.* Paris, 1973.

Poirion, Daniel, and Nancy Freeman Regalado, eds. *Contexts: Style and Values in Medieval Art and Literature.* Special issue of *Yale French Studies.* New Haven, 1991.

Quain, Edwin A. "The Medieval Accessus ad Auctores." *Traditio* 3 (1945): 215–64.

Quilligan, Maureen. "Allegory and the Textual Body: Female Authority in Christine de Pizan's *Livre de la cité des dames.*" *Romanic Review* 79 (1988): 222–48.

———. *The Allegory of Female Authority: Christine de Pizan's 'Cité des dames.'* Ithaca, N.Y., 1992.

———. "Words and Sex: The Language of Allegory in *De planctu naturae*, the *Roman de la Rose*, and Book III of the *Faerie Queene.*" *Allegorica* 2 (1977): 195–216.

Rand, E. K. "The Classics in the Thirteenth Century." *Speculum* 4 (1929): 249–69.

———. "The Metamorphoses of Ovid in the *Roman de la Rose.*" In Percy W. Long, ed., *Studies in the History of Culture.* 1942; repr., New York, 1969.

———. *Ovid and His Influence.* Boston, 1928.

Raynaud de Lage, Guy. " 'L'Histoire ancienne jusqu'à César' et les 'Faits des Romains.' " *Le Moyen Age* 55 (1949): 5–16.

———. "Les 'Romans antiques' dans l'Histoire ancienne jusqu'à César." *Le Moyen Age* 63 (1957): 267–307.

———. "Les Romans antiques et la représentation de la réalité." *Le Moyen Age* 67 (1961): 247–91.

Regalado, Nancy F. " 'Des contraires choses': La Fonction poétique de la citation et des *exempla* dans le 'Roman de la Rose' de Jean de Meun." *Littérature* 41 (1981): 62–81.

———. "The Medieval Construction of the Modern Reader: Solomon's Ship and the Birth of Jean de Meun." Forthcoming.

Reno, Christine. "Feminist Aspects of Christine de Pizan's 'Epistre d'Othéa à Hector.' " *Studi francesi* 24 (1980): 271–76.

———. "The Preface to the *Avision-Christine* in ex-Phillipps 128." In Richards, ed., *Reinterpreting Christine de Pizan*, pp. 207–27.

Reynolds, L. D., and N. G. Wilson. *Scribes and Scholars: A Guide to the Transmission of Greek and Latin Literature.* Oxford, 1974.

Ribémont, Bernard. "Froissart, le mythe et la marguerite." *Revue des langues romanes* 94 (1990): 129–37.

Richards, Earl Jeffrey, ed. *Reinterpreting Christine de Pizan*. Athens, Ga., 1992.

Riffaterre, Michael. "L'Intertexte inconnu." *Littérature* 41 (1981): 4–7.

———. "Sémiotique intertextuelle: L'Interprétant." *Rhétoriques, sémiotiques. Revue d'esthétique* 1–2 (1979): 62–81.

Rollinson, Philip. *Classical Theories of Allegory and Christian Culture*. Pittsburgh, 1981.

Roncaglia, Aurelio. "Les Troubadours et Virgile." In *Lectures médiévales de Virgile*, pp. 267–83. Rome, 1985.

Rousse, Michel. "Le Pouvoir, la prouesse et l'amour dans l'Enéas." In Dufournet, ed., *Relire le 'Roman d'Enéas,'* pp. 147–67.

Rudd, Niall. "Daedalus and Icarus (I): From Rome to the End of the Middle Ages." In Charles Martindale, ed., *Ovid Renewed: Ovidian Influences on Literature and Art from the Middle Ages to the Twentieth Century*, pp. 21–35. Cambridge, Eng., 1988.

Ruhe, Doris. *Le Dieu d'Amours avec son paradis: Untersuchungen zur Mythenbildung um Amor in Spätantike und Mittelalter*. Munich, 1974.

Rychner, Jean. "Le Mythe de la fontaine de Narcisse dans le *Roman de la Rose* de Guillaume de Lorris." In *Le Lieu et la formule: Hommage à Marc Eigeldinger*, pp. 33–46. Neuchâtel, 1978.

Sanford, Eva M. "The Use of Classical Latin Authors in the *Libri Manuales*." *Transactions of the American Philological Association* 55 (1924): 190–248.

Sasaki, Shigemi. "Le Poète et Pallas dans le 'Chemin de long estude' (vers 737–1170 et 1569–1780)." *Revue des langues romanes* 92 (1988): 369–80.

Scaglione, Aldo. "The Classics in Medieval Education." In Bernardo and Levin, eds., *The Classics in the Middle Ages*, pp. 343–62.

Schibanoff, Susan. "Taking the Gold out of Egypt: The Art of Reading as a Woman." In Elizabeth A. Flynn and Patrocinio P. Schweickart, eds., *Gender and Reading*, pp. 83–106. Baltimore, 1986.

Schnapp, Jeffrey T. "Dante's Sexual Solecisms: Gender and Genre in the *Commedia*." In Kevin Brownlee, Marina Brownlee, and Stephen G. Nichols, eds., *The New Medievalism*, pp. 201–25. Baltimore, 1991.

Schneider, Norbert. *The Art of the Portrait*. Cologne, 1994.

Schöning, Udo. *Thebenroman—Eneasroman—Trojaroman: Studien zur Rezeption der Antike in der französischen Literatur des 12. Jahrhunderts*. Tübingen, 1991.

Schreiber, Earl G. "Venus in the Medieval Mythographic Tradition." *Journal of English and Germanic Philology* 74 (1975): 519–35.

Segal, Charles. "Circean Temptations: Homer, Vergil, and Ovid." *Transactions of the American Philological Association* 99 (1968): 419–42.

Seznec, Jean. *The Survival of the Pagan Gods: The Mythological Tradition and Its*

Place in Renaissance Humanism and Art. Trans. Barbara F. Sessions. Princeton, 1953.

Simon, Marcel. "Les Dieux antiques dans la pensée chrétienne." *Zeitschrift für Religions- und Geistesgeschichte* 6 (1954): 97–114.

Singerman, Jerome E. *Under Clouds of Poesy: Poetry and Truth in French and English Reworkings of the Aeneid, 1160–1513*. New York, 1986.

Smalley, Beryl. *English Friars and Antiquity in the Early Fourteenth Century*. Oxford, 1960.

Smit, A. M. M. *Contribution à l'étude de la connaissance de l'antiquité au moyen âge*. Leyden, 1934.

Smith, Nathaniel B. "In Search of the Ideal Landscape: From 'Locus Amoenus' to 'Parc du Champ Joli' in the 'Roman de la Rose.'" *Viator* 11 (1980): 225–43.

Solodow, Joseph B. *The World of Ovid's Metamorphoses*. Chapel Hill, N.C., 1988.

Spence, Sarah. *Rhetorics of Reason and Desire: Vergil, Augustine, and the Troubadours*. Ithaca, N.Y., 1988.

Spiegel, Gabrielle M. *Romancing the Past: The Rise of Vernacular Prose Historiography in Thirteenth-Century France*. Berkeley, 1993.

Stecopoulos, Eleni, with Karl D. Uitti. "Christine de Pizan's *Livre de la Cité des Dames*: The Reconstruction of Myth." In Richards, ed., *Reinterpreting Christine de Pizan*, pp. 48–62.

Steinhagen, Harald. "Zu Walter Benjamins Begriff der Allegorie." In Haug, ed., *Formen und Funktionen der Allegorie*, pp. 666–85.

Steinle, Eric M. "Versions of Authority in the *Roman de la Rose*: Remarks on the Use of Ovid's *Metamorphoses* by Guillaume de Lorris and Jean de Meun." *Mediaevalia* 13 (1989 for 1987): 189–206.

Stierle, Karlheinz. "Mythos als 'Bricolage' und zwei Endstufen des Prometheusmythos." In Fuhrmann, ed., *Terror und Spiel*, pp. 455–72.

Stock, Brian. *Myth and Science in the Twelfth Century: A Study of Bernard Silvester*. Princeton, 1972.

———. "A Note on Thebaid Commentaries: Paris. B.N., lat. 3012." *Traditio* 27 (1971): 468–71.

Strubel, Armand. "'Allegoria in factis' et 'Allegoria in verbis.'" *Poétique* 23 (1975): 342–57.

———. *Le Roman de la Rose*. Paris, 1984.

———. *La Rose, le renart et le graal: La Littérature allégorique en France au XIIIe siècle*. Paris, 1989.

Sturges, Robert. *Medieval Interpretation: Models of Reading in Literary Narrative, 1100–1500*. Carbondale, Ill., 1991.

Tesson, Françoise Guichard. "La Glose des Echecs amoureux: Les Idées et le genre de l'oeuvre d'après le commentaire du verger de Déduit." Diss., University of Montréal, 1980.

———. "La *Glose des Echecs amoureux*: Un Savoir à tendance laïque: Comment l'interpréter?" *Fifteenth-Century Studies* 10 (1984): 229–60.

Thiry, Claude. "Allégorie et histoire dans la 'Prison amoureuse' de Froissart." *Studi francesi* 21 (1977): 15–29.

Thomas, Antoine. "Guillaume de Machaut et L'*Ovide moralisé*." *Romania* 41 (1912): 382–400.

Thut, Martin. "Narcisse versus Pygmalion: Une Lecture du Roman de la Rose." *Vox romanica* 41 (1982): 104–32.

Todorov, Tzvetan. *Symbolism and Interpretation*. Trans. Catherine Porter. Ithaca, N.Y., 1982.

Trousson, R. *Le Thème de Prométhée dans la littérature européenne*. 2 vols. Geneva, 1964.

Tuve, Rosemond. *Allegorical Imagery: Some Medieval Books and Their Posterity*. Princeton, 1962.

Uitti, Karl D., with Michelle Freeman. "Christine de Pisan and Chrétien de Troyes: Poetic Fidelity and the City of Ladies." In Norris Lacy, Douglas Kelly, and Keith Busby, eds., *The Legacy of Chrétien de Troyes*, 2 vols; vol. 2, pp. 229–53. Amsterdam, 1988.

———. "From 'Clerc' to 'Poète': The Relevance of the *Roman de la Rose* to Machaut's World." In Cosman and Chandler, eds., *Machaut's World: Science and Art in the Fourteenth Century*, pp. 209–16.

———. *Story, Myth, and Celebration in Old French Narrative Poetry, 1050–1200*. Princeton, 1973.

Van Dyke, Carolynn. *The Fiction of Truth: Structure and Meaning in Narrative and Dramatic Allegory*. Ithaca, N.Y., 1985.

Varvaro, Alberto. "I nuovi valori del Roman d'Enéas." *Filologia e letteratura* 13 (1967): 113–41.

Vauchez, André. "Lay People's Sanctity in Western Europe: Evolution of a Pattern (Twelfth and Thirteenth Centuries)." In Blumenfeld-Kosinski and Szell, eds., *Images of Sainthood in Medieval Europe*, pp. 21–32.

Vicari, Patricia. "*Sparagmos*: Orpheus among the Christians." In Warden, ed., *Orpheus: The Metamorphoses of a Myth*, pp. 63–83.

Vickers, Nancy. "Diana Described: Scattered Woman and Scattered Rhyme." In Elizabeth Abel, ed., *Writing and Sexual Difference*, pp. 95–109. Chicago, 1982.

Vinge, Louise. *The Narcissus Theme in Western European Literature up to the Early Nineteenth Century*. Lund, 1967.

Vitz, Evelyn Birge. "The *I* in the *Roman de la Rose*." *Genre* 6 (1973): 49–75.

von Wartburg, Walther. *Französisches Etymologisches Wörterbuch*. Vol. 3. Berlin and Leipzig. 1934.

Wallen, Martha. "Biblical and Mythological Typology in Machaut's *Confort d'Ami*." *Res publica litterarum* 3 (1980): 191–206.

Walters, Lori. "Chivalry and the (En)Gendered Poetic Self: Petrarchan Models in the 'Cent Balades.'" In Margarete Zimmermann and Dina De Rentiis, eds., *The City of Scholars: New Approaches to Christine de Pizan*, pp. 43–66. Berlin and New York, 1994.

Warden, J., ed. *Orpheus: The Metamorphoses of a Myth*. Toronto, 1982.

Warren, W. L. *Henry II*. Berkeley, 1977.

Waugh, Patricia. *Metafiction: The Theory and Practice of Self-Conscious Fiction*. London and New York, 1984.

Weinrich, Harald. "Structures narratives du mythe." *Poétique* 11 (1970): 25–34.

West, M. L. *The Hesiodic Catalogue of Women*. Oxford, 1985.

Wetherbee, Winthrop. *Platonism and Poetry in the Twelfth Century: The Literary Influence of the School of Chartres*. Princeton, 1972.

———. "The Theme of Imagination in Medieval Poetry and the Allegorical Figure 'Genius.'" *Medievalia et Humanistica* n.s. 7 (1976): 45–64.

Whitman, Jon. *Allegory: The Dynamics of an Ancient and Medieval Technique*. Cambridge, Mass., 1987.

Willard, Charity Cannon. *Christine de Pizan: Her Life and Works*. New York, 1984.

———. "Lovers' Dialogues in Christine de Pizan's Lyric Poetry from the *Cent Ballades* to the *Cent Ballades d'Amant et de Dame*." *Fifteenth Century Studies* 4 (1981): 167–80.

Williams, Sarah Jane. "An Author's Role in Fourteenth-Century Book Production: Guillaume de Machaut's 'livre ou je met toutes mes choses.'" *Romania* 90 (1969): 433–54.

———. "Machaut's Self-Awareness as Author and Producer." In Cosman and Chandler, eds., *Machaut's World: Science and Art in the Fourteenth Century*, pp. 189–97.

Wilson, Katharina M., and Elizabeth M. Makowski. *Wykked Wyves and the Woes of Marriage: Misogamous Literature from Juvenal to Chaucer*. Albany, N.Y., 1990.

Wittig, Joseph S. "The Aeneas-Dido Allusion in Chrétien's *Erec et Enide*." *Comparative Literature* 22 (1970): 237–53.

Zink, Michel. "Froissart et la nuit du chasseur." *Poétique* 41 (1980): 60–77.

———. "Héritage rhétorique et nouveauté littéraire dans le 'Roman antique' en France au moyen âge: Remarques sur l'expression de l'amour dans le *Roman d'Enéas*." *Romania* 105 (1984): 248–69.

———. *La Subjectivité littéraire: Autour du siècle de saint Louis*. Paris, 1985.

———. "The Time of the Plague and the Order of Writing: Jean le Bel, Froissart, Machaut." In Poirion and Regalado, eds., *Contexts: Style and Values in Medieval Art and Literature*, pp. 269–80.

Zumthor, Paul. *Essai de poétique médiévale*. Paris, 1972.

Index

In this index an "f" after a number indicates a separate reference on the next page, and an "ff" indicates separate references on the next two pages. A continuous discussion over two or more pages is indicated by a span of page numbers, e.g., "57–59." *Passim* is used for a cluster of references in close but not consecutive sequence.

Coláiste na hOllscoile Gaillimh
3 1111 30093 6935